# Women Making History

## THE REVOLUTIONARY FEMINIST POSTCARD ART OF HELAINE VICTORIA PRESS

Julia M. Allen and Jocelyn H. Cohen

LEVER PRESS

Copyright © 2023 by Julia M. Allen and Jocelyn H. Cohen

Lever Press (leverpress.org) is a publisher of pathbreaking scholarship. Supported by a consortium of higher education institutions focused on, and renowned for, excellence in both research and teaching, our press is grounded on three essential commitments: to be a digitally native press, to be a peer-reviewed, open access press that charges no fees to either authors or their institutions, and to be a press aligned with the liberal arts ethos.

This work is licensed under the Creative Commons Attribution-NonCommercial-NoDerivatives 4.0 International License. To view a copy of this license, visit http://creativecommons.org/licenses/by-nc-nd/4.0/ or send a letter to Creative Commons, PO Box 1866, Mountain View, CA 94042, USA. The proposal for this work was subjected to a partly closed ("single-blind") review process; the complete manuscript was subjected to a closed ("double-blind") review process. For more information, please see our Peer Review Commitments and Guidelines at https://www.leverpress.org/peerreview.

DOI: https://doi.org/10.3998/mpub.12737267
Print ISBN: 978-1-64315-035-2
Open access ISBN: 978-1-64315-036-9

Published in the United States of America by Lever Press, in partnership with Michigan Publishing.

Contents

| | |
|---|---|
| *Member Institutions Acknowledgments* | v |
| *List of Illustrations* | vii |
| *Acknowledgments* | xvii |
| *Preface* | xxi |
| Introduction | 1 |
| Chapter One: Inception | 31 |
| Chapter Two: Printshop in Indiana | 81 |
| Chapter Three: Nonprofit Status | 153 |
| Chapter Four: Change and Growth | 201 |
| Chapter Five: Storefront in Bloomington | 263 |
| Epilogue | 319 |
| *Glossary* | 337 |
| *Appendix* | 353 |
| *Notes* | 401 |
| *Bibliography* | 431 |
| *Index* | 437 |

*Member Institution Acknowledgments*

Lever Press is a joint venture. This work was made possible by the generous support of Lever Press member libraries from the following institutions:

Amherst College
Berea College
Bowdoin College
Carleton College
Central Washington University
Claremont Graduate University
Claremont McKenna College
Clark Atlanta University
College of Saint Benedict & Saint John's University
The College of Wooster
Davidson College
Denison University
DePauw University
Grinnell College
Hamilton College
Harvey Mudd College
Hollins University
Iowa State University
Keck Graduate Institute
Knox College
Lafayette College
Macalester College
Middlebury College
Morehouse College
Norwich University
Penn State University
Pitzer College
Pomona College
Randolph-Macon College
Rollins College
Santa Clara University
Scripps College
Skidmore College
Smith College
Spelman College
Susquehanna University

Swarthmore College
Trinity University
UCLA Library
Union College
University of Idaho
University of Northern
  Colorado
University of Puget Sound
University of San Francisco
University of Vermont

Ursinus College
Vassar College
Washington and Lee
  University
Whitman College
Whittier College
Whitworth University
Willamette University
Williams College

*List of Illustrations*

1. Savoy cabbage painting by Jocelyn Cohen. 1973. Courtesy of Jocelyn H. Cohen and Indiana University, Kokomo     2
2. Women's Christian Temperance Union Officers postcard. Courtesy of Helaine Victoria Press, Inc. Reproduced from Anna Gordon, *The Beautiful Life of Frances W. Willard* (Chicago, IL: Woman's Temperance Publishing Association, 1898).     9
3. Frances Willard on Her Bicycle postcard. Courtesy of Helaine Victoria Press, Inc. Photo reproduced from Frances E. Willard, *A Wheel Within a Wheel* (New York: Fleming H. Revell Company, 1895).     11
4. Women of History postcard accordion set, interior, 3-D view. Courtesy of Helaine Victoria Press, Inc.     14
5. Mary Astell notecard. Title page to her 1694 treatise, published anonymously, advocating for equal educational opportunities for women and career options beyond mother and nun. Courtesy of Helaine Victoria Press, Inc. Title page reproduced from [Mary Astell], *A Serious PROPOSAL to the Ladies, For the Advancement of their true and greatest Interest*, By a Lover of her SEX., London, Printed for K. Wilkin at the King's Head in St. Paul's Churchyard, 1694).     25

6. Nancy Poore and Jocelyn Cohen in Venice, CA, 1974. Courtesy of Helaine Victoria Press, Inc. and Smith College Special Collections. 33
7. Women in Art: A Special Issue of *Sister*. 35
8. Radclyffe Hall and Una Troubridge postcard. Courtesy of Helaine Victoria Press, Inc. 40
9. *Flair* magazine cover, New York issue, September 1950. 42
10. 1893 Woman's Building & Sophia Hayden postcard. Courtesy of Helaine Victoria Press, Inc. Photo reproduced from Mary Kavanaugh Oldham Eagle, ed., *The Congress of Women held in the Woman's Building World's Columbian Exposition, Chicago U.S.A. 1893* (Chicago, IL: Monarch Book Company, 1894). 49
11. Sojourner Truth postcard. Courtesy of Helaine Victoria Press, Inc. Photo reproduced from Jacqueline Bernard, *Journey Toward Freedom, The Story of Sojourner Truth* (NY: Norton, 1967). 50
12. Equal Rights Amendment postcard, front. Courtesy of Helaine Victoria Press, Inc. 52
13. Connie Marsh memorial print. Courtesy of Jocelyn H. Cohen. 55
14. Three Singular Women in Concert, Margie Adam, Susan Gluck, and Judy Grahn flyer. Courtesy of Helaine Victoria Press, Inc. 58
15. Photo of collective from inside Lesbian History Exploration packet, 1975. Courtesy of Jocelyn H. Cohen 62
16. Woman Voter bookplate. Courtesy of Helaine Victoria Press, Inc. Illustration reproduced and adapted from the book review page of *The Woman Voter* magazine, N.Y., 1915. 66
17. Elizabeth Gurley Flynn postcard. Courtesy of Helaine Victoria Press, Inc. Photo reproduced with permission from Elizabeth Gurley Flynn, *The Rebel Girl, an autobiography; my first life 1906-1926* (NY: International Publishers, 1986). 73

18. Elizabeth Gurley Flynn postcard, back, "Rebel Girl" inset photo. Courtesy of Helaine Victoria Press, Inc. Image reproduced from Joe Hill, "The Rebel Girl" (Chicago, IL: Rayner Dalheim & Co., Music Printers & Engravers, [1915]). 74
19. Fanny Bullock Workman notecard with the message: "What can a woman do; Anything she pleases. Congratulations!" Courtesy of Helaine Victoria Press, Inc. Photo reproduced from Fanny Bullock Workman, *Two Summers in the Ice Wilds of the Eastern Karakoram* (New York: E.P. Dutton and Co., 1916); border reproduced from Martha Louise Rayne, *What Can a Woman Do: Or Her Position in the Business and Literary Worlds* (Detroit, MI: F.B. Dickerson, 1884). 77
20. Madame Blanchard First Day Cover Envelope Stamp Block, numbered. Courtesy of Helaine Victoria Press, Inc. 83
21. Emily Carr postcard. Courtesy of Helaine Victoria Press, Inc. 85
22. Book Sale Invitation notecard. Courtesy of Helaine Victoria Press, Inc. 89
23. Chandler & Price printing press. Courtesy of Helaine Victoria Press, Inc. and Smith College Special Collections. 93
24. Columbia, Helaine Victoria Press logo. Courtesy of Helaine Victoria Press, Inc. 95
25. Jocelyn Cohen on woodpile. Courtesy of Vicki Leighty. 98
26. Nancy Poore and Jocelyn Cohen working in the print shop. Courtesy of Helaine Victoria Press, Inc. and Smith College Special Collections. 99
27. Thanksgiving broadside. Courtesy of Helaine Victoria Press, Inc. 104
28. Women of History postcard accordion set, back cover. Courtesy of Helaine Victoria Press, Inc. 107
29. Ida B. Wells-Barnett postcard. Courtesy of Helaine Victoria Press, Inc. Photo courtesy of Alfreda Duster. 111

30. Nancy Poore printing on the Chandler & Price press, 1977. Courtesy of Helaine Victoria Press, Inc. and Smith College Special Collections. 112
31. Jocelyn Cohen at the Michigan Women's Music Festival, 1983. Courtesy of Helaine Victoria Press, Inc. and Smith College Special Collections. 115
32. Knock Knock, Jazz Age notecard. Courtesy of Helaine Victoria Press, Inc. 117
33. Suffragists & the Statue of Liberty print. Courtesy of Helaine Victoria Press, Inc. Verse from Alice Duer Miller, *Are Women People* (New York: George H. Doran, 1915); illustration by Christine Eber. 120
34. 1978 Helaine Victoria Press Catalog. Courtesy of Helaine Victoria Press, Inc. 121
35. Harriet Tubman, Black Women Heritage First Day Cover. Courtesy of Helaine Victoria Press, Inc. 123
36. The Fairy Melusine broadside. Courtesy of Helaine Victoria Press, Inc. 124
37. Jocelyn Cohen printing on the Chandler & Price press. Courtesy of Helaine Victoria Press, Inc. and Smith College Special Collections. 125
38. Olive Schreiner postcard. Courtesy of Helaine Victoria Press, Inc. 129
39. Break-Time at the Defense Plant postcard. Courtesy of Helaine Victoria Press, Inc. Photo courtesy of the Walter P. Reuther Library, Archives of Labor and Urban Affairs, Wayne State University. 135
40. Bread & Roses emblem. Courtesy of Helaine Victoria Press, Inc. 137
41. Lucy Parsons postcard. Courtesy of Helaine Victoria Press, Inc. Photos courtesy of the Labadie Collection, University of Michigan. 139
42. Ellen Swallow Richards postcard. Courtesy of Helaine Victoria Press, Inc. Photos courtesy of Massachusetts Institute of Technology Historical Collections. 141

43. Helaine Victoria Press logo used on letterpress printed postcards. Courtesy of Helaine Victoria Press, Inc.  147
44. Alfreda Duster, Nancy Poore, and Rosa Horn. Courtesy of Jocelyn H. Cohen.  149
45. Trackwomen on the Baltimore & Ohio Railroad postcard. Courtesy of Helaine Victoria Press, Inc. Photo courtesy of the National Archives.  162
46. Nancy Poore, Camille Saad, Merry Bateman, and Jocelyn Cohen. Courtesy of Helaine Victoria Press, Inc. and Smith College Special Collections.  164
47. 1980–81 Helaine Victoria Press Catalog featuring many new offerings. Courtesy of Helaine Victoria Press, Inc. Photo reproduced from *The Woman Citizen*, May 1918.  165
48. Vicki Leighty, Jocelyn Cohen, and Nancy Poore, ca. 1981. Courtesy of Vicki Leighty.  169
49. Kimura Komako postcard. Courtesy of Helaine Victoria Press, Inc. Photo reproduced from *The Woman Citizen*, May 1918.  170
50. Whiskey Crusade postcard. Courtesy of Helaine Victoria Press, Inc. Photo of Lucy Thurman reproduced from Elizabeth L. Davis, *Lifting as They Climb* (Chicago: National Association of Colored Women, 1933); photo of the sidewalk scene at Corcoran's courtesy of the Ohio Historical Society; photo of the saloon interior courtesy of the Kansas Historical Society, Topeka; photo of the temperance hatchet courtesy of the Smithsonian Institution.  175
51. Susan B. Anthony in Her Study postcard. Courtesy of Helaine Victoria Press, Inc. Photo by Frances Benjamin Johnston, courtesy of the Library of Congress.  177
52. Zora Neale Hurston postcard. Courtesy of Helaine Victoria Press, Inc. Photo courtesy of the Library of Congress.  184
53. Holiday Rebus broadside, handmade paper. Courtesy of Helaine Victoria Press.  193

54. Rosies with cakes celebrating their defense work during WWII. Courtesy of Helaine Victoria Press, Inc. and Smith College Special Collections. 196
55. Phyllis Carter postcard. Courtesy of Helaine Victoria Press, Inc. Photo courtesy of the Library of Congress; photo and fieldwork by Beverly J. Robinson. Information and quotations are from her interviews (1977–79) and subsequent report on the project. 199
56. Adrienne Rich, "Split at the Root," broadside. From *Nice Jewish Girls: A Lesbian Anthology,* ed. Evelyn Torton Beck (Watertown, MA: Persephone Press, 1982.) Courtesy of Helaine Victoria Press, Inc. 206
57. Bernice Schipp. Courtesy of Helaine Victoria Press, Inc. and Smith College Special Collections. 210
58. Lawrie Hamilton. Courtesy of Helaine Victoria Press, Inc. and Smith College Special Collections. 212
59. Paula Worley. Courtesy of Helaine Victoria Press, Inc. and Smith College Special Collections. 214
60. Michelle Cliff, from *Abeng,* broadside, handmade paper. Courtesy of Helaine Victoria Press, Inc. 222
61. Otomi woman postcard on handmade paper. Courtesy of Helaine Victoria Press, Inc.; picture courtesy of Lilly Library, Indiana University, Bloomington, IN. 224
62. Women and Papermaking folio, front cover. Courtesy of Helaine Victoria Press, Inc. 225
63. Displays at the Ten-Year Retrospective show. Courtesy of Helaine Victoria Press, Inc., and Smith College Special Collections. 228
64. Ten-Year Retrospective Exhibit Opening Invitation postcard. Courtesy of Helaine Victoria Press, Inc. 229
65. Nancy Poore & Jocelyn Cohen before the Ten-Year Retrospective Opening, 1983. Courtesy of Helaine Victoria Press, Inc. and Smith College Special Collections. 229
66. Nan Brooks performing at the Ten-Year Retrospective opening. Courtesy of Jocelyn H. Cohen. 230

67. Paula Worley, Bernice Schipp, Toba Cohen, Vicki Leighty, Beth Robinson, and Jocelyn Cohen. Courtesy of Vicki Leighty. 232
68. Jane Addams & Mary McDowell postcard. Courtesy of Helaine Victoria Press, Inc. Photo courtesy of Jane Addams Memorial Collection, University Library, University of Illinois at Chicago. 236
69. Mary McLeod Bethune postcard. Courtesy of Helaine Victoria Press, Inc. Photo courtesy of Bethune-Cookman College. 237
70. Madam C. J. Walker postcard. Courtesy of Helaine Victoria Press, Inc. Photo courtesy of Madam C. J. Walker Manufacturing Co., Indianapolis, IN; research and caption by A'Lelia P. Bundles, great-great-granddaughter of Madam Walker. 238
71. Emma Tenayuca postcard, inscribed to Vicki Leighty, 1984. Courtesy of Vicki Leighty. 247
72. Uprising of the 20,000 and Clara Lemlich postcard. Courtesy of Helaine Victoria Press, Inc. Photo "Calling for a vote for a general strike" courtesy of the American Jewish Archives; photo of Clara Lemlich reproduced from *Munsey's Magazine*. 248
73. Women in the American Labor Movement folio, front cover. Courtesy of Helaine Victoria Press, Inc. 251
74. Edmonia Lewis postcard. Courtesy of Helaine Victoria Press, Inc. Photo courtesy of the Schomburg Collection, New York Public Library; research by Bernice Schipp. 257
75. Rosie the Riveter postcard. Courtesy of Helaine Victoria Press, Inc. Photo of WWII poster courtesy of the National Archives. 258
76. Women Making History, Queen of the Cards T-shirt. Courtesy of Helaine Victoria Press, Inc. Design by Donna Fay Reeves. 265
77. Jocelyn Cohen with Helaine Victoria Press Women's History Shop sign. Courtesy of Vicki Leighty. 269

78. Jovita Idar postcard. Courtesy of Helaine Victoria Press, Inc. Photo courtesy of Institute of Texan Cultures, originally taken by A. I. Idar in Laredo, TX, 1914, in the print shop of *El Progreso* for which Idar wrote; caption by Vicki L. Leighty using interviews with Jovita Lopez, 1985. 273
79. Yoshiko Hayakawa postcard. Courtesy of Helaine Victoria Press, Inc. Photos by Marcelina Martin; caption by Marcelina Martin and Edith Millikan. 277
80. Helaine Victoria Press women's history bookmarks over the years, a sampling. Courtesy of Helaine Victoria Press, Inc. 278
81. Latina History and Culture bookmark. Courtesy of Helaine Victoria Press, Inc. 279
82. Elsa Gidlow postcard. Courtesy of Helaine Victoria Press, Inc. Photos: 1924 (left) and 1965 in her garden (right) courtesy of Booklegger Publishing; 1983 (middle) courtesy of Marcelina Martin (photographer); caption by Celeste West. 280
83. Donna Fay Reeves with photographer Lori Sudderth at the Helaine Victoria Press Women's History Shop opening on November 8, 1986. Courtesy of Helaine Victoria Press, Inc. and Smith College Special Collections. 282
84. Herschel and Toba Cohen at the Helaine Victoria Press Women's History Shop opening on November 8, 1986. Courtesy of Helaine Victoria Press, Inc. and Smith College Special Collections. 282
85. Prof. Audrey McCluskey reading at Black Women: History opening, 1987. Courtesy of Helaine Victoria Press, Inc. and Smith College Special Collections. 286
86. Mary Fields postcard. Courtesy of Helaine Victoria Press, Inc. Photo courtesy of Wedsworth Memorial Library (Cascade, MT); caption by Audrey McCluskey. 288
87. Nadine Stair, "If I Had My Life to Live Over" broadside. Courtesy of Helaine Victoria Press, Inc. 292

88. WWI Rivet-gang Workers postcard. Courtesy of Helaine Victoria Press, Inc. Photo courtesy of the National Archives; caption by Deborah Hoskins. 297
89. Jocelyn Cohen at the National Women's Music Festival in Bloomington, Indiana, 1986. Courtesy of Vicki Leighty. 301
90. Women in Social Protest postcard set, front cover. Courtesy of Helaine Victoria Press, Inc. Design by Laura Sparks. 307
91. Chinese American Garment Workers Strike postcard. Courtesy of Helaine Victoria Press, Inc. Photo copyright 1974 by Cathy Cade; caption by Judy Yung. 310
92. Disability Rights, Sharon Kowalski, Lesbian and Gay March postcard. Courtesy of Helaine Victoria Press, Inc. Photo courtesy of copyright JEB (Joan E. Biren), 1987; caption by Donna Fay Reeves. 311
93. Dine (Navajo) Women, the Longest Walk postcard. Courtesy of Helaine Victoria Press, Inc. Photo courtesy of copyright JEB (Joan E. Biren), 1978; caption by Brad Howard. 313
94. Sisters of the Harlem Renaissance postcard set, front cover. Courtesy of Helaine Victoria Press, Inc. Design by Sharon L. Sklar; photo courtesy of the Moorland Spingarn Research Center, Howard University Archives, Howard University, Washington DC. 320
95. Sisters of the Harlem Renaissance postcard set, back cover. Courtesy of Helaine Victoria Press, Inc. Design by Sharon L. Sklar; photo of Nella Larsen courtesy of the Estate of Carl Van Vechten; photo of A'Lelia Walker courtesy of A'Lelia P. Bundles. 322
96. A'Lelia Walker postcard. Courtesy of Helaine Victoria Press, Inc.; photo courtesy of A'Lelia P. Bundles, great-great-granddaughter of A'Lelia Walker; caption by A'Lelia P. Bundles). 324

97. Chandler & Price press headed for Seneca Falls, NY. Courtesy of Jocelyn H. Cohen. 329
98. Laura Sparks at the Women's Rights National Historical Park, The Suffrage Press print shop, 1995. Courtesy of Jocelyn H. Cohen. 330
99. Lily Press to Helaine Victoria Press, broadside. Courtesy of Helaine Victoria Press, Inc. 332
100. Jocelyn Cohen in front of the Women's Rights National Historical Park, The Suffrage Press print shop, 1995. Courtesy of Jocelyn H. Cohen. Photo by Patricia Antelles. 333

## Acknowledgments

This book, like the products of Helaine Victoria Press, is the result of a host of collaborative relationships. We are very grateful for all of them and for the new and renewed friendships they have provided.

We are deeply indebted to the women of Convivial Design, Melinda Hess and Patricia Antelles, who scanned hundreds of postcards and related ephemera, gave these items their correct file names, and figured out how to digitize the postcard captions. We are especially grateful to Patricia Antelles for the video she captured in 1994–1995, documenting key events in the history of Helaine Victoria Press and adding moving images to the visual archive. We are thankful that Melinda Hess brought her filmmaker skills to shaping, editing, and perfecting our audio and video clips. We also appreciate the work of Perrie Levitt, the data wrangler who proofread the postcard captions, repairing the errors produced by optical character recognition scanning software, and who worked with Convivial Design to execute the comprehensive metadata plan necessary to produce a digital book. Finally, we are grateful to Robin Hackett for her enthusiastic production of the index for the print edition of this book.

When contacted, many women cheerfully offered their memories of working with Helaine Victoria Press in a variety of capacities. Many thanks to all who responded to our queries. Nancy

Poore and Vicki Leighty provided hours of consultative help in addition to detailed audio interviews. Vicki Leighty also searched her personal archives, offering photos and documents unavailable elsewhere.

Early in our process, Donna Fay Reeves took Julia Allen on a tour of key Helaine Victoria Press sites in Martinsville and Bloomington; later, she shared her memories of working for the press in an audio interview. Susan Gubar, Jean Robinson, and Barbara Ann Caruso generously shared their memories of Helaine Victoria Press in either in-person or telephone interviews; Merrie Bateman and Camille Saad, Joan Sterrenburg, and Ellen Dwyer responded thoughtfully to our sent-out-of-the-blue questionnaires.

The Helaine Victoria Press records are now housed in the Special Collections at Smith College, where Mary Biddle helped both of us—at different times—access and use the papers. We are especially appreciative for all the digital copies of Helaine Victoria Press photographs made by a technician at Smith.

The process of compiling all of the Helaine Victoria Press products, photographs, audio files, and digital files has meant seeking permission from many individuals and entities to reproduce these assets. In some cases, it has meant locating people with whom we have not had contact for many years. Many thanks to those who helped us with this process and who gave us permission to include their images and voices.

This book would still be wishful thinking on our parts without the enthusiasm, coaching, and extraordinary patience of our editor, Beth Bouloukos at Lever Press; her assistant, Hannah Brooks-Motl; our editor Sean Guynes; and the publishing team at the University of Michigan, Jason Colman and Amanda Karby, to all of whom we offer our sincere gratitude.

Acknowledgments come in many forms—not only in offering thank-yous, but also in recognizing good timing, opportunity, and luck. Before much of the country shut down to slow the progress of the novel coronavirus COVID-19, the Smith College Special Collections kept regular hours, and traveling from the West Coast to gather information from the twenty-three archival boxes seemed like a long trek, but not impossible. Most of the collaborative work for the manuscript occurred during three years of four-day, in-person retreats each season. We want to acknowledge that the experience of writing this book would have taken on a very different rhythm and form if our meetings had not been possible, and the three research trips to Smith College in Northampton, MA had not occurred. We also wish to thank Sonoma State University for providing unlimited Zoom access, without which our last year and a half of pandemic-enforced online collaboration would have been far more difficult.

Loving support from partners nourished the project. Julia M. Allen offers heartfelt thanks to Jane B. Cedar for her generosity and willingness to live with this project for several years. Jocelyn Cohen is deeply grateful to Alma Hecht (1955–2019) and for her own arboreal work, with the respite offered by the trees and gardens she cared for throughout the bookmaking journey.

Despite, or along with, the pandemic and loss of loved ones, the book progressed and came to fruition. As we worked on the manuscript, we came to recognize again the large and dedicated network of feminists/womanists, of which Helaine Victoria Press was a part, who continue to question, rethink, and remake the world around us.

In spite of our best efforts, we may have overlooked or misconstrued some events in the history of Helaine Victoria Press and those related years in the feminist movement. We alone are responsible, and we apologize for any errors of fact or interpretation that appear in our narrative.

*Preface*

This book is the story of the nearly two-decade evolution of Helaine Victoria Press, a Lesbian feminist small press that published the first postcards and other educational non-book materials about women in history. It is a story that folds in layers of politics and culture, as well as anecdotal stories—from print, art, craft, rural living, and economics—that bookended what we saw at the time as the Women's Liberation Movement. It also is the story of a dream envisioned by two women, Nancy Poore and myself: the dream to weave a life that was built on telling *everyone* about women's achievements, caring for the land, keeping the craft of letterpress printing alive, making art that was for the masses, and all the while earning a living wage.

Before the idea of making postcards about women occurred to us, Nancy and I were already talking about moving from Los Angeles (LA) to the country. Nothing about the idea had a structure, and although land was cheap in the 1970s, neither of us had any savings. Already a seasoned journalist, Nancy was intent on writing fiction, and I was still committed to painting and exploring what a female sensibility in art meant or could reveal through my large, would-be expensive oil paintings. I had wonderful support in the Feminist Art Program (FAP) from both Judy Chicago and Miriam Schapiro. Producing the cards was to be a side pursuit and even as the venture grew, both Nancy and I were sure we could do both—

research, print, publish, and distribute women's history postcards while she wrote her novels and I continued to paint.

In Los Angeles, we each were juggling multiple jobs. Nancy was doing freelance writing, and I was finishing my BFA at Cal Arts in the FAP and working part-time in the library. During those early years, the press was called Helaine Victoria Enterprises because we were not printers at first, so calling it a press seemed presumptuous. "Enterprises," we both decided, made us sound bigger than two women designing postcards at a kitchen table, and thus more respectable. As vibrant as the feminist LA art scene was in the early 1970s, I felt alienated as my new interest in printing and mass-producing a form of art did not seem to meet with the feminist art community approval. It was OK to print, but not in the volume of 500 to 1,000 copies. The divisive politics and dissolution of the collaboration between Judy Chicago and Miriam Schapiro left me feeling like I was on an island, and Nancy was one person who understood. She and I shared not only our romantic connection, but political and ideological agreement as well. There seemed to be something sexy about sharing everything.

I wanted out of LA with a passion; I wanted to create a harmonious, somewhat utopian place where Nancy and I would create and craft wonderful postcards about lost women in history. And that is what we did.

The move to rural Indiana in 1976 was serendipitous. Lacking financial resources, time, knowledge, or a skill set for relocating in the country, I felt stuck in LA, and that dream to live in the country seemed nothing more than that. My brother, Marty, had moved from his small home in the Indiana countryside and had been renting it out for $130 a month, enough to cover his mortgage and taxes. Marty had moved there at the encouragement of his friends, the Amys, who lived at the end of the road. Ultimately, country life did not suit his lifestyle. When I found out he was looking for a new tenant, I grabbed the chance, and Nancy agreed on my proposal to move.

But southern, rural Indiana was neither a welcoming nor a hospitable place for progressively minded people, let alone Jews or gays and Lesbians. Martinsville, the closest town ten miles away, was the home of William Chaney, Grand Dragon of the Ku Klux Klan in Indiana. There was little overt daily discrimination against Black people in Martinsville, because locals had managed to intimidate just about anyone who was "different" from coming there, including Black and Jewish residents or others culturally different from the generally white population.

In spite of the cloud of prejudice and bigotry, some people, both in town and country, wanted to do better. For the most part, our country lane appeared to be a small haven of such people, and was a bit different than the surrounding community; the seven neighbors on the mile long, one-lane road were of the mindset that "it is none of my business what my neighbor's lifestyle or politics is." When Marty told the Amys that his sister was moving into his place, they encouraged us, knowing well that I'm Jewish and that Nancy and I were gay. With the support of my family sixty miles away in Indianapolis, the assurance of friendly neighbors, and a place in the country that came to us with such ease, I balanced my fear of Martinsville with the possible dream. However, more than once as a school bus or a carful of teenagers drove down the road, we heard "lezzie queers" yelled at our house. I liked to think it was no one I knew.

Our new home on ten acres included a 400-square-foot garage that we turned into a printshop, office, and distribution center. Because I never envisioned the press beyond Nancy and me, the thought of other women coming out to work did not cross my mind before we moved there. However, as our enterprise grew, the help, camaraderie, and company of other women had a growing appeal. Guests helping out was a treat, and my parents came often on their Sundays off, enabling us to keep up the land and manage the staggering amount of work involved in running a publishing company. The one-hour drive to the Martinsville printshop from the two feminist enclaves, Indianapolis and Bloomington, posed one barrier. In addition, driving from Bloomington, Martinsville with its racist reputation, lay ominously in between.

The distance and need for a car, time, and courage to go through Martinsville meant that coming out to Helaine Victoria Press was no easy task. Plus, we had no funds to pay anyone. The press paid the $130 monthly rent which covered both the business and our 500-square-foot home on ten acres. We took a draw when possible for daily living, grew our own food, and I had a cash red raspberry crop. As much as Nancy and I wanted to make the cards available inexpensively, when it came time for needing more help with the business, we also wanted to be able to pay women who otherwise could not work there. The economics of a subsistence style of life and work did not allow for much room to pay women a wage of any sort, let alone a living wage. With some effort and determination, some women from varied class backgrounds made their way out to us, but there were few women of color in both the Bloomington and Indianapolis feminist communities, or they had formed their own coalitions and movements. The unique situation we had made our lifestyle possible. And even with that, my family pitched in time and resources, like a heater for the printshop, a new refrigerator, and a small loan for the printing equipment.

Before moving to Indiana, Nancy and I mostly combed the stacks of libraries in search of women for the postcards. We felt like detectives, yet almost all of the women we found were white: white artists, white suffragists, white activists. If white women's history seemed buried to us, the histories of Black women, Latinas, Chicanas, Native women, and Jewish women alike were further lost or hidden. As our awareness and consciousness grew, we realized we were missing out on critical slices of women's contributions and involvement in—well, the world. Although all my teachers in the FAP were Jewish, as a Jewish woman, it did not even occur to me that there seemed to be few women artists from earlier periods historically who were Jewish. Later, I found that

Jewish women, mostly from poor immigrant families, were in the forefront of many labor and working-class movements. Finding out about this grassroots rebellion and determination to reform working conditions and improve women's lives strengthened my identity as a Jewish woman. In our early research, we did discover Rosa Luxemburg, the Jewish German socialist activist. Even so, her Jewish identity was often obscured in the library sources. When we produced the postcard of Luxemburg as part of our first eight postcards, I recall feeling a bit of surprise and pride to learn she was Jewish. If I felt additionally proud discovering amazing women from my culture, it stood to reason that others would feel similarly as their heritage and identity was revealed.

As we realized those omissions in earlier cards, we called ourselves to task for more diversity and inclusion and better representation in future research and publishing. What could we do better, to whom could we give greater representation, and what did we need to do to engage and focus on others who had been left behind or left out? Our change in focus noticeably occurred when Nancy and I moved to the Indiana countryside in 1976 and became devoted full-time to the press. As our research skills developed, Helaine Victoria Press (meaning Nancy and I) worked to mitigate the omissions. Our shift from using libraries to archives and special collections for research provided new avenues for discovering and recovering marginalized women. That said, it seemed like each community, culture, or marginalized segment of the population had its own nuances of how and where to look, taking us on another journey each time. As popular historians of women's history, we made up everything we did along the way. Discovering how to find these diverse populations was a learned practice not just for us, but in academia, as well. It was not as though others had already made these discoveries and had a vision to share with the world.

Across the country, the women in print (WiP) community challenged publishers to address race and diversity issues. The white, feminist print community overall had to reckon with our publishing material and our business practices. Reaffirmed by the voices within the WiP community, we felt more compelled to fill the gaps in women's history. Helaine Victoria Press co-evolved with the ideologies and what was deemed most urgent and important in the feminist publishing world.

As Nancy and I pursued our research, the voices of women of color, particularly Black women and Chicanas at the WiP conferences, articulated the additional economic, social, and political obstacles they encountered. These included less access to money, discrimination, and lack of interest in their manuscripts from mainstream publishers, and, if works did get published, fewer reviews in magazines, tabloids, and journals. Their leadership and words in workshops and in print in the women's publications helped point the way and solidify how we would move forward. Their work and energy, as exhausting as it must have been for them, was truly monumental. It continued to fuel Helaine Victoria Press's passion to uncover women's accomplishments. For example, our Women in Social Protest series wove together the activism of Chinese Americans, Native women, African Americans, women with disabilities, Lesbians, and Mexican Americans. We also published specific series on Latinas, Jewish women, and women in the Harlem Renaissance. We began reaching out to women all over the country who were familiar with or specialized in particular subjects, inviting them to write postcard captions. That not only gave an appropriate voice to the card caption but also provided recognition for the researcher to have her/his name on the back of the postcard.

Ironically, the strength of the WiP movement and all our voices collectively insisting on better representation and highlighting the lack of diversity in the publishing world did not go unnoticed by mainstream publishers and distributors. This in turn had some adverse effects on many of the smaller feminist presses and their efforts to publish diverse works. Having led the way and created a niche audience for all women's writing, small feminist publishers watched as larger corporations stepped in, making it difficult for the smaller feminist enterprises to compete and thus survive. We watched this scenario unfold, and although book publishing did not directly affect Helaine Victoria Press, many more postcard publishers and book publishers branching out began producing postcards on women. However, as far as crafting the postcard as an educational tool, multi-dimensional with extensively researched captions on the back, Helaine Victoria Press held a unique space.

Nancy and I had an idealistic philosophy about shared roles: as much as possible, there was to be no division of labor in any part of the printing and publishing processes or in the care of the land. Over the years, I have also found that some of the best collaborations occur when people actually have different strengths, or small egos, and the load can be equally carried by all parties. In the beginning, Nancy, an editor by profession, knew more about the print and journalism world than I did. Final edits of the captions went to her. But in the printshop, we both had similar skills. Her design sense was more based in movements, such as Art Deco, Art Nouveau, or Victorian; for me, with a fine arts background, it was more what I thought looked nice, sometimes bordering on a handmade look, like the Women & Ecology series. I was also striving toward a female sensibility in art or craft. We both treasured earlier craft traditions where time and skill embellished a product. We shared setting type, printing, packaging the cards, filling orders, and the day-to-day business tasks and chores. We shared equally and passionately our friendship and vision, as well as the breadth of interest and skills necessary to run a small press; shared, too, was our desire to push the craft of letterpress, experiment, and innovate in our artistry.

What I learned about collaboration over these last five decades came into play in writing this book. In the 1970s, I watched the collaboration of my two mentors, Judy Chicago and Miriam Schapiro, crumble. Then, in the early 80s, my collaboration with Nancy dissolved. As Helaine Victoria Press grew, I reinvented models for collaborating. In the 1990s, before the internet was readily available, I worked with fast-paced, highly collaborative teams in interactive multimedia.

My connection with my coauthor, Julie Allen, began in 1990, when we were roommates at the Berkshire Conference on the History of Women at Rutgers University. The organizers paired us up based on each of us requesting a "quiet, non-smoker, no scents or perfumes." I did not expect someone I would like so much, let alone become longtime friends with, let alone write a book together. A few years after Julie's book, *Passionate Commitments: The Lives of Anna Rochester and Grace Hutchins*, came out in print and her travels promoting it became less time-consuming, I had posed an idea: "Julie, would you like to work on a book about Helaine Victoria Press?" With no pause, no hesitation, she replied unabashedly, "YES!" I am still struck by that moment.

We began meeting every season, alternating between my home in San Francisco and her home in Portland or beach cottage nearby. As the book evolved and stories came back to life, we framed a panorama of issues and politics roaring at the time, ranging from race and culture, sexual identity, socioeconomics, class, disability access, love, heartbreak, art versus craft, isolation, and more. In terms of collaborating for this book, Julie and I have different skill sets for its crafting. She comes from an academic background, a professor of rhetoric, English, and women's studies. She reads voraciously, and her research skills on the internet keep pace with the times. She has a broad perspective on history, social movements, all the isms—and, of course, feminism. And she brought a very unexpected gift: Beth Bouloukos, her editor from SUNY Press, had accepted the position of Senior Acquisition Editor with the new blossoming Lever Press. Beth reached out to Julie asking if she was working on anything new. We were over a year into writing, and a publisher was a distant item on our to-do list. We quickly shifted gears and spent our next seasonal retreat filling out the proposal application, and the book was accepted for initial submission. We asked for five years to submit; Lever Press offered us two. Thus, the unexpected part Julie's resources helped play in making this venture possible. Transparency of opportunity is important to acknowledge. It is interconnected with race, culture, class, gender and other considerations as varied as how good one's internet connection is, physical disabilities, and if you have a "room of one's own." Ideologically and politically, privileges make way for opportunities that allow ventures and certain kinds of life possible.

These past three years, I have been the storyteller. As cofounder and director of Helaine Victoria Press, I know the facts and details of the press's everyday activities, challenges, hardships, successes, and all the ways in which we worked. I have enjoyed writing vignettes that filled in factual and anecdotal material. The stories woven throughout the book provide a picture or feeling of the times and the place. Very early on in our process, Julie and I established a collaborative rhythm: me reminiscing and recalling notable and not-so-notable events, and she overlaying the story with context, framing it in history as well as current critical thinking. Her phone interviews with Nancy Poore, my cofounder, added precious facts and anecdotes to the first decade of Helaine Victoria Press's story. Julie and I also reached out to Vicki Leighty, Donna Fay Reeves, and several other participants for memories and confirmations on events. Chapters went back and forth with edits and highlighter ribbons, mine in yellow, hers in green, and questions for both of us in purple.

Whether in painting, printing, publishing, multimedia, or caring for land, within a feminist perspective, collaboration and inclusiveness go hand in hand. My current work has a different kind of collaboration, where I design the look and feel of gardens, creating spaces in nature for people to love and enjoy. As an aesthetic arborist, I work in collaboration with the trees and shrubs to show off their natural form and habit, and from time to time I share this work with others in my field. These past five years collaborating with Julie have been a special joy and spice in my life in the continuum of feminist evolution. As we wrote the book, I could look in retrospect at the ways Helaine Victoria Press evolved, from two women's dream into an organization reckoning with a broad spectrum of challenges. Opportunities come from many places and do not necessarily happen out of hard work, making the right choices, or doing the right thing; this book could not have happened without the collaboration and all Julie brought to it, just as she could not have written it without me.

Today, social action movements continue naming and highlighting the issues we tangled with during feminism's second wave. The journey's path keeps expanding, and hands and arms open wider. Just as my journey with Helaine Victoria Press was one of learning to understand the importance of inclusion, this is the path of feminism as well. I learned at the press how much it meant to individual women who suddenly felt recognized. When history and historians leave out your culture, gender, or race, whether by burying it or through neglect, it is unfair, degrading, and dishonest both on a personal level as well as in the larger scheme of things.

Framing this book historically also made me realize that Helaine Victoria Press had been left out of our history, out of the history of feminist publishing, feminist art, the small press movement, and the second wave of feminism as a whole. We hope this book helps remedy that, as well as re-featuring the women and movements Helaine Victoria Press brought to light for nearly two decades during that exuberant revolution.

Jocelyn Cohen

# INTRODUCTION

> *Nancy Poore remembers the moment she met Jocelyn Cohen: "I walked into the gallery area, and here was this little thing in overalls trying to hold up a canvas bigger than she was. I went over to help, and when we turned the canvas around, there was the painting in all its glory. 'Is it a vegetable?' I asked. She said, 'Yes, it's a Savoy cabbage.'"*[1]

In October of 1972, Jocelyn and Nancy had each joined a group of women in Los Angeles, working to transform an old laundry at 11007 Venice Boulevard into the first women's art gallery, to be called Womanspace.[2]

A freelance journalist at the time, Nancy volunteered as a paste-up artist for LA's feminist newspaper, *Sister*.[3] Jocelyn was enrolled in the Feminist Art Program at California Institute of the Arts, studying with Miriam Schapiro, Judy Chicago, and Arlene Raven.[4]

For many women, Nancy and Jocelyn among them, this was an era of gender awakening. Women questioned and changed laws, institutions, and preconceived perceptions of women's worth, igniting bursts of expression and creativity, along with scrutiny within most disciplines. At the time, this ferment was referred to as the Women's Liberation Movement; now it is more commonly called second-wave feminism. Examining politics, history, philosophy, the sciences, and the arts, women questioned assumptions

1. Savoy cabbage oil painting by Jocelyn Cohen.

around race, class, identity, discrimination, accessibility, exclusion, and equality, not only within patriarchal institutions but among women and within the women's movement, as well.

Rooted in this movement and nourished specifically by the Feminist Art movement, and later, the Women in Print movement, would grow Helaine Victoria Press, the first publisher of women's history postcards, founded in 1973 by Nancy Poore and Jocelyn Cohen. As Lara Kelland has pointed out, Helaine Victoria Press was, above all, an effort to elevate cultural expectations and prospects for women by reshaping "collective memory"— the ways in which people select and sculpt elements of the past in order to articulate and celebrate their aspirations in the present.[5, 6]

The founders did so not by trying to establish monuments or museums, but by blanketing the country with postcards featuring women who had contested the social limits of their eras. The press, which flourished for seventeen years, ultimately published and marketed hundreds of postcards, plus notecards, broadsides, bookmarks, bookplates, and T-shirts, all documenting a history that Nancy, Jocelyn, and later participants excavated from old books and archives.

In this way, the work of Helaine Victoria Press was not just reshaping collective memory, but actively *generating feminist memory*, with feminist memory understood as dynamic and participatory. While the women of Helaine Victoria Press produced the cards, they were purchased by thousands of people across the globe who then made use of them in a multitude of ways, becoming participants in a multidirectional, open ended, rhetorically evolving process of transforming feminist consciousness. Thus, although general terms such as collective memory and public consciousness are widely used, what distinguishes the work of the press and similar organizations is, more specifically, that their efforts were horizontal and mutable, as the cards were designed to travel with intentionality through many hands and cross many fields of vision, acquiring messages, stamps, and addresses, and/or landing on bulletin boards or refrigerators, with meanings constructed by their senders and viewers and their locations and surrounding images.

Moreover, not only did Helaine Victoria Press's images and text reveal women's accomplishments in new ways and through new methods, but much about the way that Jocelyn and Nancy lived and worked challenged standard expectations for women's lives. Using communication media available in the 1970s and 1980s, the cofounders of Helaine Victoria Press re-centered women in the historical record, upended conventional notions of art, insisted upon women's access to technology, and challenged cultural limits on women's relationships with each other—and, throughout the lifespan of the press, they struggled to answer a question they posed to readers of *Sister* in 1975, "Can Women's Businesses Succeed?"[7]

## RECENTERING WOMEN IN THE HISTORICAL RECORD

Nancy and Jocelyn's efforts, originally named Helaine Victoria Enterprises[8] as they did not yet have their own printing press, extended the work of feminist historians such as Eleanor Flexner and Sheila Rowbotham,[9] exemplifying what Michel Foucault would later call an "insurrection of subjugated knowledge."[10] Their research methods illustrate Foucault's concept of "genealogies [...] a combination of erudite knowledge and what people know."[11] Although some scholars make a strong distinction between history and memory, Helaine Victoria Press occupied a middle ground, providing expansive information in the postcard captions, but less, of course, than one might find in an article or book.[12] Marita Sturken's view seems more appropriate when considering the work of Helaine Victoria Press: she sees history and memory as "entangled."[13] The cards were, in short, history recovered in the service of generating feminist memory.

Public memory, as Greg Dickinson, Carole Blair, and Brian Ott point out, is profoundly rhetorical: "Groups tell their pasts to themselves and others as ways of understanding, valorizing, justifying, excusing, or subverting conditions or beliefs of their current moment."[14] Encompassing all the ways that we collectively talk to ourselves about our past and, thus, about who we are, public memory often involves specific locations, including museums, such as the Smithsonian in Washington, DC, or monuments, such as the statues in a local park. Libraries often have the names of authors painted on walls or chiseled into stone facades; even street names and names of schools serve to reinforce public memory (Washington, Adams, Madison, Lincoln, Grant). These frequent reminders of a collective past work to form our identities and reinforce our sense of belonging to a given population.

At the same time, public memory is usually partial rather than inclusive, selecting as significant only those individuals and events deemed (by those controlling the narrative) to represent the values of the collective. It is no surprise, then, that this partiality leads to struggles, which is exactly what happened during the second wave of feminism: women realized they had been largely left out.

Feminists at the time, striving to overcome years of indoctrination into circumscribed lives, were hungry for new possibilities. As Lesbian-feminist photographer Joan E. Biren later commented, "There was nothing in the culture that nourished us."[15] Writing in the early 1970s, poet and author Mary Mackey expressed the longing that many women shared at the time: "Women need models to grow up on [ . . . ]. Models in our society are women who haunt magazines and fashion shows, showing other women how to dress, how to stand, how to become perfect glossy objects. Now we need new kinds of models. Models for our minds."[16]

Altering public consciousness, however, is no simple matter.[17] "Public memory speaks primarily about the structure of power in society because that power is always in question in a world of polarities and contradictions and because cultural understanding is always grounded in the material structure of society itself."[18] Taking on that structure of power directly, some feminists engaged in local actions, seeking to rename streets, parks, or schools, and to memorialize in this way the courage and accomplishments of women such as Rosa Parks. Naming is an important feminist process, from calling out the ways in which women are subjugated— "rape culture," "domestic violence," "glass ceiling"—to coining new terms, such as Ms. as a counterpart to Mr., in order to avoid defining a woman by her marital status. Naming also enables us to remember those, human or mythical, who resisted that subjugation. Feminist institutions such as presses, bookstores, and restaurants were often named in honor of the resisters—Persephone Press, Diana Press, Jane Addams Bookstore. With these naming processes, women claimed both concepts and locations.

However, Nancy and Jocelyn chose a different avenue, one that would disperse images and text across the country (and, as it would turn out, across the world), building the movement by placing small memorials into as many hands as possible. Through personal and archival work, the women of Helaine Victoria unearthed photographs and researched corresponding historical and biographical information for the detailed captions on the backs of the cards, countering the degrading images of women plastered across public spaces. They recovered untold—or forgotten—stories about the labor movement, women artists, women in politics, women and animals, and women and nature, reinstating a collective ancestry exhibiting creativity and strength.

As Nancy and Jocelyn searched libraries and used bookstores, and later delved into unopened archival boxes of photos, they realized that some of the stories had not always been considered insignificant. There had been times when some women were featured in headlines, when their books had been published, and when they were celebrated, at least in some circles, for their achievements. Nancy, who had graduated from Scripps College in 1962, said later, "The women's movement started me reading on the suffragettes' struggle to win voting rights for women. These very proper upper-middle-class Englishwomen were bombing buildings, being thrown in jail, and going on hunger strikes, and no one ever told me about it [ . . . ]. And then I began to wonder what else I didn't know."[19] Jocelyn and Nancy believed that learning these stories would introduce possibilities and galvanize women to action. For some of their earliest cards, they drew on images from Jocelyn's classes in the Feminist Art Program.

## UPENDING CONVENTIONAL NOTIONS OF ART

The Feminist Art Program fueled much visionary feminist recovery work. Initiated by Judy Chicago in 1970 at Fresno State College,[20] the program infused art education with feminist consciousness-raising, construction projects, and efforts to track down the art and accomplishments of women. In 1971, Judy Chicago and Miriam Schapiro collaborated to bring the Feminist Art Program to the new Walt Disney-sponsored California Institute of the Arts, located in the Los Angeles suburb of Valencia. Art historian Arlene Raven joined the faculty in the fall of 1972. Students and faculty predicated much of their work on the relationship between art and feminist consciousness, reading the few available texts on women's history and creating art based on personal and collective experiences. Their work echoed the larger movement's emphasis on challenging from the inside-out the social roles assigned to women, as well as the systematic erasure of women whose lives and work fell outside the limited scope of women's propriety.[21]

As Arlene Raven later commented, "Education became a part of artmaking and artmaking a part of education; the private fed public consciousness, and women's public culture, including women's art, enriched and changed the private hearth."[22] According to Faith Wilding, one of the first students, the program's approach reflected feminist sensibilities, including:

> consciousness-raising; building a female context and environment; female role models; permission to be themselves and to make art out of their own experience as women; collaboration and collective work; and exploring the hierarchies of materials and high-low art practices as well as recovering the positive values of denigrated or marginalized practices.[23]

Realizing the shared nature of experiences previously considered singular and private, then challenging the hierarchies of materials and high-low art practices, opened up fresh possibilities for feminist expression as well as a renewed understanding of the social responsibilities of art. Indeed, a primary goal of the program was to shift the hierarchical structure of the male-controlled art world. Art critic Lucy Lippard articulated this stance, insisting "that feminist art replaced the modernist 'egotistical monologue' with a dialogue—between art and society, between artist and audience, between women artists of the present and those of the past—

and with collaboration as a creative mode."[24] What's more, Lippard suggested, feminist art should be engaging in dialogue with the community. Logically extending this innovation, the founders of Helaine Victoria Press were determined to create forms of feminist memorializing that were not place-bound, but rather that were mobile, reproducible, multipurpose, and modifiable.[25]

Many discussions of public memory concentrate primarily on museums and monuments, calling into question matters of place and public responses to varieties of locations.[26] From the start, however, Nancy and Jocelyn had no intention of creating lasting museum-bound works of art—although collections of Helaine Victoria Press cards are now held at numerous libraries and archives—but rather sought to produce timely, impermanent commodities to intervene in the zeitgeist. They pushed the Feminist Art movement farther away from the capitalist emphasis on gallery and museum cultures of rarity toward a greater degree of collectivity and self-sufficiency. They joined Lucy Lippard and others in shifting the movement toward a rhetorical stance, concerned with the *effect* of a discourse (broadly interpreted to include expression in many forms) on an audience, creating a dialogue that extended into a boundary-less multilogue.

How would viewers take in the images and captions on the cards? In "The Rhetoric of the Image," Roland Barthes outlined the functions of the elements in similar representations. Each card, he argued, has three messages: a linguistic message (as noted above); a coded iconic message; and a non-coded iconic message.[27] The linguistic message responds to the question, "What is it?"[28] and, in the case of Helaine Victoria Press, serves to constrain the image on any given card: this is not just any old photograph of a woman; this is a particular woman in a particular time and place, and what's more, she is significant for the range of her accomplishments in that given time and place. The non-coded iconic, or literal message serves to reinforce the caption, and vice versa. The coded iconic message, then, is the interpretation provided by the viewer, using

2. Women's Christian Temperance Union Officers postcard

Officers of the World's Women's Christian Temperance Union. Left to Right: Anna Gordon, Assistant Secretary; Agnes Slack, Secretary; Frances E. Willard, President; Lady Somerset, Vice President at Large; Mary Sanderson, Treasurer. Often thought of as a handful of elderly fanatics, the WCTU was in fact among the top few groups of social and political influence in the late 19th and early 20th centuries. Flourished chiefly under the dynamic and legendary leadership of Frances Willard (1839–1898). Although best known for its concern over the moral and physical effects of alcohol and drugs, the WCTU's interests and activities extended to every sphere of social reform. They accomplished much for woman's suffrage, education for the poor, and labor reform. A large part of their complaint against the liquor industries included the money and manpower which booze tycoons poured into anti-suffrage campaigns for decades; and the saloons which were male preserves where poor laborers spent their week's pay on escaping in drinks instead of feeding their families. For these reasons, the famed "Polyglot Petition" for world temperance easily collected more than 7 million signatures.

her cultural and ideological background. Although given some direction by the caption, viewers read the images through their own lexicons, making of the image their own personal and elaborated significance.

In order to allow for interpretive possibilities, Nancy and Jocelyn looked for active images rather than simply posed portrait shots. Barbie Zelizer has referred to photographs taken mid-action as being in the "subjunctive voice," further explaining: "Grammatically, the subjunctive qualifies the word of action by situating it within the hypothetical [...]. We come to remember whole events through condensed images that reduce complex and multidimensional phenomena into memorable scenes. Often, they are memorable because they activate impulses about how the 'world might be' rather than how 'it is.'"[29] As Jocelyn and Nancy found, the active images often lent themselves to varieties of feminist meaning making.

Jocelyn, Nancy, and other contributors constructed the postcards, like any rhetorical effort, out of the available means of persuasion, both image and text, conforming to their ideological schema. Viewers would reconstruct the card according to their own lights. For some, the cards never left home; instead, they became the foundation of a personal art gallery.[30] As Donna Fay Reeves, a volunteer and later employee of Helaine Victoria Press, pointed out: "[...] most of the people that I knew that bought the cards weren't mailing them anywhere. They were putting them on their wall, [or] they were buying them as gifts."[31] In other words, the cards functioned as semi-public memorials in a world where women are rarely accorded any public acknowledgment and where women's accomplishments and contributions are often considered transient. While many cards served as low-cost memorial sites, even more did go into the mail, where friends, relations, letter carriers, and shoppers viewing the cards along the way would be at the very least jolted from their certainties.

Writing about the revolutionary potential of feminist art in

3. Frances Willard on Her Bicycle postcard

Frances Willard (1839–1898) was photographed on her bicycle "Gladys," which she learned to ride at age 53. Willard was the best known and most dynamic president of the Woman's Christian Temperance Union and founder of the World W.C.T.U. She was a pioneer suffragist, pacifist, and educator, and was the first Dean of Women at Northwestern University. Witty, resolute, and progressive, she greatly influenced her students despite opposition from Charles Fowler, conservative president of the college—and the former fiancé with whom Willard had broken ties. She said, "Dr. Fowler has the will of Napoleon, I have the will of Queen Elizabeth." She left, explaining: "I would not waste my life in friction when it could be turned into momentum," which is exactly what she turned it to when she moved on to the National W.C.T.U. and made it into the largest women's organization in the country. It was typically venturesome that she took up cycling when she did. Her own delightful account of the adventure is in her 1895 book, *A Wheel Within a Wheel*.

a 1975 article for *Quest: A Feminist Quarterly*, Alexa Freeman and Jackie MacMillan insisted, like Nancy and Jocelyn, that finding negative images of women was easy, but pointless. On the other hand, "[b]y providing us with a positive image of ourselves, art can help us develop the strength to struggle. Feminist art, by definition, must be a force for change, rather than a reflection of society as it is."[32] Key among the ways that artistic content should function was "by helping women develop a sense of identity with each other rather than with the oppressor. Women's history has begun to serve this function," they noted. Moreover, meaningful content should include "a portrayal of revolutionary struggle. Processes of change, including concrete victories, should be emphasized."[33] Nancy and Jocelyn could not have agreed more, and worked to find images and to craft those images into more evocative cards.

By choosing postcards as their medium, Nancy and Jocelyn had also anticipated another of Freeman and MacMillan's mandates: accessibility. "Without exposure," they said, "art is useless and becomes merely an individual exercise. The problem of accessibility in art is manifested both in terms of content (is it convincing?) and exposure (what kind of distribution will it get?)."[34] What could receive wider exposure than a postcard?

In fact, by using the postcard medium to create feminist art, Jocelyn and Nancy were anticipating the current conversation on multimodality—the use of multiple modes to convey a rhetorical message. Drawing out a theory of multimodality, Gunther Kress insisted—echoing, consciously or not, the forty-year-old arguments of Cal Arts graphic design program director Sheila de Bretteville—that "design" is the key term, because it "foregrounds a move away from anchoring communication in convention as social regulation. Design focuses on an individual's realization of their interest in their world."[35] In an unstable social world, design looks into the future, aiming to affect that future. De Bretteville, in fact, had already pushed this concept beyond the individual, pointing out that "the audience is not an audience; it's a co-participant with you." Moreover, she said, "Feminist design looks for graphic strategies that will enable us to listen to people who have not been heard before."[36] Helaine Victoria Press cards gave voice to women who had not been heard before by portraying a woman or women taking action for change, or working for their rights, or for the protection of animals, of a prairie, or of a way of life.

Modes are the materials engaged by design; "a mode is a socially shaped and culturally given semiotic resource for making meaning."[37] Helaine Victoria Press's designs drew upon a range of modes: the paper (in some cases, handmade by Jocelyn), the press, the typefaces, the ornaments,[38] the colors, the images, the biographical and historical sources, and, for delivery, the US Postal Service.[39] Postcards were an early, portable/mobile technology delivering public memories to one's doorstep. In the case of Helaine Victoria Press, postcards provided an inexpensive mobile technology for moving feminist images and information to any location where a postal service delivered mail.

Postcards themselves flourished during the early part of the twentieth century, coinciding with the early women's rights movement and often being used as vehicles to argue for and against woman suffrage and other forms of feminist social change. Indeed, at that time, postcards had only recently become an accepted mode of postal communication. When first introduced, the postcard was considered scandalous. In Germany "in 1865, [General Postal Director] Philipsborn [ . . . ] rejected its introduction due to the 'indecent form of communication on exposed post pages.' The nudity of communication, as Philipsborn recognized, would be nothing but communication of nudity."[40] This anxiety did not prevent postcards from becoming extremely popular across the world during the early part of the twentieth century. Helaine Victoria's revival of the postcard built on this popularity—and on the very feature to which General Postal Director Philipsborn objected: the ready viewability of the card by all those through whose hands it passes.

In addition to individual cards, Helaine Victoria Press com-

4. Women of History postcard accordion set, interior, 3-D view
Women of History accordion album of eight postcards, viewed with album open. Helaine Victoria Press's premier offering, showcasing their creative letterpress style and craft.

bined—or linked—cards in series, placing various scenes of women alone or in groups in close proximity, thus multiplying the meanings by the possible connections.[41] One series was fixed in their orientations—the cards were attached to each other in an accordion strip—and others were simply bundled together, making for even more possible combinations.

Kress viewed representation and communication as two separate "social practices," although in the case of Helaine Victoria Press, the two practices were rarely considered independently. Representation offers an individual's interest in the world, while communication makes that interest available to others. Thus, rhetoric, according to Kress, "is oriented to the social and political dimensions of communication; design is oriented to the semiotic;" in other words, the making of meaning.[42] A designer draws together a multiplicity of modes, all invested with meaning, to shape the larger meaning of the whole. Over time, Jocelyn and Nancy adjusted their printing techniques and their image choices in order to convey their meanings more clearly. Moreover, they deliberately chose subjects with extensive histories, such as women working or engaging in social protest, by this means conveying the long trajectory of feminist activism and women's accomplishments.

In order to create each card, press workers asked, without prompting, the questions Kress considered standard for any communication situation:

> What is the environment of communication? What relations of power are at issue? Who are the participants in communication? What are their criterial characteristics? What is the phenomenon to be communicated? What resources are available to make the message?[43]

They were not alone in working to fuse art and persuasion; indeed, the Feminist Art movement was predicated on the elimination of traditional distinctions. The editors of *Womanspace*, a periodical published briefly by women involved in establishing the eponymous gallery, insisted that they were "consciously attempting to overcome false divisions of disciplines."[44] Likewise, in an article written during this time, graphic designer Sheila de Bretteville pointed to the importance of feminist textual and graphic influence on public consciousness, declaring,

> The design arts are public arts, and as such are major vehicles for forming our consciousness. Consciousness, in turn, is illuminated by communications [ . . . ]. For me, it has been this integral relationship between individual creativity and social responsibility that has drawn me to the design arts [ . . . ]. [I] try to project alternative values into society in the hope of creating a new, even utopian culture, by acting in accordance with values of my own choosing.[45]

Nonetheless, within feminist print culture, Helaine Victoria Press occupied a liminal space. While Nancy and Jocelyn found the dissolving of disciplinary boundaries liberatory and established Helaine Victoria Press on exactly the intersection of these old fence lines, the practical systems of marketing were not keeping up with the new forms. As Kress pointed out, Western societies have long emphasized language over image for serious rhetorical tasks. Having been trained in linguistic skills, many feminists started newspapers and journals, wrote books, founded publishing houses, established bookstores, and wrote song lyrics that provided a soundtrack for the movement. Feminist knowledge was created, by and large, through linguistic means. At the same time, craftswomen infused popular art forms with feminist content, taking advantage of the various festivals and conferences to sell a range of products—clothing, jewelry, and ceramic arts.

Helaine Victoria Press's postcards were clearly artistic material objects, yet they bore rhetorical messages and were motivated by a desire to broadcast information and to educate. However, bookstore shelving still required spines for display, and festivals, often held outdoors, were subject to weather changes that postcards, unlike other crafts, could not withstand.[46] As Donna Fay Reeves recalled, "I remember the problems with having a paper product at an outdoor festival [ . . . ]. I mean, if our product got wet, it was ruined."[47]

Still, every practical impediment led to a creative solution as Nancy and Jocelyn pursued their multifaceted dream of generating feminist memory. The pair were firm supporters of a primary goal of the Feminist Art Program—and the women's movement as a whole—which was to increase women's access to resources. Judy Chicago stated emphatically, "Feminism is a set of principles, and a way of looking at the world that, for me, is rooted in a redefinition of power—from power over others to empowerment."[48] Having been drawn to the Feminist Art Program because of its enthusiastic overthrow of a system that not only isolated artists but also held women's creativity in contempt, Jocelyn welcomed the new emphasis on empowerment. She found the challenges to traditional hierarchies of media, often expressed in terms that set "art" against "craft," especially liberating.[49] Commenting on these challenges, Miriam Schapiro later said, "We tried to erase the harsh line between high art and craft, and now craft has found its way into ideational art and political art in a highly energized manner."[50]

This innovation was especially important to Nancy, who, as a native Chicagoan, was drawn to the Arts and Crafts movement, which aimed to produce beautifully handcrafted material objects. The proponents of the movement strove to eliminate the lines between traditional art and applied and decorative arts. However, although the movement honored women's visual and creative contributions to design and craft, it still upheld the Victorian concept of womanhood. So, while Nancy appreciated the social and political aims of the movement, she was aware of the ways in which the men of the movement restricted women's participation, and she welcomed feminist efforts to claim all aspects of design and print culture. Craft, on the other hand, while in many cases celebrating women's traditional skills, also sometimes meant acquiring skills not taught to young girls; in Jocelyn and Nancy's case, it meant learning how to print.

## INSISTING UPON WOMEN'S ACCESS TO TECHNOLOGY

For activists within the second wave feminist movement, gaining access to technology was not simply about learning a skill. It was, rather, a means to an end—enabling women to control the means of communication and artistic production. Because accessing technology was part of a larger political effort, women in both the Feminist Art and the Women in Print movements consciously fused skill-sharing work with probing discussions of the feminist direction and significance of that work.[51]

Within the Feminist Art Program, Judy Chicago recognized the importance of women learning how to use construction equipment, especially how to handle power tools. She insisted that her students at Fresno State construct their own classroom and studio space, and she herself at one point enrolled in a welding class in order to create large-scale metalwork. As artists, students needed to be able to work in any form that fit the content they wished to portray; as women, they needed to be independent.

Applying these principles, Jocelyn sought out Helen Alm of the Cal Arts graphics program to ask for her advice about learning to print, especially about learning to operate the Rotaprint offset press in the school's graphics lab.[52] Although Nancy was not a student in the program, when Helen Alm learned that Jocelyn and Nancy were trying to print their postcards, she declared, in true feminist fashion, that they should do so at Cal Arts. Jocelyn enrolled in her class for two terms, and Nancy came in after hours to work in the graphics print and production lab.

For Jocelyn, embarking on this journey into graphic design and the process of learning to use the production tools to disseminate words and images meant taking a fork in the road from her previous trajectory as a feminist painter. For Nancy, however, the opportunity easily bridged her life as the daughter of a successful graphic designer in Chicago and her career in journalism with the specialized print work that she had dreamed of doing but had been prevented from accessing because she was a woman. In her youth, Nancy had treasured the times she had spent accompanying her father into small printshops filled with job presses and cases of type. Later, in the mid-1960s, when she had worked as the only woman editor at the *Chicago Tribune*, she had spent years handing off copy to the linotype operators who were typesetting the words for the women's section she edited. Then, she had only been able to watch as men managed the daily newspapers rolling off the large web presses. While Jocelyn initially saw learning to print as a way to produce an art form that could reach more people, for Nancy, the new skill meant she had finally found an avenue to a craft that she had longed to learn.

Printing on the offset press was just the beginning, though. Ultimately, both Nancy and Jocelyn wanted to learn to use a letterpress. No courses were available to them, as almost all printing education, not to mention apprenticeships or printshop jobs, was closed to women, despite the fact that women had been engaged in the printing profession in America since the early Colonial era. In fact, most trades were limited to male applicants, although Title IX, passed in November 1972, was beginning to have an effect. Nonetheless, the culture of discrimination was hard to uproot, and it took innumerable attempts before Nancy and Jocelyn were able to find an instructor, Robert Wilkinson at Santa Monica City College, willing to let them into his course.

Gender discrimination in the trades was widespread and continues to this day. According to Gunseli Berik and Cihan Bilginsoy, two theories attempt to explain the dearth of women in the trades. "The human capital theory emphasizes women's own choices," alleging that women simply don't want to work in the trades. However, in a second, more cogent, theory "accounts by women employed in the skilled trades strongly suggest that the key factor in women's low representation in the skilled trades is discrimination rather than women's choices."[53] Indeed, that was Nancy and Jocelyn's experience. So, how did this discrimination affect the process of generating feminist memory?

In his account of the development of collective memory, Jacques Le Goff organized the history of public memory around shifts in communication technologies.[54] While tracing this history, however, it behooves us to explore *who controls* the communication technologies of a given time. Until the 1970s, access to control of the primary communication technology—print—was effectively denied to half the population, and even after laws were passed to enable women to learn printing, the culture did not change with the laws. It is no wonder that the second wave of feminism saw the rise of a number of women-run printshops, as those who had managed by whatever means to gain skills taught others, and, with the presence of women-run printshops, there ensued a corresponding explosion of publishing houses and feminist bookstores around the country and around the world.[55] Women were determined to gain access to the "culture's meaning-making apparatus."[56]

In 1976 June Arnold, cofounder of Daughters, Inc., a feminist publisher, pointed out that

> [t]here are now more than a hundred and fifty feminist presses or journals in over thirty states. Including women's book stores, we have created a circle of media control with every link covered: a woman writes an article or book, a woman typesets it, a woman illustrates and lays it out, a woman prints it, a woman's journal reviews it, and women read it—from Canada to Mexico and coast to coast.[57]

Women active in this feminist print culture coalesced during the 1970s into the Women in Print movement, prompted by a national conference organized by Arnold. The goals of the conference combined practical skill-sharing and discussion of common problems with work on political questions and forging of connections between feminists in all aspects of print culture. Like the Feminist Art Program, the Women in Print movement merged the acquisition of skills with the elaboration of feminist concepts to create a wholistic approach to expanding the discourse of second wave feminism. Reporting in *off our backs* on the second Women in Print conference, held in Washington, DC, Fran Moira emphasized that the movement was "a many-tentacled network to communicate women's words and works."

Helaine Victoria Press joined the "many-tentacled network" as one of the few printers, uniting with other printers at the conference to establish the US Alliance of Lesbian and Feminist Printers, an organization that published a newsletter and collaborated with other women in print-related fields to organize the Midwest Women in Print conference in Chicago in 1982. According to Fran Moira, "The US Alliance of Lesbian and Feminist Printers was established at the conference. Founded on principles of noncompetitiveness and skills sharing, it is open to individual women in the printing trade and women-owned printshops."[58] The Women in Print movement grew to be a guiding cultural and political force in the development of feminist and Lesbian feminist consciousness. It encompassed women publishers, bookstores, magazines, women's studies programs, newspapers and journals, presses, writers and designers, historians, librarians, and print distributors. Each of these entities in turn created its own hub of activity, networking, and support, bringing together women and creating safe spaces for conversations, whether they be via the written word or one on one exchanges or group discussions. When Jocelyn and Nancy attended the second Women in Print conference, they first shared their own printing expertise at a skills workshop and then joined in ground-breaking discussions of racism and classism in feminist print enterprises.

As the Women in Print movement evolved, the participants faced troubling and complex issues around race discrimination and barriers to equal access to publishing for women of color. Conference participants from the Black, Latina, and working-class communities questioned and challenged the scope of publishing by feminist presses. Emotions ran high as participants struggled to figure out ways for women in grassroots, undercapitalized organizations to deal with the structural and systemic racism that permeated feminist periodicals, bookstores, and publishers, despite the fact that many of these organizations were run by diverse groups of women.

Fran Moira reported that

> [t]here was a spirit of respect and admiration for one another's work and integrity and, in one workshop particularly, there was the unleashing of the fury and anguish of some women of color and some white working-class women. Riding out the fury and anguish were the underlying commonalities and the intention, based not on guilt but desire, to share resources and support one another. [59]

Although issues of race and class were at the forefront of many conversations, WiP also tangled with a complicated and diverse web of people and ideologies. These included—and, to be sure, this is not a comprehensive list—rights of women with disabilities, transgender issues, questions around sexual practices and religious beliefs, and matters of editorial ethics, most especially the question of who, if anyone, has the right to edit the work of someone from a different culture, class, race, or spiritual belief system. The issues were vast, and the workshops, dialogues, and conversations provided a space for women from many marginalized communities not only to find each other and arrange collaborative relationships but to address the gathering as a whole, challenging those with access to publishing technologies and spaces to rethink the ways in which they deployed those resources.

These challenges were central to the ongoing dialogue between Jocelyn and Nancy as they worked to create a comprehensive collection of images and captions. Although Helaine Victoria Press was publishing more and more cards on African American women, women at the conferences insisted upon the importance of searching for women from all racial and ethnic heritages and socioeconomic classes. Thus, the issues raised by WiP discussions both reaffirmed and worked to advance the politics and emphases of Helaine Victoria's publishing choices. And, in turn, Helaine Victoria Press moved others by making visible the accomplishments of neglected and overlooked women, often women of color and/or working-class women, publishing them in a way that invited engagement, whether by adding a message and mailing a card or by posting it in a visible location. Although it was true that the histories of marginalized women were more difficult to recover, Jocelyn and Nancy thrilled to every new discovery. They welcomed the difficulty as an opportunity to expand their skills and learn new strategies for finding women and women's movements concealed in unfamiliar resources and institutions.

While Helaine Victoria Press was committed to generating feminist memory in the most comprehensive sense through mobile and reproducible systems of communication—most notably postcards—their Chandler & Price press and printshop signified more than simply a workplace. Celebrated in all of Helaine Victoria's catalogs and on the backs of the cards, the press represented metonymically women's insistence on access to technology within feminist print culture.[60] Recognizing that the power of the press belongs to those who own it, Jocelyn and Nancy used their press not only to produce the cards, but to engage customers in their semi-annual catalogs with photographs of the press and reports of publishing plans, demonstrating their pleasure and expertise in using this significant piece of communication technology.[61] They also supplied lovingly detailed reports of garden harvests and pictures showing year-by-year tree growth. In this way, they invited readers to share vicariously in their independent and sustainable rural way of life.

## CHALLENGING CULTURAL LIMITS ON WOMEN'S RELATIONSHIPS WITH EACH OTHER

Just as the Chandler & Price letterpress represented women's access to technology to Helaine Victoria Press customers, the ten acres with organic garden and pond figured metonymically as women's independence. As a whole, Helaine Victoria Press epitomized the revolution in women's relationships with one another.

The gay liberation movement that had been building for decades had finally burst forth in 1969 with the Stonewall rebellion, and, although women's participation was not publicly as formidable as was men's, the energy crossed the gender divide and led to a fusion of feminist and Lesbian activism. A key document expressing the logic of Lesbian-feminism is "The Woman Identified Woman" published in 1970 by Radicalesbians. Arguing that sexual categories are socially constructed for the purpose of maintaining masculine power dynamics, the writers assert that "[i]t is the primacy of women relating to women, of women creating a new consciousness of and with each other, which is at the heart of women's liberation, and the basis for the cultural revolution."[62]

The second wave of feminism had led to changes in women's perceptions of one another, opening up new possibilities for self-sufficiency, solidarity, and companionship. At the same time, pressure from women had led to the passage of significant anti-discrimination laws, enabling some women to move into formerly gender-restricted positions. Across the country, inspired by the "back to the land" movement and energized by feminism's avowal of women's strengths, a significant number of women began to form collectives to relocate outside of the cities, seeking to live sustainably and independently. Many of these locations were remote and required that women have and share with each other a wide range of skills. Jocelyn and Nancy were among those seeking a sustainable life outside the city. The press moved to rural land in Indiana, where Jocelyn and Nancy could grow their own food as well as house and operate their beloved Chandler & Price letterpress. They were inspired, as were many people at the time, by Helen and Scott Nearing's book, *Living the Good Life*, which describes the Nearings' efforts to claim rocky-soiled land in Vermont and live a self-sufficient lifestyle there.[63]

Nancy and Jocelyn also found inspiration in centuries-old women's writings. While they were searching the libraries at UCLA and Scripps for neglected images and narratives of women, they found two books that served to add another dimension to their foundational feminist ideology.

In 1694 in London, Mary Astell had written and published *A Serious PROPOSAL to the LADIES for the Advancement of their True and Greatest INTEREST*, offering the book anonymously as "A Lover of Her Sex." In it, she explained her vision of a community, a "religious retirement,"[64] within which women would be able to learn and develop themselves, expanding their choices beyond the standard opportunities for women at the time: mother or nun.

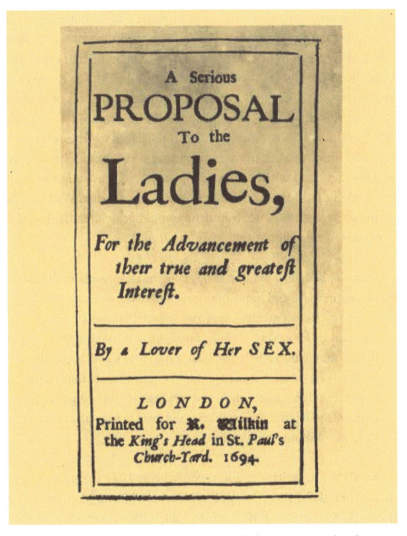

5. Mary Astell, title page to her 1694 treatise, published anonymously, advocating for equal educational opportunities for women and career options beyond mother and nun.

*A SERIOUS PROPOSAL To the Ladies*, attributed to Mary Astell, refutes the 17th century theory of women's incapacity. It is the lack of education, Astell says, which brings about untrained judgment in women and leads them to wrong decisions. She proposed a college with a double aspect: a retreat from the world for those who desire it, and also an institution to fit women to do the greatest good in their own time and to improve the future. The teachings were to be not only religious but secular, including languages, philosophy, literature. In 1697 she wrote Part II, wherein she stirs her reader (whose equality she has already proven) to carry out her own development. Women, she says, should reason things out for themselves, determine their own acts and not rely on custom or be imposed upon by their fathers and husbands.

"Let us learn," she said, "to pride ourselves in something more excellent than the invention of a Fashion, and not entertain such a degrading thought of our own worth as to imagine that our Souls were given us only for the service of our Bodies and that the best improvement we can make of these is to attract the eyes of men."[65]

How was this to be accomplished? Astell proposed a community in which women could devote themselves to "the service of God and improvement of their own minds."[66] As part of her vision, Astell articulated what Nancy and Jocelyn couldn't help but read as a coded description of the Lesbian feminist spirit. Within this community, Astell wrote, friendship would grow unsullied by the demands of the competitive world, so that

> what should hinder but that two Persons of a sympathizing disposition, the make and frame of whose Souls bears an exact conformity to each other and therefore, one would think, were purposely designed by Heaven to unite and mix, what should hinder them from entering into a holy combination to watch over each other for good [ . . . ]. And therefore nothing is more likely to improve us in virtue and to advance us to the very highest pitch of goodness than unfeigned friendship, which is the most beneficial, as well as the most pleasant, thing in the world.[67]

Sarah Scott, writing some seventy years later from her home in Bath, England shared with Lady Barbara Montagu, produced a novel, *A Description of Millennium Hall*, which imagines and narrates such a community as Astell envisioned. She, too, chose to publish anonymously, listing the author as "A Gentleman on his Travels." The community Scott described is constructed on both a biblical and an English political foundation, drawing from one to comment upon the other. Most significantly, however, this imagined community placed women at the center of the commentary, thus shifting their efforts from drawing the attentions of men to their abilities to create a superior form of society.[68] Although neither Nancy nor Jocelyn subscribed to the religious doctrines that framed these two documents, they recognized the essence of women's connections and community that both authors had celebrated. Both books emphasized women's friendships, which were centrally important to both Jocelyn and Nancy and were also fundamental to the emerging Lesbian feminist movement.

It was the combined visions of all of these documents plus the energy of other women who felt the liberatory potential of women's reconceived relationships that powered Nancy and Jocelyn's partnership and the founding of Helaine Victoria Press in 1973. As powerful as the energy and ideas were, however, economic conditions were often equally challenging.

## "CAN WOMEN'S BUSINESSES SUCCEED?"

Throughout the seventeen years of the press's existence, the question that Nancy and Jocelyn asked in 1975 in their article for *Sister*, "Can Women's Businesses Succeed?", dogged the efforts of all who came to work for the press. In that article, Jocelyn and Nancy argued that women's businesses could succeed if the following steps were taken: 1) women were encouraged to support other women; 2) women running businesses made it a point to court women who had money; and 3) women running businesses supported other women-run businesses. They made every effort to follow their own advice. After the press was established, they offered the work of other women for sale through their catalog, and whenever possible they marketed their products through women-run distributing companies, women's bookstores, and women's festivals and conferences. Although they developed a substantial list of mail order customers, their courtship of women with access to wealth was never notably successful.

Nancy and Jocelyn did all they could to streamline expenses, moving to the country and subsistence living to reduce the costs of overhead, running the business on a cash basis, and never accumulating debt. Finally, they applied for and received nonprofit status for Helaine Victoria Press, Inc., which allowed them to seek grants and accept donations. A board of directors was formed from women in the area, many associated with Indiana University and other local institutions. Students were able to use work-study funds to work at the press. Volunteers were welcomed. Nonetheless, the continuing dearth of resources exacerbated conflicts and finally led to Nancy's departure for her hometown of Chicago.

Vicki Leighty, who had been working part-time at the press, took on the position of assistant director. When the isolation of the workshop and office became increasingly problematic, Jocelyn and Vicki moved the office functions to a space in Bloomington. Simultaneous with this move, Vicki promoted the establishment of the Helaine Victoria Press Women's History Shop in Bloomington. More women became involved, fundraising, writing captions, and working in the shop; Donna Fay Reeves, who managed mail order sales, was one of the few paid workers.

Helaine Victoria Press outlasted many women's businesses, as the changing economic circumstances in the 1980s led to the demise of feminist publishers and bookstores in community after community. By 1990, however, it was clear that because of a fundamental lack of capital alongside changing technologies and the incursions of large commercial publishers, Helaine Victoria Press would not be able to survive.[69] Although the press officially closed in 1991, the cards live on and still garner interest from collectors and those seeking to illustrate articles and displays. Several years after the press closed, the printshop, along with the Chandler & Price letterpress, moved to the Women's Rights National Historical Park at Seneca Falls, New York where busloads of children came to learn about the women's suffrage movement, the power of the press, and the technology of that era.

The following chapters document the history of Helaine Victoria Press in more detail. Chapter One, "Inception," explains the genesis of Helaine Victoria Press in Los Angeles. Chapter Two, "Printshop in Indiana," details the press's move from Los Angeles to Martinsville, Indiana, the purchase of the Chandler & Price letterpress, the transformation of the garage into a printshop in which it was housed, and Nancy and Jocelyn's dream to live self-sufficiently and care for the land. Chapter Three, "Nonprofit Status," outlines the decision to apply for nonprofit status, and Chapter Four, "Change & Growth," traces Nancy's departure and the influx of local feminists eager to support the press. Chapter Five, "Storefront in Bloomington," describes the relocation of the office and the establishment of the Helaine Victoria Press Women's History Shop, while the Epilogue depicts the final years of the press, the decisions that led to its closure, and the continuing influence on feminist memory of Helaine Victoria Press. See the glossary on page 337 for explanations of specialized printing and papermaking terms.

Finally, on page 353, the Helaine Victoria Press Chronological Publication Catalog offers readers a record of almost all editions of the press's publications—postcards, prints, posters, bookplates, notecards, cachets, T-shirts, and broadsides. The list includes many assorted 'not for sale' publications such as invitations and fancy promotional items. To view more full-size images of Helaine Victoria Press cards, bookmarks, bookplates, photos, and other ephemera, see the EPUB edition of this book at www.leverpress.org. The EPUB edition also contains audio and video clips of commentary about the history and workings of the press.

CHAPTER ONE

## INCEPTION

*The beginning of the press in 1973 and the end of the press in 1990 brackets the kind of extraordinary, exuberant women's revolution both within the academy as well as throughout aspects of life in the Western world.*[1]

—Prof. Susan Gubar

### LOS ANGELES, 1973

After Nancy and Jocelyn met at Womanspace, their relationship flourished during the exhilarating early years of the women's movement. Yet Nancy lived in Venice, California, and Jocelyn lived an hour's drive away, on the far edge of the San Fernando Valley. How would they stay in touch with each other? There was no such thing as Wi-Fi or the internet, and telephones were wired to the wall. Bell Telephone, Inc. held a monopoly over phone service and charged "long distance" rates by the minute between towns and even between parts of big cities, so calling was limited. That left the United States Postal Service (USPS). It may have been slow by today's standards, but it was cheap and reliable. A postcard could be mailed anywhere in the United States for six cents.[2]

There was only one problem: commercial postcards, called "scenics" and intended for tourists, were irrelevant, at best; museum cards showcased work by male artists; and postcards featuring images of women were downright awful.³ During the early years of the twentieth century, suffragists published cards celebrating the struggle for suffrage, but anti-suffrage forces countered with alarming postcard images of what might happen if women were to have equal rights or work outside the home (never mind that many already did). These stereotypes continued into the modern 4.25" x 6" glossy chromes readily available in the latter half of the twentieth century. Where were the images that celebrated women's struggles and achievements? Where were the images that reflected the nascent Women's Liberation Movement—that "extraordinary, exuberant women's revolution"? Jocelyn and Nancy turned to each other. "Let's make our own!"

For women of this generation, who had been raised with the belief that they must compete with other women to snag the best man, the notion of collaboration was revolutionary. Jocelyn had witnessed feminist collaboration when she had attended the Corcoran Conference on Women in the Visual Arts in Washington, DC in April 1972. The conference was a response to the poor representation of women artists in the major galleries; only 6% of the artists represented in the Corcoran Gallery were women. Other galleries reported similar numbers. Annette Polan described the event:

> Fed up with the status quo of the male-dominated art world, a small group of women from Washington organized the conference not just as a protest aimed at the Corcoran Biannual which included no women; but also as an opportunity to draw women together to exchange ideas. This forum was a democratic gathering of young, old, well-known and emerging—women who were able to reach out to each other and collaborate to bring about imperative sociological changes. It was a time of great ferment after a long history of isolation.⁴

Jocelyn was riveted as she listened to Judy Chicago and Miriam Schapiro reveal their explorations of a female aesthetic in art and

6. Nancy & Jocelyn in Venice, CA 1974.

describe their own collaboration as they created the Feminist Art Program at the California Institute of the Arts in Los Angeles (Cal Arts). The budding movement on the west coast stirred strong opinions, and Jocelyn witnessed an east coast/west coast schism taking place, as some established women artists denied the notion that women's art was, or should be, any different from that by men. Art was art, they argued. Although Jocelyn was already an artist, that was not enough: she wanted to be part of just such a cooperative effort, articulating a female aesthetic and making substantive change. Jocelyn did not know to what extent these two women artists would change her life, but she did recognize the power of asserting what one wants, the possibility of integrating her art with Lesbian feminist politics, and the potential of words and visuals to articulate a visible female aesthetic.

Although feminists active in the Women's Liberation movement were drawing attention to and organizing campaigns against discrimination and oppression, including unequal pay, rape, and domestic violence, at the same time there was a hunger for positive images of women, as well, as women realized the extent to which they had been expunged from public memory. Lesbian feminists were especially determined to emphasize women's strengths and accomplishments, having been told for years by medical, religious, and legal authorities that theirs was a diseased and abject identity. Lesbian feminism as a movement fed personal relationships, encouraging women to feel that they could effect change. Nancy and Jocelyn were experiencing decades of barriers collapsing—hitherto undreamt-of possibilities were beginning to materialize.

Before producing their first postcards, the pair collaborated on a special issue of *Sister* celebrating women in the arts.[5] Like women across the country, they were seeking out heroes, challenging the insubstantial gendered assumptions on which they'd been raised, and they were eager to share their findings as widely as possible. Because Nancy had been volunteering in the production of *Sister*, she had little trouble convincing the other staff members to let her and Jocelyn edit and produce this issue. The "special supplement: women in art" presented first Nancy's and then Jocelyn's choices of women artists—from many eras and many parts of the world—who had been ignored, neglected, defamed, and otherwise erased from the standard histories as well as from museums and other public spaces. They pored through books and went to the UCLA main library as well as the Cal Arts library in search of reproductions of artworks and portraits of the artists.

Jocelyn and Nancy not only researched and wrote the special edition—they produced it, as well. These were the days of paste-ups, each section of text and every little image pasted onto the large, blue line grids for a newspaper tabloid. This method was rife with possibilities for things to go wrong. The day before they were to take the pasted-up sheets to the tabloid printer, the self-portrait of Sofonisba Anguissola went missing. They searched everywhere for the tiny picture to finish the paste-up, finally finding her on the floor behind a piece of furniture in Nancy's dining room. Once the

7. Women in Art: A Special Issue of *Sister*
The art issue of *Sister*, August 1973, the first collaborative venture between Nancy Poore and Jocelyn Cohen, researching and publishing historical material on women.

paste-up was done, they drove out east of Los Angeles to the press, a newspaper that did jobs such as theirs late at night after finishing their regular work. Quality issues ensued, but many hours later, the papers were loaded into Nancy's Volkswagen, and off they went back to Los Angeles for distribution.

Titling her choices "An Alphabet Soup of Heroes," Nancy wrote: "Any child can assure you that certain letters tend to surface repeatedly in a bowl of alphabet soup; and, in very much the same way, certain women, from our spottily clouded history have been resurfacing persistently in my awareness."[6] *What caused this persistence?* Nancy mused. "If there is something alike about them all, I decided, it must be this: *Each integrated her art and her life uncompromisingly, and each asserted that integrity without equivocation*—even when faced with the loss of all external support."[7] She went on to list twelve women from the seventeenth to the twentieth centuries, including Aphra Behn, Julia Morgan, Isadora Duncan, George Eliot, Pauline Oliveras, Sarah Siddons, and Mai Zetterling. For each one, she provided a rationale for their inclusion, beginning every sentence with "Because" and listing over and over the remarkable accomplishments of each one against all odds. Demonstrating her passion for print, Nancy illustrated her article not only with cameo photos of some of her heroes, but also with letters of the alphabet displayed in elegant typefaces. Ever since college, she had admired and studied typography and the art of printing.

Drawing upon her studies with Lesbian feminist art historian Arlene Raven in the Feminist Art Program, Jocelyn titled her article: "Opening: A Personal Gallery." Likewise choosing from among many, she selected twenty-four visual artists from the sixteenth through the twentieth centuries, contesting the ways in which their work had been described:

> At the turn of this century, critics began changing the history of women artists. Women who were recognized as great artists in

their own times began taking on a new form. They became "mere illustrators for books" (said of Rosa Bonheur), "superficial portraitist" (Rosalba Carriera). The work of Angelica Kaufman was referred to as "aenemic little decorative history pieces" and she is remembered for her bigamous marriage.[8]

Jocelyn's pages featured the words and photographs of the visual artists, mostly painters, themselves, including reproductions of their art when possible. Some of those she featured were: Emily Carr, Diane Arbus, Lavinia Fontana, Artemesia Gentileschi, Kathë Kollwitz, Mary Cassatt, Georgia O'Keeffe, and Rosa Bonheur. In allowing the artists to speak for themselves, she hoped

> that the personal statements of struggles, ambition and impressions will begin setting an historical outline from which women can learn and with which they can identify [ . . . ]. It is a necessity for me to reconstruct the history which was stolen from me. From it I am gradually developing a context for understanding my struggles, pain, strength and visions as a woman and an artist.[9]

The pictures and small biographical sketches that made up their articles became their first step in generating feminist memory, producing the multimodal postcards that Helaine Victoria Press sent around the world for years.

These were the early, heady days of the women's liberation movement. Within the feminist art movement, women were asking questions: how can we make our art visible outside of the male-dominated art establishment which controls access to most galleries, museums, and schools? How can we reach other women? Three parallel lines of thought began to develop: the desire to infiltrate the established art scene, the aspiration to create a separate, more openly available and significant art movement, and the need to codify a female aesthetic in art.

Sometimes the conversations led to ideas such as hanging art in places where women congregate—laundromats, for example. However, both the effort to gain access to the gallery and museum edifice and the laundromat scheme assumed that art was not reproducible—that there was only one of any given art object available to be placed somewhere. This alone meant that viewing would be limited. What's more, if one were to dedicate oneself to subverting the art establishment, an enormous amount of energy would have to go into changing that centuries-old system.

Neither Jocelyn nor Nancy had any interest in such a project. They wanted to produce art that would be accessible to anyone regardless of their economic circumstances, citizenship, or community—urban or rural.

Postcards, they realized, would be the perfect reproducible medium. Most significantly, the sender could modify the card by writing a message on it, perhaps even commenting on the image. Then, as the card traveled to its destination, the image and caption would be seen along the way from sender to postal clerk, to mail carrier and recipient. And who knows who else would see and react to it after it arrived? The cards, thus, were an incipient form of multimodality involving many participants. Making and selling postcards was also intended to subsidize their own art—Nancy Poore's writing and Jocelyn Cohen's painting. By then, Jocelyn had solved the distance problem by finding a live-work painting space for her studio in Santa Monica, renting it for $65 per month.[10]

A storefront studio was every artist's dream. Jocelyn had been looking for one for months and had almost given up when she saw a "For Rent" sign one evening while she and Nancy were headed into Chez Puce, a crepe restaurant across the street on Pico Boulevard. They went over to look and, lo and behold! it was the ideal space. Newly painted, glossy, clean white walls, a gray concrete floor, and a high ceiling and flood lights. There was a small bathroom with a sink and toilet, a back window with cast iron safety bars, a back door leading down a narrow alleyway to parking, and a transom over the front door. Large glass windows which, when covered with white paper, would allow filtered light. She signed the lease on the spot.

However, this ideal studio had no amenities to serve as a live-in space—no place to sleep or bathe, and it was not zoned for living. Here, the skills that Judy Chicago had encouraged women to learn in the Feminist Art Program became critical as Jocelyn remade the studio. Nancy, familiar with the rudiments of design and architecture, drew up exacting blueprints for the project. She had a friend who worked in the trades, so Jocelyn hired her to help build a loft and a closet. They built a small half-wall to create a separate kitchen and bathing area under the loft. They even cut and fitted the ladder to the loft with no nails or screws.

But the *piece de resistance* for the living area was the claw-foot bathtub which Nancy and Jocelyn picked out at a junkyard. In fact, they thought the find was so good that they would go into the claw-foot bathtub business to subsidize their art and their new enterprise. (This was the first of many such attempts.) So, they purchased seven of the behemoths at between five and eight dollars each and had them delivered to Nancy's backyard, feeling sure that they could resell the rescued tubs to high-end designers and make a handsome profit. Unfortunately, things did not work out as planned.

Helaine Victoria Enterprises' first postcards were designed on Nancy's kitchen table, until space issues forced a move to Jocelyn's all-purpose drafting table, where they carved out a business office as well. Both women worked after hours, Nancy after her day job editing a trade magazine and Jocelyn after painting, classes, and her job in the Cal Arts library. But there was no shortage of excitement for the venture, which might explain why they were convinced that their efforts would be so profitable. This move became the first in a series as Helaine Victoria Enterprises evolved over nearly two more decades.

Like the subjects of the *Sister* art supplement, the women Nancy and Jocelyn chose to place on these first eight 4.25" x 6"

## 8. Radclyffe Hall and Una Troubridge postcard

Radclyffe Hall (left) and Una Troubridge (both British). Lived and traveled together most of their adult lives, until Hall's death in 1943. Hall was a wealthy author, noted for *The Well of Loneliness* (1928), a partly autobiographical novel. She was decorated for valor as an ambulance driver in World War I. Both women were well known in cultural salons of the time, including that of Romaine Brooks, an American-born Parisian portraitist who later painted Lady Troubridge.

cards were drawn largely from Arlene Raven's art history class, from scouring the Cal Arts library, or from excavating trips to the UCLA stacks: Mary Cassatt, Emily Carr, Rosa Bonheur, Radclyffe Hall and Una, Lady Troubridge, Rosa Luxemburg, Aimee Semple McPherson, plus two images drawn from antique woodcuts. One of the woodcuts, showing two women together on a bobsled, was taken from a Victorian printer's sample. Jocelyn and Nancy gave the image a new focus, with the title: "Sisterhood is Warm." The other woodcut, taken from a catalog of printers' designs, depicted two women representing a bountiful harvest. Nancy and Jocelyn named it "American Amazons." They called their first eight cards the Kitchen Table Series.

As they sat down to create their first cards, both knew they needed and wanted to embellish the images with something more than just the photograph, extending the multimodal character of the cards as far as possible. Having grown up with a father who was a graphic designer, and then having been one of a very few woman section editors at the *Chicago Tribune,* Nancy understood and felt at home in the design world. For Jocelyn, however, this new venture meant making a grand leap from the bohemian world of painting to the world of reproducibility. Nonetheless, she brought her painterly sensibilities to the new endeavor.

For inspiration, Nancy and Jocelyn sought models in published materials. They knew the more their efforts were complex, interesting, and attractive, the more successful they would be at inviting participation and building out feminist memory. As they combed through old books and magazines looking for lost women, they also scrutinized and admired design motifs of previous eras. Although the cards in Helaine Victoria's first series were very simple, adorned with stock border tapes typically used in newspaper production, the process was far more detailed than appearances suggest: they had spent hours looking at the photo and the border options like a seamstress holding up a roll of ribbon or pearly button for a shirtwaist. One of their early discoveries was *Flair,* an

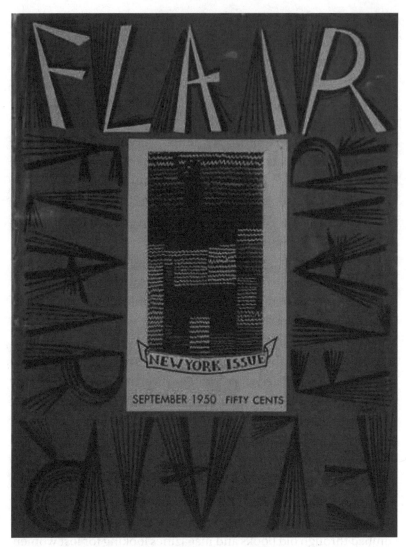

9. *Flair* magazine cover, New York issue, September 1950.

elegant magazine published from 1950 to 1951 and noted for its extravagantly produced pages, mixtures of paper, cutouts, papers glued and folded, and objects in pockets.

They studied the ways in which a flourish initial cap from the 1700s or the 1920s looked in comparison to the elegantly designed typography of *Flair*. They did not know at the time that the magazine was the creation of Fleur Cowles, born Florence Freidman, who had married her way up into the publishing industry.[11]

In some ways, discovering *Flair* sublimely affected the look and feel of things to come. Like the early greeting postcards with odd and intriguing attachments—anything from little beaded eyes or a fuzzy tail pasted on or a tiny envelope glued with a secret message inside—the multimodal handmade and hand assembled touches made the object seem more personal for Nancy and Jocelyn. Even though a page in *Flair* or an antique postcard had been reproduced in relatively large quantities for sale, they were nonetheless affordable and popular art forms—although, to be fair, the postcards were more affordable than *Flair* ever was. In their own way, over time, Jocelyn and Nancy would find and define their own style of hand-assembled touches. Perhaps it was just as well that they did not know that this magazine they so admired had folded after only one year due to the high cost of production.

With these first cards, Helaine Victoria Enterprises began their signature practice of providing detailed biographic details on the reverse side of the card, much as Nancy and Jocelyn had done in their *Sister* articles. While it is true that the six historical women portrayed might have been a bit puzzled by the company they were keeping in the series, ideological purity in this moment was not the point. Energy and invincibility were far more heroic—and necessary.

It was an overcast late afternoon during the California version of winter when they picked up the finished cards from the neighborhood printshop, 500 copies of each. They took out ads in *Sister* and in *off our backs,* another tabloid feminist newspaper, published in Washington, DC: "Send $2.00 plus $.50 shipping for 8 women's history postcards." They rented a post office box, had order forms printed, and waited for the Art Subsidy Checks to start rolling in.

Despite their enthusiasm, the experience of locating and contracting for printing services had not been uniformly wonderful. In the 1970s, even the pre-press work for printing was not a do-it-yourself at home on the computer affair. Printing equipment was large, complex, and expensive—and the printing trade was very much a male preserve. Printers did not welcome Nancy and Jocelyn as customers and often made snide comments about the images and content to be printed. After a few such encounters, they decided the only solution was to learn to print themselves.

During the winter term of 1973-1974, Jocelyn signed up for Basic Techniques of Graphics with Helen Alm at Cal Arts. There, she received instruction in all aspects of offset printing graphics—halftones, line shots, typesetting on the Diatype. She first learned to use a Gestetner (an elaborate mimeograph) for inexpensive printing and developed understandings of layout, paper, and the outside graphics and printing market. Then she tackled the Rotaprint, a small format offset press, and the ancillary preparatory equipment. When Jocelyn confided to Helen Alm about the difficulties she and Nancy were having with local printers, Helen, in true feminist fashion, insisted, "Let's just print them here!" She then gave them a key to the graphics lab so they could practice using the equipment after hours and on weekends.

Thus began several months of all-weekend print production sessions as Jocelyn and Nancy let themselves into the graphics lab when no one else was using it, experimenting with shooting halftones and converting black and white photographs to two-color images using the equipment they would need to print the images and captions on the Rotaprint offset press.

They would arrive in the morning, bringing meals with them, and practice using the equipment until late in the evening. Because

Nancy was not a student, they had to be rather circumspect about their activities.

The lab had a large graphics process, or "stat camera," for shooting halftones and line shots—again, another indispensable piece of expensive equipment at the time. It consisted of the camera portion, which is inside the darkroom, and a long-extended platform where they mounted the image to be shot/copied. They would set the scale, focus, and then mount the light-sensitive film from inside the darkroom. As they set the size and focus, the platform moved closer or farther away. After shooting the image, they took the negative and processed it in the photo chemicals. The lab had halftone screens, all the chemistry, light tables—everything they needed for pre-press print production. They did purchase their own film, and Helen suggested they buy a 150 dots-per-inch (dpi) halftone screen for better quality than the screen that was already in the lab. Learning to shoot a good halftone took some experimenting; most of their learning was by trial and error.

While they were learning to print, Nancy and Jocelyn were also developing expertise in locating information about women from history whose images they could feature on the cards. In addition to the Cal Arts library, they frequented the UCLA Graduate Library and the library at Scripps College, Nancy's alma mater. They would go to UCLA on Sundays, stopping first at the vending machines to buy coffee and veggie burritos (which seemed heavenly at the time though, in retrospect, perhaps not so much). They would spend hours and hours in the stacks, especially appreciating the air-conditioned space on hot Los Angeles days. Since they didn't yet have subject terms to guide their searches in the Library of Congress listings, they started with simply "women" or "woman." Gradually, they began to acquire keywords for card catalog searches, discovering that terms such as "explorers," or "aviation," or "religion" might have subcategories that included women. All they needed were a few catalog numbers, and with those they could go to the shelves and start searching. Certain subjects, such as temperance and suffrage, were sure to provide more material. They wanted to feature women who had been actively engaged in challenging gender restrictions and/or had sought to improve conditions for women during their lives.

At the Scripps library, "a beautiful twenties gothic revival" building, there was "an alcove with lovely furniture" that held the Ida Rust Macpherson collection of "books by and about women." Students, Nancy recalls, "gave it a wide berth, because we thought that if you loitered nearby, people would think you were a Lesbian, or if you went in there, what would there be to read?"[12] With new appreciation for the beneficence of Ida Rust Macpherson and others who had understood the importance of recognizing and celebrating women's achievements and had established this place of feminist consciousness for future generations of young women, Nancy and Jocelyn made several trips to Scripps in search of pictures and ideas to reanimate the tradition.

Used bookstores became another site yielding unexpected riches. A favorite bookstore was Acres of Books in Long Beach, whose name was not as hyperbolic as one might imagine. What they learned from used bookstores even more than from libraries was how many women had been acknowledged in their day—and then subjected to *mnemonicide*, erased from history and public awareness.[13] Having been erased from history is a different matter, they realized, than never having been acknowledged at all. To Nancy and Jocelyn, it signified that some women had had a degree of respect, honor, or even notoriety, but as decades or centuries passed, they were diminished or dropped entirely. Frances Willard of the Women's Christian Temperance Union and the French painter Rosa Bonheur were two such women whom they found early on. As they continued their research, they would find many more.

Jocelyn spent two terms studying with Helen Alm and practicing the new techniques with Nancy on the weekends. By late June of 1974, they were ready to print the cards themselves. Jocelyn remembers the first successful press run:

I still can picture the day we did our first press run. The lab was bustling, and Nancy was there, too, unusual for a school day. We burned the plates, and Helen helped us put the first one on the press, load the paper, and ink up. She needed to help others and said she would be right back. She had been teaching us how to print, so we knew how the Rotaprint worked, but we certainly lacked expertise. Helen was always busy, but she would be "right back to get rolling." We waited [ . . . ] and waited. Finally, with the press all set up, we decided to turn it on and roll. With much trepidation, we engaged the rollers on the plate and hit the paper feed lever, and there we went, sheets of our expensive paper going through the press and out the other end with our images. Helen returned, and we all were like little excited kids in a candy store as the 17.5" x 23" sheets of cards, six different images up, came off the press. We always had technical difficulties and always had trouble with even ink and always wasted a lot of paper, but we did it.

One of their innovations this year was the move to "jumbo" sized cards, 5.5" x 7.25". The choice to go with a larger format was fraught with a variety of unanticipated challenges. They found, for instance, that deltiologists—postcard collectors—preferred the 3.5" x 5" original postcard size, although they tolerated the newer 4.25" x 6" cards increasingly being produced by modern postcard manufacturers. They also discovered that the extra half inch on the 5.5" side meant the cards did not fit in the standard notecard racks in most greeting card shops. And, what's more, the large format cards required letter-rate postage. Nonetheless, they wanted the images to be large, and they wanted more space for captions on the backs.

While 1973 saw the production of eight cards, 1974's list added twelve new jumbo postcards, a press run reprinting of some of the first run of 4.25" by 6" cards plus four more new ones the same size, eight notecards printed later in the year, and a poster, their first. The new cards this year featured a two-color run in sepia and gray with Carrie Chapman Catt, Louise Sykes, Belle Starr, a promo card (not for sale) of Nancy and Jocelyn at the drafting table, Carry Nation, and reprints of Rosa Bonheur, Radclyffe Hall and Una Troubridge, Rosa Luxemburg, "Sisterhood is Warm" and American Amazons. The women they chose to generate feminist memory were international in scope: American suffragists Catt and Sykes, temperance activist Nation, and sharpshooter Starr, French artist Bonheur, English writer Hall with her lover Troubridge, and Polish-German revolutionary Marxist philosopher Luxemburg. What distinguished each woman was her determination to make her way regardless of limitations imposed by notions of female propriety; most of those honored with cards also worked throughout their lives to improve conditions for other women.

As they printed the cards in the continental 4.25" x 6" size at Cal Arts, Nancy and Jocelyn experimented with creating a two-color photo from a one-color, black-and-white image. They wanted to create a different, more complex look from that on the previous year's cards, and so they played with techniques like over- or under-exposing the screen shots, or shooting the images as a halftone and a line shot. Then they mimicked a color separation by executing two press runs for the image, one in gray and the other in sepia. Although this scheme with the 4.25" x 6" cards did not quite achieve the results they anticipated, the press runs for the next twelve jumbo cards were much more successful. Each press run consisted of six cards, with many of the photographs on the front printed in two colors, which therefore required two passes of the paper through the press, two sets of negatives stripped up, and two different printing plates. The back was just one pass through the press.

Two press runs with six different new, jumbo-size cards, each one in deep green and ochre, included more women, both American and European, who had, through extraordinary efforts, challenged social norms and thus opened space for themselves and for others who would follow. These cards were: Sophia Hayden & the 1893 Woman's Building; Two Irish women, Constance Markievicz

10. 1893 Woman's Building & Sophia Hayden postcard

Sophia G. Hayden (1868-1953) Architect. Became the first woman graduate in architecture from Massachusetts Institute of Technology, 1890. In 1891 she entered a competition for the design of the Woman's Building of the World's Columbian Exposition of 1893. Her winning design, completed at age 23, was to be her only major building. It was intended to house the art, crafts, groups, clubs, and activities of women from around the world. Its dimensions and purposes were predetermined by a Board of Lady Managers, headed by Bertha Honore (Mrs. Potter) Palmer, Chicago's leading socialite. Hayden was awarded $1,000 plus expenses and went to Chicago for construction. She worked to exhaustion as the Lady Managers introduced last minute changes. The central hall with a clerestory featured a Mary Cassatt mural of women harvesting fruit on the south tympanum. Part of the 2nd story was a roof garden. Most criticism was favorable, but some dismissed the building as merely a woman's work. Hayden was not present at official opening ceremonies and was rumored to be in a state of collapse. She abandoned architecture and after a few years married an artist. Although she lived some 85 years, there is little of her life on public record after the Chicago Fair. The inclusion of a woman architect and woman managers was originally the handiwork of Susan B. Anthony, who began to agitate in 1889 for women's control of their own events at the fair. Anthony appeared at the fairgrounds often and was paid more homage by the crowds than any other visitor.

and Maud Gonne; Mary Walker with Rev. Susanna Harris & Belva Lockwood; Two Women in the Klondike, Mary Evelyn Hitchcock and Edith Van Buren; Gertrude Stein and Alice B. Toklas; and the British Suffragettes, including Sylvia and Emmeline Pankhurst.

In designing the Woman's Building card featuring the architect Sophia Hayden, Jocelyn and Nancy used a photograph of the building taken on a busy day at the Chicago World's Fair. For the

### 11. Sojourner Truth postcard

Sojourner Truth (1797-1883). There were many Black women involved with the abolition movement who were known at the time but whose names are obscured today. Harriet Tubman, Frances Harper, Mary Ann Shadd Cary and Sojourner Truth. Although she was illiterate, she was a stirring and eloquent speaker and preacher and taught abolition, equality of the sexes, temperance and prison reform. She understood the relationship between freedom for the slave and equality for all women. She was born into slavery as Isabella in New York and was freed by the antislavery law of 1827. In 1851, Sojourner Truth came forward at a women's rights convention in Akron, Ohio and saved the meeting. A clergyman had just given a speech ridiculing woman as too weak and helpless to entrust with the vote. "The man over there says women need to be helped into carriages and lifted over ditches, and to have the best place everywhere. Nobody ever helps me into carriages or over puddles, or gives me the best place—and ain't I a woman? Look at my arm. I have ploughed and planted and gathered into barns, and no man could head me—and ain't I a woman? I could work as much and eat as much as a man—when I could get it—and bear the lash as well! And ain't I a woman? I have born 13 children and seen most of 'em sold into slavery, and when I cried out with my mother's grief, none but Jesus heard me—and ain't I a woman?"

border, they chose an Italian acanthus leaf pattern in keeping with Hayden's Italian Renaissance architectural design, further framing the upper two-thirds of the building. Above the roofline, Nancy set in a cameo of Hayden, which required a separate pass through the press. They shot traditional halftones of the building and of Hayden, printed in deep green. They also shot a line in high contrast and reversed it so only the lightest colors on the building printed in ochre, the second color. On other cards, they sometimes repeated the border on the back to separate the side depicting the caption and space for a written message from the address side; in this case, they repeated the leaf pattern as this dividing line.

The second jumbo run of six cards, printed in dark blue and ochre, included the WCTU officers, Frances Willard in her study, Sojourner Truth, Amelia Earhart and her aviation class, Susan B. Anthony and Elizabeth Cady Stanton, and Emily Carr.

While the 1973 cards were printed in black on either brown or white cardstock, these new cards featured multiple colors as well as elegant borders, some with elaborate designs chosen specifically to represent the era and the energy of the woman depicted therein.[14] Although some of the cards in these two runs were quite striking with the color separations, the techniques were time-consuming and resulted in a great deal of paper loss in the printing. The Rotaprint did not have an exacting paper feed which meant that some sheets were out of register, making the image imperfect.

Another of the year's innovations, a poster—a visually arresting argument for the passage of the Equal Rights Amendment (ERA)—became one of Helaine Victoria's most popular items. Using the lines from a well-known poem by seventeenth-century English poet Richard Lovelace, "Stone walls do not a prison make, nor iron bars a cage," Nancy added her own words, making a four-line poem: "Stone walls do not a prison make, nor iron bars a jail; But 'til the E.R.A. is won, we're only out on bail." They illustrated the poster with a picture of a London women's prison, circa 1860. An antique printing ornament, a bald eagle carrying a banner reading:

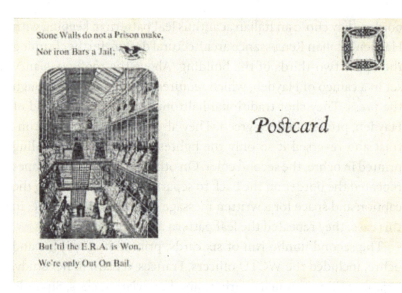

12. Equal Rights Amendent postcard, front.
Equality of rights under the law shall not be denied or abridged by the United States or by any State on account of sex. The Equal Rights Amendment.

"our rights and our liberties," was placed near the top, directly after the word "jail." Later, when Jocelyn and Nancy made it into a postcard, they printed tens of thousands of them to support the ERA campaign run by the Indiana chapter of the National Organization for Women (NOW).

As her art continued to merge with her revolutionary feminist aspirations, Jocelyn wrote an article for the February 1974 issue of *Sister*, arguing that "[t]his is the juncture at which we must decide our standards and objectives, and in what ways they require the creation of new alternatives to the known art world." Articulating for a wider audience the process she had been working through over the past several years, she called for the definition and development of a new aesthetic—"actually the equivalent of our politics."[15]

While studying fine arts at Indiana University before coming to Los Angeles, Jocelyn had had excellent, supportive instructors. One instructor, in particular, thought she should drop the images and paint abstractly. Her work, he said, was about color, not images. But she kept feeling an attachment to the fruits and vegetables she was painting. What Judy Chicago and Miriam Schapiro fostered and drew out in her were the meanings of these images. They were metaphors for her life and growth as a woman. When Judy had looked at her first painting of the semester, a small 3' x 4' canvas with a lovely, colorful still life, she said, "You need to work bigger; your energy is bursting off the canvas."

The first in her larger series, Pomegranates, a 6' x 6' canvas of fruit bursting open, expressed how she was feeling and growing as a Lesbian feminist. The second painting, the Savoy cabbage that had drawn Nancy's attention, was about Jocelyn's unfolding and opening up in this new rich, supportive feminist art niche. This was the kind of environment where the teachers/mentors looked at and interpreted the students' art in an entirely different way than most men would have. Each student explored her artistry through a feminist perspective, and worked to define, and then refine, a female aesthetic.

The revolutionary fusion of aesthetics and politics was not always as obvious to others, however, or at least not in the same way. One day, before she graduated from the Feminist Art Program in June of 1974, Jocelyn was in the program's large studio with Judy Chicago for her final semester review. Judy turned to Jocelyn and, comparing her to another student who was merging her activism and her art, said, "Jocey, you should be painting. You are a painter, not a politico." Although she felt honored that Judy had praised her painting ability, Jocelyn struggled to understand the meaning of this message, which seemed to run counter to all that Judy Chicago had stood for and had been teaching. For two years, the principles Judy and Miriam had taught and the questions they had raised had ignited an entirely new way of viewing the world of aesthetics: a female aesthetic that also encompassed and questioned the traditional hierarchical status quo in the fine arts world. What was Judy trying to say about the politics of feminist art?

This conversation with Judy Chicago was a moment of mixed feelings and ultimately a turning point for Jocelyn. Here she was, being supported by one of the women she admired most, who perhaps would continue to support her as her painting evolved and matured. Yet she was already seeing the nerve-wracking competition of the museum and gallery system. The verdant, curly leafed Savoy cabbage was not a flower; it was, above all, an ingredient. With a few additions, it made a fine borscht—not just for one person, but enough to feed many. Although Judy and Miriam disagreed with the east coast artists at the Women in the Arts conference about the notion that women's art was different than men's, they nonetheless ultimately competed well in the established art world. For Jocelyn, however, the idealism and lure of that art world was fading. Gradually, the meaning of the Savoy cabbage shifted to embrace a movement, and a more popular, readily available, reproducible, and modifiable art form began to make more sense. Furthermore, the collaboration between Judy and Miriam, which was as important to her as the feminist art itself, was crumbling at Cal Arts; a rift developed which was never discussed with the students and which continued to trouble Jocelyn throughout her career.

Tragedies and disasters, of which this falling-out was just one element, continued to plague the feminist art movement and the Feminist Art Program at Cal Arts in particular, the worst of which was the disappearance of twenty-one-year-old Feminist Art Program student Connie Marsh on April 3, 1974. Marsh had arisen early and left her dorm room at 6:00 a.m. in order to paint in nearby Pico Canyon. Newspaper stories from the time suggest that law enforcement efforts to locate her were focused on attempts to determine her psychological state, raising the possibility of a psychotic fugue that might have led her to wander off and foregrounding any mixed feelings she might have had about her work. It was typical of attitudes at the time to think that Connie's disappearance was her own fault. Students struggled with Connie's disappearance and the official reactions to it in their consciousness-raising groups. When students and faculty published a small book, *Anonymous Was A Woman*, they dedicated it to her.[16] Months later, it became clear she had been murdered.[17] Grief and anger over her death still smolder.

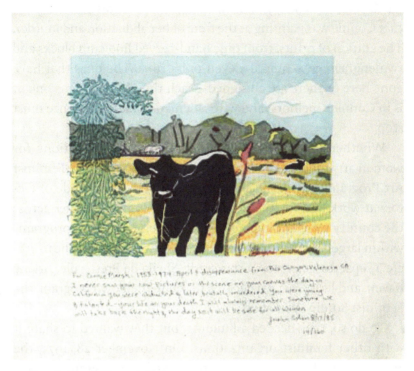

13. Connie Marsh Memorial Print
"For Connie Marsh 1953-1974. April 3 disappearance from Pico Canyon. I never saw your cow pictures or the scene on your canvas the day in California you were abducted and brutally murdered. Sometime we will take back the night and the day and it will be safe for all women. You were young & talented—your life as your death will always be remembered. JHC 8/17/1985 14/160."[18]

Like others, Jocelyn was devastated. She and Connie had talked about the beauty and quiet at Pico Canyon; both marveled at the light and color and the cows roaming in the canyons and hillsides. Jocelyn knew Connie went there to paint; neither had any knowledge that there were risks. Jocelyn later learned that the Cal Arts administration had known the area was unsafe, but they failed to tell the students. Connie's death was the kind of violence against women that the feminist performance artists in the program were addressing, but perhaps this time it was too close to home, as there was silence.

Ten years later, Jocelyn created a beautifully luminous linoleum block print in memory of Connie. The print represents the scene that Connie was painting at the time of her abduction and murder. The edition of prints, from nine hand-carved linoleum blocks and two engravings, required eleven press runs. The ones that have gone here or there are all signed—each time Jocelyn signs one, it is in Connie's memory, and with a demand that the violence must stop.

Whether this underscoring of the perilous conditions for women art students had hastened the dissolution of the Feminist Art Program is unclear. Certainly, there were a multitude of factors at work in this situation, and women in many venues across the country were finding it difficult to operate feminist programs within larger institutions. Often, the solution seemed to be to create a separate space, so, in this spirit, Sheila de Bretteville, Arlene Raven, and Judy Chicago decided to set up their own program, the Feminist Studio Workshop.

To do so, they needed a building, but they wanted to share it with other feminist organizations. On November 28, 1973, the Woman's Building had opened on Grandview Boulevard. As Judy Chicago recalls, it was "[b]ased upon the model of the Woman's Building in the Chicago Columbian Exposition of 1893 and run, like its predecessor, by a Board of Lady Managers (in this case representing the various organizations)."[19] These organizations included three galleries devoted to art by women (Womanspace, Grandview, and 707), Sisterhood bookstore, the National Organization for Women, feminist travel agency Womantours, a coffeehouse, and three feminist theatre groups.[20]

With the departure of Judy Chicago and Arlene Raven, the Feminist Art Program at Cal Arts dissolved after Jocelyn's class graduated in 1974. Judy Chicago, Sheila de Bretteville, and Arlene

Raven then shifted their energies to the Woman's Building. Helen Alm also left Cal Arts to direct the Women's Graphic Center at the Woman's Building, making printing equipment and instruction available to women; she also joined the Feminist Studio Workshop faculty. Jocelyn and Nancy, too, shifted their printing operations to this new venue, hoping to expand the types of products they offered.

As the women's movement grew in Los Angeles in the spring of 1974, word was getting around about the two feminist printers, and soon Jocelyn and Nancy were designing and printing flyers, posters, and programs for Good Taste Productions, a company consisting of Jan Oxenberg and Evan Paxton, committed to producing women's concerts and other Lesbian feminist cultural events.

One of the first was Three Singular Women in Concert: "Music by Margaret Adam, Dance by Susan Gluck, Poetry by Judy Grahn," held on June 28 and 29, 1974. Jocelyn and Nancy printed the programs and flyers on the Gestetner at Cal Arts. "It was an impressive piece of work," Jocelyn recalls, "as we registered and printed it in three colors, not an easy feat for those early copy machines."[21]

A few months later, in September 1974, realizing that Helaine Victoria was outgrowing both Nancy's apartment and Jocelyn's live-work space, the two entrepreneurs rented an office space at 1505 Fourth Street, Suite 219, in Santa Monica. Located in an Art Deco building, the office was upstairs from a traditional and homeopathic pharmacy. On the Fourth of July, they could see the fireworks on Venice Beach. There were three rooms. They furnished the one furthest back with a substantial vintage couch, the large middle room with a lovely secretary desk and books, and the front room with an engineer's drafting table. The room in the front of the office had a view of Catalina Island to the west and the San Bernardino mountains to the east, visible on a clear day. The floor was covered with clean, old linoleum. "It was a wonderful place to go and work," Jocelyn remembers.

The rent was low, food was cheap and abundant, and fuel costs

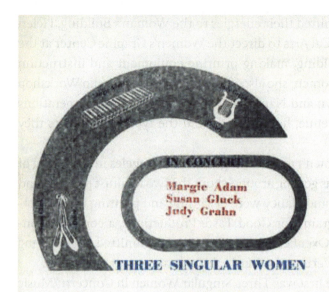

14. Three Singular Women in Concert, Margie Adam, Susan Gluck, and Judy Grahn flyer

This concert was produced by Evan Paxton for Good Taste productions. The event ran for two nights, June 28 & 29, 1974. Paxton produced a variety of concerts and cultural events for women in the Los Angeles area.

had not yet begun to rise. Despite the obstacles Nancy and Jocelyn frequently encountered, so much seemed possible in that moment.[22] They signed a partnership agreement which stated that the purpose of the partnership was the "[d]esign and sale of post cards, greeting, & note cards, stationery items, giftwares, including printing, manufacturing and packaging procedures or delegation thereof to outside suppliers and services, upon agreement of both partners. The firm also offers writing, design, and related services and consultation to clients on a fee basis." According to the agreement, the partnership would continue for at least one year and otherwise was of indefinite length. Each of them, the agreement stated, had supplied "cash, labor, skills, fixtures and other materials valued approximately at $1,000."[23] Thus, although Nancy intended to continue working on the manuscript of her novel, and Jocelyn planned to keep painting, they were both committed to Helaine Victoria Enterprises and the process of creating an inclusive feminist memory by producing women's history postcards.

About the same time, a local newspaper, the *California News-Banner*, ran an article describing Helaine Victoria Enterprises. This article, their first piece of free publicity, included photos of both Nancy and Jocelyn as well as full-sized photographs of two of their postcards, Belle Starr and Two Irish Women (Maud Gonne and Constance Markievicz), including the detailed captions. The newspaper was careful to include copyright information as well, unlike some later publications that simply reproduced the photos without attribution. Under a large banner headline reading "Focus on Freedom" was "Heroes for Women," the article on Helaine Victoria. "Their main objective," the article stated, "is to give women and events the deserved recognition history books have left out." The article's unnamed author quoted both Nancy and Jocelyn, pointing to their motivation in establishing Helaine Victoria and signaling the energy behind the cards pictured. Quickly grasping the press's vision of generating feminist memory, the writer explained that they were endeavoring to provide contemporary women some historical precedents, giving them a sense of continuity. Nancy was quoted, saying: "'I had never realized the historical precedence women had set [ . . . ]. They were saying things in the nineteenth century that could be quotes from me today." Jocelyn, for her part, focused on the process of transmission, saying: "People, for some reason, are afraid of women being knowledgeable in a political way." She went on, insisting that

> [f]or women to understand the position we are now in it is essential we understand our history both economically and politically. Women have traditionally been at the tail-end of production and distribution. They have nothing to do with the distribution of wealth. Women have no economic power, and in this country, that's important. Men control the money. They publish the history books and the greetings.[24]

Grateful for this generous and accurate account of their work, both Nancy and Jocelyn were keenly aware of the importance of publicity to marketing and sales. Nancy had been editing trade publications, and Jocelyn had grown up in a family that owned and ran a small shoe store with footwear geared to working people. By 1974, they had located the trade publication for the greeting card industry, titled, appropriately enough, *Greetings*. In the July 1974 issue, the editor wrote an article in response to a letter he had received from Barbara Calder of the National Organization for Women, calling out the sexism frequently found in commercial greeting cards.[25] Seizing the opportunity, Nancy and Jocelyn wrote to *Greetings*, announcing their own line of cards—which, they pointed out, accomplished precisely what Calder was seeking. In their letter, published in full in the October 1974 issue, they said, "Our designs give recognition to some of the leading figures who have contributed to the history of all women. We include detailed biographical captions and focus on women as complete, accomplished individuals who transcend prevailing stereotypes."[26]

As committed as Nancy and Jocelyn were to their project of making and selling postcards, their larger aim was to generate feminist memory. This dedication to accuracy in feminist memory led Jocelyn to write a letter to the editor of the *Feminist Art Journal*, published in the Fall 1974 issue, offering some corrections to an earlier article which had credited Bertha Honore Palmer with the idea of creating a Woman's Building at the 1893 World's Columbian Exposition in Chicago. In her letter, Jocelyn explained in detail the role Susan B. Anthony had played in bringing about the establishment of the Woman's Building. Although, having achieved her goal, Anthony stepped aside and allowed women with greater social status to take over, Jocelyn argued persuasively that "[i]f it had not been for the work of Susan B. Anthony, the organizers of the Columbian Exposition would have made the same mistake as the 1876 Centennial Management and left women out of the plans."[27] Jocelyn's letter was illustrated with Helaine Victoria's postcard of the 1893 Woman's Building at the Chicago World's Fair, with its inset portrait of the architect, Sophia Hayden. The letter demonstrated, among other things, the depth of research that went into the writing of the captions on Helaine Victoria's cards; in closing, Jocelyn supplied a four-item bibliography to support her arguments.

Providing this counter-narrative to the standard, and often demeaning, representations of women continued to be the foundation of Nancy and Jocelyn's work. To this end, they joined with several other women in the Los Angeles area to organize the Lesbian History Exploration, to be held at a summer camp outside Los Angeles in early May of the next year. The group was loosely affiliated with Good Taste Productions (Jan Oxenberg and Evan Paxton). Other members of the group, calling themselves the Lesbian History Collective, included Nancy Toder, Alice Bloch, Jan Aura, and Judith Silverwoman.

In addition to working on organizing the event, Nancy and Jocelyn were pressed into service as designers, publishing both the

15. Photo of collective from inside Lesbian History Exploration packet, 1975
Organizers of the Lesbian History Exploration held at a summer camp outside Los Angeles: Jan Aura, Alice Bloch, Jocelyn Cohen, Jan Oxenberg, Evan Paxton, Judith Silverwoman, Nancy Toder, Nancy Victoria [Poore]. Over two hundred Lesbians came to explore Lesbian history with a strong political and activist emphasis.

poster and the November 1, 1974 invitational packet. If ever they might have questioned the need to form separate businesses and institutions, their printing experience in this case left no doubt. The packet was designed to be printed on a single large sheet which was then to be folded into a booklet-like shape. They first had trouble finding a printer willing to deal with the Lesbian content; printer after printer would look at the job and make a snide remark that suggested for them an unpleasant experience in the offing. The printshop that finally accepted the job did reasonably well with the poster and quality of the printing.

However, when it came to the brochure, the printers apparently forgot the instructions and decided that the large sheet needed to be perforated for cutting and binding. Before finishing the job, someone reviewing the specification order must have caught the mistake and stopped making the perforations. Because Jocelyn and Nancy had pre-purchased the paper, and the printshop manager apparently didn't want to pay for the printers' mistake, he simply buried the perforated sheets at the bottoms and placed the corrected brochures on the tops of every box.

Jocelyn and Nancy didn't see the perforated pages until they were unpacking the brochures. By the time they realized what the printers had done, they had, of course, already paid for the print job as well as the paper. When confronted with the error, the printers refused to reprint the perforated copies or refund any of their money. Although they were glad to have found a printer "willing" to do the job, seeking compensation for the printers' error felt laced with danger. This experience only served to reinforce Nancy and Jocelyn's commitment to the conference and their awareness of its crucial significance in the movement to change social and economic conditions for women. It also did not escape their notice that "freedom of the press is guaranteed only to those who own one," as the often-quoted saying goes.[28]

In the Invitational Packet for the Lesbian History Exploration, the group announced their intentions: "The orientation of the

Exploration is Lesbian Prime, Lesbians as a group rather than a sub-group." They listed their goals for the gathering, a list that makes obvious the difficulties inherent in articulating a history of people who have not only been written out of past histories but have been actively discouraged from existing altogether:

* research on known lesbians and lesbian communities of the past
* personal testimony about the variety of ways that women have lived as lesbians—our triumphs and our struggles to survive
* first-hand reports by women who have participated in the major events that have shaped the recent lesbian movement
* historical fantasy; mythology; folklore; re-creations of our lesbian past
* stories about the lost women: women who should have been lesbians, women who were "cured," women who committed suicide[29]

Before launching that venture, Jocelyn and Nancy turned to another printing and design project: bookplates, small decorative pieces of paper glued onto the inside front covers of books indicating the names of owners. As they had gone through the shelves at Acres of Books and other stores, they had been charmed by the many old and beautiful bookplates. In their research, they discovered there were many women who designed bookplates, and they found a lovely, well-illustrated book entitled *Ladies Book-plates,* which included an entire chapter on "Lady Designers and Women Bibliophiles."[30] So, using images they found in old periodicals, they created new designs and printed them on gummed paper, calling them the "Educated Female Bookplates" and selling them in packets of twenty-four for $1.00 apiece, each packet including three different designs and detailed information about the sources of those designs, as with the postcards.

Now well into their second year, 1974, and with a growing number of products and ads placed in a variety of feminist periodicals,

Nancy and Jocelyn decided it was time to create a catalog, specifically one that included an order form. Each item in the catalog was described in loving, and sometimes amusing, detail. Nancy heralded the Educated Female Bookplates, for instance, with a question and answer:

> Should we be allowed to read and write? If you are among the uppity, put your beliefs out front—on the title page! Great antique designs with space for your signature. Protect your library [ . . . ]. Free bookmark included. Makes a nice economical gift, too.[31]

The outside cover of the single-page folded catalog was interactive, featuring a picture of three bookmarks, each with a picture of a woman from a Helaine Victoria postcard. The picture, captioned "Which is the real Frances Willard?", invited recipients to figure out which of the three photos was Willard and then who the other two were.

Continuing their own work, Jocelyn and Nancy renewed their substantive efforts to generate feminist awareness and build memory. On January 11, 1975, a show entitled "Women and the Printing Arts" opened at the Woman's Building on Grandview—the first-ever show of work by women printers. The exhibit featured work by twenty-five women printers from across the country, plus cards by Helaine Victoria Enterprises.[32] The fact that most of the work shown—although inclusive of posters and cards—was books, and that Helaine Victoria was not only the single collaborative entrant but also the only enterprise, pointed to the ongoing tension between the traditional notion of the singular artist producing the book as the standard printed object and Helaine Victoria's radical feminist vision of reproducible, modifiable, mobile art. Nancy and Jocelyn continued to support Arlene Raven's definition of feminist art as art that "'raises consciousness, invites dialogue, and transforms culture.'"[33] While Jocelyn and Nancy could not help being aware of their outlier status, they hoped that their

16. Woman Voter bookplate
Adapted from the book review page of *The Woman Voter* magazine, NY, 1915.

work would provoke others to think beyond the traditional ways of doing things.[34]

At about the same time, though, they received a cheerful, enthusiastic letter from a woman named Judy Kaplan of the New York chapter of NOW, who understood the transformative nature of what they were doing. Kaplan had amassed a collection of some

250 first day covers celebrating stamps honoring women.[35] Having seen Helaine Victoria's ad in *Majority Report,* a feminist publication from New York, Kaplan offered to sell Nancy and Jocelyn some of her collection at about forty or fifty cents apiece. They, in turn, she suggested, could sell them for $1.00 or $1.50 apiece. In a warm, collaborative gesture, Kaplan even offered to help them write advertising copy for the first day covers. It did not take Jocelyn and Nancy long to realize this would be an easy way to subsidize their labor-intensive postcard business, as well as expand their efforts to re-center women in the historical record. First day covers, as Kaplan had realized, offered a way to continue the process of returning to active memory women who had, at one time, been nationally recognized.

In August of 1975, Helaine Victoria Press issued a press release announcing a special package of first day covers for International Women's Year. Not long after, in October, Jocelyn went to the eighth National NOW convention in Philadelphia. Because this year the United States was anticipating the celebration of the Bicentennial of its creation as an independent republic and the anniversary of the adoption of the Declaration of Independence, Nancy and Jocelyn decided to assemble a commemorative packet of postcards with a descriptive header to sell exclusively at the NOW convention. The set contained a variety of Helaine Victoria postcards, each recognizing someone who had done political work on behalf of women in the US. In addition, the set had a small insert with two to four old US postage stamps honoring women as part of the design.

At the NOW convention, Jocelyn met up with Judy Kaplan for the first time after having corresponded with her for several months. As Jocelyn was setting up, Judy came by—and poured out a bag full of beautiful first day covers onto the Helaine Victoria Press table. Almost immediately, women started grabbing them up. Some first day covers were quite old, bearing 1¢ Virginia Dare stamps, with others showing the Hundred Years of Progress of

Women stamp with Elizabeth Cady Stanton, Carrie Chapman Catt, and Lucretia Mott. Although card sales at the convention were good, especially the commemorative postcard packet, the first day covers acted like a lure, catching the eye and enticing customers to the table.

From then on, Judy would send Nancy and Jocelyn bundles of first day covers to sell. Having seen how well they sold, Jocelyn and Nancy also started going to stamp shows and stores to collect them. For the most part, first day covers with stamps recognizing women at that time were cheap and plentiful, but it took some effort to get them—unless, of course, Judy sent them. There was nothing too difficult to learn about buying them, and they found it fascinating to collect the same first day cover subject—for instance, the Susan B. Anthony stamp—from as many different cachet designers as possible.[36] Some were embossed, others had enhanced portraits or a little story scene, and some were simply produced by an individual, perhaps even one of a kind.

The first day covers offered another way to generate feminist consciousness, and the wholesale purchases did produce some profit after resale; however, they were never a major source of income for Helaine Victoria Press. Nonetheless, with this introduction to another way to create accessible art celebrating women's history, Nancy and Jocelyn would venture into making their own first day covers the next year.

The "Art Subsidy Checks"—sufficient income from postcard sales to support their own artistic ambitions—that Jocelyn and Nancy had trusted would come rolling in had yet to appear, despite their low cost of living and best efforts at creating desirable products, as well as diversifying the items they sold. They joined an ongoing conversation among Los Angeles feminists about the prognosis for businesses catering to women and selling products by and to women. Their commentary on the issue appeared in the April 1975 issue of *Sister* in an article titled "Can Women's Businesses Succeed?" Nancy and Jocelyn thoroughly analyzed the economic status of women, focusing especially on women running businesses in the United States. For emphasis, the issue's cover featured their poster "Stone Walls do not a Prison make," an argument for the passage of the Equal Rights Amendment.

They began by pointing out how the issue of women's businesses' viability was not limited to their own small concern but had also been the topic of conversation in several feminist periodicals in recent months. They continued describing the current economic climate, with ongoing corporate efforts to erase small and minority-run businesses: "These giant cartels operate in gentlemanly conspiracy, not competition. By polite agreement, they divide the globe into their various territories, like morsels of a succulent pie."

Suggesting that the women's movement could take some combination of three possible paths, they insisted that "[t]he women's movement cannot fail economically, for if we fail there, we will fail politically." The most likely downfall, they said, was that of assimilation: "a few token rewards and job opportunities to quiet us down." Unfortunately, they pointed out, women tend to succumb to the convenience of the current economic possibilities, working for corporations then spending their resultant inadequate pay at the malls and shopping centers run by affiliated corporate overlords. How can women escape this cycle? Jocelyn and Nancy's suggestions were thoughtful, if perhaps not sufficient to change a very entrenched system.

Basing their ideas in their historical research, they noted the deep participation of women of wealth in the suffrage movement and related organizations. Calling for a similar participation on the part of women who had access to capital, they suggested activists work to change attitudes—to ensure that financial largesse came with sufficient class consciousness and was not labeled "charity." In addition, they recommended solidarity: women should deliberately seek out the services and products of other women rather than taking the path of convenience. Finally, they advocated education. Read Charlotte Perkins Gilman's *Women and Economics* (1898), they said. Add to that "*The Lady* (1910) by Emily Putnam, Volume IX of the U.S. Senate report on *Women and Child Wage-Earners in the United States* (compiled 1908–1911), and today's classic *Born Female* by Caroline Byrd." They called for awareness of the past in order to avoid similar mistakes in the present and future, noting the tens of millions of dollars fed by the liquor industry into anti-suffrage coffers in the early twentieth century and the efforts of the insurance industry and other right-wing groups in the mid-1970s to stop the passage of the Equal Rights Amendment.[37]

After a year of planning, Nancy and Jocelyn took a slideshow demonstrating some of their research discoveries and incipient understandings to the Lesbian History Exploration they had helped to organize. The event, held May 2–4 in 1975, deliberately drew a small audience, perhaps 200 Lesbians from across the country. The conference was a resounding success, a grand show of solidarity and enthusiasm for the accomplishments of women in the past. Elsa Gidlow, a poet and lifelong out Lesbian born in 1898, was the guest of honor. She recounted the event in her autobiography:

> About this time, I was invited to meet with a group calling itself The Lesbian Herstory [sic] Collective [ . . . ]. There I met women who became my friends, including Jocelyn Cohen and Nancy Poore, who started Helaine Victoria Press, moved to Indiana, and created wonderful historical postcards of feminist women.[38]

After reading her poetry, which was especially well received by the conference participants, Gidlow played a tape recording of herself reading her article "Ask No Man Pardon: The Philosophical Significance of Being Lesbian." This, she later reported, led to so many requests that she published it as a small pamphlet—and it went through four printings.

For some, this conference provided an opportunity to present work they had been doing for years, like Liza Cowan who presented a historical slideshow on "What the Well-Dressed Dyke Will Wear."[39] Her presentation contained history, humor, and thoughtfulness on the topic of fashion. A representative of the recently formed Lesbian Herstory Archives in New York City came to explain the vision and work of the archives. Other slide talks, like the one Nancy and Jocelyn gave, also looked at Lesbians in the past, revealing their unique places within the cultures of their times and, in the process, commenting on efforts to create a new culture in the present.

Jocelyn and Nancy's presentation provided an overview of Lesbians from a variety of walks of life. It included artists and writers; members of Natalie Barney's circle, Gertrude Stein and Alice B. Toklas; women such as Emily Carr, who were clearly independent; and Georgia O'Keeffe and Vita Sackville West, whose identities shifted over the course of their lives. The presentation brought up some uncomfortable politics, especially regarding some of the famous Paris Lesbians who aligned themselves with fascist politicians or political parties during the 1930s and '40s. For many of the 200 participants, this was their first introduction to the concept of Lesbian history.

While organizing the conference, learning about first day covers, selling books, and researching women's history, Jocelyn and Nancy also produced several new postcards this year. Still under the Helaine Victoria Enterprises name, they introduced cards featuring Olive Schreiner, Elizabeth Gurley Flynn, Rosa Luxemburg and Clara Zetkin, and three women pioneers in the field of education, Mary MacLeod Bethune, Emma Willard, and Prudence Crandall. They also reprinted a number of cards from the two previous years; reprints, however, were rarely the same as the originals. If a card had originally been printed in black or sepia, it might be reprinted in three colors or a border might be added. Sometimes they would revise the captions with newly recovered information.

This year's new cards were originally printed in dark green and rose. On the Educators card, they chose to print the photographs in dark green. They then set off the photos with an ornate, rose-colored capital "P" beginning the title "Pioneers in Education," adding the subsequent letters in a Gothic font. This typeface, and the word "Education," were repeated on the back. For this card, they had selected three very different kinds of educators from widely divergent backgrounds, all acknowledged progressive groundbreakers. In a design departure they would not repeat, they printed the caption on the front. They framed it in a spiral-bound notebook border, a motif that they decided, in retrospect, was probably a bit too modern for the eras of the three women pictured. As is evident, Helaine Victoria designs were becoming more advanced and technically proficient. The Elizabeth Gurley Flynn card, for example, had a photograph of Flynn on the front, and on the back, next to the caption, they placed a reproduction of the cover of the sheet music for Joe Hill's song celebrating Flynn, "The Rebel Girl." Nancy and Jocelyn had introduced this design the year before on the Emily Carr postcard.

Although they sought publicity in the form of newspaper and magazine articles, Nancy and Jocelyn also continued to place ads in feminist journals, including *Ms., off our backs,* and *Majority Report,* supplementing these ads, when they could, with letters to the editor. Because they had been trying to break into the college bookstore circuit, they had been pleased by a short article in the January 1975 issue of *College Store Executive* with two of their cards pictured: "Eye-catching design and storytelling captions are among the points of twenty-one new postcard designs from Helaine Victoria, a young California firm."[40] However, they found that college and university bookstores were a difficult market to penetrate, as they were dominated by large corporate publishers, mainstream agents, and distributors.

Feminist periodicals and catalogs were more generous, understanding Helaine Victoria's mission to create a participatory medium producing feminist awareness and memory. Kirsten Grimstad and Susan Rennie, editors of *The New Women's Survival*

## 17. Elizabeth Gurley Flynn postcard, front

Elizabeth Gurley Flynn (1890–1964). Irish American labor and free speech leader. Born to an adamant socialist father and feminist mother, she was an expert champion of the Bill of Rights all her life. In her New England childhood, she was irrecoverably shocked by laborers with 12-hour shifts and no safety provisions. She met children and women (some pregnant or nursing) with missing fingers and other permanent injuries. Her career as a spellbinding speaker began at 16, when she was arrested during a pro-labor speech in New York. Her long association with the Socialist and later Communist parties was simply based on her belief that they offered the best break to the working classes of her times. A travelling organizer for the Industrial Workers of the World, she was a leader in the New England and New Jersey textile strikes of 1912–13 and the Spokane 1909 Free Speech demonstrations. She was a devoted worker in defense of Sacco and Vanzetti in the '20's. She was jailed many times, lastly as an elderly woman during the infamous sedition trials of the McCarthy Era in 1952. The major work of her youth and prime is beautifully told in her autobiography, *The Rebel Girl*. She was travelling in Russia, working on further memoirs, when she died in 1964. Flynn never considered her activities at all un-American, but rather was an ardent champion of Constitutional freedoms and responsibilities.

18. Elizabeth Gurley Flynn postcard, back.

*Sourcebook*, for instance, gave the press over a full page of coverage, reproducing the images from five different cards, including the card with the photo of Nancy and Jocelyn together. In a column-plus of text, the two editors enthused about the press, saying that "Helaine Victoria Enterprises have devised a splendid means of encouraging communications among feminists that simultaneously raises consciousness as it conveys feminist information."[41] Carol Anne Douglas, who wrote a column for years in *off our backs* under the name "Chicken Lady," frequently gave Helaine Victoria a kind mention. In the November 1975 issue, she commented specifically on how readers could get their own products: "Postcards and bookplates from Helaine Victoria, a feminist archive publisher, can be ordered from 1505 Fourth Street, Suite 219, Santa Monica, CA 90401."[42] While the reference was brief, *off our backs* was widely read across the country, and women scoured its pages for purveyors of feminist products to support. In this issue, Helaine Victoria's line appears next to a news item, an article about two women who applied for a marriage license in Niles, IL and were arrested and jailed for their efforts. Such reports underscored the need to sustain feminist endeavors as much as possible.

Professor Ellen Dwyer of Indiana University was one who understood this need early on. She not only sought out but also shared Helaine Victoria's products. Writing to Jocelyn in early December of 1975, she asked for ten more copies of the Helaine Victoria catalog, because "[t]here are a number of women who would be interested in your products. I wish," she added, "more feminist products were available."[43] Then serving as Coordinator of Women's Studies at Indiana University, Dwyer was a consistently loyal patron of the press, and would later join in researching subjects and writing captions for cards, coordinating the publication of one of the press's series in the late 1980s. Looking back, she recalled that

[f]rom its beginning, the press understood the importance of highlighting the range and diversity of women's experiences. As someone who taught women's history in the mid-1970s, I found the press's postcards a valuable supplement to the relatively few basic texts available at that point. I much appreciated the inclusion of working-class history, women in science, the issues of race and disability—the list goes on and on.[44]

This year saw another innovation at Helaine Victoria Enterprises. Nancy and Jocelyn introduced a series of eight notecards, produced at the Women's Graphic Center. Printed in black ink on 8.5" x 11" sheets of golden ochre paper, the cards were machine-folded to 4.25" x 5.5" so they could be opened to full-letter size, providing space for writing on the back.

One card celebrated Fanny Bullock Workman, a world traveler, photographer, and writer of the late nineteenth century. "What Can a Woman Do?" queried the front of the card over a photo of Workman, the answer appearing below: "Anything She Pleases." While the interior of the card read Congratulations and featured another photo of Workman, the back of the card listed some twenty-one possible uses for the card, along with Helaine Victoria's signature detailed biographical caption. Some of these possible uses included: "Graduation, New job, Getting rid of a job, Marriage/Divorce, Winning a lawsuit, Winning an election," all working to generate feminist memory—Fanny Bullock Workman's image and brief biography—for purposes in the present. Another card presented a cartoon of women in bloomers from a *Harper's Magazine* of 1851, while a third featured the title page of Mary Astell's *A Serious Proposal to the Ladies,* a book that had let Jocelyn and Nancy know that some current feminists—themselves included—were not the first to suggest that women-run communities might offer more egalitarian arrangements.

Although the Women's Graphic Center provided both offset and letterpress equipment, it was becoming clear to Nancy and

19. Fanny Bullock Workman notecard with the message: "What can a woman do; Anything she pleases. Congratulations!"

Fanny Bullock Workman (American, 1859-1925), documented her travels in numerous books, filled with opinions, observations, and Fanny's excellent photographs. She was an important Himalayan explorer and geographer and an enthusiast of bicycling, hiking, and women's rights. She and her husband explored India, Algeria, Europe, and the Far East on bicycles. They covered as much as 86 miles per day, fording rivers and pushing their bikes through sand with 10 to 12 pounds of baggage on the handlebars—plus Fanny's kettle—and mending 40 punctures or so each day. Her most challenging and successful trip was her last, recorded in *Two Summers in the Ice Wilds of the Eastern Karakoram*. This expedition mapped the area accurately and produced a wealth of Fanny's unique photos. Our shot of her was taken by another climber in 1912, from an eminence she called Silver Throne, at 21,000 feet.

Jocelyn that their use of it for profit-making purposes was not consistent with what many women understood to be the goals of the Center. With this, the pair knew it was time to come up with a better plan. Formulated in late 1975, their new plan had three key parts: they would shift from offset to letterpress, they would buy their own equipment, and they would move to the country, away from the intense politics of Los Angeles and urban living. In fact, Nancy had long wanted to do letterpress printing, having grown up imbued with the spirit of William Morris and the Arts and Crafts movement.[45] While a student at Scripps, an all-women's college, she had been one of a select few allowed in to a printing course with a master printer. But at that time, the students, being women, were only allowed to compose—that is, set the type in a composing stick. They were not allowed to run the press, both an annoyance and a disappointment to Nancy.

Jocelyn, for her part, saw type, printing, and design as a compatible adjunct to her painting. She knew by this time that she didn't care for offset printing.

> It made my stomach hurt a lot. I didn't like the way that offset treats the design, as a real separate element [ . . . ]. Every step in the offset process seemed to separate the original material farther away from the end product. Offset can be a really alienating method—strictly a job [ . . . ]. Usually the designer and the printer and the plate-maker are separate people, and they don't know much about what each other's job is. To have any control over the end product, you can do it all by yourself, which we did. But even then I found the materials I was working with separate from each other. Not everybody feels this way; some women do love offset printing.[46]

With their newfound goal of learning to operate a letterpress, they set off to find a class in which to enroll. Acquiring the skills for letterpress printing was a big part of their scheme for subsistence living. Job presses were made of cast iron, and as long as one was not dropped in a move, very little could go wrong; they were one of those brilliant mechanical inventions made to last. If Nancy and Jocelyn were to live self-sufficiently in the country, they required dependable equipment, as well as the skill to use and care for it properly.

As excellent students, neither Nancy nor Jocelyn was accustomed to being summarily turned away when applying to an educational institution. What's more, legislation, specifically Title IX of the Education Amendments, had passed in 1972, making sex discrimination illegal in educational settings that received federal funds in any form. Their encounters with printers by this time, however, should have let them know that finding a printing class that would accept them might be different from their previous experiences.

Sure enough, when Jocelyn approached the instructor at Los Angeles Technical College, he told her in no uncertain terms that women were not allowed in his classes. Despite hearing variations on this response at other schools, they persisted, until finally, they found an instructor who welcomed them into his class. They would begin studying letterpress printing with Robert Wilkinson at Santa Monica City College, and in doing so, they would master a heretofore inaccessible technology, and soon be able to create new forms of reproducible, multimodal, participatory art.

CHAPTER TWO

## PRINTSHOP IN INDIANA

> *The new lesbian sensibility associated with feminism can develop only in a support community, not in isolation, because it is the expression of a social experience lived in community. But where do we find our communities? In consciousness-raising groups, alternative institutions, communes and collectives, or in the informal network of female creators nationally and internationally.*
>
> —Arlene Raven, Through the Peephole (21)

While they were studying letterpress printing, Nancy and Jocelyn continued to imagine ways they might be able to have their own press. They knew that they wanted a letterpress—a Chandler & Price, if possible. With such a press, they could print more cards, cultivating their artistry and expanding the material means of growing the feminist multilogue while, at the same time, rewriting more women back into history. But how could they possibly house such an item in a small Los Angeles office space? Several friends were talking about moving to land in northern California—should they join that venture? While Helaine Victoria blossomed, the two talked about how they might move out of the city. The desire was there, but neither the time to look for land nor the means to purchase it were available. The dream persisted unresolved.

Although the future seemed cloudy, they moved forward with two new creative projects. After having learned about first day covers from Judy Kaplan, they decided to make their own cachet, a picture printed on an envelope celebrating the release of a new stamp. With an original cachet, they knew that they could reach many new viewers. When they learned a new stamp acknowledging commercial aviation was due to be issued on March 19, 1976, they determined to find a woman to honor. This task required a significant amount of research, as the usual female aviator who comes to mind is Amelia Earhart. Of course, a number of women had preceded Earhart, but Jocelyn and Nancy wanted to find the *first* professional female aviatrix. They discovered that one Madame Blanchard holds that title, and was, in fact, much admired by Earhart.

Madame Blanchard, it seems, was a pioneering balloonist who served as Napoleon's chief of air services, both civilian and military. The cachet they created depicted Mme. Blanchard standing aloft on a platform raised by a balloon, holding the ropes with one hand. Next to her was an inset illustration of an aerial balloon.[1] This project, too, elicited a less-than-hospitable response when Nancy and Jocelyn sought professional engraving services to make the photoengraving plate of Madame Blanchard. Nancy recalls the encounter:

> One day, we walked into a place that made engraving plates. We wanted to have some images made up [ . . . ]. The guy behind the counter was flabbergasted. He didn't know how he'd do the job. [He'd do it the way he did it for anybody else, but he'd never had a woman customer before.] This hippie kid from some shop down the street came in and said, "Hi!" And the guy behind the counter said, "Hi!" And then he said, "Hey, kid, what do you say to a couple of girls who do printing?" The hippie fellow said, "Hi?" The old guy muttered, "Times have changed. I'm not ready for this."[2]

20. Madame Blanchard, First Day Cover Envelope, stamp block

Madame Blanchard: Napoleon's Chief of Air Services and Pioneer Aeronaut 1810–1819. Commercial Aviation • First Day of Issue. MME. M. BLANCHARD headed the commercial and military air forces (one balloon) under Bonaparte and Louis XVIII, until she was killed by an accident aloft over Paris in 1819. Her work often included appearances at weddings and festivals, etc., where her ascent was the dramatic feature of the day. She was the widow of J. P. Blanchard, first balloonist to carry international air mail (France to England).

Although they succeeded in making the cachet, Jocelyn and Nancy were more convinced of the need to find ways to do as much of their own press work and pre-press work as possible.

By late 1975, having printed over twenty different postcards plus note cards, bookmarks, bookplates, and a poster, Nancy and Jocelyn had spent a fair amount of time scouring the shelves of Acres of Books and other stores for pictures and information about likely postcard candidates. Jocelyn's mother, Toba Cohen, had also joined in the bookstore searches in her hometown of Indianapolis, finding several signed editions, including Elizabeth Cady Stanton's autobiography, Frances Willard's *A Wheel Within a Wheel*, and Vera Brittain's *Testament of Youth*. They realized they had brought home rather more than their space could accommodate—and they wanted to share their bounty with others. It was time to sell some of the books. Using the best English booklists as models, they constructed the first of several Helaine Victoria booklists to distribute to customers. Each book was described in brief but informed, occasionally opinionated detail, following the standard format.

Toba Cohen came up with a code to guide book pricing. She used the word SUPERWOMAN, assigning a number to each letter: S=1, U=2, and so on, up to N=0. They would then erase the bookstore's price and substitute the letters for the bookstore's numbers. Then, adding their markup, they would price the book accordingly.[3] For example: if they had bought a book for $1.00, they would erase the $1.00 price on the book and substitute the letters SNN. Then, when it came time to sell, they could figure whatever markup made sense at the time. Bookselling, while not quite as easy as selling first day covers supplied by Judy Kaplan, nonetheless offered a reasonable way to add to their income while also working toward their larger goal of recentering women in the historical record.

Jocelyn and Nancy's next landmark event was the publication of their third catalog, issued in early 1976.[4] This was the first time many, though not all, of the cards were illustrated. In it, they tried out the language and concepts they had been developing in their advertising copy on a larger scale. They had headlined a classified ad in *Ms.* magazine earlier that year as "Discover Our Heritage," and suggested that readers "[s]hare your pride and discovery every time you write a note on our postcards, notes & greetings." Their aim, after all, was not to produce art for just one viewer, but modifiable art to be shared as widely as possible with customers who would put it to use—post it on an office door, write to a friend on it—in short, reinscribe it with more meaning for a new audience.

In their catalog, they offered three groups of "Women from History" postcards in the 5.5" x 7.25" jumbo format, six cards in each group, for $1.75 per group or $4.00 for all three, eighteen cards in all. Individually, cards sold for thirty cents each. The first group included: Amelia Earhart, Sophia Hayden and the Woman's Building, Emmeline Pankhurst and British suffragettes, Gertrude Stein and Alice B. Toklas, Sojourner Truth, and Frances Willard of the

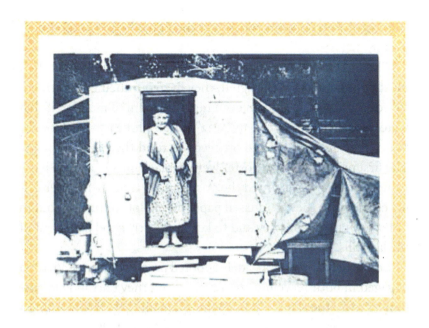

21. Emily Carr postcard

Emily Carr (Canadian, 1871-1945). A powerful painter and writer who devoted her life to expressing what she felt and saw in the British Columbia woods, including the totem poles and villages of the Native American West Coast Indians. She grew up in Victoria when it was under English rule and studied in San Francisco during the Chinatown tong wars. She was a true Canadian who lived in the woods simply with her animals including her many beloved sheep dogs. In the conservative atmosphere of 19th-century Victoria, she was considered eccentric and felt a sense of "otherness," often remaining isolated. She grew produce, raised hens and rabbits, made pottery and rugs, and took boarders to supplement her art. Overdue recognition and fame arrived in the 1920's and increased with the publication of two of her books, *Klee Wyck* and *The Book of Small*. A vivid picture of her life and the places she went and people she met are revealed in these and her other books. All of her work, from painting to writing to rugmaking, remained uninhibited by academic standards.

WCTU. The second group was comprised of Susan B. Anthony and Elizabeth Cady Stanton; Emily Carr; Two Irishwomen: Constance Markievicz and Maud Gonne; the officers of the WCTU; Radclyffe Hall and Una Troubridge, and Belle Starr. The third group had Elizabeth Gurley Flynn; Rosa Bonheur; Carrie Nation; Olive Schreiner; Three educators: Prudence Crandall, Mary McLeod Bethune, and Emma Willard; and Rosa Luxemburg and Clara Zetkin. Beyond this array of cards representing an enormous range of previously subjugated histories, the catalog listed packages of eight different note cards: "because <u>you</u> asked for them!", plus the first three

"Educated Female" bookplates[5] and the Equal Rights Amendment poster.

The Equal Rights Amendment poster had become one of their most popular items. Through it, they lived out their commitment to women's liberation in an even more substantial manner, if that were possible. Selling the 17" x 22" posters for $1.50, or four for $5.00, they gave 25% of the proceeds to fund the ERA campaign. The first printings of the poster were in black ink on antique ivory paper. Because they printed the poster many times, the paper colors changed, as they purchased paper in odd lots or on closeout in order both to save money and to keep perfectly good paper out of the landfills.

Before recycling was a widely adopted practice, Helaine Victoria engaged in both recycling and reusing, and they encouraged customers to do the same. Upon opening a mailing tube containing a poster, customers were often charmed to find a half-sheet memo on reused newsprint, with the following message from Nancy:

> If you return your TUBE
> We'll send you 2 cards FREE,
> Save yourself a PENNY
> And help us save a TREE
>
> You just pulled this note out of a perfectly good, re-usable tube that was ridiculously expensive and could still do a lot more to earn its keep [ . . . ]. It's not only a nifty bargain; it will also make you feel good. Thanks.

Although the poster was a huge success along with the ERA postcard, Nancy and Jocelyn were committed to the postcard as their medium.

With a developing list of mail order customers—a list they had been compiling from previous orders and from those who had visited their tables at conferences—Jocelyn and Nancy wanted to be able to offer more printed feminist products beyond what they could publish themselves. They knew that only women living near large urban areas would have access to retail sites, and even those were rare. Having already successfully begun to sell the first day covers from Judy Kaplan, Jocelyn and Nancy sought permission from Elsa Gidlow to market her books. She readily accepted their offer. At about the same time, Christine Eber wrote to them requesting they consider selling her note cards. Realizing the possibilities inherent in expanding their list, they agreed. The cards, a series titled "Women of Greatness," featured Eber's meticulously drawn portraits of Dorothea Lange, Kathë Kollwitz, Lorraine Hansberry, and others. In a letter to Nancy and Jocelyn, suggesting the idea of their handling sales for her, Christine Eber articulated the exponential logic of their common motive and horizontal method: "I know we all want to see more women praised—and more women and men reached through this effort."[6] Thus, Helaine Victoria Enterprises enlarged their list of distributed items, while also increasing their own offerings.

In addition to the catalog sent to their mailing list, Nancy and Jocelyn sent out a separate catalog to retailers. This one offered many reasons that a given retailer might want to stock Helaine Victoria products. "All Helaine Victoria products are ideal fundraisers," announced the catalog. In a paragraph inside the pages, Nancy and Jocelyn argued that shops with an ecological, feminist, ethnic, or international focus should be selling Helaine Victoria cards. Moreover, they insisted, there were "no hidden built-ins, such as postage, wrapping, schlepping, etc. [ . . . ] Your customers," they stated, "really welcome such high quality so inexpensively." Not trusting the shops to display Helaine Victoria materials properly, they advised sellers to open the all-alike packages of cards for individual sale and to put examples on a wall or in a rack "so they can't get lost under countertop merchandise. Put like items together," they counseled. "Remember holidays."[7]

The combination of learning to print on a letterpress, researching and publishing cards, locating and selling books, printing their first cachet, and marketing their products, all while trying to find a way to have their own press, was beginning to overwhelm Jocelyn and Nancy. And although they were surrounded by feminist organizations and activities, plus having reasonable rent and access to good, fresh food, the city felt oppressive. Neither Nancy nor Jocelyn had any attachment to Los Angeles; Nancy had moved to the city for a job with Wells Fargo bank, and Jocelyn had come only for the Feminist Art Program. Although she had profited immensely from her experience, the disbanding of the Program had been discouraging to her, especially as she watched the inspiring collaboration between Judy Chicago and Miriam Schapiro dissolve before her eyes. At the same time, she felt the radical goals of the larger feminist art movement evaporate as artists began to revert to the hierarchically driven system that rewarded "stars" who produced single objects for galleries and museums. It was not surprising, then, that Jocelyn became ill. She succumbed to a particularly virulent flu that turned into pneumonia. In her worst moments, Jocelyn lamented, "I don't want to die in LA!"

It was in this condition that Jocelyn called Toba, her mother, on Mother's Day in 1976. Her brother, Marty, answered the phone. As they chatted, he mentioned that he was about to rent his ten acres with cottage and garage outside Martinsville, Indiana, to new tenants, and was going to be showing the place to potential renters the next day. "*Stop!*" Jocelyn pleaded. "Maybe *we* want to move there." Marty agreed. She then wrote a long letter to Nancy, outlining the benefits of Marty's country place. Ten acres! A garage for a printshop! A cottage to live in!

After Nancy, too, agreed to the plan, they had six weeks to sell everything and move to Indiana, with Marty even flying out to help with the sale and packing. Liquidating much of their book collection and selling as many cards as possible, they figured, would give them some sorely needed cash for their cross-country drive. The sale itself was an event, complete with invitations: black and white folded cards with an image from an earlier Edwardian bookplate of

# BOOK PREVIEW

Sunday, April 25, 1976 at Helaine Victoria
1505 Fourth Street, No. 219, Santa Monica
4 to 9 p.m.

## 22. Book Sale Invitation notecard

Inside: You are invited to a preview of the Helaine Victoria book collection for our friends and customers. Our Spring and Summer Booklist will be mailed immediately afterward, and this first showing is a unique opportunity to add to your collection or just browse through our hundreds of unusual, out-of-print, and rare books by and about women. Light refreshments in the research room. R.S.V.P.

Jocelyn Cohen and Nancy Poore mailed this elegant letterpress invitation in a red envelope. At this event, both the first and last at the Santa Monica office, they not only sold used and out of print books by and about women that they had been collecting, but, because this event occurred shortly before they moved to Indiana, they sold all manner of office furnishings as well.

three women reading, mailed inside red envelopes, hand-printed at the Woman's Graphic Center in the Woman's Building.

The sale was a great success. They sold all the lovely, mostly antique furniture they had carefully purchased and, of course, downsized their library. With that cash infusion, they set off in Nancy's un-airconditioned Volkswagen Bug, crossing the desert in the middle of summer with all their belongings packed around them along with Nancy's cat, Ducky. Five very long, very hot days later, including an overnight visit with Nancy's mother in Scottsdale, Arizona, they arrived at Jocelyn's parents' house in Indianapolis on July 5, 1976. When Toba drove them out to the country house the next day, what they saw was a vastly different world from the one they had left in Los Angeles. There were fields extending to the horizon, all green with corn at least five feet tall. The thick, warm, humid Midwestern air smelled of fresh soil and newly cut hay. Everything was verdant—roadside trees formed arching canopies as they drove down narrow lanes. There was no hazy smog; there were no congested freeways.

Excited by the possibilities and eager to get to work, Nancy and Jocelyn gave little thought to what they had left behind: a vibrant community full of bookstores, libraries, schools, restaurants, and farmers' markets—and, within it, a strong Lesbian feminist community that had provided the foundation for their partnership. The views on their morning walks along their beloved palm-lined Santa Monica bluff, sipping coffee and discussing the plans for the day, would be replaced by another kind of beauty in this new country life. Now they were on their own, ten miles outside Martinsville, Indiana, which, as far as they could tell, had nothing approaching a feminist community, but instead was home to the Grand Dragon of the Ku Klux Klan. Indianapolis was over an hour away by car, and Bloomington, home of Indiana University, was forty-five miles. However, Nancy and Jocelyn had both dreamed of living self-sufficiently and having space for their own press, where they could work to generate feminist memory without worrying about the conventional attitudes of job press printers. And so, undaunted, they immediately set to work transforming their new home into a productive space.

Nancy and Jocelyn knew they should plant a vegetable garden so they could harvest some food while they still had warm soil and sun, but the work required to reestablish the garden seemed overwhelming. In a generous and welcoming gesture, a neighbor came over with his little tractor and offered to plow their garden. They were even more grateful for this gesture because he knew where the garden had been in the past; it was long-neglected and now very overgrown. With the garden plowed, they prepared the soil, using the French intensive method of double-digging each three-foot-wide bed and making pathways in-between. Then Chuck and Polly Amy, neighbors who were friends of Marty and lived a half-mile down the dead-end road, told them of the best nursery for vegetable starts and seeds, a vast country business the likes of which Jocelyn and Nancy had never before seen or imagined. Chuck and Polly Amy's neighborly acts and otherwise unintrusive but watchful presence helped give them a sense of safety in an area where they were often viewed with suspicion. They came home from the nursery with a car full of flats and seed packages, and even though they planted late in the season, they were able to harvest a supply of vegetables that first year.

Jocelyn's parents, Herschel and Toba Cohen, provided key elements that made the move successful, although Toba later confessed that when the pair had announced their plan, she could not envision what they would be able to do in that space. Nonetheless, she provided a modest loan to enable them to buy materials as well as a press. Jocelyn's parents had always been supportive of her endeavors, and liked to share in her success. Both Toba and Herschel came out to the country to help build shelves in and insulate the garage in preparation for bringing in the press and storing supplies and the precious inventory. They also purchased the propane heater, making the garage a workable space. Marty, too, came out and helped to line the garage with simulated wood paneling. Herschel then helped Jocelyn plant 300 bare-root trees on the property, each between six and ten inches tall, as part of a state-funded effort to control erosion and improve wildlife habitat. He would help plant another 200 the following year.[8]

It was through Toba's connections that they were able to find the press that they wanted. She knew a woman who was a print broker, who knew, in turn, Paul Egenolf, a man who bought, sold, moved, repaired, and restored presses. He knew Indianapolis printshops, and he showed Jocelyn and Nancy around. Many of the presses, though, were too large or had an automatic feed. But when Egenolf showed them a Chandler & Price hand-fed platen press, they were delighted. They learned that the hand-fed presses, which once were the work horses of all printshops, were usually candidates for metal recycling, so they felt particularly fortunate to find one. They paid $150 for the press itself, which included delivery; by the time they bought much of the equipment required for a functioning shop, they had spent $500 of their loan.[9] Still, excitement overrode their anxiety about the enormity of their undertaking. Within two weeks of their arrival in Indiana, their new (seventy-five-year-old) Chandler & Price New Series press was purchased, the press of their dreams, along with a trim saw, stone and galleys, a lead snipper, a proof press, spacing furniture, and cabinets for the furniture and cases for the leads and slugs.[10]

When Paul Egenolf found the press for them, it was hooked up for 220 volts. He converted it to 110, changing out the motor for another one he tracked down. There were only three more things they needed to do in order to make the press and printshop workable: have the rollers resurfaced, as they had melted in storage; have the platen ground down so it was uniformly flat;[11] and locate type, preferable a complete family. Paul Egenolf also gave them an extra set of rollers and told them where to send the first set to be rehabilitated. When Paul and his son delivered the press in August of 1976, Jocelyn and Nancy immediately named it: Helen (for Helen

23. Chandler & Price press and printshop
View of the Helaine Victoria Press printshop. The photo was taken shortly after Nancy Poore and Jocelyn Cohen acquired the equipment from various old letterpress shops and after they had renovated their garage into a shop and office.

Alm) R. (for Rotaprint) Wilkinson (for Robert Wilkinson). They easily could have added Paul Egenolf to the name, as his help and generosity expedited their efforts and removed many obstacles. At a time when so many men were committed to maintaining barriers to women's success, there were also people like Paul who helped in their own way to open doors for women.

Through a printers' newsletter, Nancy and Jocelyn found a complete family of Munder, an old style "Roman" typeface, cast in 1926 by Barnhart Brothers and Spindler (BB&S) in Chicago. The foundry, one of the foremost in the country, had been acquired by American Type Foundry in 1911, but remained BB&S and subsequently closed in 1933, several years after producing the new typeface, as the linotype process took over in most printshops. The fifty-four cases were in excellent condition, much of it still wrapped in the brown craft paper for each size font from six-point (pt) to seventy-two-point in Venezian (Roman), italic, bold, and bold italic, never having been used since it was purchased some fifty years before. The book-size fonts were included in double and triple quantity, in the anticipation of someone setting entire books by hand. Having acquired this superb foundational set of type, they continued, over time, to search for additional type and ornaments to enhance their printshop. They also continued to add a few pieces of equipment, including a larger proof press and a small guillotine paper cutter. Paul Egenolf would tell them about shops going out of business or selling their letterpress equipment, and they would go and see what was available.

Their printshop established, Nancy and Jocelyn were eager to reconnect with their customers, to reenter the conversation and let everyone know about their new home and shop. One of their first publications from Indiana was their second booklist. In their press release announcing the booklist, Nancy emphasized one of the features of the list that distinguished it from others: "One is reminded that every book before 1890 was set with foundry type, one letter at a time; and beautiful or unusual typography are included in our notes." Each book was described in brief, feminist-inflected detail. About Louis Albert Banks, D.D.'s *Hall of Fame,* they said: "Based on the author's concept of what an American Hall of Fame should be. Nominates many contemporaries who contribute statements. Women get a few pages at the back."[12] Margaret E. Sangster's 1909 novel *Happy School Days* is offered with the caveat: "If you can get through Sangster's syrupy tones, there's lots of sound advice: how to cope with algebra, eat a proper lunch, understand boyfriends, and become class president."[13]

Continuing to furnish their printshop with elegant and charming ornaments, Nancy found a copper engraving of Columbia, which became Helaine Victoria's trademark. Columbia, or Freedom, or Liberty, as her various representations are called, is among this country's earliest national symbols, predating Uncle Sam by many years. They knew when they saw this female representation of freedom with such a strong yet suppressed history that she was the perfect representation for Helaine Victoria Press.

**24. Columbia, Helaine Victoria Press logo.**
Columbia, also known as Freedom or Liberty, became the trademark for Helaine Victoria Press. She was rescued from an old-time printing plant. Her original size as a copper engraving was only about 2″ tall.

One day, Jocelyn, Nancy, and Toba visited a printshop that was going out of business in Indianapolis to see whether there were any ornaments they could acquire inexpensively. The city had a Printing Arts building at the time, a large, old warehouse filled with businesses in the print trades: printing, embossing, binding, gold stamping, and typesetting on monotype and Linotype machines. When they arrived in the late afternoon, the owner said all the remaining paper was going to be tossed, so they should take whatever they wanted. An entire cabinetful was headed to the landfill! It was near closing time, so they quickly began packing the best odds and ends they could find. There was paper for catalog covers, shorter runs of postcards, invitations, and signage. At 5:00, the proprietor told them he was closing up, and they would need to leave. They left, pleased with their haul but disappointed they could not take more. What a waste of precious paper they could have used! By then the building was empty, as most of the trades began by 6:30 or 7 a.m.

It's unclear who came up with the idea, but they all saw that there were two doors: the main large ones accommodating shipments of paper and equipment in and out, and then a smaller one, similar to a regular house door. "Let's try it," someone said—it was locked, of course. Then Toba opened her wallet, pulled out a credit card, and slipped it into the crack between the door and the frame. Voila! They went through the now-open door, somehow justifying their pilfering, since the paper was headed for the dump the next morning. They found it all very exciting and nerve-wracking at the same time. Here they were, engaged in one of the very few, small crimes any of them ever committed before or since. But they came home with a large amount of paper, saving Helaine Victoria Press a lot of money and rescuing the paper from the landfill.

As they dashed from one printshop to another seeking supplies, Jocelyn and Nancy knew that they didn't have much time before the Indiana winter would set in. They needed to maintain their focus on Helaine Victoria Press—their whole reason for making this extraordinary move. At the same time, so much needed to be done: insulating the house, installing a wood stove in the house, and splitting an adequate supply of wood.

Being Midwesterners, both Jocelyn and Nancy knew enough to take the approaching winter seriously. That first year, they purchased a beautiful, black enamel Swiss woodstove and a cord of wood, having it delivered to the house. However, because the stove was smaller than standard cord wood, they had to chop the wood into smaller pieces. Jocelyn became adept with a wedge and sledge. As they settled in, they found that almost half their time would be taken up with subsistence chores—growing food, gathering and cutting wood for the winter, and caring for the land.

One morning, late in the summer, they awoke, terrified, to the sound of a helicopter overhead, going back and forth across the property. Was this some sort of surveillance? If so, what for? Although they had not been living in the Indiana countryside long, already their sense of isolation was providing fertile ground for worries about their vulnerability as feminists and Lesbians. Finally, the helicopter left, and they were left to wonder who had been so interested in them or their property. It was only when, a few days later, the entire swath of an Indianapolis Power & Light easement that ran through their property turned brown that they realized the land had been aerial sprayed with a nonselective herbicide to kill all the trees.

Horrified, Jocelyn tried to convince the power company to change their practices. Company officials were unmoved. Finally, she was able to work out a very bad deal: Power & Light would cease dumping herbicide all over them if Jocelyn and Nancy would maintain the easement, which amounted to approximately four acres. From then on, someone had to go in every year with a self-propelled small bush hog (a type of rotary mower), chain saw, scythe, and loppers to remove all the species of trees that would exceed the height designated by the power company. Because they had little money for hiring outside contractors, that someone was usually Jocelyn.

25. Jocelyn Cohen on woodpile
When a load of firewood was delivered, the delivery person would quickly dump it off their truck in the vicinity of the woodshed. Then it needed to be neatly stacked for the winter. Vicki Leighty snapped this after they had completed the job, circa 1983.

By fall, in addition to establishing themselves on the land and in their house, Nancy and Jocelyn continued to set up the printshop. They acquired some ornamental fonts, many dingbats and wooden type, and many decorative borders and flourishes. Beyond the Munder family of type, they had more drawers with beautiful specimens of wooden type. These were made for large fonts that would be too heavy in lead. The wooden fonts were very old and decorative, mostly used for signs and posters. In addition to the type, they obtained lots of decorative piece borders—individual pieces that one composed just like type to form a border. Oftentimes, an ornamental border came with a variety of different designs that could be composed together harmoniously. They also came with corner pieces, enabling a printer to create a frame for

26. Nancy Poore and Jocelyn Cohen in the Helaine Victoria Press printshop
Nancy Poore on left by press; Jocelyn Cohen on right by type cabinets, 1977.

the main element—that is, the photograph, or whatever was the centerpiece. The borders could be used to divide the composition or as a flourish. They had several cases of these piece borders as well as borders on Linotype slugs (longer sections of thirty picas, or about five inches, with the border design). With all this, they had, in Jocelyn's words, "the most beautiful, functional letterpress shop one could imagine!"

The first order of business was to produce a holiday catalog for their retail and wholesale customers. While they had endeavored to continue supplying cards during the move, they were determined to expand the means to generate an active feminist memory. In the wholesale catalog for stores and fundraisers, they offered a $55 package:

> ... 18 handsomely packaged sets of postcards, plus six alike of each of the 18 designs (216 postcards in all). There are also eight pack-

ages of the assorted notes and greetings with envelopes, plus eight alike of each design (128 in all). Every assorted set of greetings and postcards has a different card facing up. You will also receive half a dozen posters and one dozen packages of bookplates. The perfect introduction to our line for $55.[14]

For their retail customer list, they sent out an autumn brochure consisting of one page with the new address and telephone number. In a paragraph on the back, they announced:

> Greetings from our new location in the Indiana countryside. We are temporarily out of our regular brochure, but will have a new one for winter. We can still supply your established favorites in *Helaine Victoria* postcards, note cards, bookplates, and ERA poster. Our First Day Cover and book selections are described on their own separate literature.[15]

Despite the power company annoyances, within six months they had converted the garage to a printshop and office, they had heat for both the house and shop, they had harvested their first crops, they were printing their first catalog from Indiana, and they were already planning a new series of postcards. Although their sales that year topped those of the previous year ever so slightly, their expenses with the move far exceeded their gross receipts, challenging them to continue to come up with ways to maximize income while minimizing costs.[16]

With the move to Indiana, the press officially became a full-time effort for both Nancy and Jocelyn. While the original idea had been to sell postcards to support their art, Nancy now had less time to write, and Jocelyn had less time—and less inclination—to paint. Jocelyn and Nancy had met in the context of the Feminist Art Program, that brief but powerful articulation of what Judy Chicago and Miriam Schapiro considered a female aesthetic.[17] Although Jocelyn had been discouraged by the collapse of the Feminist Art Program, she and Nancy knew that their work at Helaine Victoria Press was part of a larger movement toward generating feminist historical awareness expressed by art historians Arlene Raven and Ruth Iskin that year. After the dissolution of the Feminist Art Program, and immediately following its successor, the Feminist Studio Workshop, Arlene Raven and Ruth Iskin attempted again to explain the artistic sensibility they had experienced.

In "Through the Peephole: Toward a Lesbian Sensibility in Art," Raven and Iskin argued that "the lesbian is an exemplary symbol—the woman who takes risks, who dares to be a creator in a new territory, who does not follow rules, who declares herself the source of her artistic creation."[18] Insisting that while the term "lesbian" historically has been used reductively, to limit and to discard, Raven and Iskin point out that in this historical moment, it is being reclaimed and expanded:

> Lesbian sensibility does not describe an aesthetic quality only. Lesbian sensibility is an active manifestation of the transformation of personal identity, social relations, political analysis, and creative thought which has long been among the aspirations of revolutionary thinkers. Work produced in a feminist/lesbian community has the possibility of acknowledging the radical transformation of self through revolutionary social practice.[19]

They also made it clear that they found no necessary link between Lesbian sexual experience and lesbian sensibility. To reclaim a Lesbian sensibility is to disavow the hierarchical structures of patriarchy and is instead to immerse oneself in community and find love in its widest, most comprehensive sense, they said.

> The new lesbian sensibility associated with feminism can develop only in a support community not in isolation, because it is the expression of a social experience lived in community[ . . . ]. In our

feminist community, the concept of the lover in its fullest sense has been reclaimed. But it is a love transformed in work, which is what I believe Rita Mae Brown intended in saying, "An army of lovers cannot fail."[20]

While Raven and Iskin used language commonly associated with physicality and, most especially, sexuality, they tried to reclaim this language and infuse it with new meanings. Unfortunately, once words have been colonized by the powerful for their own purposes, reclaiming them is extremely difficult. Raven and Iskin's efforts were no exception; while the women's movement in general made every effort to undo the social disapprobation accorded to close relationships between women and to celebrate love in its infinite varieties, the freighted language could not easily be redefined and reclaimed. Nonetheless, Raven and Iskin's analysis spoke to a moment in feminist history and articulated the rhizomatic principles of inclusivity that informed the work of Helaine Victoria Press. Their words in many ways echoed both Mary Astell and Sarah Scott, centuries before, as these early feminist writers were challenging religious and patriarchal ideologies constraining women's friendships and communities. Nancy and Jocelyn were in the vanguard of the movement, and the work of Helaine Victoria Press continued to exemplify all that Iskin and Raven attempted to put into words.

Nancy and Jocelyn had traded the extraordinary community in Los Angeles that had fed Raven and Iskin's work, as well as their own, for a life of relative isolation on a dead-end road in rural Indiana. Yet, their work was motivated and fueled by a community of women that was not bound by time or location, but, rather, transcended the limitations of borders and extended from the past into the present, the "informal network of female creators nationally and internationally." Using the medium of postcards and the USPS system, Nancy and Jocelyn created a means to connect feminists with each other all over the country, if not the world. The USPS, always a key element in the success of their work, now became central, as almost all their communication depended upon it.[21] The USPS "is obliged, by law, to provide daily pickups and deliveries to every community in the country and cannot pick and choose where they deliver based on profit."[22] Nancy, Jocelyn, and Helaine Victoria Press lived in one of those hard-to-get-to rural communities. For the press, this daily delivery and/or pickup was the mainstay of their existence, and the dissemination of the messages they were creating relied upon this still-revolutionary communication model.

As Nancy and Jocelyn settled into the Indiana culture, Jocelyn produced a small broadside in tribute to their new home with a quote by Etta Macy, an Indiana Uplands Quaker:

If thee needs
Anything & cannot
Find it,
Just come to me
and I'll tell thee
How to get along
Without it.

Each copy of the broadside was priced at two dollars, and the edition of 100 copies sold out quickly at conferences and festivals, never appearing in a catalog.

Over the years, Jocelyn and Nancy produced many items in small editions or as give-away ephemera. To celebrate their first Thanksgiving in Indiana, they took some of the cardstock they obtained from the out-of-business printshop and printed a greeting for friends and family using their dingbats and an ornamental initial cap. Having their own printshop gave them the power of the press, whether to create a printed gift for friends, family, or customers; a sign for conferences; announcements of things to come; a special bookmark—or even an emergency printing of more ERA postcards.

> **J**ocey & Nancy wish to thank Nature for providing some of her resources today and through out the season. With respect and joy we will all partake of the varied life she shares with us on this Thanksgiving Day. We also thank Sarah Hale, editor of *Godey's Lady's Book,* for making this a national holiday so we can be together at this special time of year.

27. Thanksgiving broadside
Jocey and Nancy wish to thank Nature for providing some of her resources today and throughout the season. With respect and joy we will partake of the varied life she shares with us on this Thanksgiving Day. We also thank Sarah Hale, editor of *Godey's Lady's Book,* for making this a national holiday so we can be together at this special time of year.

As ideal as their location seemed at the time, Jocelyn and Nancy nonetheless found that it was often difficult to escape the fact of isolation and the burdens that placed on their partnership. The "army of lovers" seemed especially distant, until one day, they received a letter from Donna Fay Reeves that confirmed some of their suspicions about Martinsville, but also gave them a welcome glimpse of local subterranean feminism.

Donna lived in Bloomington, but her mother, Jo Reeves, worked in the Martinsville post office, and had met Jocelyn and Nancy when they set up their PO box and when they came in occasionally to buy stamps or to send out a large mailing. "I came out in 1969," Donna said,

> so mom knows a Lesbian when she sees one, and she asked me if I knew any women who lived out on Dynasty Lane who might be doing something with pictures or something. She had seen some pictures come through of Belle Starr.... She told me that, at the post office, if somebody has the address wrong, [letter carriers] can guess on the address if they recognize the name. What they normally do is try to get the package to the person, and she said that these guys, if there was anything wrong with your address, they would purposely put it on hold and say: *Wrong Address*. And she knew that they were doing that, and so she somehow got your phone number and called you when they had packages on hold for you ... and then when you came in, I mean, she suspected, just from the pictures. And so she told me all that, and so I thought about it, and then I wrote a letter telling you the whole story and saying, sounds to me like you might be Lesbians, and if you need to know—if you want to know some Lesbians in Bloomington, I mean maybe you already know some, but if you want to contact, here's my number and all that. So, I think it was maybe a couple of weeks later or something, I got a letter, and you guys said that you thought about it a little bit, because you didn't know who I was, but then it just sounded all right, and so you contacted me. And I came out to your house, on Dynasty Lane, and that's how we met. And that's also how I heard about the press.[23]

What better evidence could they have had of the effects of postcards as multimodal rhetorical devices, speaking to all through whose hands they pass as they travel to their destination? Nancy and Jocelyn were thrilled to know they had a friend in the Martinsville post office as well as a friend in Bloomington. Donna Fay

Reeves became a strong supporter of the press, frequently volunteering her time, and years later, after the press's business office moved to Bloomington, she took over the mail order operations.

Because Jocelyn and Nancy's work was rooted in community, it was no mistake that their first publications beyond the cards were their catalogs, reaching out to all those who had responded to their work in the past, their larger community. Their next effort would be even more elaborate cards, celebrating women whose lives they were continuing to search out in books and archives, and offering customers more reasons to write messages and send the images out into the world. For the first time, they would also try to find family members of their subjects, hoping to gain access to personal accounts and unpublished photographs.

Thus, Nancy and Jocelyn spent the fall and winter of 1976–77 researching and printing cards and planning trips to conferences and festivals in the summer. Their collaborative process in the printshop, sparked by mutual commitments, felt easy. Allowing the subject, content, and/or message to drive the design, they rarely, if ever, experienced conflicts over how to produce a given card. Like a painter's palette and brushes, a quilter's boxes of fabric scraps and remnants, or a woodworker's assorted tools and woods of many species, the printshop housed a rich collection of typefaces, ornaments, dingbats, linoleum blocks, and ink colors, all ready to be assembled in a variety of artistic ways to complement and enhance the meanings of the women being recalled on cards—their photos, their words, and their spirits.

Helaine Victoria's premier new offering would be Series IV: Eight new postcards in an "elegant handmade album folder." This series included Mother Jones, Aphra Behn, George Sand, Victoria Woodhull, Ida B. Wells-Barnett, Isadora Duncan, Margaret Fuller, and Amelia Earhart with Betty Gillies, Elvy Kalep, and Frances Marsalis, members of the 99's, a women pilots' organization. The accordion-folded album was a salute to the old-style souvenir tourist folders that offered multiple views celebrating a given location.

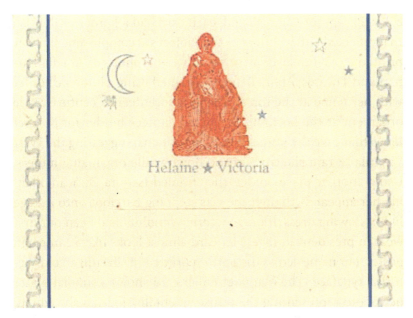

28. Women of History postcard accordion set, back cover
Women of History accordion album of eight postcards, viewed with album open. Helaine Victoria Press's premier offering, showcasing their creative letterpress style and craft.

In this case, however, the album was "embossed in silver, red, and blue."

After the two browsed through their piece borders, they decided on a design. Nancy composed the border out of separate segments, carefully aligning them all to give the impression of continuity. The cards offered multiple views celebrating and memorializing eleven women "who shared a certain quality Janet Flanner captured when she wrote of Isadora Duncan, '... She lifted from their seats people who had never left theater seats before except to get up and go home.' In this spirit, each of these women, in different eras and on different continents, gave to her particular kind of work a new importance, which she made the world experience as it had never done before."[24]

This series, representing women with a wide range of achievements, held together as a cohesive unit both in content and design. All the photos were printed in black, some with a silver accent

PRINTSHOP IN INDIANA    107

color. Except for George Sand, each card had a border or flourish that reflected either the era or the subject's accomplishment. They printed a playful silver airplane above the photo of Amelia Earhart and The 99s; Aphra Behn was framed using a linotype border with her name at the top and a silver seventeenth-century castle ornament at the bottom. They chose a piece border for Mother Jones that gave the impression of mountains, suggesting the West Virginia terrain she trod up and down while organizing miners. Using another piece border, they framed Isadora Duncan, making her appear as though she was stepping barefoot onto a stage in her flowing dress. If only Victoria Woodhull had been our first woman president in 1872! Her card almost looks like a campaign poster, her name across the bottom printed in silver in an old Victorian typeface. The Margaret Fuller card shows a sundial under her photo representing the transcendentalist journal she edited, *The Dial*; the sundial and a garden heliotrope, her personal symbol, are printed in silver at the bottom of the card, along with her name in an 1870s decorative typeface, Grimaldi. For Ida B. Wells-Barnett, sitting in her backyard looking at the viewer straight in the eye, they chose a handsome linotype border with thin multiple lines. Lastly, George Sand is simply the image, looking noble; we would hardly know she had such a rebellious life. Although each card stands alone, the design process took into account how each card looked next to the others in the album.

The album was limited to a run of 1,000. This series and the album debuted the new press and demonstrated again their skill and artistic sensibility as well their patience for the repetitive tasks required to assemble the elegant folio. The album constituted eighteen press runs; the cards were hand-glued into the album cover, then hand-folded with the flap inserted into the die-cut slit and closed.[25] Always aware that their goal was to create images and captions that both traveled and invited commentary and communication, they printed individual cards, as well, in case customers were reluctant to tear the cards apart from the folio.

By now, Nancy and Jocelyn were hoping to find photographs that had not previously been published, or at least were not sourced from materials still under copyright. Knowing that Mother Jones had been active in West Virginia, they wrote to the library at West Virginia University, asking for a photograph that had not been as widely reproduced as others. Likewise, for a photograph of Amelia Earhart, they wrote to Purdue University, location of the Earhart papers, where librarians offered them several possible images. Librarians were often happy to respond to their requests, as they were pleased to see otherwise rarely used materials receiving some attention.[26]

Realizing that active or otherwise unusual images were more likely to draw attention and encourage viewers to engage in conversation, Jocelyn and Nancy chose a picture of Earhart, not alone, but with three other women: all pilots, all on roller skates. They were even more delighted when they were able to locate one of the women pictured, Betty Gillies, and correspond with her. What they discovered through this correspondence, though, was one of the cracks in the foundation of the women's movement. In her letter, Betty Gillies wrote:

> I can't say that I am thrilled with the prospect of the cards being at the National NOW conference! Personally I am very much opposed to the methods employed by NOW, particularly in respect to their support of the Equal Rights Amendment. I am a worker for <u>STOP</u> ERA! I believe that women, as such, should continue to receive the protections heretofore granted to them by law.[27]

Nancy and Jocelyn began to grasp the ways in which this was a complex issue with no easy resolution. They were pleased to hear from her, nonetheless—and impressed to learn she was still flying and had served as Squadron Commander of the WASP Squadron, stationed at New Castle Army Air Base during World War II.

Of the remaining cards in the series, the card honoring journalist and anti-lynching activist Ida B. Wells-Barnett led to the most memorable experiences for Jocelyn and Nancy. They knew they wanted to make a card celebrating Wells-Barnett and her work. What they did not have was a photograph that they felt was appropriate for their purpose. So, with some research, they determined that her daughter, Alfreda Duster, lived in Chicago. They wrote her a letter explaining their mission and asking whether she might have an unpublished photograph that she would be willing to let them make into a postcard. She responded quickly, sending a small photograph, about 2.25 x 2.25 inches, in a plain white envelope. This photo became Helaine Victoria Press's Ida B. Wells-Barnett card, part of the Series IV album and a widely circulated individual card, as well.

Nancy and Jocelyn's request began a correspondence and friendship that lasted until Alfreda Duster's death in April, 1983. She was very appreciative of their work, and, at the same time, understood that they were young and relatively inexperienced in the ways of publishing. In her letters, she shared her own activities, especially her speaking engagements and published work, and then suggested books for them to read, and gave them marketing advice, explaining how they should approach bookstores, schools, libraries, churches, clubs, and PTAs. Writing in March of 1977, when they were working on the caption for Wells-Barnett's card, Alfreda Duster clarified the relationship between her mother and Susan B. Anthony, saying,

> Beginning on page 227 of *Crusade for Justice*, you will find an interesting story about Susan B. Anthony which will clarify her position concerning the Negro race, and my mother's activities with her. I have heard my mother state that the basic criticism Miss Anthony had of her was that mother married, and Susan B. Anthony thought she should have kept all her energy and activities for the suffragist cause.[28]

### 29. Ida B. Wells-Barnett postcard

Ida B. Wells-Barnett (1862–1931). As a young editor, she investigated lynchings and published the first news campaigns to expose their true nature and extent in the U.S. She was a lecturer, women's rights leader, and organizer of civic clubs for Black women. She criticized do-nothings, Black and white, and defied mobs even though a price was on her head. At the 1893 Chicago Fair she circulated a booklet, "Why the Colored American is not in the World Columbian Exposition." Her honors and leadership positions were many, and her hallmark was refusal to compromise.

30. Nancy Poore printing on the Chandler & Price press, 1977

All was offered with extraordinary warmth and generosity, and would continue buoying Jocelyn and Nancy for the next several years.

In the spring of 1977, after producing the Series IV album, they printed their first full catalog on the Chandler & Price press, using Jocelyn's sketch of the two of them printing the catalog for the cover, an approximation of the mid-action illustrations they sought for the cards. Inside, they reached out to readers with photographs of each of them, each of the cards, the garden, and the two of them in a field across the road, with cornstalks lining a path and trees in the distance. Most significantly, the catalog allowed them to show off the type and ornaments they had acquired. Announcing the new Series IV album, they said it "illustrates the historical women most requested of us." Inside, the catalog offered a reprise of their previously printed poster, bookplates, and cards, including the Kitchen Table series; two pages devoted to first day covers; and an entire page featuring cards by Christine Eber—all demonstrating rather complicated typesetting. Eight pages were devoted to the Helaine Victoria Booklist #3, including "Limited Editions, Privately Printed by Women," plus a page of "Memorabilia and Miscellany, Etc." with a unique assortment of old postcards, women's magazines, and art prints. Each book came accompanied by a free bookmark and bookplate. Featured in a special box in the booklist was *Crusade for Justice,* Ida B. Wells's autobiography, edited by Alfreda M. Duster.

Another special section of the booklist was titled "Books for Insomniacs, Riding the Bus, Waiting in Lines." Accompanied by an illustration of a bus, this section offered ten books for $9.00 postpaid. "Are you addicted to the expensive paperback Gothic habit? Romance and stuff?" Nancy wrote. "You can get swell novels for less from Helaine Victoria—hardbacks, no less. These are guaranteed first-rate potboilers, with a few classy items thrown in to keep you on your toes and cultured."[29] Readers might have wondered how Nancy and Jocelyn happened to have such a collection.

Perhaps it was through the catalog that Mary Powers, a reporter from the Louisville *Courier-Journal,* discovered them and later wrote a detailed two-column article on the press entitled "Postcards give mini-lessons on women throughout history." Powers successfully articulated the essence of Helaine Victoria's work, providing a brief history of the press and noting that the standard heroines, such as Eleanor Roosevelt, Helen Keller, and Virginia Woolf, would not be found among the cards. Instead, she said, "the cards feature a picture and a 100- to 200-word biographical sketch of obscure women that never turned up in conventional history classes." Responding to Powers' question about how they decide whom to research and honor with a card, Jocelyn explained that "'the most obscure women are the minority ones, but I really feel a responsibility to find these women and just not let their accomplishments fade.'" Then she added, "'We also walk a fine line with how we handle the women selected for the postcards. We've had cards returned by persons criticizing them for being too radical, but the opposite also happens, and some radical feminists accuse us of being too middle class.'"[30] It wouldn't be long before this question would erupt in front of them again as women struggled to locate themselves in the burgeoning movement.

With the new Series IV album, individual cards, poster, bookplates, and first day covers, they began to seek out feminist conferences and festivals where they could rent or, better yet, be offered a table to sell their products to an appreciative audience. As it happened, their first Indiana foray into the world of conference and festival selling was the Indiana State Meeting of International Women's Year, "Hoosier Women Make History," held in Indianapolis July 13–16, 1977. It was a very large conference, attracting women of all political persuasions. The conference offered a fine opportunity to sell cards, though the audience was more diverse than the community to which they were accustomed, and Jocelyn and Nancy found themselves challenged at times. The Helaine Victoria table was located next to the Planned Parenthood table, and Jocelyn watched in alarm as several women from the Republican party, who had lingered and admired Helaine Victoria's cards, went over to harangue the women at the Planned Parenthood table. *What message are the cards sending? And what messages will be sent on the cards?* she wondered.

A month later in August 1977, Nancy and Jocelyn traveled up to northern Michigan for the second (their first) annual Michigan Women's Music Festival, which offered a very different audience for their cards. Unfortunately, it also offered a much less comfortable location for selling them. The Michigan festival was an outdoor event, with all participants camping on a large piece of farmland. Wind, rain, and hot, dusty days followed by humidity wreaked havoc on the cards. Nancy and Jocelyn were constantly trying to figure out better ways to keep their products from lifting off into the atmosphere or scuttling across the sandy ground. But the wild enthusiasm of festival attendees for Helaine Victoria's

31. Jocelyn Cohen at the Michigan Women's Music Festival, 1983
Helaine Victoria Press founders, staff, and volunteers took their wares to many women's festivals and conferences. They attended the Michigan festival from 1977 on for many years, as well as academic events such as the Women in Law conference, the Berkshire Conference on the History of Women, and the annual meetings of the National Women's Studies Association.

products made the effort worthwhile; here was part of the community that they had worked for all winter.[31]

In contrast to the fixed and unyielding arguments that Jocelyn had witnessed at the International Women's Year conference, the Michigan festival and others provided a strong response to Arlene Raven's question: "The new lesbian sensibility associated with feminism can develop only in a support community, not in isolation, because it is the expression of a social experience lived in community. But where do we find our communities?" Hundreds of thousands of women participated in these women-only cultural events. In Raven and Iskin's terms, each was "the woman who takes risks, who dares to be a creator in a new territory, who does not follow rules, who declares herself the source of her artistic creation." All these women, representing multiple differences, came together for a few days of learning, sharing, arguing, and formulating new individual and collective perspectives. For Nancy and Jocelyn, these women-only, woman-identified events filled their minds and spirits before they returned to their rural outpost in Indiana.

After the festival in Michigan, they were ready to produce a catalog for the holiday season and for the coming year, as well as to continue harvesting vegetables and cutting wood for the approaching winter. Having established a printshop, they changed their name from Helaine Victoria Enterprises to Helaine Victoria Press. The holiday catalog's front and back covers featured Columbia, their logo, for the first time.

Nancy especially enjoyed making cards using the dingbats, ornaments, and engravings they had acquired for the press. For this year's catalog, she made a bright two-color holiday card reading "All the Best of the Season," using dingbats or stock cuts of holly, three Santas, a Star of David, and a fanciful calendar reading "Jan. 1." She also produced a special series of note cards she called the Jazz Age series, for their use of dingbats and charming found engravings, repurposed for feminist cards. Leaving aside serious historical matters for a moment, these cheerful note cards encouraged light-hearted conversation. One card had a woman looking through a telescope; inside, it read, "I've been looking for someone like you," giving the sender the opportunity to take an active romantic role rather than the traditionally feminine passive role. Another card read "Knock - Knock," followed by the typical "Who's There?" with an elaborate picture of a woman's shoe followed by "Shoe who?" Opening the card, one read, "Gesundheit!" The back of each card read: "This series of our cards is printed directly from type & ornaments of the 1920s & '30s. The messages are also true

32. "Knock - Knock" Jazz Age notecard
Created by Nancy Poore as part of the four-card Jazz Age series. "Knock - Knock. Who's There? Shoe. Shoe Who? Gesundheit!"

to the conversational modes of the day. After all, a smooth line is the shortest distance between two friends."[32]

Jocelyn and Nancy endeavored to make the catalog itself reflect their values and artistry and their vision of producing active feminist historical awareness. They printed the catalog in two colors, in multiple typefaces, and with many ornaments. The cover, reminiscent of early advertising art produced in job shops with a set up similar to Helaine Victoria's, looked like a type sampler. "Cover printed on reclaimed paper from reclaimed foundry types," they announced on the first page. The interior offered photos of all of the cards, the largest selection yet—twenty-seven images—and the booklist was divided into categories for the first time and adorned with dingbats and illustrations. First day covers on related topics were inserted into the booklist, drawing connections and dissolving boundaries between art, commerce, and information. A late-year addition to the catalog was a card introducing Ernestine Rose, the daughter of a rabbi who emigrated from Poland to England and later to America, becoming a well-known nineteenth-century feminist orator. For this card, Jocelyn and Nancy dispensed with a border, instead placing a red rose, another of their ornament finds, in the lower left-hand corner of the card over the blue-ink photograph. They had the card commercially offset printed, then ran it through the letterpress themselves to add the red rose.

That winter's production included a new collaboration "demonstrating a lesbian feminist aesthetic," as Arlene Raven and Ruth Iskin had articulated it, in both process and finished creation: a 14" x 18" print of Alice Duer Miller's 1917 poem "An Unauthorized Interview Between the Suffragists & the Statue of Liberty," illustrated by Christine Eber. Jocelyn and Nancy had discovered Alice Duer Miller while combing the shelves of Acres of Books in Long Beach. This poem came from Miller's *Are Women People*, published in 1915. Having found one book, they looked for more and learned that Miller was not only a suffrage activist and poet, but a novelist and screenwriter. She had authored the book which led to the script for the 1932 film *Roberta*, as well as a host of others.

The Alice Duer Miller print challenged them, stretching both their printing and collaboration skills. Miller's words were provocative, and they knew that an illustration would enhance the meaning of those words. They asked Christine Eber, who had designed and produced the Women of Greatness note cards that Helaine Victoria was distributing, to do some sketches to accompany the poem. The "Interview" was comprised of two parts: a question from the suffragists asking why liberty was not extended to women and a response from the Statue of Liberty, suggesting that she is "a milestone, not a destination" and that true liberty exists in the spirits of the suffragists themselves. With this print, not only were they generating feminist memory, but Nancy and Jocelyn were also reminding customers that the movement belonged to all women, and the press was doing its part by offering the materials for building connections.

Selecting from the illustrations Christine Eber sent, Nancy and Jocelyn arrived at two line drawings for the engravings: the upper half of the Statue of Liberty beneath the moon and stars occupied the lower right of the print while, centered above, stood a group of suffragists in early twentieth-century dress seeming to hold the script of their question up to the Statue of Liberty as though it were a banner. A colophon within a rectangular wreath below the statue included biographical information about Alice Duer Miller. The two illustrations diagonally bisected the sheet, upper left to lower right. To the left of the illustrations was the text of the "Interview;" the upper right, above the Statue of Liberty, was blank, seeming to offer a space next to the suffragists for them to fill.

Because the size of the sheet, 14" x 18", exceeded the platen size, they had to dip the sheet, printing half at a time. They printed it in four colors, the poem in sepia and other elements in red, blue, and reddish brown, on a speckled, heavy recycled paper called Speckletone. They offered the print in a "numbered limited edition of 550," their nod to the art world's desire for rarity. Helaine Victoria, however, only charged $6.50 postpaid for this rare item, still making it widely accessible.[33]

Another item produced that winter, "Seed Catalog," available as a large note card or as a postcard, was made using Jocelyn's hand-carved linoleum blocks and a photoengraving from an old seed catalog. The seed catalogs represented Nancy and Jocelyn's attachment to the land and to growing their own food. Behind

33. Suffragists & the Statue of Liberty print
This print enhances the 1917 poem by novelist, screenwriter, and poet Alice Duer Miller, bringing to light the wit and political irony she was known for in her writing.

the seed catalog engraving were the hours and hours the two of them spent selecting seeds for the upcoming spring crop. "These designs," they said in the 1978 catalog, "grew from our commitment to recycle useful & beautiful materials wherever possible. We make them from old cuts, types & paper rescued from neglect, combining them in our own designs and messages."[34]

ANNOUNCING
NEW
DESIGNS FROM

Helaine Victoria Press

FAMOUS for STYLE & CHARM

ALICE DUER MILLER SUFFRAGETTE POSTER!

Engla's New Series on Great Artists

Plus Super Letter-Press SPECIALTIES

Catalog for
1978

OLDE BOOKS & RARE
NEW YORK NOW FIRST DAY COVERS

& OF COURSE FABULOUS FEMALE FEATS OF THE  ON HELAINE VICTORIA POST CARDS & NOTES

34. 1978 Helaine Victoria Press Catalog
Front cover for the 1978 Helaine Victoria Press catalog.

This year marked one of Nancy and Jocelyn's last efforts to produce new bookplates.[35] The seven elegant designs, most featuring women reading or writing, were packaged in cellophane bags with charming headers proclaiming, "Be sure your books (before you lend) Their Homeward Way will always wend." Unfortunately, they were learning that living in the country sometimes created hardships for paper products. In this case, the glue on the backs of the bookplates proved irresistible to the Martinsville mouse population, and Helaine Victoria Press lost a large number of bookplates to rodent appetites. The little interlopers found their way in to the rescued steel library card catalog cases and chewed their way up and down the corners of thousands of bookplates.

With the holidays coming, Nancy and Jocelyn wanted to print a special card for friends, family, and colleagues. Using some of their found papers and the Copperplate Gothic font, they printed a 5" x 7" flat note card titled "Winter Greetings to You." Four lines followed, each preceded with a little dingbat: "super solstice wishes; happy hanukkah knishes; lots of Christmas cheer; and a brave new year." They later turned the card into a postcard and made both versions available for sale.

They learned that winter that the US Postal Service was going to issue a stamp on February 1, 1978, commemorating the life and work of Harriet Tubman. Seizing the opportunity to reach an audience of stamp enthusiasts (as well as all those who would view the envelope en route), Nancy was eager to make another cachet, this time honoring four women, including Tubman, in a limited edition of 400. She used black, maroon, and pale bronze inks, hand-mixed especially for the cachet. The cachet, "Our Heritage of Black Women," presented Elizabeth Freeman, Litigator; Ida B. Wells-Barnett, Rights Leader; Zora Neale Hurston, Folklorist; and Harriet Tubman, "Conductor," framed in stylized pale bronze foliage to form a contrasting backdrop.

Inside the envelope, they provided an insert, or "stuffer," with a detailed account of the accomplishments of the four women,

35. Harriet Tubman, Black Women Heritage First Day Cover
OUR HERITAGE OF BLACK WOMEN: Elizabeth Freeman (?-1829) Litigator, Ida B. Wells (1862-1931) Rights Leader, Zora Hurston (1901-1960) Folklorist, Harriet Tubman (1820-1913) "Conductor." Tubman blazed Underground Railroading trails; Hurston logged Afro-America's Tales; Wells the Crusader said "Justice be done!" And Freeman—Free Woman—sued & won! Harriet Tubman, First Day of Issue.

including sources for the images, much as they had done on each of the postcards they had published. Nancy printed the stuffer on an ivory-laid paper, folded to allow for more description. The press also offered fifty of the covers with the regular issue Frederick Douglass stamp, printing stuffers for these with additional information about Douglass and the early women's rights movement.

Two more broadsides completed Helaine Victoria Press's new products in 1978. Nancy found a medieval illustration of the European folk tale of the fairy Melusine and told her story beneath the illustration in a numbered edition of 100 9" x 12" broadsides: "The Fairy Melusine, Countess of Poitou (circa 10th century), flying from the Tower of Lusignan in her demi-serpent shape. Her husband violated the secret of her enchantment & she departed her castles and her territories forever." Below that, Nancy drew from Elizabeth Gould Davis's *The First Sex* to explain the significance of the story of Melusine: "Throughout the ancient world, *women* held the secrets of *Nature* and were the only channel through which flowed

36. The Fairy Melusine broadside
Throughout the ancient world, women held the secrets of Nature...

the *wisdom & knowledge of the Ages.* This is reflected in the priority of female *Oracles, Prophets, Priests, Sybils, Pythonesses & Maenads.*"

Jocelyn, meanwhile, bracketed the millennium of women's history with a twentieth-century letter from English writer Violet Trefusis to Vita Sackville-West, illustrated with woodcuts from Djuna Barnes's 1928 *Ladies Almanack,* entreating her to fly away

37. Jocelyn Cohen printing on the Chandler & Price press
On a typical day of printing, Jocelyn Cohen and Nancy Poore would trade off as printers during long press runs.

with her and to "Live fully, live passionately, live disastrously! Let's live, you and I, as none have ever lived before!"

Jocelyn and Nancy were aware of the passionate relationship between Violet and Vita, having included them in the slide talk they gave at the Lesbian History Exploration in 1975. As they were buying books, they had come upon *Ladies Almanack*, a book Djuna Barnes had written and illustrated with her own exceptionally detailed and whimsical woodcuts. Jocelyn designed the print using the words of Violet Trefusis, combined with engravings made from the woodcuts in Barnes's book. The print sold out almost immediately, so Jocelyn printed a second edition before distributing the type.

When Nancy and Jocelyn received an invitation from Sheila de Bretteville to enter their work in a graphic arts show and sale celebrating the birthday of the Women's Graphic Center at the Los Angeles Woman's Building, "Poster, Books & Postcards—by Women," they were delighted to have the opportunity to demonstrate the ways in which their work embodied the principles of the feminist art movement. They chose to send the two broadsides, plus the postcard album. De Bretteville responded, thanking them and saying, "Your work is really beautiful. I wish you were here to see the show—to be at our birthday party."[36] Although they were glad for the opportunity to show their multimodal work, Jocelyn and Nancy were happy to be in rural Indiana with their beloved printshop and garden.

Once in a while, however, their printing efforts came with small catastrophes. Nancy recalls one especially grievous moment: she was working outside when suddenly Jocelyn came flying out of the printshop, sobbing. Nancy waited a few minutes for the storm to pass, then learned that apparently Jocelyn had forgotten to check the placement of the gripper bars before running the press, and had smashed one of the few seventy-two-point Munder "W"s. Fortunately, these were headline letters they rarely used, so the event was not as tragic as it could have been. But such times were rare, and the printshop was a source of joy where they produced hundreds of beautiful postcards and broadsides. The land, too, provided their sustenance as well as a home from which they could travel to archives, conferences, and festivals throughout the country.

Working in the printshop had no designated hours. Sometimes the weather governed the best times to do chores outside versus in the shop. Or perhaps the press was all inked up with a special hand mixed color, and the press run had to finish regardless of the time. Fatigue would set in. One evening, as it was getting later and later, Jocelyn thought a drink would be a nice pick-me-up. Despite both Nancy and Jocelyn's interest in the temperance movement, they enjoyed a cocktail now and again. So, Jocelyn invented the signature Helaine Victoria cocktail, a hearty mix of whisky, Amaretto, and orange juice which they dubbed "The Printer's Devil." (In printers' lingo, a printer's devil was an apprentice who performed a number of tasks, such as mixing ink, cleaning up, and distributing type back into the cases after the job was over.) The liquid "printer's devil" helped them accomplish all of the above tasks.

This year marked their first table at the Berkshire Conference on the History of Women, an annual conference then meeting for the fourth time. They learned that the conference, known colloquially as "the Berks," would be held at Mt. Holyoke College in Massachusetts. Here not only would they meet women historians and Lesbian and feminist thinkers who loved and appreciated the cards, but they would form lasting associations and friendships with scholars such as Ruth Perry, who was researching Mary Astell, and poet and feminist theorist Adrienne Rich. Rich, in fact, came up to the Helaine Victoria Press table and said to Jocelyn, "I am so glad to meet you," to which Jocelyn chirped, "And who are you?" When Rich replied, Jocelyn, of course, was thoroughly mortified. Rich never held it against her, though, and later worked with the press on the publication of a broadside of an excerpt of her work. The Berkshire conferences were pivotal in the life of Helaine Victoria Press, giving Jocelyn and Nancy a chance to chat with historians about their work as it related to one card or another and be embraced by a welcoming and astute audience.

Because the conference was held in South Hadley, Massachusetts, in late August, Nancy and Jocelyn thought: Why not try to visit Helen and Scott Nearing while we're in that area? The Nearings, who had authored *Living the Good Life*, an account of their self-sufficient lives on land in southern Vermont, had inspired a generation of young people, including Jocelyn and Nancy, and had encouraged them to take up their own experiments in sustainable living. Because of their roles as elders in this movement, the Nearings attracted large numbers of people wanting to come and see how they did it. By this time, however, Scott Nearing was ninety-five years old, and the social calls were often less than welcome.

When Jocelyn wrote to the Nearings, asking for permission to visit, Helen Nearing's initial response was cool, a mass-produced "Dear Friend" letter. However, a later note, probably prompted by a gift of postcards, offered the possibility of an afternoon visit. What they learned during this brief social call served to cast doubt on some of the claims in *Living the Good Life*—and to explain why their life did not match the book's idyllic account.

To Jocelyn and Nancy, this trip was a pilgrimage, not a visit. Their politics and lifestyle, like the cards they produced, represented a variety of sources and historical periods, ranging from socialism to the back to the land movement to woman-identified self-sufficiency. Obviously, Mary Astell, who wrote *A Serious Proposal to the Ladies,* and Sarah Scott, who wrote *Millennium Hall,* and even those from the more recent Arts and Crafts Movement were all long gone. The Nearings were the closest living model they had for how to live sustainably in the country. As they drove from South Hadley to the Nearings' home in Vermont, they felt both excited and nervous to be meeting these famous people whom they admired so much.

Their arrival, however, was greeted with, at best, indifference. It appeared that the Nearings had forgotten they were coming. Scott was nowhere to be seen, though Helen said he was out back splitting wood. According to Nancy, Helen Nearing's memora-

### 38. Olive Schreiner postcard

Olive Schreiner (1855–1920). South African novelist and social theorist. Largely overlooked today, Schreiner was one of the best-known writers in English from the 1880s to the 1920s. Born to English and German missionary parents, she personified rebellion against Victorianism at the height of the Victorian age. She was a passionate pacifist, feminist, and critic of organized religion (although very religious). Her novel, *The Story of an African Farm*, about a defiant unwed mother, the first specifically feminist work in English fiction, stunned the reading public in 1881. She was both pro-Boer and a supporter of rights for Black Africans; and was militantly opposed to Cecil Rhodes. While imprisoned by the English during the Boer war, she wrote *Woman and Labor*, a major nonfiction socio-economic treatise. She married S.C. Cronwright in her late thirties, and they shared the surname of "Cronwright-Schreiner." Hampered by money troubles and asthma all her life, Olive retained a vibrant personality even in her last years. Contemporary accounts use the word "genius" more than any other in describing her. And a poor Lancashire working woman who had read *African Farm* said: "I think there is hundreds of women what feels like that but can't speak it, but she could speak what we feel."

ble welcoming line was: "Hurry along, gurruls. The light draws in early in September, and we still have three and a half acres of berries to go!"[37] And, with that, she handed them a couple of pails and sent them off to pick blueberries, making it quite clear that she had other things to do. Their attempts at conversation were unproductive.

As they prepared to leave, Jocelyn and Nancy gave Helen a stack of Helaine Victoria cards as a thank you. Then everything changed. Scott came in as Helen was looking through the cards. She pulled out Olive Schreiner and said, "Scott look, Olive Schreiner! Doesn't she look all fat and bougie, but don't we know otherwise?!" They spent some time looking at the cards, and suddenly, Nancy and Jocelyn were "remembered."

They talked a little while, and then Helen wanted to show them around the house. She was very proud of their bathtub, which had heating pipes that ran from the woodstove and kept the water in the tub hot. Then they visited the food storage cellar, and she offered them numerous pieces of produce to take with them. It ended up being a very nice and enlightening visit. The Nearings, like Jocelyn and Nancy, also had a cash crop, their blueberries, while Nancy and Jocelyn grew and marketed red raspberries. But they also learned that not only did the Nearings have visitors picking berries from the large shrubs, but they also had help with work around the farm in general. The Nearings were famous, and people interested in them or in the back-to-the-land movement flocked there to learn and help.

Nancy and Jocelyn could not keep up on their own, and they lacked the financial means to pay for much beyond the bare minimum. People did not flock to work in their garden or cut wood for them, although Toba and Herschel did spend much of their free time, mostly on Sundays, their one day off from the shoe store, helping with the land. Nancy and Jocelyn had had difficulty understanding how the Nearings could manage in the way their books described. Although they shared the Nearings' views on not using mechanized equipment, they were not able to cut wood with hand saws and then split it, too. The pilgrimage had illuminated details that the books had left out. Discovering the reality behind the Nearings' published accounts bolstered Nancy and Jocelyn's spirits; it reassured them that they were not doing anything "wrong," and that, in fact, all their publishing work and their care for the land was phenomenal for two women. The fact that there was no time for Nancy to pursue her writing or for Jocelyn to continue painting made perfect sense.

With this new insight into the likelihood of continuing challenges and a dearth of rest, Nancy and Jocelyn plunged ahead, applying for matching funds to build a pond on the land and planning for the National NOW conference to be held that year in Washington, DC. Jocelyn had already established a relationship with the Indiana Department of Agriculture, as she had planted trees and created wildlife habitat. The next step in conserving the natural resources on their small piece of land was to apply for funding for a pond. The Soil and Water division of the Department of Agriculture sought to prevent erosion and maintain water quality through the establishment of ponds on farmland. A creek ran through the ravine, and properties below theirs had already enhanced the land with small ponds. Jocelyn applied for and received matching funds for the project. The state surveyed the property and provided the plans. Chuck Amy, the friend at the end of the road, provided all the necessary equipment and labor to excavate for the pond and build the dam at a very neighbor-friendly rate. The pond proved to be the most wonderful addition for Jocelyn, Nancy, and the wildlife. Marty, Jocelyn's brother, arranged for a little sandy beach and helped to fulfill other specifications from the state program, such as stocking the pond with fish, both to help keep it clean and also to provide food for wildlife. Needless to say, friends and volunteers who came out to the country enjoyed the pond as well, skinny-dipping on hot summer days.

The Washington, DC location for the NOW conference gave

Nancy and Jocelyn the perfect opportunity to stay on and visit the Smithsonian, the Library of Congress, and the National Archives, all of which proved to be excellent sources for recovering lost and forgotten women. They made the happy discovery that policies of both the Library of Congress and the National Archives aligned with Helaine Victoria Press's values, making the photos easily available and offering reproduction services at cost.

They had begun their research in libraries, then had branched out into bookstores, and now they were finding photographs that had never before been published. Locating unpublished images in archives or in personal collections rather than in books made the process of writing a caption more challenging, but at the same time enabled Helaine Victoria Press to bring to light more women whose lives and work had been disregarded for decades. They began searching not just for women who had once been recognized and then had been forgotten, but for women whose lives and work had never been acknowledged or celebrated in the first place. This was a more profound step in their efforts to generate feminist memory, and they knew that, with these new images, more women would be drawn to the cards.

All the images Jocelyn and Nancy used from the Library of Congress and the National Archives they found by going through thousands of images, just looking. Mary Mallory, a government documents librarian at the University of Illinois at Urbana-Champaign and devoted Helaine Victoria customer whom they had met at the National Women's Music Festival, had given them tips on how to navigate through the government archives. She told them that often the arrangement of a given archive is dependent on the archivist who has organized it. Thus, communicating with that particular person could facilitate accessibility as well as provide insights into nuances of a collection that might help in locating a given person or subject or especially compelling photographs.

They found themselves repeating the location practices they had honed in the UCLA library: finding a catalog number in general and combing the shelves all around the area for possible hits.

Obviously, "women" was a possible search term, but then they realized that they had to learn the departments each of the two institutions housed that might be reservoirs of photographs. The path was not straight. They searched through photos from the Farm Security Administration; the War Relocation Authority, which oversaw the Japanese internment camps; the Women's Bureau; and the collections of each of the photographers who had worked for the Works Progress Administration (WPA), to name a few.

Although the Library of Congress and the National Archives are incomprehensibly large institutions, the photography archive department research room in each, at the time, was rather small, and Jocelyn and Nancy were often the only ones there. Staff were generous about bringing boxes of a particular subject, photographer, or government department. Nancy and Jocelyn would request certain collections such as the WPA, or Dorothea Lange or, at the National Archives, women and the war effort. Often, they would not look for a particular woman, but for a photo that seemed interesting, and then they would try to find the story behind the photo, piecing it together.

During this visit, they found new photographs of both Alice Paul and Elizabeth Gurley Flynn, which they subsequently used to create new cards for devotees of the two women. Sometimes, if they knew a name, they were able to use that name to locate engaging photos. They knew, for example, that Frances Benjamin Johnston had photographed Hampton Normal and Agricultural Institute, a historically Black college that began its mission during the late nineteenth century as a trade school. They wanted to do a card on Hampton Institute, so they looked through all the photos in Johnston's papers in the Library of Congress to find the one they thought best for their purposes, finally locating an unusual picture of the students making upholstered furniture using barrels as framing material. Like their best images, this photo showed the students in action, opening the photo to interpretation. This photo they made into a card the following year.

When Nancy and Jocelyn went to the Smithsonian, they had

no idea that they would find not just a curator ready to do her job, but also an enthusiastic supporter in Edith Mayo, who shared their commitment to locating and honoring women's achievements. She would tell them about photographs she knew of as well as search the collections on their behalf. Mayo's clear interest in collecting and sharing information about the significant contributions of women to American civic life led Jocelyn and Nancy to link her with Alfreda Duster, to ensure that all of Ida B. Wells-Barnett's papers and photographs were preserved. The friendly connection between Helaine Victoria Press and Edith Mayo continued for years, enabling the press to access many more images for publication. In gratitude for the help they had received from Edith Mayo, Jocelyn and Nancy sent a large package of Helaine Victoria cards to the Smithsonian, where they were duly registered and cataloged, and now reside as a tangible reminder of the press's work.[38]

As much help as archivists provided, Nancy and Jocelyn still needed to locate the pertinent archives and travel to them to search the collections. Helaine Victoria Press had no travel budget; Nancy and Jocelyn simply hopped into the Volkswagen and stayed with friends when they could or looked for the most inexpensive lodgings they could find. This scheme had its drawbacks. Because they were planning a series focused on women and labor, to be called Bread & Roses: Women in the American Labor Movement, Nancy and Jocelyn drove up to Detroit to first visit the Walter P. Reuther Library, Archives of Labor and Urban Affairs at Wayne State University, then the Joseph A. Labadie Collection at the University of Michigan, Ann Arbor. They took off without bothering to make a motel reservation, and when they arrived in Detroit, they drove along the river looking for an inexpensive place to stay. Seeing a motel with a vacancy sign, Jocelyn commented, "Oh, this place must be nice—look at all the fancy cars in the lot." Although they were a little puzzled when the clerk asked whether they were going to stay all night, it wasn't until later that they realized that they were in a motel that rented rooms by the hour. Nice and quiet

39. Break-Time at the Defense Plant postcard
Break-Time at the Defense Plant. Women took over hundreds of thousands of factory jobs during World War II, and a few well-publicized plants had pleasant lounges, day-care centers, cafeterias, etc. This scene at an aircraft parts factory (about 1943) was enacted many times over across the country at any spare moment. The jitterbug led the dance craze, and one out of every four juke box nickels went for a Glenn Miller platter. Leading big band vocalists included the Andrews Sisters, McGuire Sisters, Helen Forrest, Vaughn Monroe, and Billie Holliday.

during the day, the place became bedlam at night, with pimps yelling prices at the prostitutes and people pounding up and down the stairs. They left as soon as they could the next morning, and made the happy discovery that the very upscale Renaissance Hotel had a special going that, with a little negotiating, was even less than what they had paid for their night in the brothel. The fact that they were researching the history of women's struggles to make a living wasn't lost on them: *what would Emma do?* they mused. 39

When they arrived at the Walter P. Reuther Library, they were looking for images of women protesting over working conditions, women on the frontlines of the labor movement, and women who were effecting change from within, such as Frances Perkins, Secretary of Labor during the Franklin D. Roosevelt administration.

Asked later, "What did it do to your consciousness to look through hundreds of thousands of photographs of women?" Nancy replied, "I find it incredibly moving. I think of the vast numbers of women—a whole procession through history. I find it really touching, the sheer impact of it, the cumulative effect."[40]

While searching among the photos in the labor archive, they happened upon an upbeat WWII-era photo of women dancing in a defense plant lounge. Probably used originally as propaganda to entice women workers, the image, they knew, would be a sure hit for a jumbo postcard. Nancy wrote a witty caption, titling the card "Break-Time at the Defense Plant," placing the image in its historical context along with noting who might have been singing on the radio, perhaps the Andrews Sisters or Billie Holiday. Nancy could not resist framing the photo in an Art Deco piece border which had just been waiting in the printshop for the appropriate card. She printed the elegant border in silver metallic ink and the photo in a contrasting warm sepia. The production of this card illustrates exactly why Nancy and Jocelyn so loved their printshop: cases of type, ornaments, and borders, plus a cabinet of paper stock, all ready and waiting so that if something came up that enticed them, they could design the piece, send out for a photo engraving using the USPS, write the copy, shift a few priorities, and *voilà!* They had a new postcard to offer their customers.

While they were searching in this archive, Jocelyn became particularly interested in women's brigades and auxiliaries. Marjorie Long, the head archivist, was instrumental in bringing their attention to this kind of activism. She noted women's involvement in the labor struggles and how women's brigades and auxiliaries provided critical support to the strikers. The Women's Brigade at the Flint auto strike would become one of the cards in Helaine Victoria Press's upcoming Bread & Roses series. Over the next ten years, Jocelyn reached out to many libraries and institutions in search of photos documenting these forms of support and protest, in hopes of creating a dedicated series entitled "Women's Auxiliaries & Bri-

40. Bread & Roses emblem
Bread and Roses Women in the American Labor Movement, Bread & Roses emblem.

gades."⁴¹ Marjorie Long exemplified what Mary Mallory had said to them about archival organization: that archives, in her experience, did not necessarily follow a set format like the cataloging systems used for books, and the head archivist could often direct a researcher to material otherwise difficult to uncover.

Leaving Detroit, they drove to Ann Arbor, where, following another suggestion by Mary Mallory, they searched through the Labadie Collection at the University of Michigan Library. The collection houses a large archive of anarchist materials, and they were hoping to find there an unpublished photograph of Emma Goldman. (They did.) As they sorted through the photographs, they also found one of Lucy Parsons, with whom they were unfamiliar at the time. With a little research, they knew that they had to publish a card featuring her.⁴²

Because the labor movement was still largely male-centered, despite efforts by some organizations, unions, historians, and publishers to recognize women, Jocelyn and Nancy created the Bread & Roses series to emphasize women as workers and as leaders, both struggling for better conditions and contributing selflessly in a national crisis. The series consisted of nine cards, eight featuring various views and a ninth that was a composite of the eight views.

This series illustrated both Helaine Victoria's commitment to artistry as well as Nancy and Jocelyn's skill in using multimodality to engage viewers. As the cards, printed in three colors, moved through the mail or came to rest on someone's fridge or bulletin board, viewers were met with the following images: Women's Trade Union League; Women's Emergency Brigade; women workers in an "ideal" factory; WWII railroad workers; Lucy Parsons; Crystal Lee Jordan Sutton; Frances Perkins; Rose Schneiderman; and Dorothy Bellanca.

In another effort to counter the static nature of images, Helaine Victoria Press created the cards in such a way that if they were laid out together in the correct order, the viewer saw a Bread & Roses center. This circular insert intersected each photo so that each card had a quarter of the ornament. When one pieced four cards together, the ornament became whole, reminding viewers of the interconnectedness of the women's labor movement over time and across industries.

Having learned that deltiologists preferred 3.5" x 5.5" cards, Jocelyn and Nancy decided to print the Bread & Roses series in that size. Their press would print sheets up to 10" x 15"; to print the eight-card set, however, would have required an 11" x 14" sheet. To solve this problem, they divided the set into two sheets of postcard stock 7" x 11" each, printing four up at a time. Each sheet would then be cut into four cards.

Sending out to the finest photoengraver they knew of in the area, they had eight halftone engravings made of the images they had selected. They would print these images in sepia. To make

41. Lucy Parsons postcard

Lucy Parsons (1853–1942), American free speech and labor leader. A Black with Hispanic and Native American heritage, she was a dramatic speaker, noted equally for her powers of analysis and of voice. She was a central figure in Chicago and the working-class movement nationally, especially after her husband and colleague, Albert, was hanged following the infamous Haymarket "riots" maneuvered by the Chicago police in 1886. She was a founding member of Industrial Workers of the World and one of the original woman members of the Knights of Labor. Variously described as an anarchist and socialist revolutionary, she was mostly remembered as a life, long champion of the hungry, jobless, and foreign born. She spent her life organizing, travelling, writing and leafletting, giving all she had to her causes for 70 years. When she died in poverty at 89, her large literary and political library was confiscated by the F.B.I. and never released.

the borders, which they would print in blue, they chose a linotype border frame which combined both straight and wave-like, curving lines. The border was simple without being stark or meaningless, which felt appropriate, given the amount of action and activity in the photographs on the eight cards. They then pulled four proofs of the border on the proof press and pasted them up so the borders would register around the run with the photos. Where the borders intersected on each of the cards, they cut out a circle where they would place the Bread & Roses emblem on a separate press run. They sent this border image out to have a photoengraving made, and with this engraving, they were able to print all the blue borders on each of the two sheets as one press run. After the eight cards were printed and before the sheets were cut, they pasted the eight finished cards up on a board and sent this to the engraver for a photoengraving for the composite card, the ninth card in the series, which described what the term Bread & Roses means.

Each set of nine required 13 press runs. The set consisted of eight cards; thus, each set utilized two sheets of 7" x 11" cardstock. Because a 10" x 15" format Chandler & Price press is not robust enough to print more than two halftone images at a time, four images required two press runs. Nancy and Jocelyn created the Bread & Roses emblem using two found engravings in their collection. One was a round ornament of wheat symbolizing bread, and another was of a rose which they repeated four times to form a spiral bouquet within the wheat. They had this composite made into an engraving as well. After the photos were printed in sepia and the borders were printed in blue, the emblem was registered and printed in copper.

The backs of the cards were line art, with hand-set, six-point type for the captions, requiring yet another press run. How many do we have so far? Five press runs. But there are eight cards, not four—so double that: ten press runs. The ninth card required three press runs: one for the engravings, one for the type, and one for the line art engraving of the postcard logo and caption on the back. Thus, thirteen press runs.[43]

Each set was assembled into a plastic bag with the eight cards, plus the composite card on top. Jocelyn and Nancy printed a header, showing the title on the front and listing each card on the back, which was folded and stapled to close the packet. They punched a hole at the top so the sets could be hung in shops, either on their displays or on one that Helaine Victoria Press would supply later. Over and over again, Helaine Victoria Press produced labor-intensive products inspired by the artistic legacy they found in the Arts and Crafts movement and *Flair* magazine, all in an effort to grow the women's movement and generate feminist memory.

In a surge of productivity, Helaine Victoria Press also published a series on women and ecology this year. The environmental

## 42. Ellen Swallow Richards postcard

Ellen Swallow Richards (1842–1911). A chemist, she defined the modern study of interaction between organisms in their environments, which she called "Ecology." She was primarily concerned with using science to improve the quality of life in everyday home and work environments. In 1899, she organized the first conference on home economics. Her landmark water purity research was complemented by her analyses of pollution in everything from wallpaper to prepared foods. She formulated the Normal Chlorine Map, the standard map for sanitary surveys. She worked her way through Vassar (MA) and the Massachusetts Institute of Technology, becoming the first woman graduate of M.I.T. in 1873. In 1884 she was appointed Instructor in Sanitary Chemistry at M.I.T.

movement at the time was also largely depicted as a men's effort, with men heading the large organizations, such as the Sierra Club, and engaging in widely publicized confrontational tactics through groups such as Greenpeace. Jocelyn and Nancy wanted to counter this public impression of environmentalist men battling corporate men for control of resources. The series featured four individual women: Velma Johnston, leader in mustang and burro protection; Irene Herlocker, Hoosier prairie conservationist; Hope Sawyer Buyukmihci, who maintained a wildlife refuge; and Ellen Swallow Richards, who defined the study of ecology as a science, plus a composite card of all four.

This series brought its own set of problems. To honor the work and devotion of their subjects, Jocelyn and Nancy wanted to use the best in environmentally sound printing practices. This meant using ink in earth and forest colors on 100% recycled paper. For the first press run, they had chosen a recycled cover stock which was not coated, and the dots on the halftone engravings tended to run together, creating slightly blurred images. Finally, after considerable searching, they found a very heavy coated cardboard that was recycled but wasn't being marketed as such. With that, they printed the cards again.

When they printed the series, Jocelyn created a linoleum block print frame that, like the border in the Bread & Roses series, encircled all the cards when they were laid out together in the proper order. To make the frame, she pasted up pictures of simple elements from nature: flowers, animals, fish, birds, and plants in a rectangle. She had an engraving made of this, and pulled a proof on the proof press. She then cut a linoleum block to the same size as the engraving, seven by ten inches. Linoleum blocks can be purchased for printing already mounted type high on wood, in the same way an engraving is mounted type high on wood. Placing a sheet of carbon paper on top of the block, she laid the proof over that, and traced the outline of the little images; this left a carbon copy on the linoleum block. With the images transferred to the linoleum block, she was able to take her linoleum block carving tools and remove or carve out the linoleum everywhere on the block except where she wanted the fill color to print. This would be the background color for the line engraving of little creatures. Nancy and Jocelyn printed the line engraving in green, the background tint in ochre, and the photos in sepia. Although each card was separate, when pieced together, the border went around all four cards in the series.

For the set, they added a composite card, just like in the Bread & Roses series. This time, they came up with a nifty way to combine the header for the set's package with the front composite card. They had an engraving made of the four cards before they were cut from the sheet. Then, instead of printing a separate header for the package, they had the paper cut long enough to add the series title and descriptive header, the title on the front, and a list of contents with a brief description of each card on the back. After they printed the front and back of the sheet, they did another press run with a piece of brass perforating rule so that the composite card could be detached from the header and sent as a regular postcard—a little bonus. The set was assembled into a plastic bag and a hole punched so that stores could hang it from a rack.

Jocelyn and Nancy felt the series was very close to their hearts and, like other series, could have been much larger. Both were ardent animal protectionists, and they were trying to blend the love of the land and guardianship of the ten acres they rented into their work life. In this way, the series was a personal statement as well; the women they chose were not widely known and, except for Swallow, worked within their own communities on local concerns or crises, which reflected the way Jocelyn and Nancy were caring for their small niche in southern Indiana. This set exemplified their aim to draw attention to women who were otherwise largely disregarded both within and outside of their communities.

Occasionally, organizations and individuals asked Helaine Victoria Press to print something special for them. Whenever possible—especially if the mission of the person or group aligned with their own—Jocelyn and Nancy tried to fulfill these requests. They were especially apologetic, however, when they were forced to turn down a request from Elsa Gidlow to print her "Creed for Free Women." As Nancy said in a letter to Elsa,

> Our type is a family which went out of production over 50 years ago. There are simply not enough letters in the sizes large enough to look like anything, and no way to send to a foundry for more. Our longest single piece to date has been our Alice Duer Miller verse on the Statue of Liberty, and it is eight lines shorter than your creed. We almost didn't make it on that one, and some of the printing difficulties were so large that we might not have attempted it had we known.[44]

If the press had to decline specialized printing jobs on occasion, Nancy and Jocelyn were still happy to participate in local and regional events. In early January, Gloria Kaufman, professor of English and Women's Studies at Indiana University South Bend, invited them to come to South Bend for a Susan B. Anthony Birthday Party, to include a Feminist Fair. She would arrange for them to have a booth at the fair, which she expected would be quite lucrative for them. Could they send some cards ahead of time that she could reproduce in the publicity materials? And would they be willing to donate something for the winner of an essay contest being held in the local schools?[45] Of course, they would.

Likewise, when Dave Long, publisher of a deltiology newsletter that reached 750 members of a postcard collectors club, sought an article about the press from Nancy—plus 750 postcards to send to club members, Nancy happily responded, aware that this would be a fine way to reach a cohort of women postcard collectors. In the article, Nancy briefly explained the press's origins, described the usual output of small letterpresses such as theirs (with emphasis on rarity), and then said that "Jocelyn and Nancy both felt that more outreach would be accomplished by a widespread popular art form such as postcards. They had fun breaking tradition to work with pictures and color, and felt that these departures would provide fun and interest for their customers as well."[46]

Because Jocelyn and Nancy had moved into archival research and away from books as sources for images, they decided it was time to stop collecting books. There would be no more Helaine Victoria Press booklists. The booklists had served them and their many subscribers well. They had modeled their lists on the finest catalogs from English rare book sellers, writing careful, sometimes whimsical descriptions. People read them for the sheer pleasure of the commentary as well as for the revelations of unknown texts. Scholars purchased rare items from them and often found leads to materials unavailable in libraries. However, by 1979, other booksellers were beginning to realize that they should publicize the books on women in their collections; some books were even being republished, mostly by small presses. The need for the Helaine Victoria booklist was waning, while the desire for more cards was strong. They did, however, continue collecting for their own purposes, searching for lost women or buried movements. Often a few boxes of books accompanied them to conferences and festivals.

Having completed their newest offerings, Jocelyn and Nancy constructed their 1979–80 catalog, chatting on each page with their customers, drawing them into their process and demystifying the technology. The opening two pages of the catalog contained "Highlights from the History of Helaine Victoria Press," a continuing effort to share with customers the story of the press and to include them in the ongoing events in the life of the press and the land. "Those of you who are as interested in method as in madness and motivation, read on," they invited. Offering customers a glimpse into her deep understanding of letterpress printing, Nancy wrote:

Letterpress is the process which uses three-dimensional forms to make an <u>impression</u>. The wonder of what can be done with it never wears off. Impression turns up everywhere in art and nature—footprints, mountain valleys, ocean floors, sculpture, cuneiform, etc. Letterpress suits the country printer because it doesn't rely on a constant flow of supplies that requires a big city nearby. The experience of being so in touch with one's craft and learning perpetually from its practice is the characteristic which keeps letterpress alive in the hands of a few artisans. We "job out" occasional work (e.g., this catalog) to an offset shop, so that we can concentrate our own presswork on bringing out new designs for you.[47]

Both the Bread & Roses and Women & Ecology series were introduced in this catalog, along with several new jumbo cards, including Jane Addams at Hull House, Dian Fossey, Margaret Sanger, Alice Paul, and Amelia Earhart with Eleanor Roosevelt. The handsome, fifteen-page catalog announced "Over 20 NEW cards & letterpress specialties printed right here by hand at HV press." Also included: a "handy self-mailing order form" stapled into the center. The front of the catalog featured an old engraving of a woman at a large press (although, they conceded, it could have been a loom).

To save time, they sent the catalog out to a small independent offset printer who seemed comfortable working with women and feminist material, but they still used proofs set with their Munder type or other ornamental fonts to make some of the special headlines and cover copy. The front copy, especially, was made in this way:

"Helaine Victoria Press
Catalog 1979-80
We dedicate this catalog to you, our wonderful customers, friends and colleagues. We thank you every one."

Why go to this trouble? By using proofs of Munder, they could incorporate the beautiful *ct* and *st* ligatures which were part of the charm of this family of type—and, of course, it was their signature typeface.

In another fine moment of celebrating feminist memory, the 1979 Helaine Victoria Press catalog also included an explanation of Columbia as their logo, or trademark. "We rescued a copper engraving of her from an old-time printing plant," they explained. "Now we find from the Smithsonian," they went on, "that she is among our earliest national symbols. The familiar version of Uncle Sam, with stripes and topper, didn't become general until the 1870's. So, look for Columbia where fine cards and admirable traditions are displayed." And with that, they printed a picture in the catalog of Columbia. Next to her is Uncle Sam, labeled "Latecomer."[48]

With the new postcards also came a new signature logo Jocelyn and Nancy designed specifically for cards printed on their Chandler & Price letterpress. In 1901, the Postmaster General had issued

43. Helaine Victoria Press logo used on letterpress printed postcards
The special postcard logo was first used in 1979 and was reserved only for those postcards printed letterpress.

an order which allowed the words "Post Card" instead of the longer "Private Mailing Card" on the backs of postcards. Often, publishers would design an ornate logo associated with their company. But none were as elegant and descriptive as Helaine Victoria's. The border was hand-set from piece borders, the type a combination of Munder and Parsons, and the image a line art illustration of a platen press. They pulled proofs of the components and pasted them up, then sent this out to an engraver for multiple size engravings to use on their postcards. A few years later, while attending the Michigan Women's Music Festival, they discovered a postcard with Helaine Victoria's signature logo. Although it was a copyright infringement, the pirating also attested to the beauty of their logo. However, to make matters worse, the postcard in question was produced using an inferior printing method on a xerox machine. The woman responsible apologized and later reissued her card with her own "postcard" logo.

While the press grew, the relationship between Helaine Victoria Press and Alfreda Duster continued to grow as well, as Duster wrote encouraging letters to Nancy and Jocelyn and they, in turn, continued to promote the Ida B. Wells-Barnett postcard. Early on, Alfreda Duster had suggested that they come visit her in Chicago. When that visit never came to pass, she decided in May of 1979 that she would visit them in Indiana the following month. Seventy-four years old and indefatigable, she told them that she and her niece would be taking the Greyhound bus from Chicago to Martinsville; they could then pick the two of them up in Martinsville and take them out to see the press and the land.

Given Martinsville's history, Nancy and Jocelyn were terrified that, at the very least, Alfreda Duster and her niece would be treated poorly upon their arrival in the town. In 1969, Carol Jenkins, a twenty-one-year-old Black woman from Rushville, Indiana, was stabbed to death with a screwdriver while selling encyclopedias door-to-door in Martinsville. What's more, Martinsville was still the home of the Grand Dragon of the Ku Klux Klan. Thus,

44. Alfreda Duster, Nancy Poore, and Rosa Horn

Photo by the pond at Helaine Victoria Press on a warm summer day in June, 1979. Left to right: Alfreda Duster, Nancy Poore, and Rosa Horn. Alfreda Duster, Jocelyn Cohen and Nancy Poore had developed a friendly relationship through their correspondence about Alfreda's mother, Ida. B. Wells-Barnett. Ms. Duster had invited the two of them to Chicago, but ultimately decided to take the bus and come to Martinsville bringing her niece, Rosa Horn. They spent the day, walking, talking in the printshop and discussing Wells-Barnett and many of her associates.

they were frantic to get into town to retrieve their guests as soon as the bus appeared. When Nancy arrived to collect them, however, she learned that the bus had pulled in early. She was enormously relieved to find that Alfreda and her niece were visiting the 5 & 10 cent shop in town, where the women behind the counters were ever so friendly, and they were having a lovely time.

During her visit to the press, Alfreda Duster talked about the people she knew and admired, especially anti-apartheid activist

Bishop Desmond Tutu of the Anglican Church in South Africa, then general-secretary of the South African Council of Churches. Nancy and Jocelyn took the opportunity to ask what she thought about people who had shown themselves to be heroic in some matters, but flawed in others. They were thinking, they said, of discontinuing the card featuring Frances Willard, president of the Women's Christian Temperance Union in the early twentieth century, after learning of her racism.[49] "Oh, you mustn't do that, girls," Alfreda said, "We mustn't forget Miss Willard's wonderful work for temperance."[50] Jocelyn, at one point, expressed her feelings of discouragement at the state of the world, saying, "Oh, well, you know, now that they've perfected the atom bomb and they poisoned all our food, the earth is doomed." To which Alfreda responded, "Oh, no, honey, God will maybe let us go to the brink if we're that foolish. But somehow, we'll pull back, and it'll all be all right. I never doubt it."[51]

Before she left, Alfreda looked through every card they had. Of course, she wanted more copies of the card about her mother, but also any other cards honoring African American women, Susan B. Anthony, and several others. Jocelyn and Nancy were so grateful that she had let them use her mother's image, they made up a big box of everything she liked and said, "Please, take it." But she insisted on counting every single card and paying for them, even calculating Indiana sales tax. When they demurred, saying they couldn't possibly take her money after she'd been so generous in helping them, she said, "Well, then give it to a good cause."[52]

By 1979, a profusion of feminist publications—*Spokeswoman* and *New Directions for Women,* among others—offered opportunities for advertising, and even mainstream publications such as *Publishers Weekly* saw the value in writing about Helaine Victoria's products.[53] Indeed, *Spokeswoman* printed Helaine Victoria's ERA poster on the cover of the November 1979 issue. Conferences and festivals continued to proliferate. In July of that year, shortly after the National Women's Music Festival in Champaign-Urbana, Illinois, Helaine Victoria Press joined Planned Parenthood, Mary Kay

Cosmetics, the Belton, Indiana Business College, and Headstart in having a booth at a women's fair in Columbus, Indiana, a town of about 29,000 people.

Despite these indicators of development and progress, Jocelyn and Nancy were startled and dismayed by a letter they received in mid-summer 1979: Cynthia Gair and Helaine Harris were announcing the closure of their business, Women in Distribution (WinD). At the inception of the business in 1975, Gair and Harris had encouraged feminist publishers to give them the exclusive rights to distribute their books, and, with the notable exception of Diana Press, many did. As a result, the numbers of publishers and the numbers of bookstores grew substantially every year. Nonetheless, although the business was growing, when they had an accountant analyze their books, they found that the operation was unsustainable—they would not be able to make enough money to pay people to do the work required, and they could not keep doing it all themselves. Thus, they would be closing their business immediately, though trying to make payments to their small feminist business clients before bankruptcy court took over.

As national and international as the women's movement had become, those who were working in publishing had formed a close-knit community. Looking through the WinD catalog at the number of women's presses and publishers or at *Feminist Bookstore News* or at *Women Printers Newsletter*, one finds a whole subculture of Lesbian feminist and feminist enterprises, organizations, and individuals. All these entities woven together created an empowering movement of writers, craftswomen, activists, theorists, visual artists, and musicians, as well as academics forming Women's Studies programs. The print component was the most significant communicator of the when, where, and how of everything that was taking place.

Although the closure precipitated a crisis among feminist publishers and bookstores, Jocelyn and Nancy had a diverse selection of cards; they published a catalog every year; and they had created a substantial mailing list that led to a thriving retail mail order business. Moreover, they were able to transport the cards to conferences and festivals, where they made a large percentage of their annual sales. Nonetheless, like WinD and many other feminist enterprises, they were an undercapitalized business.

How to manage in an era of rising inflation and shrinking support was a frequent topic of conversation among the representatives of various organizations at events such as the Michigan Women's Music Festival, which they attended again that August. It was beginning to seem that the answer to Nancy and Jocelyn's question: "Can Women's Businesses Succeed?" did not reside entirely in feminist loyalty. Larger economic forces were at work. As Julie R. Enszer has commented: "Macroeconomics illuminate successes and failures within the context of the economic and political realms of women's lives, relocating causes of successes and failures from the personal and interpersonal to the structural and institutional."[54] More and more frequently, they heard from women whose organizations had been in operation longer than Helaine Victoria Press about the many benefits available to those holding nonprofit status.

As they learned more about the possibilities inherent in nonprofit status—not the least of which would be lower postage costs on bulk mailings and the credential that would give them easier access to photo and publishing rights—Jocelyn and Nancy decided that they should fill out the 501(c)3 application. This Internal Revenue Service application, predictably detailed and complicated, is usually written by an attorney. Buoyed by Alfreda Duster's optimism, and unable to afford the luxury of hiring a lawyer, they determined to do it themselves. That weeklong process would be their next achievement, and it would bring with it many changes to Helaine Victoria Press.

## CHAPTER THREE

## NONPROFIT STATUS

*We hope by mixing neglected archival materials with the art of letterpress, a feminist perspective, and the power of the press, some new thoughts, ideas, and feelings will result from our work.*
—Nancy Poore, interview with Maide Tilchen, *Sinister Wisdom,* Spring 1980

*I am [...] amazed by the revolutionary nature of the images and texts, given the times in which they were produced.*
—Professor Ellen Dwyer, personal communication, March 16, 2017

Convinced that trying to operate as a profit-making enterprise was slowing their efforts to reach more women and build feminist consciousness, in mid-January of 1980, Jocelyn and Nancy applied for nonprofit status for Helaine Victoria Press. They drove up to Chicago to the home of Nancy's friend Susan Korn, cataloging librarian at DePaul University. There they spent five days at Susan's kitchen table, away from the demands of the press and the woodstove, writing the Application for Recognition of Exemption Under Section 501(c)3 of the Internal Revenue Code, a document whose name mirrors its length and complexity. They listed Helaine Victoria's assets, explained the mission of the organization, wrote bylaws, and named their first board of directors. When asked to explain Helaine Victoria's sources of financial support, Nancy and Jocelyn said that, in addition to the sales of educational postcards and posters to schools, libraries, other educational institutions, and private individuals, they would be offering paid lectures, slideshows, panel discussions, and exhibits and displays of Helaine Victoria's work. These presentations would serve to educate attendees about the publishing crafts and processes used and the historical sources from which they were drawn.

Jocelyn and Nancy had always welcomed opportunities to display the work of Helaine Victoria Press, even though it meant pausing their work at the press. Conferences and festivals had, for several years, allowed them to visit and interact with women who had many different interests, and whose reactions to the cards provided them with direction and ideas for their next efforts. They rarely saw these reactions otherwise, as they sent cards off through the mail or shipped them to bookstores. What's more, these events offered a respite from the isolation of the Indiana countryside and a space to build friendships, as they became acquainted with the other vendors and conference-goers came to know their work in a welcoming atmosphere of feminist solidarity. Now, they were increasing the exposure of the press by proposing to offer workshops and presentations—which would entail even more production delays. They probably didn't realize, as they filled out the 501(c)3 paperwork, how much work they were adding to Helaine Victoria's obligations.

As much as Jocelyn and Nancy felt they were generating feminist awareness and memory, they were learning that various populations appreciated the cards for their own reasons. Most of those reasons, though, overlapped with their own in one way or another, offering a lesson in coalition-building. Not long after they returned from Chicago, they drove down to Cincinnati, where, at the invitation of one of the organizers, they had been invited to show and sell Helaine Victoria cards at a national conference on the history of women in the Methodist church, convened by the General Commission on Archives and History of the United Methodist Church under the auspices of its Women's History Project. Members of this group enthused over the postcards featuring Frances Willard and the officers of the WCTU, among others.

If the Methodist women appreciated the WCTU cards, Fred Whitehead, writing in the *Daily World*, the newspaper published in association with the Communist Party, was equally keen on the Bread and Roses series. In an article titled "U.S. Women and Labor," Whitehead reviewed the series, providing complete ordering information, listing the content of several cards, and offering two cards as illustrations. "Not only are these little cards attractively printed," he wrote, "they also include well-written accounts of the history and significance of the women they depict. Each one thus presents a kind of chapter summary of the history of American working women."[1]

Likewise, Earlham College, an institution associated with the Society of Friends (Quakers), invited Helaine Victoria Press to participate in the Lucretia Coffin Mott E.R.A. Festival.[2] The program announced the press, saying "Helaine Victoria Press is a Feminist Graphics company located in Martinsville, Indiana and known throughout the country. Their work celebrates famous and should be famous women and issues. Their latest work is a Lucretia Mott post card." For the first time, Nancy and Jocelyn did more than set up a table or booth with the cards. They offered a workshop on feminism and business and a slide show entitled, "A Graphic Collection of Women: Post Card Politics," demonstrating the years of misogynistic images purveyed on postcards published during the nineteenth and first half of the twentieth centuries.

Helaine Victoria Press, as a matter of principle, worked to change the cultural landscape by publicizing the achievements of women rather than giving yet more space to the cultural hegemony of men, even if by means of critique. Nonetheless, Nancy and Jocelyn had collected postcards depicting women in an endless variety of demeaning situations. For the slideshow, they drew from this collection, which they later labeled the Pre-1950 Postcard Archive. This collection ultimately numbered approximately over 500 commercial postcards dating from 1880 to the early 1950s with a strong emphasis on early-twentieth-century cards.[3] Although the collection they drew from to create a consciousness-raising slideshow also contained some pro-suffrage and temperance cards, as well as places of historic significance to women such as Carry Nation's home, the majority were sexually suggestive, belittling to women, or generally less than complimentary, emphasizing the "battle of the sexes." Nancy also most likely presented this slideshow in some form a few days later at the National Women's Studies Association conference in Bloomington.[4, 5]

Helaine Victoria Press's participation in the Lucretia Coffin Mott Festival prompted a letter of gratitude from Professor Barbara Ann Caruso, who had organized the event:

> Students and assorted other persons are continuously (2 this a.m.) telling me how wonderful it was to have you here. Good to know you're appreciated—yes? . . . Don't be surprised if you get a call from this semi-organized, would-be Helaine Victoria go-fer. There's something real tantalizing about the possibility of working with you for a while.[6]

Over time, Barbara became a welcome volunteer at the press in the country. In fact, the press offered a chance for many academics to escape from their colleagues' scrutiny of their feminist and/or Lesbian feminist politics or even teachings. Barbara was not the only professor who volunteered for a day or a few days here and there. A host of women faculty from local colleges enjoyed what to Nancy and Jocelyn seemed like mundane tasks: collating postcards into sets, stapling headers, and counting cards for inventory. Martha Vicinus, Indiana University English Department faculty and proponent of the Women's Studies Program, was an early volunteer who excelled in packaging postcards. It took Jocelyn and Nancy a while to realize that some of what they considered tedious and repetitive tasks could actually be an enjoyable respite for others. Barbara Ann Caruso remembered her visits to the press: "Jocelyn, or Nancy, I'm not sure which of you, said that PhDs were particularly good at putting cards in cellophane envelopes, and that it was a skill we had. So, I did that. I was glad to be able to do something well."[7]

Despite the "extraordinary and exuberant" times, most colleges, universities, and academic disciplines did not welcome feminist scholarship. Prof. Jean Robinson's experience was not unusual:

> I still remember this conversation I had with one of the senior women in the Political Science Department where my tenure line was back in the early '80s, and she didn't think I should be "wasting my time on things that wouldn't count." And things that wouldn't count were like working on HV or doing the postcards. None of those things counted for academic work even though they involved research and writing, and they were publications in a way, and I always listed them on my CV. But from the point of view of the mainstream Political Science Department, and probably the rest of the university, they didn't count, count as in count toward the things I'm supposed to be demonstrating that I'm good at or as superb, excellent at in order to get tenure.[8]

Despite such messages, most feminist scholars continued undaunted. Working with Helaine Victoria Press gave a few in the central Indiana area a way to circumvent, if momentarily, their workplace challenges. Barbara's dignified response to the less-than-inclusive attitudes of her colleagues exemplifies the stance many took:

> [ . . . ] I was not at all in many ways like my colleagues. So, I had a whole world of knowledge or hopes or aspirations or visions and

concerns, politics, that they didn't have. I can remember them talking about how not well-educated I was and that I didn't go to Princeton or Yale or Oxford. And one day I had all these books laying on a table in my office, and cards as well [ . . . ] lots of feminist books that I'd gotten mostly at the time at those [women's] bookstores. And my colleagues, a couple came in, and they didn't know one of those books. And I thought to myself, you're the ones who are not well-educated. This is what it is to not be well-educated.[9]

For many like Barbara, coming to the country and helping out provided a "good place to breathe." A day in the country seamlessly wove together printing, gardening, eating, and business. In addition to putting PhDs to work slipping cards into cellophane envelopes, Nancy and Jocelyn encouraged volunteers to learn how the Chandler & Price press worked. "I did Zora Neale Hurston's red border," Barbara recalled. "Yes, I remember it very well. And I remember thinking, 'Oh, my God, I'm gonna get my fingers stuck in here.' But I loved it."[10]

Operating on very slim budget, Nancy and Jocelyn were grateful for the help and friendship of volunteers. In their application for 501(c)3 status, they had explained that they were the only two employees of the press. They each worked seventy hours per week and received salaries of $200 per month. More discreetly, in the catalog, they advised customers that this was the fourth year of their French intensive double-dug garden: "Since our cards don't quite do the whole job of supporting us, the garden provides for a large part of our vegetarian lifestyle."[11] Customers could make of that what they would.

Overworked and underpaid, Jocelyn and Nancy told each other privately with every innovation that *this* was going to be the idea or product that would change their fortunes. Perhaps their attitude exhibits what Lauren Berlant would call "cruel optimism," as they continued to attach themselves to a vision that, by its very nature, would wear them out.[12] Unlike Cynthia Gair and Helaine Harris of Women in Distribution, however, Nancy and Jocelyn did not ask an accountant to analyze their books to determine the likelihood of their financial success within the unavoidable structure of capitalism. Rather, they maintained an unflagging determination that their work could help enlarge the space for women in the world. If not attacking the structure of capitalism directly, they were working to establish a "more perfect union," one in which feminist concepts of equality and cooperation replaced celebrations of the beneficence of competition.

That spring, when the NOW National Board met, Indiana representatives told the others about Helaine Victoria Press's ERA poster—and the special offer the press had made to sell thirty of the posters for $10. With that offer, board member Teresa Bergen of Brooklyn realized that for $10 she could enable more women to go to the upcoming ERA march in Chicago. She wrote to the press, explaining her scheme:

> I have been traveling around the NYC area trying to drum up support for people to go to the Chicago ERA march. I have been collecting money and offering a free poster to anyone who contributes $5 or more. I only have 9 left and we have collected over $200. I have one more speaking date to go and I feel that the remaining posters should bring in at least another $100.
>
> Thank you! Your kindness in reducing the price of your beautiful posters sparked my imagination and now more people will get to Chicago.[13]

Teresa Bergen's letter cheered Nancy and Jocelyn and served to reinforce their deeply held belief that their horizontal, multimodal, cooperative method could, in fact, generate new ideas and feelings.

Nonetheless, Helaine Victoria Press was operating within an economic system that required frequent change from its participants, and Nancy and Jocelyn had to respond accordingly. This pressure to adapt to changing circumstances would accelerate, as 1980 was a presidential election year, and President Jimmy Carter was being challenged by conservative Republican Ronald Reagan. If this ceaseless need to adjust and innovate was stressful, Nancy and Jocelyn also were determined to find opportunities for creative development.

Using the archival sources with which they were now familiar, Helaine Victoria Press published four new jumbo cards in 1980, in addition to reprinting many of the most popular cards from past years. The new cards were: Helen May Butler and Her Ladies Brass Band; Women of Colorado You Have the Vote; Trackwomen on the Baltimore & Ohio railroad, 1943, originally also part of the Bread & Roses series; and Students Making Barrel Furniture.

For Jocelyn and Nancy, the Chandler & Price letterpress was more an artistic tool than a production machine. While they happily printed many cards, when it came time to reprint a given card, they were more inclined to send it out to an offset printer for reproduction.[14] They had found a small offset shop in a nearby town whose owner treated them and their products as he would any others: respectfully. With this resource, they decided that, in order to release these four new cards more quickly, they would job them out to this printer. Most of the designs were simple, with plain borders, although each differed slightly from the others. However, for the Helen May Butler card, they found among their linotype borders that they had a lovely twelve-point border that resembled a bar of music with little flowers interspersed among the notes. They pulled a proof of this and used it to frame the photo along the top and bottom of the card. This border, with the feminine flowers among the musical notes, echoed and reinforced the visual message of the photograph it framed: the women pictured were elaborately dressed according to women's fashion dictates of the era, and, at the same time, were holding instruments ranging from clarinets and saxophones to trombones, tubas, and bass drums. Helen May Butler herself stood in the center, holding her baton, clearly in charge. With this card they envisioned messages sent by and among the many feminist musicians and their fans.

Like some of the cards in the Bread & Roses and Women & Ecology series, what distinguished these jumbo cards from several earlier cards was the fact that none of the women pictured was even remotely well-known or famous, although Helen May Butler may have had a small local following during her time. Moreover, other than Butler, the women pictured remained nameless: Helaine Victoria's cards were the first public acknowledgement of their anonymous accomplishments. Feminist memory, by definition, was not about making "stars," but rather about recognizing the lives and accomplishments of many women. Edith Mayo had enabled them to find two of the photos: Women of Colorado, and the Ladies Brass Band. Developing personal ties with curators and archivists facilitated Nancy and Jocelyn's access to otherwise hard to find material on many occasions. At the same time, these connections helped to establish a network of people committed to and involved with women's history nationally and internationally.

Despite the fact that the women in these photographs were not named, the Trackwomen on the B&O card, like all the cards, was in its essence mobile and accessible. Because of this mobility, it found its way to a railroad worker in a remote, rural area in the Midwest. She later wrote to the press, telling Nancy and Jocelyn how much she treasured the card. She kept it posted on her fridge, she said, to remind herself of the importance as well as the history of the work she was doing.

The Trackwomen image epitomized the kind of photos they looked for, images that drew one's eye and hinted at a multitude of untold stories. Not only were the women unnamed, but the photographer was nameless as well. Perhaps s/he was working for the WPA or the Woman's Bureau? The five African American women in the photograph stand looking directly toward the viewer, holding their shovels with hands in gloves, some mismatched, and each wearing a cap or wrap of sorts on her head.[15] Their ages varied and demonstrated the fact that jobs during the war opened up opportunities for different kinds of women:

45. Trackwomen on the Baltimore & Ohio Railroad postcard

Trackwomen on the Baltimore & Ohio, 1943. The wartime manpower shortage opened more jobs of more kinds to women than ever before. Employers hired Black women, over-35's, and married women—3 groups previously barred from most offices and industries. About 90% of Black working women were domestics or farm workers before the war, but 18% worked in factories by war's end, and those on farms were halved. Equal pay and promotions were decreed by new laws, but these were not fully enforced, especially for Blacks and older women. However, wages and opportunities were better than ever before. Peacetime put more than 2 million women in nontraditional jobs out of work, but most found other jobs in the postwar boom, contrary to all predictions—even their own.

Black women, women over thirty-five, and married women, all previously barred from most offices and industries. Here they stood, not dressed in work clothes supplied by the railroad, but rather wearing what could have been their Sunday best, including street shoes perhaps now wearing thin. But the faint smiles give us pause: what are they thinking or feeling with this new, better-paying job, perhaps one offering the possibility of promotion? Is this a hopeful opportunity? Will their nice coats get ruined in their day's work? It is hard to pull one's eyes away from their faces, especially knowing that, as the caption tells us, they would lose their jobs with the return of peacetime.

Other copies of the Trackwomen on the B&O traveled widely and were reproduced in magazines and newspapers, where they reached more audiences. They were posted on school and library bulletin boards, as well as on other refrigerators, drawing different, but nonetheless significant, affective responses to this reminder of the competence and collective effort demonstrated by women during WWII. In this way, the cards were not only multimodal, but also multifunctional: put to use in myriad ways to generate feminist memory.

In another portent of change, that winter, Helaine Victoria Press made what would be their last first day cover cachet, celebrating the release of a US first-class postage stamp honoring Frances Perkins. The Bread & Roses series had included a card with a photo of Perkins and a caption describing her work as Secretary of Labor in the Franklin D. Roosevelt administration. It was a short step, then, to producing a first day cover. For the cachet, they chose a different photo of Perkins, one taken prior to her position as Secretary of Labor. She was doing fieldwork, researching working conditions in the factories for one of the many investigative committees she worked on after viewing the Triangle Shirtwaist Factory disaster in 1911. Nancy and Jocelyn enclosed a copy of the Perkins card from the Bread & Roses series in each envelope to explain her significance.

Although the change from an (allegedly) profit-making corporation to a (more accurately) nonprofit organization would serve to bring several new women into Helaine Victoria's circle, a few friends had already been helping out. Jocelyn's mother Toba was primary among them. When she was not needed at Herschel's Shoes, the family shoe store, she came out to the country many weekdays to help with mail orders and bookkeeping, sometimes staying overnight in order to be able to work the next day as well. Merry Bateman, a marketing specialist, and Camille Saad, a graphic designer, were two of the first Helaine Victoria fans to contact the press and offer their services.

46. Nancy Poore, Camille Saad, Merry Bateman, and Jocelyn Cohen, 1980
Merry Bateman, a marketing specialist, and Camille Saad, a graphic designer, were among the first Helaine Victoria Press fans to contact the press and volunteer their services. The four are standing here with one of the 400 pine trees Jocelyn and her dad, Herschel, had planted a couple of years earlier.

Merry had been active in the women's movement in college during the early 1970s. Majoring in women's history, she became familiar with Helaine Victoria postcards. From then on, whenever she and Camille found a women's bookstore, they would look for Helaine Victoria products, especially the jumbo cards. "Working in the direct marketing business," Merry said,

> we had a lot of ideas to help them lift response rates and sales through their mail order catalog. We got to know Jocey and Nancy. In fact, we had an amazing inside look at their business, all the

**47. 1980–81 Helaine Victoria Press Catalog featuring many new offerings**
The 1980–81 Helaine Victoria Press catalog featured a picture of Japanese suffragist Kimura Komako on the front cover. Columbia, plus a small representation of the ERA poster and postcard, decorated the back, leaving room for a mailing address and stamps.

trials and tribulations. Their work came across as coming from a large organization, while in reality it was two enterprising women committed to building this comprehensive card line.[16]

Camille Saad designed the 1980–81 catalog for the press, featuring Kimura Komako, Japanese suffragist, against a light blue background on the cover. This catalog cover was the first to have an image taken from a Helaine Victoria card; beneath the image of Komako was printed a quotation from her, dated 1917. In this way, the cover demonstrated to readers the multimodal fusion of image, text, and color that characterized Helaine Victoria cards.

Inside, the blue-and-white theme continued, with page after page of illustrations of cards, larger than they had been in previous catalogs, thus more easily viewed. One page was devoted to photos of Jocelyn and Nancy at work, alongside a narrative history of Helaine Victoria Press and an argument for the importance of mail order as "an antidote to the high cost of shopping by car."[17] The photos of Nancy and Jocelyn showed them almost exclusively engaged in printing-related activities—operating the press or returning type to the cabinets—reminding readers that not only were they producing exemplars of accessible, modifiable feminist art, they had also mastered the technology and claimed the printing trade for women.

Camille and Merry made another significant contribution to Helaine Victoria. When they came out to the country, they had been working at Abbey Press, the largest religious mail order gift outlet at the time, located two hours away in St. Meinrad, Indiana. There they had befriended Bernice Schipp, also a marketing specialist, and thought both that she would enjoy working with Helaine Victoria and that the press could greatly benefit by Bernice's knowledge and experience. This connection would soon prove to be rewarding beyond expectations.

In 1980, Nancy and Jocelyn announced one of their new ideas on a sheet of goldenrod paper, folded and stapled in the center of the catalog: "A Keepsake from Helaine Victoria Press," it read. "A marvelous little selection of letterpress ephemera that you probably never knew we printed. It comes in a big (10 ½" x 13" when open), beautiful **Folio** with the history of the Press printed on the inside face." In order to print the folio on the Chandler & Price press, they had a large size engraving made of Columbia from a proof of their original one. The outside was simple, featuring the six-inch-tall image of Columbia centered above a line reading "Helaine Victoria Press" and with the word "FOLIO" below in their Munder type, followed by a line under that using one of their hand-set piece ornaments. The inside of the folio, 6.5" x 10.5" folded, with a flap to hold an assortment of cards, provided a brief narrative of the press's history, including small, captioned photos. They offered the folio for "only $3.00. A mere fraction of its worth,"[18] and used it, like the catalogs, to chat with customers as if they were sitting together at the picnic table overlooking the pond. "We are printers of pictorial documents on women's history," the folio began, "including labor, suffrage, civil rights, ecology, arts and ideas, lifestyles, and certain renegade individuals[.] People sometimes think this is a big outfit. They address mail to a department or a title[.] The real point about being small is that H.V. is personal. If you have ever phoned, visited, or met us traveling, you already know that."[19] With this offer, they hoped to entice customers to acquire a few more cards to send or give or post, creating more conversations and more viewers.

Continuing the order form innovation from the 1979–80 catalog, they included a form in the 1980 catalog that did not have to be cut from the catalog and that was folded in such a way that it could simply be taped or stapled closed, a stamp and return address could be affixed, and then it could be mailed back to the press. This one clearly listed every item so it was even easier to fill out than the previous one. In the catalog, Nancy and Jocelyn acknowledged Merry and Camille, along with several other volunteers, saying,

MORE SPECIAL THANK-YOUS: to Merry Bateman and Camille Saad for layout, ideas, talent, and energy, generously given to the new catalog, and to promoting Helaine Victoria in general; and to Toba Cohen, Becky Alexander, and Martha Vicinus, who helped us out in the office at times when we didn't know how we could get it all done; and . . . to all our customers and friends who make it possible to continue our work.[20]

With catalogs, festivals, conferences, and presentations, Helaine Victoria Press was becoming known, gaining participants locally, nationally, and internationally. Even *Publishers Weekly* included Helaine Victoria Press products in a special annual section on notecards, greeting cards, and stationery of interest to bookstores. The remote location of the press, however, did not encourage a large number of visitors or volunteers. Those who did make the effort to come were dedicated to the mission of the press. One such volunteer was Vicki Leighty, who had grown up in the Martinsville area. Vicki had been working in the anti-nuclear movement but had returned, and wanted to find a way to be involved in the women's movement. A friend in the Indianapolis area advised Vicki to try to find Helaine Victoria Press, which she knew was located somewhere near Vicki's home. Vicki found the press —and continued to volunteer and work for the press for the next seven years.

Helaine Victoria Press gave Vicki what she was looking for: a deep introduction to both the larger field of women's history and the current Lesbian feminist movement. For her part, Vicki offered Helaine Victoria Press her passion for organizing, her willingness to take on new projects, and her local knowledge.[21]

At the same time, as more volunteers were beginning to seek out the press, Helaine Victoria cards were prompting enthusiastic responses from customers across the globe. Writing to Jocelyn in response to receiving a catalog order later that year, Adrienne Rich expressed her appreciation for the large Trackwomen on the

48. Vicki Leighty, Jocelyn Cohen, and Nancy Poore, ca. 1981

B&O card—"their faces are so wonderful"—and then wondered why they hadn't printed on the Kimura Komako card the quotation from Komako that had appeared on the cover of the catalog:

> "Liberty for woman is no idle dream. Most of them look at me aghast when I speak of it. It is not 'nice' to discuss such things. The very virtuous shudder and change the subject. But there are those that come back to me quietly, privately, and ask new questions and plead with me to tell them more. So you see we have made a beginning." —Kimura Komako, Japanese Suffragist, 1917

"The whole package was glorious to receive," Rich said. "[ . . . ] Your beautiful and caring work is much appreciated here."[22] Shortly thereafter, Jocelyn and Nancy redesigned the Kimura Komako card to include the quotation below the image, printing it as a jumbo card rather than the original 3.5" x 5" aimed at attracting deltiologists.

Liberty for woman is no idle dream. Most of them look at me aghast when I speak of it. It is not "nice" to discuss such things. The very virtuous shudder and change the subject. But there are those who come back to me quietly, privately, and ask new questions and plead with me to tell them more. So you see we have made a beginning.

— Kimura Komako, Japanese Suffragist, 1917

### 49. Kimura Komako postcard

Kimura Komako, shown on a visit to New York in 1917-18. A leading Japanese actress/dancer, Mme. Kimura came to the U.S. mainly to study the methods of American woman suffragists. She organized the first (1913) Japanese suffrage meeting, magazine and society—both called *Shin Shin Fujin* (New True Woman). It was a courageous, even shocking step, criticized but not given much real public notice. Yet it paved the way for the more famous Akiko Hiratsuka and her colleagues, who stunned the nation in 1920 by petitioning to end an ancient law against women's participation in political gatherings. They won that round and, in 1946, the franchise. On April 10, 13 million Japanese women voted for the first time in more than 25 centuries as a nation.

Like other cards, the Kimura Komako card traveled widely, just as Jocelyn and Nancy hoped. An editor for a Japanese publishing house in New York, Tricia Vita, read the notice about Helaine Victoria in *Publishers Weekly,* then went to Djuna Books, a women's bookstore in Greenwich Village, and found a selection of cards, including the Kimura Komako card. She wrote an article about the card for the Japanese edition of *Cosmopolitan,* then wrote to Helaine Victoria, letting them know about the article and thanking them for publishing the card. She translated the article's title for them: "Two Women Work Hard, Helaine Victoria Press," and said that the information in the article was taken from their catalog and from the Kimura Komako caption. "It was a wonderful surprise to the Japanese editor that you know so well about an early Japanese feminist!"[23] This evidence of the active building of feminist memory internationally through their cards elated and encouraged the two cofounders.

During the summer of 1980, Nancy and Jocelyn had received a letter from Judy Harvey Sahak, a librarian at Scripps College, telling them that Scripps would be reinstating its letterpress printing program and, to celebrate, the library would be mounting an exhibit of work by women letterpress printers. In addition, the library planned to purchase the items sent for exhibit in order to build its collection of fine letterpress printing. Would they like to participate? she asked. Of course, they would! Nancy replied with great enthusiasm, sending multiple copies of several items so that they could be displayed front and back. "You'll probably notice right away that there isn't a book in the parcel, nor a poem, and but two broadsides," she said.

> In this way I expect we'll be quite different from your other contributors, and I hope the departure from convention isn't unwelcome. We made a conscious decision at the beginning to stick mainly with postcards and various other occasional items that would be associated with an old "job" shop. This was partly because this

unusual material interested us most, and because such beautiful books and broadsides were already being produced by other fine printers.

She went on to describe how she and Jocelyn had established their printshop and to explain their philosophy about re-using and recycling their materials. "One thing that makes the H.V. style (if it can be given so precise a label) so interesting from the printing viewpoint is some of the materials we manage to find and use," she said. "We have located in diverse places, from abandoned printshops to garbage bins, wonderful old type and engravings, about to be melted or scrapped. My Jazz Age cards, for example, are made entirely of such finds, as are Jocey's piece-border flowers on the Etta Macy and Violet Trefusis prints."[24] The library bought all the items that Nancy and Jocelyn had sent for their permanent collection, and, according to Judy Sahak, the exhibit was very successful, with at least one student asking how to order Helaine Victoria cards.

More fan mail was arriving from catalog customers, confirmation that their rhizomatic method of transmitting feminist images and information was working. Jo Feldman wrote from San Francisco, saying: "I gotta hand it to you folks; I never expected to be moved to tears by a postcard catalog—and you did it *twice:* with the 'Unauthorized Interview' and with the look on Dian Fossey's face on page 7 [ . . . ]. Whoops of exultation and glee that you're doing what you're doing a) at all, and b) so unassailably well. THANKS."[25] In a quieter but no less fervent message, Ruth Perry of the Humanities Department at MIT wrote, "You are to be complimented because the information you cite on the back of your Mary Astell notecard is all right, which is more than many scholars in the field can manage[.]"[26]

By this time, Jocelyn and Nancy had figured out that many of their most ardent customers would be found in schools, colleges, and universities. As Jocelyn said in 1980,

We've had a hard time finding our niche for customers. We're making postcards, which isn't done much anymore. And when we started, doing women's history, it wasn't very popular. So, we've had a really hard time just drumming up interest in what we do. Bookstores would say that cards should go in a gift store. Gift stores would say that we were educational and political, and that they wouldn't carry us. At our first really big academic conference, I was afraid the academics would find us not academic enough. I think if that had happened, we would have quit. The amazing thing was that that was our niche. The academics loved our cards.[27]

Because they had come to realize that teachers at all levels were using their cards in outsized numbers, Nancy and Jocelyn were especially thrilled to learn in November, 1980, that Helaine Victoria Press's application for nonprofit status had been approved in record time, ten months after they had submitted it. Was this business as usual, they wondered, or did Helaine Victoria Press have a subterranean friend in the Internal Revenue Service helping to facilitate their application before a new administration took over? They would never know, of course, but they were grateful nonetheless. Days after their 501(c)3 approval, Ronald Reagan was elected president of the United States, in a move that would usher in serious cutbacks to institutions and organizations of all sorts that were supporting Helaine Victoria Press.

It was their fondest hope that their new status would help pull them out of the red, and, especially, that having a savvy board of directors with smart and varied perspectives would bring a new influx of business and imaginative ideas to the press. Although they could not foresee these consequences in the moment, the fact that the press's new status required the involvement and commitments of more women would come to serve Helaine Victoria Press well in the future. The Spring 1981 Helaine Victoria Press catalog announced this new status, saying, "This means that HV Press is officially recognized as an educational organization performing a public service. It also means," the catalog hinted broadly,

> that your donations are tax deductible. In brief, our purposes are to continue photographic research in the field of women's history & culture; to make our findings easily & inexpensively available via the postcards [primarily], to print many of these cards on a hand-fed platen press, thus helping to perpetuate the craft of letterpress; to catalog & preserve postcards which reflect the image of women in society; & to give lectures & slide presentations on various aspects of the Press' work. Nancy & Jocelyn are still the fulltime printers, researchers, order department, & clean-up crew. Together with the Board of Directors we will ensure that the Press continues to be a force in the field of women's history and culture.[28]

The new year brought more new cards. Two cards introduced this year celebrated women's strength and efforts to overturn oppressive institutions and practices. Jocelyn and Nancy had been trying by means of several cards to alert women to the liberatory foundations of the temperance movement. Their efforts had not met with much success. The temperance movement—and the women associated with it—were the butt of jokes too deeply engrained in the American psyche.

With the Whiskey Crusade card, they documented women's extralegal and often violent efforts to take down the bars that drew men and their money away from their homes. In addition, they tried one more time with this card to demonstrate the ways in which feminism, especially suffrage, and temperance sprang from some of the same roots in the late nineteenth and early twentieth centuries. How many women were aware that the primary funders of anti-suffrage efforts were the distillers? Another attribute of the temperance movement not normally addressed was the issue of wife abuse. Temperance leaders saw whiskey and the bars as the culprits for domestic violence. Just as the companion suffrage

### 50. Whiskey Crusade postcard

Alcohol consumption in Colonial through 19th century America was prodigious and almost universal. Whiskey was often on the breakfast table. Frontier people thought water unsafe and drank hard cider all day. Drinking among women and children became more secretive and/or diminished when the saloon gradually replaced home as the center of social drinking. Such mostly masculine events as the Gold Rush and the Civil War intensified the trend. Virtually all men—including clergy—drank heavily. Pay envelopes went straight to the barkeep: family violence and desperate lack of funds grew epidemic in the working classes. (It was more subtle among the rich.) Early temperance societies were all male, and later male led. Women formed their first large action-oriented, anti-saloon groups in Ohio in 1873, singing and praying loudly in the streets and taverns. Lucy Thurman, a president of the National Association of Colored Women, entered temperance work in 1875. Carry Nation (1846–1911) is credited as the first to add a hatchet to evangelical methods, smashing bars, barrels, and bottles from 1899-ca. 1910. The greatest anti-drink force was the Women's Christian Temperance Union (WCTU), led at its height by Frances Willard (1839–98). Women's efforts were essential in securing Prohibition (1919); but once we got the ballot (1920), we voted heavily for Repeal (1932).

movement thought the vote would give women equality, better working conditions, and a fairer wage, temperance saw alcohol as the reason for wife battering and economic hardship at home. Jocelyn and Nancy were aware of the complicated issues and implications of prohibition, and they realized that temperance leaders viewed whiskey as the demon rather than the more pervasive patriarchal culture. They also had become aware of the ways in which suffrage and temperance leaders had betrayed women of color in their single-minded attempts to achieve their goals. Nonetheless, they wanted to demonstrate that contemporary efforts to stop violence against women had roots in temperance reform ideology.

The jumbo Whiskey Crusade card showed a half-dozen images illustrating different aspects of the temperance movement. Because of this complicated layout, Nancy and Jocelyn designed it specifically for offset printing. They thought the card would be provocative, both in content and design, but this final effort to educate second-wave feminists about their temperance activist forebears also fell flat, the images of strong, committed women insufficient to challenge cultural attitudes that ridiculed the temperance movement. Although Nancy and Jocelyn always portrayed positive images of women, they wondered, in this instance, whether they should have shown one of those popular cartoon images of a drunk man beating a woman and, under the photo a quote in a clear, unmistakable typeface, written: "Women temperance workers understood violence against women and the need for political power long before the second wave of feminism."

The other new letterpress 4.25" x 6" postcard was a photo of Susan B. Anthony in her study, acknowledging her lifelong work to bring about universal woman suffrage. Although the image and caption are of Anthony, a close look at the image shows that she is not alone: her desk holds framed photographs of her comrades and collaborators. Later, Jocelyn and Nancy added a red heart in the lower left corner, as Anthony's birthday was the day after Valentine's Day. They then offered the card as a quintessential feminist valentine.

The card found its way to Missoula, Montana, where Diane Sands was organizing a Susan B. Anthony birthday celebration in February, 1981. She ordered a good supply of the cards from Helaine Victoria to give to attendees, reporting back that there were women from all parts of the community: "League of Women Voters, Women for Peace (all in their 60s or 70s), women attorneys, teachers, dykes, students, community rowdies, and even a woman from the state employment service!—all thrilled to receive a SBA postcard from YOU as a keepsake!"[29]

**51. Susan B. Anthony in Her Study postcard**
Susan B. Anthony (1820–1906). Her birthday, February 15. is often celebrated along with Valentine's Day. This portrait, in her study (ca. 1900) shows her surrounded by photos of many friends from her abolition, temperance, and women's rights campaigns. She had incredible reserves of courage and energy, demonstrated in a political career of more than 50 years. In Europe, aged 63, she said in her diary: "Breakfast was sent to my room and, for the first time in my life, I ate it in bed. What would my mother have said?" Her last public appearance was at a party for her 86th birthday, where she told the 400 guests: "Failure is impossible."

This year brought another innovation in postcards. For the first time, Helaine Victoria Press published cards that featured women's words with no images. There were practical reasons for this new type of card. One such reason was that they had a large supply of postcard stock just waiting to be used, much of it either scrap from larger sheets or pieces reclaimed from printshops. What's more, these cards did not involve as much research, which was often challenging in their location. Cards without images also were less expensive to create because they did not require a costly halftone engraving, nor did the printer have the challenge of printing such an engraving on a hand-fed letterpress, a practice that pushed the limits of their platen press. A less practical, but more artistic, motive behind the new cards displaying women's words was that Nancy and Jocelyn had collected so much beautiful type and so many fancy initial caps, dingbats, and ornamental foundry, monotype, and linotype that they had not been able to use to great advantage so far. These cards allowed them to use and show off some of those special elements for which the press was designed.

Even more significantly, however, Jocelyn and Nancy were, for the first time, making art from words as well as from images. Before, words, usually in the form of captions, had been complementary to the images. Now, words were centered and embellished, drawing attention even more directly to otherwise subjugated ideas. They had found yet another way to upend conventional notions of art while continuing to recenter women in the historical record and generate feminist memory. Whereas most of the recent cards that Jocelyn and Nancy had printed introduced unsung women or groups of women demonstrating against oppressive conditions, in contrast, the names of those whose words were used were often well-known, which served to draw customers' attention to them—but the words themselves were unexpected. These words, though brief, catalyzed serious reflection about women, challenging basic structures of thought about sexuality, nationhood, and economic status.

A few of the typographical "word cards" were quite intricate and included captions. For instance, a card featuring Emma Lazarus's poem "The New Colossus" offered an inset photo of Lazarus and a caption about her on the back. If time was ever accounted for, cards such as this were at least as intricate to design and print as any with a photograph. With these cards, Helaine Victoria Press emphasized the importance of women's words and ideas, offering customers another way to share their feminist commitments.

Although Helaine Victoria Press had been soliciting and responding to suggestions from customers in feminist collaborative fashion for some time, this year marked the first that Jocelyn and Nancy created a set specifically in response to a group's request. The Wisconsin Women Library Workers (WWLW) contacted the press, asking whether they could commission a set of cards honoring several Wisconsin women library workers who had made especially significant contributions to the field of library science. Nancy and Jocelyn agreed to take on the project. The arrangement they made was that the WWLW would provide the photos and captions, while Helaine Victoria would design, produce, and package the cards. The WWLW would pay for the materials, shipping, and production costs; in lieu of payment for labor, Helaine Victoria would receive half of the press run of 1000, some for sets as well as some for individual card sales. This was a generous offer on Helaine Victoria's part, because, as it turned out, most of the photos supplied by the WWLW were portraits. Jocelyn and Nancy had realized early on that most portraits were not all that appealing, no matter who the subject was. Not taken mid-action, but rather posed, the photos did not invite lengthy perusal or interpretation. Moreover, although the women depicted had made major contributions to the development of American library systems, Helaine Victoria customers were not clamoring for specialized information of this sort. Unfortunately, the sets did not fly off the shelves, though they proved meaningful for WWLW, which, in a way, was more to the point.

In the summer of 1981, with their new nonprofit status, Helaine Victoria Press held its first meeting of the board of directors. Members of the first board were: Barbara Ann Caruso, PhD, Earlham College faculty; Jocelyn H. Cohen; Gloria Kaufman, PhD, Indiana University South Bend faculty; Susan Korn, Chicago librarian and women's rights activist; Nancy Poore; and Martha Vicinus, PhD, Indiana University Bloomington faculty. Among other items of business, the board voted to increase Nancy and Jocelyn's salaries from $200 to $600 per month. The money, however, simply wasn't there, despite the optimism of the board.

Hoping for ideas to address this scarcity, in early October, Nancy and Jocelyn drove to Washington, DC to attend the second Women in Print conference. The conference, held at the 4-H Center in Chevy Chase, Maryland, was organized largely by women who wrote for and published *off our backs,* a nationally distributed radical feminist monthly tabloid newspaper. Most of those attending the conference came from bookstores, periodicals, and book publishers; Helaine Victoria Press was one of only five printers who sent representatives. Although the conference focused primarily on the interests of the aforementioned groups, Jocelyn and Nancy found several workshops that spoke to their desire to engage the power of the press to catalyze new ideas, while also letting them know that they were not alone in an unfriendly political and economic climate.

By this time, most major cities as well as large towns had a women's bookstore. These stores offered the work of presses and publishers owned and operated by women that gave voice to authors whose works and words "did not meet the needs" or "did not fit the lists" of mainstream commercial publishers. Periodicals flourished, addressing women's issues and concerns as well as offering venues for women to post or advertise their services, wares, events, and businesses. Women could more readily find those of like minds, providing a sense of solidarity and empowerment. Hungry for change, women—including Nancy and Jocelyn at Helaine Victoria Press—were creating a new feminist print culture, the largest by far since the women's rights movement of the late nineteenth and early twentieth centuries.[30]

The Women in Print conference embodied the rich diversity and complexity of the feminist and Lesbian feminist movements of the times. The associated activities, politics, and art not only were elements of a movement, but also formed a culture within which many women thrived for nearly two decades, creating and distributing a wide variety of publications, raising questions, and opening minds. Commenting specifically on Helaine Victoria Press's modifiable and multimodal contributions to this culture, Susan Gubar recalled that she "collected the cards and I kept them in the top left-hand drawer of my office in Ballentine Hall [. . .]. And, every bit of feminist business I did in the '70s and early '80s was done through those cards."[31]

On the first day of the conference, both Nancy and Jocelyn attended the general session in which Jackie St. Joan and Persephone Press addressed "The Threat from the Right and What to Do About It." From there, they went to workshops that addressed more specifically the financial issues they had been working on for the past two years. Jocelyn joined other publishers as Barbara Grier of Naiad Press led a discussion entitled "Returning to 'Helping Each Other' Ethics: Using Early Movement Techniques to Increase Our Numbers and Strengthen Our Base," a clear echo of ideas raised in the article that Nancy and Jocelyn had authored for *Sister* back in 1975, "Can Women's Businesses Succeed?" At the same time, Nancy went to a related session, hearing New Victoria Printers address the question "How Does an Alternative Press Serve the Community and Still Make Money?" After this effort to quiet the insistent demands of the economy, they turned to the more thought-provoking issues of feminist analysis.

Jocelyn went to a meeting of archivists led by Mirta Quintanales, Sonya Alvarez, and Barbara Smith entitled "Introducing Third World Women's Archives: Information Exchange Between Present Archives and One Newly Formed." The next day, both Nancy and Jocelyn attended the general session led by Maureen Brady, Betty Bird, Michelle Cliff, and Juanita Ramos, "Creating a Lesbian Literature: How Conscious Are We? Race, Class, Age, Disability." After they shared their own expertise in a workshop for printers entitled "Converting Your Idea to Finished Printing: Making the Best Choice of Form and Printing Method (Political/Technical Aspects)," they went to a forum on "Racism and Classism in Feminist Periodicals, Bookstores, and Publishing Organizations: Increasing the Availability of Writing by Women Whose Voices Traditionally Have Been Suppressed," led by Hattie Gossett and Jill Krolik. Galvanized by listening to Cherrie Moraga explain the dearth of images and voices of women of color as largely a function of the ownership of presses by white women, Jocelyn and Nancy returned to Martinsville more determined to do their part to change that dynamic. They pledged to themselves that they would, from then on, find and publish primarily images and stories of women in marginalized communities. The women in print movement, in conjunction with women's bookstores, kept the issues of class and race centered in the movement and through publishing and distribution moved words into action.[32]

The fact that Helaine Victoria's earliest cards rarely celebrated women of color reflected the lack of material in the kinds of sources they knew how to use as they were starting out—books and libraries. Because Nancy and Jocelyn were relying on secondary sources for those first couple of years, their research turned up only a few, such as Sojourner Truth and Mary McLeod Bethune. As they honed their research skills, they learned that archives are a different kind of repository with mostly untapped history and culture. When they began, they hadn't known to ask for the archival collections of libraries, which often were in another building or in a part of the building separate from the main library itself. With this new understanding, they had greater success in discovering women of a range of ethnicities. In many archives, they followed again their strategy of sifting through categories.

At Helaine Victoria Press, there was no shortage of new projects and ideas. By now, the Press had fired up the movement for women to produce cards reflecting positive and inspiring images of women, and other presses were beginning to realize that postcards with images of women from history could be popular and could function to grow the movement. Nancy and Jocelyn knew that they didn't want to duplicate what other publishers were doing, so they started actively searching out cards by other enterprises; when they found some likely cards, they offered to distribute them through the Helaine Victoria Press catalog. It was no small matter to suddenly move from having an inventory of a hundred cards to marketing several hundred, but they saw the inclusion of more cards as an important way in which they worked toward their goal of expanding feminist memory via the accessible postcard medium. Moreover, by selling other publishers' cards, they could maintain their own presence and, at the same time, make a small profit on the other cards as well.

Despite the fact that cards of various maternal lines were commingling on the pages of Helaine Victoria Press's catalog, it was clear that Helaine Victoria Press's cards were unlike any others. Helaine Victoria's cards had detailed captions, were often produced in series or in the jumbo size, and, as a general rule, represented women who were not already familiar names. Moreover, the images on Helaine Victoria Press's cards were usually active, inviting interpretation and encouraging more action. By spending hours combing through boxes of photographs in archives, Nancy and Jocelyn were able to offer images that could be found nowhere else.

The card that they produced of Zora Neale Hurston is a case in point. They knew they wanted to offer a card of Hurston. Both Jocelyn and Nancy had read her biography written by Robert Hemenway, as well as her autobiography, *Dust Tracks on the Road*. After the Women in Print conference in Washington, DC, they visited the Folklife Center in the Library of Congress and started searching through boxes of photographs, looking for Hurston and other women, scenes, and stories. Among other photographs, they found a picture and story about Phyllis Carter that they knew they wanted to make into a card.

Then, while looking through the collection of folk music collector and researcher Allen Lomax, they found a photograph labeled "an unidentified woman." She was holding a notebook and had a huge smile on her face.

They knew almost immediately it was Hurston. Her autobiography and biography had alerted them to the fact that she was traveling in Eatonville and working with Lomax at the time the photo was taken. They couldn't believe their good fortune in finding this one beautiful, unpublished photograph in a huge mass of other unsorted photos. This was precisely what they were committed to doing: finding and publishing the subjugated histories of women.

## ZORA NEALE HURSTON
Novelist, Folklorist, Anthropologist & Adventurer

She once claimed she was arrested for crossing against a red light, but escaped punishment by exclaiming that "I had seen white folks pass on green & therefore assumed the red light was for me." In this way she personalized traditional stories.

### 52. Zora Neale Hurston postcard

Zora Neale Hurston (1901?-1960) grew up in Eatonville, Fla., where she was surrounded by Afro-American culture in this self-governing all-Black town. Hurston spent much of her life seeking a form of expression that could accommodate her experience in the rural Black South, her anthropological studies at Barnard, and the artistic revolt of the Harlem Renaissance. One of her novels, *Their Eyes Were Watching God*, brought to perfection the creative artist and the folklorist. Hurston's adventuresome spirit spurred her to Haiti to study hoodoo; to look for a lost civilization in Honduras; to take her houseboat from Florida on a 1,500-mile voyage to N.Y., and made her a central figure in the Harlem Renaissance. Zora's death was tragic, but not because Zora was a tragic woman—on the contrary—but because she suffered the effects of a white, male-dominated society that didn't support Blacks, women, or artists, she died in poverty and obscurity in a Florida State nursing home. Still writing and with her visions unfulfilled, she would have to send an unsolicited manuscript to a publisher in 1959, even though she was the most published Black woman writer in America. But, as she said, "I shall wrassle me up a future or die trying." Zora's life and career have left us with a wealth of material on the Black folk community and a recent revival of her life and work has brought many of her books and other writings back into print.

At the same time, they realized that the fact that Hurston's photograph had languished for years as "an unidentified woman" spoke volumes about the racism and gender exclusion that infested the system of archival organization.[33] This instance of subjugation was not a random event, but rather was indicative of systematic and thoroughgoing suppression.

The Zora Neale Hurston card was one of the press's most successful. That it spoke to a wide audience is illustrated by a letter the press received that year from Ms. B. Sykes, whose return address was Harvard University. Ms. Sykes wrote,

> I am a Black Australian visiting student, and I recently had opportunity to see one of your cards, that of Zora Neale Hurston. I should like to place a small order, and write to enquire your multiple order costs. As I am also buying for possible distribution in Australia, through a newspaper of which I am the editor.[34]

Likewise, the card was very popular with American customers. Author Toni Cade Bambara wrote from Atlanta:

> Dear Somebody, May I please know the price of the Zora Neale Hurston postcards. And. Do you have discount rates for bulk order. And do you give discounts for unemployed writers? How about unemployed mothers? How about unemployed writer mothers working on a 90-minute TV film script on Zora Neale Hurston? How about . . . I'll think of something.[35]

When Jocelyn and Nancy returned to Indiana, in an effort to control their ever-increasing workload, they decided to limit their production to five new cards that year. This was the best idea they could muster after attending the Women in Print workshops on how to make money while maintaining a radical critical edge. Compelled by the rest of the workshops they had experienced, they remained true to their principles and determined that the five cards per year should focus on women of color and others who traditionally had been neglected by mainstream historians. To underscore this emphasis, when they began to design and produce the Zora Neale Hurston card, they pulled from her autobiography a quotation at once humorous and biting that forced the reader to confront the very thoroughness with which racism permeates American society:

> She once claimed she was arrested for crossing
> Against a red light, but escaped punishment by
> Exclaiming that "I had seen white folks pass on
> Green & therefore assumed the red light was for me."

By this time, Jocelyn and Nancy had been researching women for almost a decade, and reintroducing them, framed in ways that startled and inspired viewers—enabling them, as Sheila de Bretteville had said of feminist design, "to listen to people who have not been heard before."[36] They had pushed the limits of letterpress printing, and more and more their combined and individual artistic sensibilities for the letterpress craft and the postcard medium solidified into their vision of a female aesthetic and a method for generating feminist memory. They drew upon the tools of their shop and used their beloved Munder Venezian type, along with an accent typeface and ornament for the quote. They had uncovered a lost photo of this brilliant novelist and folklorist, and they had combined it with a signature caption, merging image and words to create something greater than each alone. Cards like the one they made honoring Zora Neale Hurston integrated all the aspects of what they loved about what they had created, Helaine Victoria Press.

If Nancy and Jocelyn were struggling to manage all of their responsibilities, the fame of the press continued to spread nonetheless. During that year, a fellow by the name of Randy Harelson published a book called *SWAK: The Complete Book of Mail Fun for Kids*. The book not only taught children about correct letter and postal formats, but was also full of grand ideas for fun ways to use the services of the USPS. Postcards, of course, are very appealing to children, and Harelson devoted a few pages to postcard sources. On one of those pages, he featured Helaine Victoria Press: reproducing the Kimura Komako card, telling an abbreviated history of the press, and suggesting that readers write for a free card and a catalog. "Their cards are wonderful," he said.[37]

Because Harelson mentioned the possibility of a free card and catalog from Helaine Victoria, all for two first-class stamps, girls wrote to the press, often telling of their special interests. A young Elizabeth Isadora Gold wrote, saying:

> I read about your company in a book on mail called S.W.A.K. Your write-up immediately caught my eye.
>
> I am a 4th grader at Friends Select School in Philadelphia, and <u>very</u> interested in women's suffrage.
>
> I wish to get your catalog and also (in S.W.A.K. it said you gave them) a free postcard. I have enclosed two first class stamps, and I hope that you will send back what I have asked.[38]

The articulate fourth-grade writer then added a postscript saying some of the women she was interested in were Elizabeth Cady Stanton, Isadora Duncan, and the Brontë sisters. We hope that she received her catalog and free card—and that it depicted one of the above-named women of interest.

In November, Mary Ruthsdottir of the National Women's History Project (NWHP), located in Santa Rosa, California, contacted Nancy and Jocelyn with a rush request: "What do you do about the copyright permissions for the images that you use on your cards and posters?" The NWHP had just received funding from the Women's Educational Equity Act to do a media piece promoting National Women's History Week (NWHW). They had many images that they wanted to use, but every source they checked seemed to offer different advice about the legalities and actualities of seeking copyright permissions. She went on to narrate their current experiences, noting that their *Curriculum Guide* was very popular and that they continued to recommend Helaine Victoria cards. "The most curious news," she said, "concerns the articles being prepared for NWHW by (get ready) *Today's Education, Glamour,* and *Peoples World!!* What a combination! On top of that, the Congress has just passed a joint resolution for NWHW '82, carried by Rep. Mikulski in the House, and Orrin Hatch in the Senate. Will wonders never cease!"[39]

Jocelyn responded quickly, explaining how to go about gaining permission to reproduce images from copyright holders. Mary Ruthsdottir wrote back, expressing her gratitude and saying, "Of the several people I've posed the question to, your description of the process was the most complete—by far!"[40] This relationship between the NWHP and Helaine Victoria Press would continue to grow over the next few years, as first the NWHP mentioned the press's materials in their curriculum guide and then later ordered cards to sell in specialized packages in their catalog.

The USPS made the work of the press possible in its country location, as they received orders and shipped out cards in response. The land gave them space not only for the printshop, but also for a garden to grow their own food. To supplement their income from the press, Jocelyn also grew a cash crop of red raspberries—both a summer crop and a fall crop—that she was able to sell to regular restaurant customers. The woodland on their land provided fallen trees for firewood for the winters. All of these features combined to make their venture successful. But the location was isolating. Occasionally, they were harassed by local teenage boys, riding down the road on their bicycles and yelling slurs at them.[41] The word "burnout" was starting to crop up in their vocabulary, and despite the shared vision of the goals of the press and a strong friendship, the joys of intimacy began to fade. There were not many places to go where they could find a peaceful retreat from each other and from the stresses of the press and the country life. The relationship began to unravel.

To combat these several pressures, Nancy and Jocelyn decided that they would arrange their work in such a way that each of them could take an occasional brief "sabbatical." For her part, Jocelyn became involved with a project in northern Indiana to help preserve the wolf population. Asked whether this work was separate from her work at the press, Jocelyn explained, "I consider my feelings about animals and nature as part of my feminism. So, I don't consider it separate, even though it was really removed from my work here."[42] Nancy sought to study with R. Hunter Middleton, a well-known type designer who had been a friend of her parents. Although Middleton's ill health precluded the week's internship she wanted, Nancy was nonetheless able to consult with him over the telephone and discuss the various typefaces Helaine Victoria had, and hear his suggestions for others. The "sabbatical" system worked well for a while, but ultimately the time off served only to create more distance between Nancy and Jocelyn rather than drawing them closer together.

During the winter, Nancy and Jocelyn struggled to hold on to their common dreams. Living self-sufficiently in the country, one of those dreams, had created its own set of problems. In order to keep the pipes from freezing on sub-zero nights, someone had to get up every two hours to stoke the stove. Nancy and Jocelyn traded off this task, which meant neither one got more than four hours of sleep at a stretch. Sometimes the electricity went out, and, as the pump was electric-powered, this compounded the pipe problem.

These conditions might help to explain why the Winter 1982 catalog, called the "Winter 1982 Picture Postcard Supplement," was an abbreviated one, simply xeroxed, while a more formal version was in production. The front cover enjoined customers to "Stock up for Celebrating National Women's History Week, March 7-13 & International Women's Day March 8." On the back cover, Jocelyn and Nancy wrote to readers in more detail: "Dear Friends, We hope you are off to a joyful New Year. We realize this must often feel difficult to you as well as us what with the extreme right's increased activity, the growth of the KKK, military and nuclear proliferation, and the ERA betrayed by the 'Justice' Dept." The missive goes on to say that, regretfully, there would be a slight price increase. "Some wonderful women from the National Women's Mailing List in San Francisco went over our records," they said, "and donated a day consulting to help HV get more solvent and found it costs 59¢ a card to produce."[43] A side note below next to Columbia read: "Isn't that a perfect coincidence?"[44]

As they contemplated their production costs and lamented the need to increase their prices, Nancy and Jocelyn appreciated the commentary added to a reproduction of their Trackwomen on the B&O card in the *Missouri Valley Socialist*: "Full employment for women and men, all age groups, and all racial and ethnic groups, without the manpower shortage created by war, is possible when the people manage the economy for the benefit of all."[45] They were also grateful, as always, for the publicity, framed for the magazine's readers.

Selling postcards for a few cents apiece achieved their goal of creating widely accessible art aimed at engendering active, participatory feminist memory, but also created a narrow profit margin problem for themselves: they had to make and sell a lot of postcards in order to make enough to live on and keep the press running. Determined keep the press running in order to grow the movement, Nancy and Jocelyn went to work producing a new 1982–83 catalog. From the small, elegant listing and display of Helaine Victoria Press products in 1981, the catalog ballooned this year to a twenty-page newsprint tabloid offering hundreds of postcards produced by Helaine Victoria Press and many other women's presses around the world. The cards were arrayed within twenty-nine subject categories, from Artists to Women/Language/Words, complete with a table of contents including page numbers. They offered the cards for sale individually or, if a customer wished, s/he could buy all the cards in a given category as a package: "Complete Art Repro[duction] Category AR 2-94 (85 cards) $30.00 or order your favorites individually."

In this larger catalog, Nancy and Jocelyn introduced a new feature, "Viewy News," a chatty letter from Jocelyn and Nancy addressed to the catalog's readers, bringing them into the fold.[46] "It wasn't so very long ago that the images of women on postcards abounded with degrading poses, humor and stereotypes. It had always been part of our purpose at Helaine Victoria," they wrote, "to create, in the realm of popular art and culture, a view of women that reflected what we really were/are doing, what are our real roles, achievements, work, and visions."[47] From that introduction, reminding customers of the power dynamics still widely in play, they moved into a brief history of postcards in the US, then located Helaine Victoria Press within that history. "Viewy News" would continue through the 1990 catalog. Some form of a letter to customers appeared in each catalog until the very last clearance catalog in 1994. "Viewy News" not only gave an abbreviated history of Helaine Victoria Press but often centered it within the politics and historical background of the times, reminding readers of the collective power of postcards to shift feminist consciousness.

To illustrate the cover of this catalog, Nancy, with her trademark humor, took several cards and added dialogue or thought bubbles. To a card that Helaine Victoria distributed depicting astronomer Maria Mitchell, she added a thought bubble that read: "My stars! Such heavenly postcards come from Helaine Victoria!" To an image of Susan B. Anthony and Elizabeth Cady Stanton, she added two dialogue bubbles: "Oh, look, Elizabeth! Our new Helaine Victoria POSTCARD CATALOG! You really could have used something like this at Seneca Falls" to which Stanton responds, "You said it, Susan! But it's at least as useful RIGHT NOW!"[48] Who could resist a catalog with such a cover?

Despite the fact that most of the catalogs after the first two sent from Indiana were not printed on the Chandler & Price letterpress, and thus all the type for them did not have to be hand-set, hours of labor were still required to create designs and paste-ups for the offset printers. Helaine Victoria Press was now distributing over 400 cards of interest to women produced by other publishers. This meant that images of these cards, plus all that Helaine Victoria had to offer, had to be pasted in exactly the correct location onto the blue-lined grids, along with the catalog numbers and descriptions for each one. Many woman-hours were required in order to create the catalog, and everyone involved in the press at this point was pressed into service to ensure that the catalog was finished in time. A photo on page nineteen of the 1982–83 catalog shows Nancy and Jocelyn on the picnic table in their yard, snow still on the ground and trees bare of leaves, toasting the completion of the catalog.

With the influx of so many cards by other publishers, Nancy and Jocelyn began to question their ability to distribute even a portion of the cards they were receiving. But, they were devoted to the postcard concept and the activist dynamic that postcards promoted in the feminist movement. They knew that images were not benign, that they had powerful cultural effects. Thus, Helaine Victoria Press was committed to sending as many new, powerful images of women around the world as possible to supersede the decades of graphic degradation to which women had been subject. Despite these innovations, the red ink continued to flow across their account books. Perhaps, they thought, if they could offer some elegantly designed, letterpress-printed broadsides featuring the words of well-known feminist writers, they would not need to sell quite such a vast number of cards and could earn enough to keep the press going.

To make the broadsides as attractive as possible, Jocelyn wanted to print a limited edition on handmade paper. Having learned to print, she realized that the one part of the process that neither she nor Nancy had yet to master was the creation of the paper itself. She began studying at the Handmade Paper Facility, an atelier created by Joan Sterrenburg in the Fine Art Department at Indiana University in Bloomington. Her goal was to make editions of paper—multiple sheets that were as close as possible to identi-

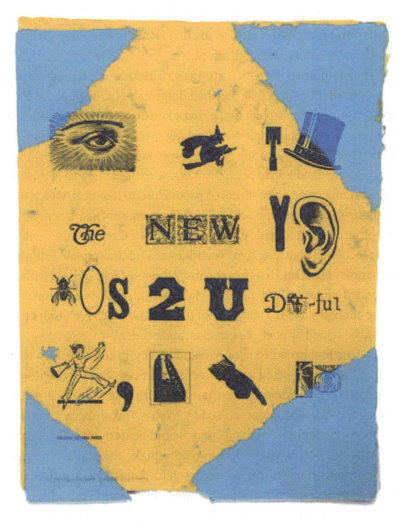

53. Holiday Rebus broadside, handmade paper
I wish that the new year brings to you delightful cheer, peace, and harmony.

cal. During the semester, she learned how to make pulp; dip and couche sheets of paper; use differing methods to apply layers of color; make both thin and thick sheets; and understand the different properties of the raw materials like cotton rag, jute, hemp and other cellulose plant materials she collected for paper on the land.

Before launching into the broadside project, and with hundreds of practice sheets in all different textures and embedded colors, Nancy and Jocelyn decided to make a rebus as a holiday greeting for friends, family, and colleagues.[49]

They composed the rebus, altering it to include words that had pictorial possibilities and that they had dingbats to fit. Inspired by *Flair*, they added a glitter droplet to the ring, like a diamond. With the rebus, they continued their tradition of making special edition printings like their Thanksgiving greeting and the Etta Macy broadside.

As Jocelyn's skills increased, she was able to meet her goal of making editions of at least sixty sheets of paper close to identical, which was necessary for a print or broadside. With the promise of a sufficient number of sheets of handmade paper, she and Nancy threw themselves into the process of producing two broadsides as a fundraiser: one featuring the words of poet and feminist theorist Adrienne Rich, and one with an extended quotation from novelist Michelle Cliff. Jocelyn determined to make enough paper to create fifty of the Adrienne Rich broadsides that would be signed by poet, papermaker, and printer.

For the first broadside, Jocelyn and Nancy, in collaboration with Adrienne Rich, selected a portion of Rich's essay "Split at the Root," a meditation on identity first published that year in *Nice Jewish Girls: A Lesbian Anthology*, edited by Evelyn Torton Beck and published by Persephone Press. Nancy would be designing and printing the broadside, while Jocelyn would make the paper. The first set of fifty Rich broadsides were to sell for $25 apiece; another 200 would be printed on commercial paper and would be sold for $10 apiece. Surely, they thought, these would serve to erase some of the press's red ink.

While they were working on the broadsides, which they hoped would fund the publication of their next postcards, Nancy and Jocelyn, inspired by local volunteer Vicki Leighty, were also planning a community gathering to celebrate the local women who had worked in the defense plants during World War II, plus women artisans in the community, specifically hand quilters and embroiderers. This program was funded by an Outreach Grant from the Indiana Committee for the Humanities (ICH), a grant they were able to apply for with their new nonprofit status. Successfully completing the requirements for a $250 grant of this kind was a prerequisite to applying for larger grants; however, the small grant did not remotely cover time, in-kind or otherwise. As Jocelyn explained in a letter to Adrienne Rich:

> One other idea (maybe crazy) we are working on is a public film showing in Martinsville of *The Life and Times of Rosie the Riveter* and a film on 4 southern women artists, [*Four Women Artists*], hopefully in time for National Women's History week[.] We have gotten a little tired of being so low profile here and just sort of at the mercy of gossip. The other day Nancy was at this VW place and the mechanic was talking about eating health foods that he'd heard it makes you feel better. A few sentences later he said, "They say you're one of those," and Nancy said, "One of what?" He said "health food nuts." Who the hell could know or bother to think about that? So we want to sponsor a really "nice evening of films" complete with free child care and refreshments (maybe sponsored by the Martinsville Homemakers Assoc.) Then if we get a cross in the yard it will be for doing something around here, not just for people <u>thinking</u> we're commies or queers or organic gardeners or Jews.[50]

They titled the event "From Handicrafts to Factory Work in Women's Lives." With her local knowledge, Vicki took on the task of finding women from the area who had worked in defense plants as well as women fabric artists in the community.

Helaine Victoria's aims for the program, apart from creating greater positive visibility for themselves, stemmed from Nancy and Jocelyn's continuing efforts to generate feminist memory by challenging cultural assumptions about women's relationships with each other, upending conventional notions of art, and rewriting women back into the historical record. On their funding application, they said that they wanted to "provide an affirmative view

54. Rosies with cakes celebrating their defense work during WWII, 1982
"From Handicrafts to Factory Work in Women's Lives," a community gathering sponsored by Helaine Victoria Press to celebrate the local women who had worked in the defense plants during World War II, plus women artisans in the community, specifically hand quilters and embroiderers. The event included screenings of *The Life and Times of Rosie the Riveter* and *Four Women Artists*, as well as an exhibit of the works of local quilters and an appearance of local Rosies. The women of the bakery at Kroger made and decorated two cakes for the occasion with frosting-crafted airplane parts on one and quilts and stitchery on the other.

of women's work, whether it be as a quilter or factory worker." Beyond that, they pointed out that "the two films also integrate Black and white women, showing a positive view of both, which may help to dispel some of the Black stereotypes which some of the Martinsville community may hold," a generous way of pointing to the history and covert presence of the Klan in the area.[51]

Eighty people came to the event, a very respectable number, although they had hoped for closer to 200. Vicki's door-to-door recruiting efforts had produced seven "Rosies," one of whom even brought assorted memorabilia from her factory work to display at the event. Fifteen quilts were on display, the work of ten quilters. Prof. Ellen Dwyer, one of their most faithful supporters, agreed to come from Bloomington to host the program, held in Martinsville's First Presbyterian Church.

She asked several of the Rosies in attendance to come forward to talk about their experiences; as they did, each was given a rose to honor her achievements. To top it off, Vicki had convinced the local Kroger grocery store to donate two large cakes for the event. When Vicki and Jocelyn explained the event to the cake decorators, they were delighted to be part of the project. Drawing upon their skills and imaginations, they decorated one cake with frosting-sculpted images of aircraft machinery parts, and the other with multicolored quilts—yet another example of women's artistry, produced daily by the unnamed women at Kroger.

By all accounts, the event was a great success. The women who were honored had returned home after the war, just as the men, but no one had given thought to their work and sacrifices. Most, now given the opportunity, were glad to tell their stories. Jean Jenson, reporter from the *Indianapolis News*, wrote a long, illustrated article, detailing the stories told by the women.[52] Writing later, Ellen Dwyer said, "I think you did an incredible job, putting together 'From Handicrafts to Factory Work;' it was by far the best ICH event I have ever attended." With that, she donated her honorarium to the press, saying that she felt that the press had done more to make the event successful than she had.[53] Prof. Susan Gubar also came down for the event, later writing to Nancy and Jocelyn: "The films, the Rosies, the amazing quilts, the cakes—it was really fine. I hope you are both feeling good about what you managed to do."[54]

Although they were pleased with the program, despite certain technical difficulties with the film projector, they were also aware that they had spent an inordinate amount of time organizing and pulling off the event—over 100 woman-hours. Aware that their primary task was the production and sale of postcards to promote national and international feminist action, they vowed not to repeat their error of underestimating the requirements of a given project, no matter how much local goodwill it might generate.

The production of postcards continued apace, after the required break for the ICH event and time spent working on the fundraising broadsides. As Jocelyn and Nancy had promised themselves, this year's cards were devoted to articulating the importance of otherwise unrecognized achievements of women across varying populations. Helaine Victoria Press continued its commitment to emphasize the lives of women of color and of other marginalized groups who were rarely considered as subjects for artistic consideration—and, if considered, usually restricted to an objectifying gaze rather than a celebration of their agency. The achievements of women the press commemorated ranged from the literary celebration of Lesbianism (Elsa Gidlow) to education and preservation of indigenous culture (Agnes Vanderburg). Other cards featured antislavery strategist, scout, spy, and nurse Harriet Tubman; anarchist organizer, writer, publisher, and free speech advocate Emma Goldman; and midwife, storyteller, quilter, oral historian, and sage, Phyllis Carter.

Of the five women, only the name of Harriet Tubman might have been somewhat recognizable. Although there had been a few small-press accounts of Emma Goldman, she was not well known until after her autobiography, *Living My Life,* was republished in 1981 (and, even then, mostly among feminists). Elsa Gidlow was an icon of strength whom they had been wanting to celebrate for years, her card serving to underscore the significance of relationships between women. Nancy had first known of Elsa through her poetry, and then, in 1975, Nancy and Jocelyn had been instrumental in bringing Elsa to the Los Angeles area as the guest of honor at the Lesbian History Exploration. One of the first women to chronicle Lesbian passion in poetry, her work was rooted in Sapphic poetry and was explicitly erotic. With her appearance at the Lesbian History Exploration, she came to represent a way of being in the world that directly contradicted the abject Lesbian identity that served to subjugate many women during much of the twentieth century.

Nancy and Jocelyn had located images of both Agnes Vanderburg and Phyllis Carter at the American Folklife Center at the Library of Congress, a result of their system of sorting through as many boxes of photos as possible. They found that folklore was a

# PHYLLIS CARTER

Midwife, Storyteller, Quilter, Historian & Sage
"There will never be enough money
when you follow what is right."

### 55. Phyllis Carter postcard

Phyllis Carter (1880–1980), midwife, storyteller, sage, quilter, and oral historian from Tift County, Georgia, was known as "a woman who never forgot." Aunt Phyllis had clear recollection of the post-reconstruction period of her childhood when fear of lynch-mobs and desperate poverty drove her family to flee their home late one night. One favorite tale concerns how a small poisonous snake was left inside the leaves of a large cabbage. Because Black cooks working for oppressive white families were not allowed to taste from the pots or cut up vegetables, the snake was undetected. "I remember once the colored woman cooked the cabbage whole, kilt the whole family out. I been here a long time, Sister." Carter bore 10 children and outlived four husbands, "two good ones and two devils." Deeply religious and unembittered, she grew up to a wide friendship with and encyclopedic knowledge of her community, both Blacks and whites. They said of her: "She was one of the very best midwives," and "She can tell you anything you want to know and never forgets a name or face." She went to school three days and acquired her vast lifetime knowledge without literacy. She charged very little for her midwifery and quilting, believing that all her skills were divine gifts, not meant for personal gain.

rich source for narrative and heroines who may have been known within their communities but who were otherwise unsung. The notes and manuscripts of the folklorists who had collected the stories provided more personal depth. In the case of Phyllis Carter, folklorist Beverly Robinson held the rights to the photo and interviews, so Nancy and Jocelyn sought her permission through the American Folklife Center to use the material on a card.[55]

Women such as Agnes Vanderburg and Phyllis Carter epitomized, for Jocelyn and Nancy, the strength and critical role that women play in our histories, politics, and community. It was just such stories that they wanted to retrieve from archives and send out into the world. A letter from Colleen Whalen in San Francisco later reaffirmed their commitment. She wrote, saying she had seen a friend's copy of the Phyllis Carter postcard: "I don't know how much this postcard sells for," she said, "and I can't find it anywhere in San Francisco. I have enclosed a check for $1.00 in the hopes that you can send me a copy of this postcard to have for my own. I don't know where else to purchase a copy [ . . . ] and I simply must have one because the look in Phyllis Carter's face just <u>bored a hole right through my soul</u>!!!"[56] In a more subdued missive, Maureen Goggin, administrative assistant to the Congresswomen's Caucus of the Congress of the United States, wrote seeking "a copy of your catalogue of postcards and posters celebrating women's history and culture."[57]

We wish we knew how many Helaine Victoria cards were sent by such feminist luminaries as Patricia Schroeder, Shirley Chisholm, Geraldine Ferraro, and Barbara Mikulski, all members of the caucus, or how many Helaine Victoria posters graced congressional office walls. The cards, all hand-printed on the Chandler & Price letterpress, were available by June of that year, 1982. By June, however, more significant changes were taking place at Helaine Victoria Press.

## CHAPTER FOUR

## CHANGE AND GROWTH

> *Some of my most erotic moments have been over the mimeograph machine.*
> —Adrienne Rich, panelist, Contemporary Female Self-Definition in Literature and Life, Modern Language Association meetings, New York, December 28, 1976

Despite the success of "From Handicrafts to Factory Work," which had created a positive impression of Helaine Victoria Press in the community, the isolation plus the stress of too much work with too little compensation had damaged Nancy and Jocelyn's partnership beyond repair. It had been a grand experiment. The ideas and models they drew from—Sarah Scott's *Millenium Hall*, Mary Astell's *A Serious Proposal*, the Nearings' *Living the Good Life,* framed in Lesbian feminist principles—had given them many of the philosophical tools for shaping their plans and aspirations. They had followed their dreams, and they had built themselves a perfect letterpress shop. With that letterpress shop, they had helped to nurture and grow the feminist movement. They had watched the seedlings they had planted grow into trees. They had grown their own organic food in a beautiful country setting with their own pond. The collaborative relationship had been new, powerful, and emotionally liberating. Exploring women's history and generating feminist memory together at the height of the second wave of feminism had created a matchless ecstasy.

At the same time, they were young and unskilled in the kinds of communication their extraordinary situation demanded. Feminist discussions were only just beginning to take place about how to create healthy relationships, especially between women—and in Martinsville they were a long way from those discussions. In May of 1982, Nancy moved back to her hometown of Chicago.

Nonetheless, both Jocelyn and Nancy were committed to maintaining the vision and work of Helaine Victoria Press. If part of their dream had dissolved, what mattered was that the press continue publishing the multimodal postcards that were fueling the movement. With Helaine Victoria Press's nonprofit status and the spread of feminist action, more women were now contributing to the work of the press as volunteers, work-study students, and interns. In time, several faculty volunteers would take on more responsibilities with the press, becoming partners in the research and writing of individual cards and the shaping of series. At this point, however, Nancy served as president of the board of directors, returning often to work at the press and continuing her involvement in the production of planned cards and sets—notably, the Haymarket Riot Centennial Commemorative set, and the special sets that had been ordered by the National Women's History Project (NWHP).

These latter sets, women from the nineteenth century in one and from the twentieth in the other, were marketed by the NWHP largely to teachers. Each set, packaged with a special header designed and printed by the press, sold for $5.95. All the cards offered ideal launching points for the study of the history of women in the US and worldwide, developing awareness in classrooms across the country.[1] The NWHP became an important customer; bulk sales meant the press could anticipate a guaranteed number of cards for each packet, and, most importantly, the outreach of the NWHP meant more exposure of the cards in the classroom and to teachers. With every set sold, Jocelyn and Nancy knew that the young students would feel encouraged to learn more and to expand their lives' possibilities.

Likewise, before leaving Indiana, Nancy worked with Claire Moses, editor of the academic journal *Feminist Studies,* to create a folio in celebration of the journal's tenth anniversary. Having been attracted to the promotional folios Helaine Victoria Press made in 1980, Claire Moses had asked whether the press could produce a similar one for *Feminist Studies.* Nancy designed and wrote the copy for the folio, telling Claire she "tried to tailor it for the various uses and audiences which you had mentioned." By April, she and Jocelyn had completed the design and had printed the folios, shipping out 300 copies in one batch and then another 1,100 in a second. The inside text was jobbed out to an offset printer, and Nancy printed the cover in the Helaine Victoria printshop. They were pleased to be asked and only wished "that there were world enough and time to do many more such creative projects."[2]

The previous year, on February 14, 1981, Jocelyn and Nancy had driven to Chicago for a Valentine's Day event for printers, publishers, and writers at Jane Addams Bookstore. They hoped to meet in person some of the customers they had known only through mail order, and to generate interest in Helaine Victoria's products among others in attendance. As they entered the store, Nancy saw Chris Johnson, cofounder and partner in Metis Press, setting up a table displaying Metis Press's publications; they talked over the display and found that they shared common passions for printing and publishing feminist materials. This connection would deepen over time, and when Nancy moved back to Chicago, she joined Chris in running Metis Press as well as in a romantic partnership lasting until Chris's death in 2015.

Was it the liberating power of the press? The deeply passionate commitments to generating feminist memory and creating political change? Or a combination of the two? Adrienne Rich was not the only one to feel that some of her "most erotic moments [had] been over the mimeograph machine." In this case, it was the possibilities of the Chandler & Price letterpress that drew together Jocelyn and Vicki Leighty, Helaine Victoria volunteer, kindling a romantic partnership, while Nancy and Chris connected over Metis Press.

Nancy, Chris, and Jocelyn were all founding members of the US Alliance of Lesbian and Feminist Printers which shared with Chicago Women's Graphic Collective the responsibility for hosting the Midwest Women-in-Print Gathering in Chicago on September 10-12, 1982. An outgrowth of the Women in Print Conference in Washington, DC, the previous October, the Gathering revisited many of the same topics but placed added emphasis on the importance of supporting women printers as well as women publishers, writers, designers, and booksellers. Participants struggled with issues around undercapitalization and invisibility, but shared a commitment to the print medium as a vehicle for fueling the movement. According to a report published in *Feminist Collections*,

> [i]f one were to try to pinpoint the central theme of the conference, it would probably be <u>education</u>. There was much discussion of how conglomerate publishing in the 1980s is socializing the book-buying public into "judging books by their covers" (and, unconsciously, by their ad campaigns), leading bookstores to expect slick, ready-made displays and standard-size books, and threatening the continued survival of small press publishers and independent booksellers.[3]

These problems would not go away, but, arguably, the Women in Print conferences, both national and regional, helped to extend the reach of feminist literacy efforts and prolong the lives of printshops, publishing houses, and booksellers for several years, thus creating a larger archive of feminist material.

As Helaine Victoria Press continued to grapple with the realities of undercapitalization, Nancy returned to Martinsville to work on the press fundraising broadside of a selection from Adrienne Rich's work, "Split at the Root." Writing to Rich just before she and Jocelyn drove up to Chicago for the Midwest Women in Print Gathering, Nancy had described the design:

> The decorative initial, from an old French alphabet, is being engraved. I [ . . . ] plan to print it in a medium-dark red. The rest of the type will of course be black, finished at the bottom with a soft gray piece border adapted from the same alphabet as the initial. The colophon will be added at the bottom in smaller italics. Besides the standard information, it will give the Persephone credit line, acknowledging them according to their specifications [ . . . ]. Happily, your first sentence justifies flush beside the initial perfectly: an especially nice effect, I think. I then broke out of justification and justified flush left, in order to avoid looking stilted with that large block of body copy.
>
> I also plan to open up the vertical space under the title and again under the opening sentence which a taller sheet will allow.[4]

To create the paper for the broadside, Jocelyn spent that summer and fall collecting rags to turn into pulp. When the next papermaking course began that fall semester at Indiana University, Jocelyn spoke with Joan Sterrenburg about her project idea: two editions of paper for a pair of broadsides as a fundraiser for the press. The paper for the Adrienne Rich broadside would be relatively simple, a single 10.5" x 16" sheet with a hint of blush and always a deckle edge. Jocelyn's main challenge was to gain the skill to make an edition of approximately sixty consistent sheets. It was one thing to make individual artistic sheets, but quite another to make sixty sheets of identical thickness. Thus, she began with a single couched sheet. Another key part of the process was learning how much pulp would be needed for an edition that size, especially

| from | Split at the Root |

KNOW that in the rest of my life, the next half-century or so, every aspect of my identity will have to be engaged. The middle-class white girl taught to trade obedience for privilege. The Jewish lesbian raised to be a heterosexual gentile. The woman who first heard oppression named and analyzed in the Black civil rights struggle. The woman with three sons, the feminist who hates male violence. The woman limping with a cane, the woman who has stopped bleeding, are also accountable. The poet who knows that beautiful language can lie, that the oppressor's language sometimes sounds beautiful. The woman trying, as part of her resistance, to clean up her act.

~ Adrienne Rich

56. Adrienne Rich, "Split at the Root," broadside
Excerpt from the essay "Split at the Root," by Adrienne Rich, printed on handmade paper.

when using rags instead of commercially prepared pulp. Just how many rags in a particular color does one require for an edition of paper? If she came up short, it would be almost impossible to replicate the pulp color and texture.

Jocelyn experienced the papermaking class with Joan Sterrenburg quite differently from the way she felt in the trade class in printing she and Nancy had taken in Los Angeles. Although Robert Wilkinson had welcomed Jocelyn and Nancy into his class, they were the only women students, and their specific interest in letterpress, a hand-fed platen press in particular, set them apart from their classmates. Still, hand papermaking, too, had once been a male domain, women only being allowed to sort rags and do finishing work. So Jocelyn was pleased to be able to take a course that covered the entire process. However, again, Jocelyn had different interests in papermaking than did her classmates, who were making one-of-a-kind pieces of art, while she wanted to make editions of paper for printing. Jocelyn always felt included and part of the studio community, never feeling that her interest in editions was any less impactful than those of the other artists' one of a kind. Joan Sterrenburg not only welcomed Jocelyn into her class, she also later said,

> I was thrilled to have Jocelyn working in the handmade paper studio, for she brought a singular knowledge, sensibility and expertise, all of which made a distinct contribution to the other students, and to me as well. I particularly appreciated Jocelyn's knowledge of Women's History, and her research in that area. It was an excellent benchmark to have someone who was creating art that evolved from historical study and a deep personal commitment. Her skill as a traditional printer, "Still printing today the historical way," was also a valuable asset to our handmade paper community.[5]

When Jocelyn had finished making the sixty sheets of paper, Nancy returned from Chicago to print the copies. In addition to the copies on handmade paper, she printed 200 on commercial paper so they could offer a less expensive edition. The colophon detailed who performed which tasks as they related to the production of the broadside: "This edition of fifty broadsides was printed on a platen press on paper handmade by Jocelyn H. Cohen. Design, hand-composition, and presswork are by Nancy Poore, using Munder Venezian foundry types and sixteenth century French ornaments." After the broadsides were printed, Jocelyn and Nancy each signed the edition.

In early December, Jocelyn sent fifty copies of the broadside on handmade paper to Adrienne Rich for her signature. When she received the copies, Rich wrote back, exclaiming:

> [t]he broadsides are spectacularly beautiful. I said to Michelle, "But how <u>does</u> anyone make paper like this?" The design, with the "split" title and the decorative initial and figures is splendid. It's an extremely strong presentation, and that, I think, will help with the up-frontness of the text [ . . . ]. I have had many (well, a few) broadsides hand-printed and never had one that so boldly and beautifully came to terms with the words. Thank you.

"I hope women will buy it," she added, "because it is such a wonderful creation of women's skill and imagination."[6]

After signing the broadsides, she returned them to the press where they would be featured in the upcoming catalog, and everyone hoped they would draw viewers' attention to the significance of Rich's words as well as bring a needed infusion of cash to the press.

Although Nancy returned to print the broadsides, the fact that she was no longer involved in the day-to-day operations of the press meant that their collaborative method of sharing labor of necessity had to change. Jocelyn and Nancy's vision had been built on the imperative that there be no specialization—that both Nancy and Jocelyn would be able to do every task associated with the press. Now, that part of the vision had to be discarded. With Nancy's departure, Jocelyn was the only skilled letterpress printer working full-time at the press. Nancy returned occasionally to print and also did specialized work from Chicago, shipping it back to Martinsville. As the press grew, and more volunteers, part time work-study students, and interns joined in the process of postcard production, job responsibilities had to be divided up, both to ensure that all necessary tasks were accomplished and also to match the skills, interests, and time availability of those working at the press.

Nancy's absence also changed the dynamic and scope of work caring for the land. Primary responsibility now fell to Jocelyn alone, although over time, Vicki shared more and more, working in the garden and helping with wood for the stove. In good weather, she arranged work parties with volunteers who would spend a day helping with outdoor chores or working on outdoor projects in exchange for a dip in the pond and a nice meal. Likewise, Toba and Herschel Cohen continued to come out on weekends to help with all kinds of chores, and the workday was always followed with dinner at the picnic table or in the little kitchen during inclement weather.

Beginning in 1980 as a full-time volunteer at the press, Vicki had become a part-time work-study student after enrolling as a freshman at Indiana University in fall 1981. Despite her part-time status, she had gradually been taking on more responsibilities at the press. Although she had learned the fundamentals of operating the Chandler & Price press, and she also would research and write captions for several cards, her gregarious nature and organizational skills led her to take on jobs that perhaps had not been attended to in the past with the rigor they deserved—managing the mailing list and setting up a current filing system as well as a system for sorting and organizing the past ten years of Helaine Victoria Press history. In a stroke of good fortune, Merry Bateman and Camille Saad's coworker, Bernice Schipp, arrived in late 1982

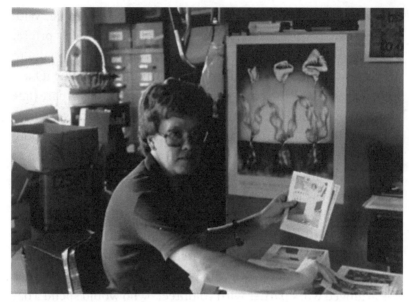

57. Bernice Schipp, ca. 1980s
Bernice Schipp traveled two hours on her weekends to volunteer her expertise in marketing advice and inventory analysis to Helaine Victoria Press. With her experience as merchandise manager for Abbey Press, the largest Catholic mail order company in the country, she created a system of logging sales and tracking inventory. She also was an expert at assembling postcard sets and was always available to discuss important business decisions.

to help the press manage their inventory, analyze their marketing strategies, and streamline their mail order procedures.

Bernice Schipp was merchandise manager for Abbey Press, the largest Catholic mail order company in the country, headquartered in St. Meinrad, Indiana. She joined other volunteers, working from home and then coming faithfully (a two-hour drive) for years to help with whatever needed to be done. Her most significant contribution, which only she could do, was logging all the orders, noting which and how many cards or other items sold. In this way, with a system she constructed for the press, she kept track of how well any given card performed.[7] The less-than-exact system of inventory control Jocelyn and Nancy had used before Bernice arrived was simply to look to see how many stacks of a given card they still had on hand and then decide whether to reprint. Often to the surprise of everyone, Bernice's numbers demonstrated that certain cards were languishing on the shelf while still taking up valuable catalog space. Such cards, she would suggest, might be moved to a less prominent location in the next catalog. Bernice's gift of her time and expertise enabled the press to sell more cards and other products and, ultimately, to distribute cards produced by other presses.

After always having collaborated with Nancy, Jocelyn suddenly had to make many daily decisions by herself. The press's nonprofit status was still relatively new, and although there was a board of directors in place, the exact responsibilities of all concerned were still somewhat unclear. Nonetheless, Jocelyn realized that the press needed a bookkeeper.[8] Soon, Lawrie Hamilton appeared. Lawrie farmed on fifteen acres of land near Salem, Indiana, about an hour-and-a-half south of Martinsville; she also did taxes for a large company and studied accounting in her spare time. As she told it,

> I had been seven years here in rural Southern Indiana, happily, when a Helaine Victoria Press bookmark appeared on my desk, accidentally left by a friend. "Women's history? A feminist press? Here in Indiana?" I'd never heard of them before, but I wrote a letter anyway, offering my professional editorial skills. Jocelyn replied. I drove up to Martinsville a year ago this Fall.

Jocelyn wrote to Lawrie in September, before heading to Chicago for the Midwest Women in Print conference, asking whether she would be willing to talk about the possibility of doing the books for the press on an hourly basis. "What the Press needed was a bookkeeper," Lawrie said, "so, I am the bookkeeper."[9]

Despite the changes in the organization, an article in the January 9, 1983 Bloomington *Sunday Herald-Times* cheered the Helaine Victoria Press team and prompted an enthusiastic return to production, marketing, and publicity work after the holidays. "Postcards tell history of women" by Cheryl Scutt offered readers a detailed

58. Lawrie Hamilton.
Lawrie Hamilton brought her bookkeeping and editorial skills to the press.

history of the press, illustrated with photos of Jocelyn and Nancy in the printshop plus three Helaine Victoria postcards: Break-Time at the Defense Plant, Mother Jones, and Trackwomen on the B & O, along with information taken from the cards' captions.[10] Having read the article about the press in the *Sunday Herald-Times*, Paula Worley, a Bloomington photographer, joined Helaine Victoria as a volunteer with the idea that she could contribute photography. What the press really needed, though, was someone to manage the Helaine Victoria Press Postcard Archive Project, so Paula became the archive manager.

Because they had been collecting cards from as many sources as they could locate for possible resale, as well as keeping an eye on the breadth of what other publishers were beginning to produce, Jocelyn and Nancy had established what they called the "Postcard Archive." Vicki had begun the process of organizing the cards, sitting at a card table and creating a file using 3" x 5" index cards, giving each a unique numerical identifier and indicating the year of publication, publisher name and contact, printing method and colors, and the subject of the card. International in scope, the cards in the archive not only documented and chronicled historical achievements as did Helaine Victoria's cards, but also offered commentary, such as inspirational quotations by women or images of sexist billboards overlaid with feminist graffiti photographed by Jill Posener, some published by The Women's Press and others under the Deviant Productions imprint. One popular card showed a billboard with a photo of a Fiat car and big letters: "If it were a lady, it would get its bottom pinched." Large handwritten graffiti on the billboard countered: "If this lady was a car, she'd run you down." Types of cards ranged from hand-colored, photocopy-produced small runs to large, slick commercial cards such as Fotofolio's reproductions of Berenice Abbott's photographs of New York City and Ylla's animal photography. The selection of art cards in full color grew, with well-known artists such as Georgia O'Keeffe, Emily Carr, and Betye Saar represented, as well as lesser-known artists whose quilts and folk art were being reproduced here and there around the country.

Realizing the importance of recognizing women who were still living, as Nancy and Jocelyn began producing cards honoring contemporary women, they made a practice of sending those honored ten copies of the card on which they were featured, asking them to sign the cards and return them in an addressed, stamped envelope supplied by the press. The press offered some of these cards to collectors at a higher price. About a dozen such autographed postcards by activists such as Sonia Johnson and Emma Tenayuca are included in the Postcard Archive.

Paula described her involvement in maintaining the Postcard Archive, another of the press's efforts to generate feminist memory:

> I was offered the opportunity to coordinate the postcard archives project of contemporary cards on women's history and culture.

**59. Paula Worley, 1983.**
Paula Worley came from Bloomington to the printshop and office in Martinsville at least twice a month. She would set up a card table and take out the piles of postcards to catalog, send thank you certificates, and solicit new cards to add to the growing collection. After the office moved to Bloomington, her hometown, she came in every week to help build the Postcard Archive, a collection of 5,000 or so postcards.

The project had been started by Jocelyn and Vicki, but needed the attention of someone on a regular basis. Every Friday I came to HV to catalog the cards (now over 1,200), seek out new ones, track down duplicates, and issue the contributors an elegant certificate which I designed and printed here [with some help from Jocelyn]. Working for HV I get information and ideas I can't get anywhere else, and it's a place where what you do as work and what is important to you are not separate. The Press tells a part of history that has largely been ignored, but which is now being told.[11]

Although at that time, the Postcard Archive had 1,200 cards, eventually Paula would catalog over 4,000 more contemporary cards by and about women, offering a "wealth of social commentary on the current attitudes towards women."[12]

The cataloging process was both detailed and thorough. Every postcard received was issued an identifying number. Paula added the card(s) to the growing sheets of 8.5" x 11" hand-typed logs with a descriptive card title, publication date, publisher, printing process and colors, and an entry in a column noting whether a certificate of acknowledgment had been mailed. She also created an index card with all this data plus contact information for the publisher, the same practice as when the cataloging began back at the card table. Every card sent to the press, whether from the publisher or a donor, was carefully archived. The sender received a personal thank-you as well as a postcard archive certificate.

In addition to the certificates, Helaine Victoria Press produced a one-page brochure explaining the purpose of the archive. Titled "The Helaine Victoria Press Postcard Archive: the only existing repository of postcards on women's history and culture," the brochure announced the press's goal: "to preserve the story of postcard publishing's vital role in popular culture and social history. Further, the Archives help ensure that the postcards will be studied and appreciated for their artistic, educational, and political significance." To accomplish these goals, the press would continue to collect, catalog, and cross-index the cards (this was done in the days before computers became widely available); make the archive available for public use; and organize a file on index cards with postcard biographical data, plus vertical files with supplemental information on each card artist and publisher.[13]

In time, the project grew so large that Paula Worley committed an entire day every week to the work. The Postcard Archive, now housed at The Arthur and Elizabeth Schlesinger Library on the History of Women at Harvard University, is the only collection of its kind, with close to 5,000 postcards produced by and/or about women between approximately 1970 and 1990, documenting the impact of women producing their own postcards, the changing times, and the kinds of cards even mainstream postcard makers designed and printed.

Even though Helaine Victoria Press no longer operated as a two-person collaboration, everyone involved made an effort to maintain the feminist culture of shared responsibility that Jocelyn and Nancy had built. Like Paula Worley, Helaine Victoria Press workers and volunteers often mentioned that the culture of the press differed from what they had experienced in other workplaces. Karen Schollenberger began working at the press in September of 1983 on the work-study program through Indiana University. She commented that she'd

> [...] always wanted to participate in a feminist organization—to be in on the inside workings. The atmosphere is different here than other jobs and more democratic. It's also different from going to feminist functions, which I've always done. I get to see how it all works, and I really enjoy it.[14]

Likewise, Kirsten Johnson, an MFA student specializing in graphics who Jocelyn had met in the papermaking classes, shared her impressions of the press:

> It was during this period that I became aware of HV's inner core: the women who make it work, the organization, the spirit behind the effort. It was a totally different business aspect than I have seen before—workers who were friends, an entire support system, a sincere interest in what each woman was attempting to add to the Press.[15]

As the press matured, women who volunteered or interned there found opportunities to challenge themselves and develop new skills, later taking these skills with them into the world. Kirsten Johnson, for instance, went on to teach letterpress and design at the University of Kansas.

Not all volunteers were local residents. Because by now Helaine Victoria Press's horizontal, rhizomatic method of developing feminist awareness had reached women across the country, women began offering their help from a distance, as well. Mary Mallory, government documents librarian at University of Illinois Urbana-Champaign, came over from time to time to help with research and correspondence. Anne Wilson, who lived in Cambridge, Massachusetts at the time, also helped by doing research in the many libraries near her and by representing the press at events too far afield for press workers to attend. Although the burgeoning cadres helped to lift some of the burdens, managing the comings and goings of volunteers and part-time workers was Jocelyn's responsibility—and maintaining her own space became more difficult, as the press's operations were spilling over into her living quarters.

Leaving aside space problems for the time being, Vicki and Jocelyn worked to build on the success of their grant-funded event, "From Handicrafts to Factory Work." They submitted another application to the Indiana Endowment for the Humanities Outreach Grant program, this time combining the press's need for publicity with newspapers' needs for copy for Women's History Week in March. Congress had designated the second week of March as "Women's History Week" the year before. Jocelyn and Vicki argued for their vision of feminist awareness, saying they sought the grant "in order that our materials might educate a wider audience and generate more participation [in Women's History Week] next year." The grant was awarded, giving the press another $250, this time to send out pictorial and informational packets to as many Indiana newspapers as possible.

In the cover letter addressed to the feature editors of the newspapers to which they sent the packets, they explained that "[a] packet is enclosed (free of charge) that will provide you with the materials to run a picture and biography of a different woman from history each day of 'Women's History Week.'" They offered a brief description of the six cards, telling the editors they were "suitable for reproduction," and alerting them to the fact that "[o]n the back are biographies which should accompany the pictures." They even offered an "optional introductory article on the importance of women's history which you could run the first day." And they suggested a courtesy line to include with each card, indicating that Helaine Victoria Press was the source of the photo-postcard and biography.[16]

To Jocelyn and Vicki's delight, newspapers in small towns across the state published articles about Women's History Week using Helaine Victoria postcards ranging from Sojourner Truth to Amelia Earhart in flight with Eleanor Roosevelt as illustrations. The cards, in this manner, traveled across the state of Indiana without benefit of the USPS, entering homes in small towns and helping to build feminist memory. The funding, however, had barely covered the cost of postage, providing no support for the press itself. Although one of the 501(c)3 goals was indeed educational outreach via programs, publishing the cards was the press's main objective. That said, they were pleased that they had fulfilled a primary Indiana Committee for the Humanities requirement to be considered for a larger grant, which was what they really needed.

In another effort to fulfill the responsibilities they had taken on as a nonprofit organization, and to encourage participation in a new audience of young women, Nancy and Jocelyn went to the College of Wooster in Ohio for Women's Week. The college invited them to present the slideshow Nancy had developed featuring images of women on postcards from the 1890s to the 1940s and, in contrast, to display Helaine Victoria cards and posters. They were the main attraction, offering, in addition to the slideshow and the display of cards and posters, a presentation on the pleasures and perils of breaking into the male-dominated field of printing.

While Nancy, Jocelyn, and Vicki were all pleased by the successes of their Women's History Week promotional projects, they continued to be grateful for the feminist publishers who often printed notices unprompted, drawing from the catalogs the press mailed out twice a year. *Equal Times* copied the first lines of "Viewy News" into a mention of Helaine Victoria Press and reproduced pictures of several postcards; *Women and Language News* listed Helaine Victoria Press under "Ideas for the Holidays," saying that the "free catalogue is a delight."[17] Spurred by this appreciation, the Helaine Victoria Press team of Jocelyn, volunteers Bernice Schipp and Toba Cohen, and work-study students Vicki Leighty and Beth Robinson worked to fill orders coming in from individuals and stores as well as to figure out who would attend the various conferences and festivals that were so critical for introducing their method of raising feminist consciousness and, not incidentally, continuing to encourage sales and an increased customer base.

One of Helaine Victoria's most important conferences each year was the National Women's Studies Association (NWSA) meetings. The field had grown exponentially, as students, community members, and faculty had applied pressure in their schools to expand the curriculum to include women and to explore the social construction of gender. This year's conference, held in Columbus, Ohio, was the site for another of Helaine Victoria's innovations: a call for postcard manuscripts. With the growth of the press and changes to the organization, Jocelyn sought more ways to spread the workload as well as to open collaboration opportunities for herself. Rather than attempting to research and write all captions in-house, as she and Nancy had done for the past ten years, Helaine Victoria opened the process to scholars and others who were now doing primary research in the newly expanded fields.

The "Call for Research," first announced at the NWSA conference in June, invited scholars and other writers to "contribute to upcoming series of cards on the following themes:"

1. Latin American and US Latinas in politics, culture, and changes which can include revolutionary activity, music and literature, folk and other art. Captions to be in Spanish and English.
2. Haymarket Riot Centennial Commemorative set, focusing

on the contributions of women to the struggle of organized labor in the US from 1886 to 1986; emphasis on immigrants, women of color, and rural working women.
3. Women's Brigades and Auxiliaries: a worldwide history of women organizing their own special groups within larger movements—for example, the Russian Women's Brigade of Death, the Pullman Porters Ladies' Auxiliary.
4. Political Action (not specified as a subsidiary or affiliate as in item #3) by women of color, poor and working class, Jewish, differently-abled, immigrants, and Lesbians, involved in such concerns as civil rights, women's liberation, environmental issues, and pacifism.
5. Additional areas evolving from work done on items #1-4, or from other suggestions by the researchers.[18]

The "Call for Research" served to extend the reach of Helaine Victoria Press, reminding all who saw it—it was reprinted in a variety of publications—that generating feminist memory must be a collaborative effort. Unlike most institutions (including those in which many women worked), Helaine Victoria understood the dangers hierarchies presented to women, at best promoting one woman as a token while erasing the rest.

In addition to running grant-funded programs, responding to mail order requests, reaching out to potential contributors, and managing volunteers and work-study students, Jocelyn continued to work on making paper, most immediately for the second in the pair of fundraiser broadsides, this one featuring a selection from Michelle Cliff's *Abeng*. Although the broadsides were undertaken to raise funds for the press, they expressed the quintessence of Jocelyn and Nancy's art, fusing feminist ideas in multiple forms and making them as widely available as possible. The fundraiser broadsides were always conceived as a pair although sold individually. They were first marketed in the catalog together and produced within months of each other. There were differences in the designs, of course, and, while Nancy had designed and printed the Rich broadside, Jocelyn was both the papermaker and designer/printer for Michelle Cliff's broadside.

Cliff had been struggling with publishing difficulties. The manuscript for *Abeng* was still not published, but, as she had retained the copyright, she was free to offer a selection to Helaine Victoria for the broadside.[19] She chose, in consultation with Jocelyn, a mytho-historical narrative of Nanny, leader of the Jamaican Windward Maroons, a band of fighters who led successful slave rebellions during the eighteenth century and freed at least 1,000 people. Nanny is a national hero in Jamaica, Cliff's homeland. With this selection, Michelle Cliff and Helaine Victoria Press could offer a mid-action glimpse of a powerful response to colonial occupation and enslavement.

To create the paper for this broadside, Jocelyn began experimenting with more elaborate techniques than those used for the Adrienne Rich broadside. With textual differences in mind, she began exploring multiple couches, creating sheets in more than one color and designs couched within the paper, enhancing the quote. Initially she played with vats of pulp leftover from other students—laying colors on color, squeezing thin pulp from squeegee bottles, playing with texture generated from different pulps, making sheets like a quilt sampler.

After some experimentation, she came up with the paper design. The Cliff sheet was three colors, meaning each sheet involved three vats of pulp, the parent sheet, and then the extra layers. This edition was signed by the author and the papermaker and printer—in this case, both Jocelyn—after the colophon. The paper was a combination of cotton rag, burlap, and manila hemp. A wide ribbon of deep blue ran across the top of the off-white paper, and another ribbon of the manila hemp ran at an angle on the upper right with the title crossing into it. It was printed in Munder Venezian foundry type with sixteenth-century initial caps. In addition to the fifty copies on handmade paper, Jocelyn printed an edition

> **FROM ABENG**
> A DESCRIPTION OF NANNY THE LEADER OF THE WINDWARD MAROONS
>
> **NOW HER HEAD IS** tied. Now braided. Strung with beads and cowrie shells. Now she is disguised as a chasseur. Now wrapped in a cloth shot through with gold. Now she stalks the Red Coats as they march toward her cave, where she spins her Akan chants into spells which stun her enemies. Calls on the goddesses of the Ashanti forests. Remembers the battle formations of the Dahomey Amazons. She turns her attention to the hunt. To the cultivation of cassava and yam and plantain — hiding the places for use in case of flight.
>
> **THE FORESTS OF THE IS-**land are wild and remind her of Africa. In places the mountains are no more than cliff-faces. The precipices of these mountains often hold caves she can use for headquarters or to conceal the weapons of her army. She mixes dyes from roots and teaches others to cast images on the walls. She collects bark from the trunk and limbs of the birch gum to touch to the skin of her enemies while they sweat — and instructs her followers in the natural ways of death. She moves on her elbows and knees across narrow rock ledges. Through corridors created by stone.
>
> **THE ENTRYWAYS ARE COVERED** in some places with vines — in others with cascades of water. She teaches her troops to be surefooted and to guard the points of access. They hunt with bow and arrow. Spears. Warclubs. They fill the muskets stolen from plantations with pebbles, buttons, coins. She teaches them to become bulletproof. To catch a bullet in their left hand and fire it back at their attackers. Only she can catch a bullet between her buttocks — that is a secret she keeps for herself.
>
> — Michelle Cliff

60. Michelle Cliff, from *Abeng*, broadside
Excerpt from *Abeng*, a description of Nanny, the leader of the Windward Maroons by Michelle Cliff, printed on handmade paper.

of 200 on machine-made paper. After printing these editions, the type was distributed.

When she received a proof of the broadside, Cliff responded, pointing to the meaning-making possibilities inherent in the very paper itself on which words were printed: "I love what you've done with the paper—it's truly magnificent [ . . . ]. This really understands my work."[20] Writing later to Vicki about the possibility of reproducing the broadside in *Woman of Power*, a magazine of feminism, spirituality, and politics, Cliff said, "It's such a beautiful piece of work. Please tell Jocey it's hanging over our dining table in our new home."[21]

While she was corresponding with Michelle Cliff and working out the details for the broadside, Jocelyn was also developing a special postcard set demonstrating the long history of women's involvement in the production of paper. In the process, she endeavored to incorporate the way the paper looked as both design and texture to complement and enhance the subject of the card, yet another of Helaine Victoria's feminist challenges to the art world's assumptions.

Titled "Women and Papermaking," the set continued Helaine Victoria's effort to locate, recognize, and publicize the accomplishments of women across time and cultures. The folio contained four 4.25" x 6" postcards:

*Otomi Woman:* A line art image of an Otomi woman in Mexico pounding bark until the cellulose became pulp-like for paper. This image was printed in sepia on paper made from burlap feed bags with some cotton rag for strength, and the border was made from cattails that grew around the pond on the land Helaine Victoria Press occupied.

*Women Sorting Rags:* A photographic image of women sorting rags ca. 1900 in the United States. This paper was particularly tricky, as the image was a halftone that required a smooth surface to hold the dot pattern. After Jocelyn couched each bright white cotton rag sheet from one vat of pulp, she dipped strips of purple paper and couched these onto separate felts. While the papers were

61. Otomi Woman postcard on handmade paper.
This Otomi woman from San Pablito Pueblo is beating the bark of trees into sheets of paper for munecos (paper dolls) which are used for witchcraft. In Mexico, before the Spanish conquest, bark paper held an important cultural role for religious ceremonies and books. Although methods vary slightly, bark paper is also found in Africa, Celebes and the Pacific Islands, at one time including Tahiti and Hawaii where the craft has now completely disappeared. The rhythmic tapping is heard as one approaches the remote villages where papermaking is predominantly performed by women.

wet, she cut the strips into triangles to become little corner pieces, placing them, by hand, onto the white sheets, then lightly pressed the two together into one on the hydraulic press. For the final step in the papermaking, Jocelyn did a second pressing using books for weight atop the wet sheets, which she laid out on the old smooth linoleum floor in the Indiana University papermaking studio. She had tested this technique and found it worked to make the paper surface smooth like a coated sheet.

*French Women in Finishing Work:* An engraved image of women in eighteenth-century France engaged in finishing work, the only other work open to Western women in the paper mills besides rag picking. The paper for this image, made from white cotton rags, had a gray, squeegeed border on two sides.

62. Women and Papermaking folio, front cover
Cover for Women & Paper: A Postcard Collection Recounting Women's Involvement in a Variety of Trades & Crafts in the Fabrication of Paper. The cover for the set of four postcards, printed letterpress on handmade paper, was made from a large, gray sheet with four flaps in a cross shape. To make this sheet in a cross shape, Jocelyn Cohen taped off the mould so pulp would not stick to those areas. She dipped the 14" x 18" mould into a vat of gray cotton rag pulp made from an easy-to-find mix of colored cotton clothing. When dry, the cover folded to 5" x 6.5" in an edition of fifty copies.

*Washi Papermaker:* An image of a Washi papermaker. Washi was the one kind of paper Japanese women were allowed to make. The Japanese method of making paper is very different from Western methods; however, this paper, although made in the Western style, was soft from the addition of burlap. Jocelyn added glitter to simulate a Japanese sensibility in the coloring.

The cover for "Women & Papermaking" was made from a large, gray sheet with four flaps in a cross shape. To make this sheet in a T shape, Jocelyn taped off the mould so pulp would not stick to those areas. She dipped the 14" x 18" mould into a vat of gray cotton rag pulp made from an easy-to-find mix of colored cotton clothing. After the sheets dried, the cards were placed in the middle and the flaps folded over to enclose them. The top flap served as a title page, on which she printed "Women & Paper" in red ink, using the antique, ornate type Grimaldi; for the subtitle, "A Postcard Collection Recounting Women's Involvement in a Variety of Trades & Crafts in the Fabrication of Paper," she used Munder Venezian. The back featured an engraving of images of papermaking tools with the headline "Some Implements for Making Paper" also in Grimaldi. The inside flap provided the colophon information, including: "Special thanks to Joan Sterrenburg from Indiana University for opening up the world of papermaking to me." The cover had deckle edges on all sides, as the shape was masked-off in the form rather than being cut after drying. Jocelyn first made an edition of fifty of each postcard on handmade paper, then another edition of 500 on machine-made paper; these were sold as a set in a plastic bag with a header.

Impressed with Jocelyn's creative reconceptualization of handmade paper as well as Nancy and Jocelyn's artful and unique conveyance of women's achievements on Helaine Victoria postcards, Joan Sterrenburg, responding to a request for exhibition suggestions from Betsy Stirrat, director of the School of Fine Arts Gallery, recommended Helaine Victoria Press.[22] With an MFA in Graphic Design, Stirrat appreciated good design; she also was a strong supporter of women's art and thus was most enthusiastic about the Helaine Victoria exhibition. This was the first time the Indiana University School of Fine Arts Gallery had held an exhibition of work by anyone other than graduate students or faculty. The Helaine Victoria Press 10-Year Retrospective was also one of the largest shows to date mounted in the gallery by a single entity, evidence that active feminist memory was continuing to develop and expand.

As luck (and feminist movement history) would have it, both Helaine Victoria Press and the Indiana University Women's Studies Program were celebrating their ten-year anniversaries in 1983. The Women's Studies Program included Helaine Victoria Press's exhibition in the publicity materials announcing their own events, and scheduled a celebratory show by feminist comedian Kate Clinton to follow the gallery opening.

In preparation for the occasion, Nancy and Jocelyn decided to repurpose the folio that they had produced in 1980 to create a Tenth-Anniversary Collection Folio. They offered the "Ten-Year Folio," which included a card from every year along with bookmarks and other memorabilia, for $10. The folio was featured on the back cover of the 1983 catalog:

> Our splendid 9" tall, letterpress cover Folio, lined with Helaine Victoria's herstory in words and pictures, is stuffed full of postcards and other memorabilia spanning the first ten years of the Press and its output.
>
> SOME FEATURES OF VERY SPECIAL INTEREST: One postcard for every year, many of them out-of-print and otherwise not available, including a rare 1973 "kitchen table" series card and other examples from our early days as offset printers; PLUS AN EXTRA-SPECIAL EXCLUSIVE: An Anniversary postcard on Jocelyn's handmade paper, created just for this collection.[23]

In addition to the Ten-Year Folio, Helaine Victoria Press produced several other printed pieces for the retrospective and celebration. Nancy came down from Chicago to design and print the invitations, using the press's ornaments and special type to illustrate Helaine Victoria's printing skills, design acumen, and quirky charm. She printed hundreds of the invitation postcards, using their stash of reclaimed paper.

They mailed the invitations to customers in Indiana and friends and colleagues all over the country. Nancy and Jocelyn also printed thousands of Ten-Year bookmarks, using up a lot of their colorful smaller scrap.

Volunteer and staff time at Helaine Victoria Press was consumed for months preparing for the exhibit, mounting examples

63. Displays at the Ten-Year Retrospective show
Ten-Year Retrospective Exhibit at the Fine Arts Gallery, Indiana University at Bloomington, September 30 through October 21, 1983. The exhibit filled the entire gallery, both on the walls and in the showcases.

of all of the cards plus their captions on fifty-five large matboards. Kirsten Johnson printed the publicity poster for the show. Nancy and Jocelyn wrote a brief overview of the press's activities during each of the ten years from 1973 to 1983.[24] All the panels were annotated, many written as joint efforts as the show evolved conceptually. Summaries of the events of each year, including photographs, were posted with each panel and, of course, included the cards, prints, bookmarks, and other ephemera produced that year. It took several days and a host of volunteers to hang the show. Arranging the panels and the settings in their glass cases was a major undertaking, and the gallery was filled with an excited buzz as the show was crafted into an impressive exhibit.

Feeling that an event of this magnitude should have more than local publicity, Lawrie Hamilton, drawing on her background in writing and publicity, wrote a charming letter addressed to Susan Stamberg, host of "All Things Considered" on National Public Radio (NPR):

64. Ten Year Retrospective Exhibit Opening Invitation postcard
On Top of the First Decade. The Ten-year Retrospective Exhibit. Opening September 30, 1983 through October 21. Fine printing, postcards, papermaking. Feminist theatrics by Nancy Brooks of Womanshine. Refreshments.

65. Nancy Poore and Jocelyn Cohen before the Ten-Year Retrospective Opening, 1983.

66. Nan Brooks performing at the 10-Year Retrospective opening, September 30, 1983.
Nan Brooks from Womanshine presented a moving one-woman performance piece during the gala opening at the Fine Arts Gallery, Indiana University at Bloomington. Almost everyone stopped looking at the exhibit and stood or sat around the perimeter of the gallery for the performance. The exhibit filled the entire gallery, both on the walls and in the showcases.

Dear Susan Stamberg:

JOCELYN: "I've been waiting for Susan Stamberg to call me, but she hasn't."
LAWRIE: "Does she have your number?"
JOCELYN: "... No...."
So here it is: (317) 537-2868.

The letter went on to describe the location and work of the press and, most critically, the fact that the press was about to celebrate its tenth anniversary.[25] Lawrie then convinced Jocelyn to create an eye-catching, hand-printed envelope for the letter and package it up with a good selection of postcards. Helaine Victoria Press had long made a practice of using stamps that honored women on all correspondence and orders, even if it meant special ordering these stamps from the Philatelic Department of the USPS and/or

230  WOMEN MAKING HISTORY

combining stamps of multiple denominations. So, this envelope included two rows of women on stamps, using a combination of values from 1¢ through letter rate, making a colorful collage of famous women.

And the scheme worked! Jocelyn received a call from NPR the day before the exhibit opening, requesting an interview. Then the call was passed on to Susan Stamberg—live. Their brief conversation about Helaine Victoria Press went across the country through the airwaves, generating not a few letters to the press, seeking information. Among others, a member of the planning committee for Women's History Week in Greenville, SC, wrote for a catalog to share with other committee members. Helaine Victoria Press's dedicated method of building feminist memory, while still grounded in accessible, modifiable postcards, had now grown to include newspapers and radio.

Opening night was the event of the season, surpassing everyone's expectations, as more than 500 people poured through the doors to view the exhibit. Mid-evening, when the room was full, Nan Brooks of Womanshine Theater captured everyone's attention as she entered, shaking a tambourine and reciting poetry.

When not so entranced, people swarmed through the exhibit, reading the panels documenting the history of the press, viewing the cards and the captions posted alongside them, and admiring the broadsides. The panels in the show, and special cases of material objects and scenes, chronicled the history of the press from 1973 to 1983. One case highlighted the accordion postcard album, illustrating and describing the various steps of production along with hand-printed promo bags. Another replicated a woman's desk, complete with a selection of beautiful, older books by and about women; a copy of the second Helaine Victoria booklist; a kerosene lantern; and an old postcard album showing examples of the not-so-funny, derogatory postcards of women printed from the turn of the century into the early 1930s. Another large case displayed tools of the printing trade, including wooden and foundry type,

67. Paula Worley, Bernice Schipp, Toba Cohen, Vicki Leighty, Beth Robinson, and Jocelyn Cohen

Photo of Helaine Victoria Press workers taken at the Indiana University Women's Center, ca. 1986. Paula Worley, a photographer, was the Postcard Archive volunteer; Bernice Schipp created a system of logging sales and tracking inventory and advised and worked on the catalogs; Toba Cohen, Jocelyn's mom, began as the bookkeeper and later assisted with order-filling and correspondence, serving as a Jill of all trades; Vicki Leighty began as a volunteer, later becoming assistant director of the press and managing the Helaine Victoria Press Women's History Shop; Beth Robinson came to the press as a work study student; she assisted with orders and other daily tasks; Jocelyn Cohen was cofounder and director.

composing stick and galleys, ink, engravings, and a pica ruler. And in case any viewer wondered whether Helaine Victoria was ever in the news, an entire case was filled with journal and news articles about the press, including a large panel all about the outreach program, Handicrafts to Factory Work in Women's Lives. Among the fifty-five panels was a series of still lifes Jocelyn had made using pulp in her papermaking classes, and another featuring one-of-a-kind sheets of handmade paper art. Countless people came up to Jocelyn and Nancy saying variations of an awed sentiment: "I had no idea you had created so much."

The Ten-Year Retrospective show honored and gave credence to the excellence of Helaine Victoria Press's research; the multimodal, participatory postcard medium they had chosen to deliver their message; and the art of the letterpress work they were producing, all from a tiny fixed-up garage in the Indiana heartland. The event showcased the press's continuing influence on a wide range of communities, as well as on multiple levels and disciplines within liberal arts educational systems.

The show lasted from September 30 through October 21, 1983. Letters of congratulations arrived from fans of the press and from friends, family, and mentors. Arlene Raven made a special postcard with a picture of Jocelyn, taken by photographer Susan Rennie, to applaud both Jocelyn and Nancy on their achievements. Longtime Helaine Victoria Press supporter Anne Wilson cabled from her home in Cambridge, Massachusetts, saying, "Thinking of HV and both of you with love and wistfulness. Have a terrific second decade."[26]

Spirits were high as work resumed. The 1983 holiday catalog had gone out, introducing "Gift Boxes." These wonderful gems not only made a nice sale, but also could be pre-assembled, ensuring the selection was already in a box and ready to go. Assembling the gift boxes was a fun task, as well, as each box might vary in selection, and, if a customer expressed interest in a particular subject, the Helaine Victoria folks would tailor the items. Initially, two boxes were offered: The Bountiful Basic for $8.95 (a $10.95 value) included a "Holiday Postcard, 5 Herstorical Notecards, 1 packet Bookplates, 15 Assorted Postcards in standard, continental & jumbo sizes." The other, larger Postcard Fans Box for $15 (a $19 value) contained a "Winter Greeting Card, Bread & Roses set, Continental size Set, Giants, both sets Plus 4 New HV Cards!"[27] These boxes were not meant to be static gifts, but to rather invite participation in the feminist multilogue.

Beth Robinson, a BFA student at Indiana University, had come to the press as the second work-study student after Vicki. Driving out to the country one day a week, she filled orders, helped package cards, and did other miscellaneous jobs necessary to the smooth running of the press. Often, Jocelyn, Toba, Beth, and sometimes Donna Fay, as well, would be working together. One day in the late fall of 1983, Beth, Toba, and Jocelyn were busy filling orders and having fun putting together the new gift boxes when Jocelyn heard what was undeniably *MOOING* nearby. Peering outside, she was horrified to see a small herd of cows trampling her beautiful French Intensive, double-dug garden beds (beds which had never had a person walk on them, let alone a 1,200-pound cow). All three women dashed outside to persuade the cows to leave. The cows, however, were impervious to persuasion.

Jocelyn knew immediately where the herd had come from. Bessie, a neighbor who lived about a mile away by road but whose property, as the crow flies, was nearby, owned the cows. They had gotten through Bessie's dilapidated fence, had crossed another neighbor's property, had traversed the dam for the pond, and had ambled up to the garden, munching their way through the greens, the tomatoes, and other late-harvest crops. She grabbed the keys to her VW and told Beth and Toba where she was going: "If I don't return, you should call the police." Then she drove around the bend to Bessie's.

When Jocelyn went up to the home's front door and knocked, Bessie greeted her with a shotgun pointed at her head and said, in her strong Indiana twang, "You goddamn lezzie queer, get out of here!" Jocelyn grabbed the barrel of the shotgun and pushed it to one side, telling Bessie that the cows were destroying her garden. She then asked her what Bessie had meant by what she had just said. It turned out that Bessie did not have the slightest idea. She had heard the kids on the bus say it, she said. Furthermore, she didn't understand why it mattered if the cows walked in Jocelyn's garden. Nor did she understand about the sensitivity of the soil. When Jocelyn explained that the garden was still producing crops, Bessie was astonished. However, with that beginning, the two gradually began to have an amicable conversation, Jocelyn nonetheless maintaining her grip on the shotgun barrel. Bessie asked why Jocelyn was not married and then confessed that her own husband had mistreated her and that it had been so hard to make dinner and do the laundry on top of all the farm work. Suddenly, Jocelyn's independence was beginning to make a lot of sense to Bessie. Finally, she agreed to get a neighbor to help her round up the cows. Jocelyn drove home to tell Toba and Beth another story of Helaine Victoria's efforts to challenge the social roles that circumscribed women's lives. It was time for a "Printer's Devil."[28]

A short while later, the cows were lured home, the fence was repaired, and the damage to the garden, they hoped, would work itself out in time. Events such as this were not in Beth's work-study job description. To her credit, however, she was unfazed, and she continued working at the press for several more years.

When writing an end-of-the-year report to Nancy on the status and condition of the press, Jocelyn did not mention the cows, but did announce that, to no one's great surprise, the press was broke. She was hoping, she said, that holiday orders would enable her to pay the outstanding bills. The season was approaching, and many workers privately cherished fond hopes that, given the publicity from NPR with Susan Stamberg and a locally prestigious Ten-Year Retrospective, the press would reap some economic benefits.

Although sales were increasing, thanks in part to Bernice Schipp's suggestions, an updated mailing list, and the growing number of festivals and conferences at which Helaine Victoria Press could set up a table or booth, so were expenses. Inflation had caused prices to rise by 110%. Knowing that their customers' incomes had not increased 110%—and that, in fact, many women had lost their jobs during the recession that peaked in late 1982—the press determined to continue their mandate to make accessible art, and thus had not increased prices accordingly. A set of six jumbo cards cost $2.00 in 1974. In 1984, a set of twelve jumbo cards would set a customer back $5.00, an increase of only 25% per card.

Despite the press's precarious financial condition, Jocelyn, Nancy, and all the other Helaine Victoria participants were deter-

### 68. Jane Addams & Mary McDowell postcard

Jane Addams (1860–1935), social reformer and pacifist. Traveling in 1888, she discovered Toynbee Hall in London, known as the prototype of the settlement house. Her belief that the settlement offered the opportunity for a mutually enriching life for herself, and others led her to found Hull House, with Ellen Gates Starr, in Chicago in 1889. The working-class, ethnic neighbors flocked to the classes, clubs, day nursery, gymnasium, dispensary, concerts, plays, exhibits, and other functions of the settlement. Hull House was a headquarters of education and labor reform, and a major political influence. An era of voluntarism began among women, and thousands of centers modeled on Hull House sprang up over the next 30 years, including the University of Chicago Settlement, headed by Mary McDowell (1854–1936). McDowell was an early resident of Hull House, and she and Addams were devoted friends. Untiring in their pursuits, they aroused public attention to improve industrial districts. Called "Mary the Magnificent," McDowell was a trade union organizer who chaired the committee advocating what became the 19-volume national investigation on women workers. Addams was a lifelong feminist and founder of the Women's International League for Peace and Freedom and McDowell worked for peace through the League of Nations. Addams believed that the passionate desire for good will and human understanding among nations would sweep away the impulses for war, and that peace education could be as infectious as war propaganda.

## 69. Mary McLeod Bethune postcard

Mary McLeod Bethune (1875-1955) was one of seventeen children of Samuel and Patsy McLeod, slaves on the McLeod plantation in Maysville, South Carolina. Born after the Emancipation, Mary McLeod was a free woman. Seeing the overriding importance of real freedom and equality, she became a powerful force in the emerging struggle for civil rights. As an educator, she established a school for Black girls in 1904, and within 20 years she transformed it into a college. She was a valued counselor to four presidents, director of a major government agency, founder of the National Council of Negro Women, and a consultant to world figures seeking to build universal peace through the United Nations. As president of NCNW, Bethune implemented programs addressing the problems of Black women, the Black community, and the world community. Her deepest interest was in the education of women, and she led a voter registration drive in 1920 for Black women. She expanded the NCNW and launched the *Aframerican Woman's Journal*. Her philosophy for the NCNW was to "visualize a growing oneness in purpose; a growing release from selfishness; . . . a growing consciousness in our own souls that we work and serve NOT FOR OURSELVES, BUT FOR OTHERS!" Bethune was a powerful speaker; she marched for civil rights and picketed businesses which discriminated against Blacks. Through her words and actions, she was one of the most influential and inspiring Black leaders in the country.

CHANGE AND GROWTH

*"I am a woman who came from the cotton fields of the South. I was promoted from there to the washtub. Then I was promoted to the cook kitchen, and from there I PROMOTED MYSELF into the business of manufacturing hair goods and preparations.... I have built my own factory on my own ground."*  — Madam C. J. Walker

### 70. Madam C. J. Walker postcard

Madam C. J. Walker (1867–1919). Businesswoman. Philanthropist. Inventor. Confidence Builder. Born Sarah Breedlove in Delta, LA, she was a laundress until 1905 when she formulated hair and scalp preparations especially for Black women. When she died at 51, she had become the first self-made American woman millionaire. She traveled extensively promoting her products and speaking out on issues affecting women and Blacks. Thousands of Walker agents, nearly all women, sold her *"Wonderful Hair Grower"* in the U.S., Central America and the Caribbean. More than 200 agents met in Philadelphia in 1917 to hear Madam speak about *"Women's Duty to Women"* at the first convention of the Mme. C. J. Walker Hair Culturists' Union of America. That same summer Mme. Walker was the only woman in a group of Black men who visited the White House to petition President Woodrow Wilson to make lynching a federal crime. Mme. Walker contributed generously to educational and other causes in which she believed, including Mary McLeod Bethune's Bethune-Cookman College. Madam's Irvington-on-Hudson, N.Y. mansion, 'Villa Lewaro', was the site for important meetings of Black leaders. The Walker Co. still is in Indianapolis, manufacturing Madam Walker's original formulas. As was her wish, the company president has always been a woman.

mined to continue their work. Certainly, the images produced by the press were upending conventional notions of art, falling well outside anything considered even remotely acceptable to the art establishment. Those same images, however, had enthusiastic audiences across the country and even beyond US borders, as the mailing list grew and orders came in.

Another grant from the Indiana Committee for the Humanities enabled the press to send out even more cards to newspapers nationwide for Women's History Week in 1984. Helaine Victoria Press sent out over 200 packets, offering a card to publish each day of the week, March 4–10, and a message about why women's history is important. Some newspapers followed their advice and published one each day, while others printed only one story with all cards together. In any case, the result was that Helaine Victoria Press cards, already multimodal, again traveled via another medium—newspapers—potentially reaching a vastly greater audience than before.

This year, Helaine Victoria Press's new cards offered yet more radical political messages, a response, perhaps, to the shrinking of possibilities for women and working people during the Reagan presidency. A new card for Jane Addams showed her in her later years with her friend Mary McDowell, both holding peace signs. Although Addams was rather well-known for her work establishing Hull House, the card demonstrated how her activism had extended well beyond the settlement house movement and into efforts to create global change, a fact often downplayed in popular accounts of her life. Another new card that year offered a fresh look at a woman previously celebrated on a Helaine Victoria card. This time, educator Mary McLeod Bethune was given her own card, and a caption that focused on Bethune's political work not only in education, but also in civil rights struggles. The caption documented her influence in the Black community and especially her work with Black women.

Helaine Victoria Press's call for postcard manuscripts—an innovation designed to draw on the growing feminist consciousness and desire to participate in generating feminist historical awareness—was beginning to produce results. Elaine Leeder, then on the faculty of Ithaca College, was one of the first to respond to the invitation, sending a photo and caption for her dissertation subject: Rose Pesotta, a Jewish immigrant, anarchist, and labor organizer with the International Ladies Garment Workers Union during the first half of the twentieth century. Norma Alarcón of Purdue University offered her dissertation research on Rosario Castellanos, Mexican journalist and feminist. Paul Avrich of Queens College submitted information on Voltairine de Cleyre, an American anarchist active during the late nineteenth and early twentieth centuries who had challenged both capitalism and the institution of heterosexual marriage, among other things.

Jocelyn, for her part, suggested a card featuring Madam C. J. Walker, who developed a line of hair products for Black women. With these products, Madam Walker then provided training and employment for other Black women as salespeople and as beauticians. Her lecture-demonstrations and savvy business model led her to become the first self-made American woman millionaire. The business, Mme. C. J. Walker Manufacturing Co., was located in Indianapolis, and Madam Walker's daughter and grandchildren, residents of Indianapolis, had shopped for years at Herschel's Shoes, Jocelyn's parents' store. So it was not hard for Jocelyn to contact one of Madam's great-great-granddaughters, asking if she would write a caption and provide a photograph for a card honoring Madam Walker. A'Lelia P. Bundles, then a field producer for NBC News and a researcher for Alex Haley's book on Madam Walker, responded with enthusiasm, even offering the possibility of another card in the future on A'Lelia Walker, daughter of Madam Walker and prominent patron of the arts during the Harlem Renaissance.

The photo that A'Lelia Bundles supplied could not have been more perfect. It showed Madam in the driver's seat of an elegant, open automobile, surrounded by three other women who were officers of her company. All four were wearing elaborate hats of the period. In designing the card, Jocelyn drew upon early advertising materials used by the Madam C. J. Walker Company to create the border. To match and emphasize the elegance of Madam Walker and her entourage, she designed the card with a handsome border using two different piece borders, alternating one in silver with another in metallic lavender. Under the black-and-white photograph, she added a quotation from Madam Walker hand-set in Munder Italic with decorative initial caps for the "M," "C," "J," and "W" in her name. The quotation, taken from a speech Madam had given at the National Negro Business League Convention in 1912, read: "I am a woman who came from the cotton fields of the South. I was promoted from there to the washtub. Then I was promoted to the cook kitchen, and from there I PROMOTED MYSELF into the business of manufacturing hair goods and preparations [ . . . ]. I have built my own factory on my own ground."[29]

With a shop full of beautiful, handsome, and frolicsome fonts, Jocelyn, in consultation with Nancy, utilized the power of typography to integrate the words with the photos, the design motifs, and the captions on the cards. Using these carefully designed typographical elements, she was able to bring the heroines to life, presenting them as if they were speaking directly to the viewers. Thus, the multimodal cards not only traveled through the mail, presenting visual elements enhanced by descriptive text on the reverse, they also created an intimate link between the viewer and the subject of the card, erasing the decades that otherwise intervened. The addition of quotations on the fronts of the jumbo postcards not only brought the images alive, but the words also gave Helaine Victoria cards a particular distinction, as if the jumbo-size format with a detailed caption and, on letterpress-printed cards, the trademark postcard logo "Still printing today the historic way" was not enough to announce to all who viewed the cards: these are Helaine Victoria Press cards.

In the press release for the Madam C. J. Walker card, Helaine Victoria Press linked two disparate, but very accomplished, Black women in feminist memory, noting that

> Ida B. Wells-Barnett, the militant Black and women's rights leader, was a guest of Madam Walker while a delegate to the National Equal Rights League in New York City in 1917. She wrote of Madam, "I was very proud of her success [ . . . ]. She had little or no education, and was never ashamed of having been a washerwoman earning a dollar and a half a day. To see her phenomenal rise made me take pride anew in Negro womanhood."[30]

When Jocelyn sent a package of cards to A'Lelia Bundles to thank her for all she had done to help make the card, Bundles wrote back on one of the cards:

I love the card!
You have given me a wonderful idea by sending the 100 cards.[31] I'm going to use them for promotion of the project, book, etc. So, I will be ordering more.
Been traveling around the country covering the Jesse Jackson campaign, so am just getting home to find your package. A nice welcome home last night. Also in my [mail] box was a note from Toni Cade Bambara on the Walker card. They're already circulating![32]

Indeed, the growing number of Helaine Victoria Press postcards featuring African American women was not going unnoticed. In the September 1983 issue of *Essence* magazine, the "Where to Find" column announced that Helaine Victoria Press was the place to find Black women's postcards: "The Helaine Victoria Press offers a large collection of postcards illustrating women's history, including cards that depict Afro-American women. The subjects range from the notably famous, such as Sojourner Truth and Mary McLeod Bethune, to women who are less known, such as the female freedom fighters of South Africa."[33] This welcome bit of publicity generated letters from women seeking more information, such as Mrs. A. Gaskins of Pittsburgh, who wrote to "Dear Wonderful People," saying, "I'm so elated to know that someone has created a Black postcard. I'm so tired of going into the card store to see nothing but cards for Caucasians." Then she added generously, "But then, I guess other ethnic groups must feel the same way."[34] Likewise, Donna B. Powe wrote from Baltimore, asking for a catalog because she collected "postcards as well as anything having to do with Black Americans." It was her intention, she said, to "have a history book to pass on to [her] daughter."[35]

In the spring of 1984, Darlene Clark Hine, then-associate professor of history and vice provost at Purdue University, contacted Helaine Victoria Press, asking whether the press would be willing to display and sell cards at the first conference/workshop of the Black Women in the Middle West Project at Purdue. Jocelyn and Vicki were thrilled. They gathered their supplies for a nice display and packed up all the available cards on African American women. Not only were they the only exhibitors invited to display their wares, but they were the only white women present. Although Jocelyn and Vicki couldn't help feeling a little self-conscious, the conference participants were delighted with the range of cards they offered. It had to have been the most enthusiastic audience for Helaine Victoria cards, Jocelyn thought, since the first Berkshire Conference on the History of Women in 1978. She and Vicki were indeed pleased, witnessing more cards, with more messages, leaving their care and going to traverse the country, expanding feminist memory.

Nancy was now working full-time in Chicago, having taken a position as a design and production supervisor at a publishing operation at Northwestern University. She was planning to coordinate what was then being called the Haymarket Riot Centennial Commemorative set, which later became the Women in the American Labor Movement series, and she was looking forward to having her own letterpress on which to work in Chicago. "As a student of letterpress printing for twenty years," she said, "I envision being able to do some projects in Chicago on equipment we hope will be donated SOON. This would not duplicate the equipment at HV/HQ, but rather supplement it so as to add to the Press's capacity for variety, giving the Indiana staff a somewhat different printing experience and practice when in town."[36]

It was a generous offer, and although Nancy did acquire a Pearl letterpress, there is no evidence that any Helaine Victoria staff or volunteers went up to Chicago to use it. Instead, Jocelyn and the cadre of volunteers and work-study students were trying to figure out a reasonable organizational structure that would serve to manage the workload, as it was taking such a different form than it had before. In a bid to revisit the critically important issue of challenging the cultural limits on women's relationships with each other and maintaining an equitable, non-hierarchical work environment, they came up with the idea of a "Working Committee," in addition to the board of directors. During the summer of 1984, after Nancy began her full-time job in Chicago, Vicki was appointed part-time Assistant Director of the press; she, Jocelyn, and Lawrie were the only (minimally) paid workers, apart from the work-study students.

Writing at the time, Vicki articulated the concept of the Working Committee succinctly:

> The belief that "knowledge is power" holds true at HV. Those who know the most information about HV influence more of the decisions. By making information available to <u>everyone</u> involved at every level of HV, more equal input is afforded to <u>everyone</u>. The [W]working [C]committee is comprised of informed women who have a clear understanding of how the press operates and how decisions must be made.[37]

The Working Committee members were all staff plus the most consistent volunteers and work-study students. At the time, this meant Beth Robinson, Vicki Leighty, Toba Cohen, Paula Worley, Lawrie Hamilton, Bernice Schipp, Mary Mallory, and Anne Wilson. The skills of the various volunteers and staff members were indeed disparate. Bernice Schipp, for instance, in addition to doing sales analyses for each catalog, was working on a scheme to add source codes to the address labels in order to track the best conferences and other sources of potential customers. "As you can see by the summary," she said, "the Michigan Music Festival seems to be the best in acquiring names. But do those customers respond to the mailings best?"[38] No one could do the catalog analyses like Bernice, but it was important for others to understand what she did. The establishment of the Working Committee provided a framework within which workers and volunteers could share information and locate themselves in relation to each other. They even instigated an internal newsletter called "Newsy Views: The Official Unauthorized Newsletter for Staff and Board of HV Inc." which became their communication medium so that even those who were not present at meetings could be kept informed.

Awareness of Helaine Victoria Press's postcards was spreading, and more publications, especially feminist magazines and journals, were taking notice and publicizing the press. Dave Long, writing in *The Postcard Collector*, stated unequivocally, "I feel the most important American publisher of women on postcards is Helaine Victoria Press from Indiana. This small company has produced over 100 different postcards of women—the most prominent in our history."[39] A new publication out of the Indiana University English Department, *Feminist Teacher*, featured the press in its inaugural issue, including an interview with Jocelyn. The first question asked by the interviewers referenced the call for postcard manuscripts, wondering whether the press had gotten much response. Despite having received manuscripts for Rose Pesotta, Rosario Castellanos, and Voltairine de Cleyre, Jocelyn said, the press's staff was discouraged by the fact that people were still sending in mostly suggestions of white suffragists.

Nonetheless, they were determined to keep unearthing evidence of movements and activists whose work had scarcely been acknowledged at the time, much less remembered later. Their dedication to this principle often required considerable searching and sifting through rumor and myth to find factual evidence. A case in point was that of Emma Tenayuca, a union organizer and strike leader of pecan shellers during the 1930s, who they also later included in a new series on Latina women. As Jocelyn said at the time,

Everybody says, "Oh, yeah. Emma Tenayuca. I heard she was important." But no one seems to know anything about her. This one source we were reading said that she was real active, and then there was this meeting, and it was invaded by right-wingers and she disappeared after that and was never heard of again [ . . . ]. We called the library historian at [one library] and she said that her brother is living in the area, so Vicki called her brother and talked to the brother's wife who said [where she is living]. She's a retired schoolteacher.[40]

Vicki Leighty was studying folklore at Indiana University, so she took on the task of contacting and interviewing Emma Tenayuca, then living in San Antonio, Texas. Using a 99-cent device from Radio Shack that plugged into her cassette recorder and attached to the phone handset with a small suction cup, Vicki called Emma Tenayuca from the press's landline, recording the interview over several calls.[41] In addition to the information she collected during the interviews, Vicki found information on Tenayuca's organizing work in two publications, one specifically documenting the lives of notable Texas women.[42] With the help of archivists, she then located photos in the *San Antonio Light* archives at the Institute of Texan Cultures at University of Texas at San Antonio.

Because they wanted to release this card along with an upcoming Jewish series as soon as possible, all five cards were sent out to an offset printer. When Jocelyn designed this particular card, she used a tint screen, much like she and Nancy had done earlier, to create a two-color card from a black-and-white photograph. In this case, the photograph showed Emma Tenayuca on the steps of the Palacio Municipal, fist raised in the air and backed by several other women and men holding large banners, addressing an audience. Two of the large beautiful fabric banners were overlaid with the mauve tint, and rather than use a typographical border, she chose to have the mauve ink frame the photograph to the edges of the card, drawing the messages of the banners outward into

Emma Tenayuca, Chicana, encabezando una manifestación de la Alianza de Trabajadores en 1937 en los escalones del Palacio Municipal de San Antonio.

### 71. Emma Tenayuca postcard inscribed to Vicki Leighty, 1984

Helaine Victoria Press asked a number of the women honored on their postcards if they would autograph ten copies. This card Emma Tenayuca inscribed to Vicky Leighty, with whom she had spent several hours on the telephone, providing information for the caption on the reverse side of the postcard:

Emma Tenayuca, born 1916 in San Antonio, Texas. A courageous Chicana labor leader whose commitment to justice led her to a militant stand against hunger, misery, and unemployment of the Great Depression. From 1934-48, she supported almost every strike in the city, writing leaflets, visiting homes of strikers, and joining them on picket lines. First knowledge of the plight of workers came from visits to the "Plaza del Zacate," the Trafalgar Square of SA where socialists and anarchists came to speak. Contact with fired workers led her to join the Communist Party in 1937 and the Workers Alliance in 1936, an organization of the unemployed founded by Socialists and Communists, 90% of whom were pecan shellers and agricultural workers. The WA held demonstrations for jobs, not relief, and demanded that Mexican workers had the right to strike without fear of deportation, and to a minimum wage and hour law. When 12,000 pecan shellers marched out of the factories in 1938, Tenayuca was unanimously elected strike leader. In retrospect she says, "What started out as a movement for organization for equal wages turned into a mass movement against starvation, for civil rights, for a minimum wage law, and it changed the character of West Side San Antonio."

the space beyond the speakers. Under the photo the Spanish text reads: "Emma Tenayuca, Chicana, encabezando una manifestacion de la Alianza de Trabajadores en 1937 en los escalones del palacio Municipal de San Antonio." ["Emma Tenayuca, Chicana, leading a demonstration of the Workers Alliance in 1937 on the steps of the Municipal palace of San Antonio."]

When the card was published, Vicki sent one to Tenayuca

"I am a working girl, one of those who are on strike against intolerable conditions. I am tired of listening to speakers who talk in general terms. What we are here for is to decide whether we shall or shall not strike. I offer a resolution that a general strike be declared – now."

Clara Lemlich speaking at Cooper Union, November 22, 1909, NYC

### 72. Uprising of the 20,000 & Clara Lemlich postcard

The uprising of 20,000 shirtwaist workers in 1909 was the "largest strike of women ever known in U.S." Idealistic Jewish women with roots in Russian socialism and union struggles were the force behind the strike. The industry employed 30–40,000 workers in NYC—2/3 Jewish and 80% women—in dismal sweatshops. Low wages, poor working conditions, and sexual abuse were among the grievances. Beginning in September 1909, women picketing against two employers were arrested, beaten, and harassed by hired thugs and police. At a mass meeting at Cooper Union on November 22, speakers debated the question of a general strike. Finally, Clara Lemlich (1886–1982), a young Jewish worker who had been among the first strikers, delivered an impassioned speech in Yiddish, the native tongue of the majority of shirtwaist workers, calling for a general strike. Instantly the crowd was on its feet shouting its emphatic affirmation. Within a few days, 30,000 shirtwaist workers were on strike. The Women's Trade Union League and wealthy and middle class women actively supported the strikers, forming a unique bond. The strike was settled on February 15. Despite a disappointing settlement, striking women awakened the public to problems facing women workers; the important issue of unionizing Black women came to the fore; the women gained an understanding of their strength in union and in number; and the "great uprising" became a catalyst for the rest of the industry.

through the mail, later beginning to worry about whether it had been a good idea. Writing a letter, Vicki apologized for the brash move: "I hope I did not do something wrong by sending you the postcard which you mentioned receiving in your last letter. I should have asked you if it was okay first to send the card without an envelope when it would come to your address. I hope your mail carrier is an okay person." Responding to Vicki's concern, Emma Tenayuca wrote,

Imagine receiving a card from you with a picture of myself on each side. My postman will now know I was once a "red." No, Vicki, many, many people in S.A. know I was once a member of the C.P. Often, quite often, recently, I agonized over my inability to return to some activity, to speak as openly as I did at one time. I have been a guest speaker at the Western Conference of the Newspaper Guild, at Texas Lutheran College, at the Chicano Conference in Austin, and at San Marcos State University. However, the surroundings and my feelings were such that I could not "cut loose" and tackle the problems as I see them today.[43]

She seemed to feel comfortable enough with Vicki, though, to declare unreservedly her disgust with then-President Reagan and those surrounding him, saying, "[W]hat could be more brutal, more callously brutal than a slight remark, 'Yes, there is poverty in America,' [and] the placing of millionaires on the Committee to investigate poverty. Or the Christianity of a Falwell, a racist, a bigot, who seeks only by prayer in the schools to hit at the crime in our country? Perhaps, perhaps, I shall be more active this year, by writing and speaking."[44] We don't know whether Emma Tenayuca was able to speak out in the way she wanted, but her card circulated widely, offering her words and a powerful image of her in action to all those who saw it, reinscribing her work in feminist memory.

One who saw the card was Sandra Cisneros who mentioned Helaine Victoria Press in a column she wrote for *San Antonio Woman,* extending the press's horizontal reach. "The Helaine Victoria Press people of Indiana just celebrated their 10th year anniversary of printing fine postcards featuring women in history and culture. Their new catalog is excellent," she said, "with information you'll want to share with everyone, including your mother. Their educational materials include postcards featuring such greats as Emma Goldman, Colette, Georgia O'Keeffe, and most recently, San Antonio's own Emma Tenayuca (hurray!)."[45]

Aiming to acknowledge another chronically underrepresented

group in women's history, Jocelyn was working on one more series this year, collaborating with Sue Levi Elwell to produce a series on Jewish feminists. Jocelyn had met Sue as a customer; she was, at the time, in rabbinical school in Cincinnati. When they talked about the possibility of a small series, they wondered who they should include. As a rabbinical student, Sue was well-versed in Jewish history, and with this background, she and Jocelyn puzzled out a list of four women, making every effort to be as broadly inclusive as possible. Jewish women had appeared throughout the cards Helaine Victoria had already published, but this small series targeted a distinctive Jewish voice and experience. They chose Mary Antin, author of *The Promised Land*, a 1912 novel describing the experience of immigration and settlement in the US;[46] Clara Lemlich, worker and impassioned spontaneous strike leader of the "Uprising of the 20,000" shirtwaist workers in 1909; Rosa Sonneschein, publisher of *The American Jewess*, a late-nineteenth-century magazine by and for women; and, for the fourth card, Sadie American and Hannah Greenbaume Solomon, both active in establishing the Jewish Women's Congress of the 1893 World's Columbian Exposition in Chicago and the National Council of Jewish Women, a permanent organization that developed from the Congress.

Sue Elwell located and provided the photos, Jocelyn designed the cards, and the two collaborated on the captions. The four cards drew from previous design motifs used on both letterpress and offset jumbo cards—borders reflecting the time, autographs on the photo, quotations from the woman pictured. One interesting diversion from this pattern was the Rosa Sonneschein card. On this card, they used the cover of her magazine *The American Jewess* from the first month it was published and, instead of the original picture in the center, they dropped in a photographic portrait of Sonneschein herself.

As dedicated and enthusiastic as the many women, such as Sue Elwell, were who offered their labor and expertise to support the press, the original energy of the press had changed, and the all-

73. Women in the American Labor Movement folio
Front cover for nine postcards in a folio set Women in the American Labor Movement: Organized Struggle in the Workplace 1886-1986, in recognition of the Centennial of the Haymarket Tragedy and the First International Celebration of May Day.

encompassing passion for every aspect of Helaine Victoria that Nancy and Jocelyn had shared never recurred. Volunteers often had differing motivations for wanting to be involved with the press, reflecting the demographics of the movement as a whole. Some were young and just beginning to explore feminism; others were experienced in political movements and wanted the press to adopt those movements' tactics; others were questioning their sexuality and saw the activities around the press as a place to investigate other possibilities. What's more, volunteers and work-study students came and went. Several new volunteers appeared during the mid-1980s, including Edith Millikan, an art history scholar who devoted many hours to managing the press's correspondence and assisted with sales and conferences and festivals; Georg'Ann Cattelona, a graduate student who worked on fundraising, outreach, and copy for the catalogs; Linda Greene, an editor who contributed her expertise to the press; and Betsy Osborne, who helped with correspondence and outreach programs at the shop and provided additional assistance wherever it was needed. Laura Sparks, another Indiana University student, brought her graphic design and newspaper production work abilities to the press, later adding letterpress printing skills, as well. Sandra Runzo, then a doctoral student at Indiana University, worked on several catalogs, helped with copyediting, and participated in all those mundane tasks like packaging at which academics excelled, perhaps as a methodical relief from more stressful intellectual endeavors. Those listed above were not the only volunteers; many other women contributed time on specific chores and projects as they were able. Work study students from Indiana University, plus one or two part-time workers rounded out the Helaine Victoria Press staff.[47]

While it is true that the press's direction changed after Nancy moved to Chicago, it is also true that the women's movement as a whole was changing, maturing in some ways, but also responding to political and economic pressures from the larger culture. The press, out of necessity, had to change in response to developments outside of itself as well as within. It was about this time that Nancy realized that the strain of trying to be involved with the press from a distance was just too much. She tendered her resignation on January 12, 1985.[48]

While Jocelyn had found the decision-making burdens difficult, the collapse of the founding partnership of Helaine Victoria Press was, for her, more profoundly disquieting, echoing as it did the dissolution of the Feminist Art Program. Drawing from the writings of Mary Astell and Sarah Scott and the utopian foundations of the Arts & Crafts Movement as well as from the contemporary Lesbian feminist movement, Jocelyn and Nancy had modeled their partnership on ideals developed over centuries; ideals in which friendship formed the core value. Their inability to maintain a close friendship, even across the distance, left both feeling bereft.

Reluctantly, Jocelyn took over coordinating the Haymarket Centennial series, which Nancy had been managing, and Indiana University Political Science professor Jean Robinson stepped in to edit the series. Mary Mallory, a frequent volunteer, handled much of the correspondence. Renamed the Women in the American Labor Movement series, the set included nine cards enclosed in a folio. On the front cover of the folio, Jean and Jocelyn gave more shape to the general subject matter, subtitling the series "Organized Struggle in the Workplace 1886–1986," and adding, "in recognition of the Centennial of the Haymarket Tragedy and the First International Celebration of May Day." The series was jobbed out to a union printshop and the union bug sat prominently in the lower right-hand corner of the folio's front cover. With this series, the press began naming those who wrote the captions.

The cards included: the sit-down strike, featuring a 1937 strike by women workers at Woolworth's, with research by labor historian Philip S. Foner; Voltairine de Cleyre, American anarchist freethinker, with research by historian Paul Avrich; Russian-Jewish labor organizer and anarchist Rose Pesotta, with research by sociologist Elaine Leeder; labor organizer and anarchist Lucy

Gonsalez Parsons, with research updated from her card in the Bread & Roses series by Jocelyn Cohen; the Haymarket memorial, with research by Mary Mallory; labor leader Maida Springer-Kemp, whom Vicki Leighty interviewed by telephone; May Day, represented by two girls wearing banners in Yiddish and English protesting child labor, with research by Jocelyn Cohen; farmworkers organizer Dolores Huerta, with research by Margaret Rose; and Blue Collar Asian Women. To create the caption for this last card, Vicki Leighty interviewed several of the women pictured. A folio provided both a general bibliography for women in the US labor movement as well as specific bibliographies for the subjects of each of the cards. Linda Preuss, an artist and designer and friend of Jocelyn from her Feminist Art Program days, provided several significant design ideas that were incorporated into the final product.[49]

The bibliographies, offered for the first time on a Helaine Victoria series, are a reminder that, despite the often-robust sales at festivals such as the Michigan Women's Music Festival, a primary audience for Helaine Victoria cards was teachers and students. Jean Robinson commented on the significance of the cards to her work developing the curriculum for Women's Studies at Indiana University, which, she said, "was a really young academic program. It had not even been in existence for five years [ . . . ]. And the first part of the curriculum, really, was trying to teach women's history and trying to help make it authentic." In teaching women's history, she said, they made it a point to emphasize the connection between feminism and the women's movement and other social movements, "so there was a strong strain of working class and labor movement stuff. And one of the things that I found really both attractive and useful about Helaine Victoria was that it didn't just produce bourgeois liberal feminist stuff. It was really tied to labor and working-class issues and the idea of what a movement is and activism."[50]

Letters, too, attested to the cards' usefulness in multiple contexts:

The project (for Women's History Week) was a huge success! Women in Herstory (postcards) are plastered all over the Learning Center wall! The girls really had their awareness raised. We have stimulated so much interest that the project will continue....
—Joan Corbett, Lincolnshire, IL[51]

I enjoy your beautiful postcards on Black women and work. Your postcard on Trackwomen on the B & O aided me in my research on a herstorical paper I wrote on women and the railroad [...]. I will be using the information from the postcard (Hampton Institute) concerning Black Women and Non-Traditional Jobs, another paper I am planning to research and write. Your postcards are very popular, and the women's bookstores in Boston, Cambridge, and Northampton cannot keep enough of them. I would like to order a whole set for myself [...]. For your pictures are an inspiration for me, a Black woman, to write about Black women and work. I am the only Black woman in my Graduate Program (Labor Relations) University of Massachusetts, Amherst.
—Yvonne Forrest, Northampton, MA.[52]

Even a Western Union Mailgram arrived, from Joanne Forman of Radio KVNM, saying, "love your postcards," and making an offer that press workers could not refuse: if the press were to send twelve cards featuring Indian and Hispanic subjects, they would be included in radio programming on International Women's Day, with credit given to the press. The press sent twelve cards, *post haste*![53]

It was no coincidence that the press was receiving responses such as these. As Jocelyn had insisted in her letter to customers in the 1985 catalog: "We constantly bring to light unpublished photos and biographies most people, including many historians, are not familiar with. Our purpose is to reach communities that would not have ready access to the kinds of materials we unearth."[54]

Hoping to continue the press's mission of recentering women in the historical record—and, to that end, seeking to stay current in the field of printing and publishing—Jocelyn went to the Third National Women in Print conference, held in 1985 at University of California, Berkeley, May 29–June 1, with over 300 women attending. This was the first time she had gone alone, without Nancy, which meant they couldn't divide up the workshops and thus cover twice as many, but rather that she had to choose only those that were absolutely the most important for the future of Helaine Victoria Press. Her choices indicate what the critical issue was for the press in 1985; she attended three workshops on finance, one on fundraising, one on bookkeeping, and one on promotion. In a last nod to the functional aspects of printing, she also went to a workshop entitled "Preparing Mechanicals So Your Printer Will Love You."[55]

Tricia Lootens quoted Jocelyn's comments at the conference in an article in *off our backs* that fall: "Helaine Victoria Press has been publishing for 13 years, she said, and barely surviving. She has periods of liking her work and periods of worrying about what they will do if the money stops. She missed the nitty-gritty of the conference: she wanted ideas to keep her going in the next year."[56] Compounding the disappointment, the conference organizers had been forced to charge participants for the tables they used to display their products. The reason for this? University of California was charging $36,000 in various fees to hold the conference on its premises, providing an illustration of the ways in which women's presses were trapped between customers with shallow pockets and businesses and institutions. In this case, the institution in question, having lost some of its tax-based funding, was having to make up the difference by charging the very people who had little to begin with.

Jocelyn came home from the Women in Print conference with one pleasant assignment. During the conference, Janet Mullaney, editor-in-chief of feminist quarterly book review periodical *Belles Lettres,* had approached Jocelyn, asking if she would be willing to write an article about Helaine Victoria Press for the quarterly.

## 74. Edmonia Lewis postcard

Edmonia Lewis (1843-1890). Sculptor. Daughter of a Chippewa Indian mother and a Black father, her heritage greatly influenced her work. Orphaned before age five, she was raised by her mother's tribe as Wildfire. When she enrolled at Oberlin College with financial support from her brother, she changed her name. During the Civil War, in 1862, she moved to Boston and began her career as a sculptor, modeling anti-slavery leaders. The sale of her work enabled her to go to Italy in 1865 to further her study and have access to marble. Although working in the Neoclassic style, her art expressed her concern with slavery and racial oppression. Her work reflected the dignity of her Indian roots and, as she put it, conveyed a "strong sympathy for all women who have struggled and suffered." She was welcomed in Rome and became part of the circle of independent women artists who included Harriet Hosmer, Charlotte Cushman and Anne Whitney. Lewis executed many large compositions herself unlike other sculptors, believing this made her work truly original. Though she confronted racial and sexual barriers, she attained professional success both in the U.S. and Europe.

### 75. Rosie the Riveter postcard

"Rosie the Riveter." Women's place in the workforce was radically changed by WWII. New popular images in propaganda, like "Rosie the Riveter," were used to recruit women to fill war-time defense jobs which suffered from the "man" power shortage caused by the war. Black women, along with older and married women, for the first time found exciting new opportunities open to them in non-traditional, skilled, and highly paid jobs. Nearly 20 million women were active in the workforce during the war, 6.5 million for the first time. The number of women in heavy manufacturing increased 460%. Overnight, women were trained to be shipbuilders, welders, riveters, and machine workers. In addition, they became the train conductors, bus drivers, lumberjacks and police which sustained the nation. When WWII came to an end, new propaganda was produced which encouraged women to leave the workforce so the returning soldiers could resume their old jobs. Although women were laid off in great numbers, 80% of them wanted to keep their skilled jobs, and many of the "Rosies" stayed in the workforce but were forced to return to their traditional unskilled positions.

What could be better than an article about Helaine Victoria that would reach the readership of a feminist book review journal? The article, "Women, History, Postcards," was published as a special feature in the journal's second issue, November–December 1985. Placed strategically next to "The Art of the Letter," a column by consulting editor Susan Koppelman, longtime friend of the press, and above a review of a collection of artist Paula Modersohn-Becker's letters and journals, Jocelyn's article explained the personal research processes that had produced the Women in the American Labor Movement series, focusing on Elaine Leeder's card on Rose Pesotta, which had grown out of Leeder's dissertation, and Vicki Leighty's research on Maida Springer-Kemp, which had culminated in a personal interview with the famed labor organizer.

In general, Jocelyn said, the development of a card begins in the archives: "First we seek an exciting photograph and then proceed with the research for the historical caption." Shifting her emphasis to the Woolworth Sit-Down Strike, the Blue Collar Asian Women, and the 1909 May Day Parade cards, she outlined the steps frequently taken in locating information. The first challenge was to identify the women in the photograph. In the case of the Blue Collar Asian Women card, photographer JEB (Joan E. Biren) was able to help Vicki contact some of the women pictured, and those women then identified the others. The next step was to learn the exact context of the photo. When researching the May Day Parade card, they read contemporary newspaper accounts which had alerted them to the fact that there had been a children's contingent in the parade protesting the use of child labor. Then they needed to determine the historical significance of the image. When they researched the Woolworth Sit-Down Strike, they learned that this event had been one of a wave of sit-down strikes—but that the Woolworth clerks had pioneered the tactic. After successfully completing these steps in the process, they found published sources for information and, if possible, sought individuals for interviews.

"Helaine Victoria's cards transcend the traditional picture postcard," Jocelyn told *Belles Lettres* readers. "The scholarly researched captions on the card backs, the use of oral history interviews, the personalization achieved by the use of quotes, and the unique design of the cards combined with the pictorial image result in a truly valuable document chronicling women's lives."[57]

While Helaine Victoria Press was soliciting postcard manuscripts from scholars around the country, Jocelyn was encouraging local talent to participate in the postcard development process as well. Vicki Leighty had now contributed material for three cards, the Blue Collar Asian Women card, one on Emma Tenayuca, and one on Maida Springer-Kemp, all involving personal conversations with the women being depicted on the card. With encouragement, Bernice Schipp took on the responsibility for researching and writing the caption for a card honoring Edmonia Lewis (1843–1890?), the first professional sculptor of African American and Native American heritage. Edmonia Lewis was able to enroll in Oberlin College, with help from her brother. From there she moved to Boston and began her sculpting career, creating likenesses of antislavery leaders. Sales of her sculptures enabled her to go to Rome, where she learned to work in marble and joined a group of independent women artists. Bernice's caption expressed the key elements of Lewis's artistic motives: "Although working in the Neoclassic style, her art expressed her concern with slavery and racial oppression. Her work reflected the dignity of her Indian roots and, as she put it, conveyed a 'strong sympathy for all women who have struggled and suffered.'"[58]

All the cards were well-received, but the most enthusiastic reception this year was reserved for Rosie the Riveter. While they were researching photographs at the National Archives, Nancy and Jocelyn had seen a postcard for sale there that was published by the National Archives as part of a propaganda series on women and the military. The card had little on the reverse side to indicate the historical background of the image. The National Archives caption read simply: "Posters like this are only one of the many types of government records preserved in the National Archives. The most famous documents, of course, are original Declaration of Independence, Constitution, and Bill of Rights." This card, direct from the National Archives, was offered first in the press's 1982-83 catalog.

Because images in the National Archives are copyright-free, Helaine Victoria Press was able to reprint the card in its full color in 1985, sending it out to a chrome postcard printer who reproduced it as it had been offered by the National Archives. Jocelyn added a caption on the reverse side of the card explaining the role of women in industrial production during World War II, a role that earned some, especially those working in aircraft- and shipbuilding, the moniker "Rosie the Riveter." The Helaine Victoria Press caption, titled "Rosie the Riveter," read in part: "Women's place in the workforce was radically changed by WWII. New popular images in propaganda, like 'Rosie the Riveter,' were used to recruit women to fill war-time defense jobs which suffered from the 'man' power shortage caused by the war."[59]

This card became one of their most popular, although few people now realize they should thank Helaine Victoria Press for distributing and articulating the significance of the image. Enthusiasm for the card reached such a pitch that the press repurposed the image in one of the next large-scale endeavors they would undertake.

## CHAPTER FIVE

## STOREFRONT IN BLOOMINGTON

> *My rationale was that there was so much going on in Bloomington: the National Women's Music Festival; Athena's, the women's art cooperative store; and the women's bookstore. We needed to have a tangible site from which to show our artistry and not just depend for sales on the catalogs and the festivals and conferences.*
>
> —Vicki Leighty, on why Helaine Victoria Press opened a store in Bloomington, IN

Cultural work—art, music, theater, film, fiction, and poetry—flourished during the early years of the women's movement, and much of this cultural and rhetorical work, like Helaine Victoria's postcards and prints, had been grounded in feminist political possibilities. However, when first Ronald Reagan was elected president, taking office in 1981, and the deadline for confirmation of the Equal Rights Amendment passed soon after without a sufficient number of ratification votes from the states, discouragement set in among many women.[1] The feeling was compounded, especially among academic women, during the Barnard Center for Research on Women's 1982 Scholar and Feminist Conference, where seemingly unresolvable conflicts emerged around the politics of sexuality. Nonetheless, some scholarly and artistic efforts to generate an active feminist memory continued to thrive, serving to maintain and build on many of the connections forged during the movement's first decade.[2]

Sensing this shift, those working at the press were keen to expand Helaine Victoria's offerings. What could be more attractive to customers—and at the same time upend conventional notions of art—than T-shirts featuring Helaine Victoria images? Not only that, but if a postcard was meant to move an image across multiple audiences, how much more successful would T-shirts be, as they moved through space on the bodies of those who wore them? T-shirts could take multimodality to a new level—and command a significantly higher price than a postcard, contributing to the press's goal of solvency. The first two T-shirts Helaine Victoria Press produced featured Rosie the Riveter and Zora Neale Hurston. Within a year, another T-shirt design had been added: Donna Fay Reeves merged Helaine Victoria's logo, Columbia, with a traditional playing card to create Helaine Victoria Press, Queen of the Cards. This clever and charming image was printed in purple, red, and blue on white shirts. Two more T-shirts followed in later years, with images taken from popular Helaine Victoria cards: Sojourner Truth and Amelia Earhart.

The press's development of a T-shirt line converged with other changes. The grassroots women's movement and the arts and academic communities in both Indianapolis and Bloomington were increasingly supportive of Helaine Victoria Press. The Ten-Year Retrospective exhibit had drawn attention to the press and had enhanced the public's awareness of the many ways that Helaine Victoria Press contributed to the cultural richness coming out of the women's movement in Indiana. During that same summer of 1986, at the National Women's Music Festival in Bloomington, Jocelyn was honored for her work with the Jeanine Rae Award for the Advancement of Women's Culture.[3] More students and volunteers stepped up to support their local source of feminist artistic/rhetorical activism.

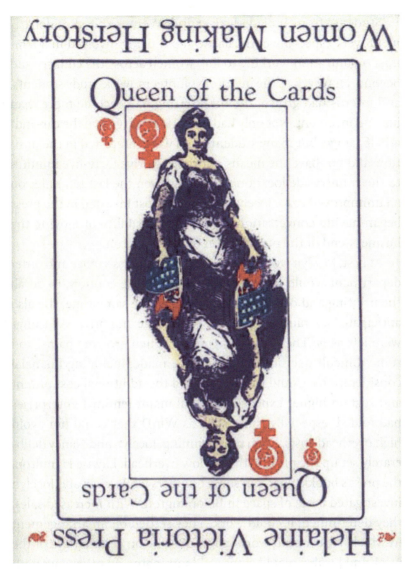

76. Women Making History, Queen of the Cards T-shirt
Donna Fay Reeves merged Helaine Victoria's logo, Columbia, with a traditional playing card to create Helaine Victoria Press, Queen of the Cards.

Students from Indiana University's Women's Studies department were especially enthusiastic about being involved in a feminist organization working to link women across the country and beyond. However, as the influx of volunteers, work-study students, and interns had grown, the rural setting had become more than just inconvenient. Not only had operations outgrown the car-and-a-half garage, but many students who were interested in the positions did not have the means nor time to drive forty-five minutes to the countryside location, especially given the last ten miles on an unimproved road. Jocelyn and those most invested in the press began having conversations about the possibility of moving the business-end of the organization to Bloomington.

At first, Jocelyn worried that moving the press's office and order department would leave her alone, out in the country, to do all the printing and other business tasks. At the same time, she also anticipated a strain on her sense of solitude and privacy if things were left as is. The press was going through growing pains, and some difficult decisions needed to be made, including financial considerations. Could the press afford the additional cost of rent and sustain higher expenses? Several major feminist enterprises had folded, especially those such as WinD that could not avoid high overhead costs. From the beginning, Jocelyn and Nancy deliberately set up the press with very low overhead. Lawrie Hamilton, the press's bookkeeper, ran some numbers while Vicki and Jocelyn investigated costs of space in Bloomington. With increased sales, they determined, it could work. They settled on an arrangement in which Vicki would work in Martinsville on certain days of the week and Jocelyn would come to Bloomington on other days with an overlap between them of a day or two.

Along with the press's move into T-shirt production, Vicki envisioned a shop offering more women's products. As a student of folklore, fascinated by material culture produced by the feminist movement, Vicki wanted to combine a shop offering such items with a permanent sales site for Helaine Victoria, thus helping to offset the cost of commercial space in Bloomington. If she could sell other cultural items such as jewelry, pottery, and buttons, she reasoned, then customers would likely also be drawn to the more challenging images and texts on the prints and postcards. With a storefront, they could replicate, in a sense, the experiences from some of their most beloved festivals, such as the Michigan Women's Music Festival and the National Women's Music Festival, where women came to the crafts booths to peruse the jewelry, pottery, and tank tops and discovered the press's postcards while there. In this way, the community's increased interest in cultural materials, along with ten years of building connections in Bloomington, made the idea of moving Helaine Victoria's base of operations into Bloomington a viable option. Under the name of her business, the Womyn's Culture Works, Vicki would be the purveyor of all the material culture items apart from press-produced products; she would pay a small portion of the rent in exchange for the space to display her merchandise.

At the same time, the press's mail order sales had been increasing, according to Bernice Schipp's analyses, and Jocelyn and Vicki realized it was time to hire someone to manage that part of the workload. Donna Fay Reeves had already been helping with the mail order business in the country. A dedicated and savvy community activist who had been working voluntarily on feminist events for years, though never receiving a dime of compensation, Donna was a logical choice. She had reached out to Jocelyn and Nancy years earlier, was familiar with and supported the press, and knew her way around the Bloomington community. At the time, Donna was working in a local restaurant, so one evening Vicki and Jocelyn went in at the end of her shift and posed a question to her: If the press were to open a mail order department in Bloomington, would she work there part-time? "Yes!"

With an agreement in place and Donna willing to join the team, Jocelyn and Vicki began looking for a location in Bloomington that could house the office, the mail order department and an accessible store, as well. It needed to be close to the IU campus to attract students and faculty. As it happened, the place they found was perfect: a two-story, house-turned-office on 4th Street, a block from Indiana Avenue which led directly into the campus. The Helaine Victoria Press Women's History Shop would be joining a range of other small businesses nearby: a vintage clothing store, several ethnic restaurants, and Caveat Emptor, a used and rare bookstore. Around the corner was White Rabbit, a large, alternative culture emporium with a coffee shop in the back that was already selling Helaine Victoria cards. Athena, the women's arts collective, was within a couple of blocks, as were a hair salon catering to the women's community, more coffee shops, and more restaurants.[4] In some ways, the new location replicated the press's original Santa Monica site, centered among like-minded small businesses in an area that supported feminist cultural work; at the same time, however, the press itself and Jocelyn's living quarters were still housed in their quiet country setting. And although the new space was indeed an added expense, Jocelyn and Vicki remained hopeful Helaine Victoria sales at the store would offset the cost of rent and utilities, and even help support the press itself. Lawrie figured that for the store to be minimally sustainable it needed to have daily sales of $30 on Helaine Victoria items—modest-sounding by today's standards, but daunting at the time.

Jocelyn and Vicki rented the entire first floor of the building they had found. The front room for the store was bright and cheery with lots of windows. There was a front yard which provided a place for the Helaine Victoria sign to be seen from the street. They even located a Lesbian feminist sign painter in Bloomington to design and paint the sign. With a lush lavender background, Columbia, the press's trademark, stood proud in purple, almost two feet tall, next to elegant lettering: "Helaine Victoria Press Women's History Shop."[5] It was the only store in the world devoted to the process of generating participatory feminist memory, and, although many major cities and university towns still had a women's bookstore,

77. Jocelyn Cohen with Helaine Victoria Press Women's History Shop sign
Vicki Leighty and Jocelyn Cohen wanted a large, beautiful sign announcing the shop when it opened in 1986. They discovered a Lesbian feminist sign painter in Bloomington to design and paint the sign. With a lush lavender background, Columbia, the press's trademark, stood proud in purple, almost two feet tall, next to elegant lettering: "Helaine Victoria Press Women's History Shop."

there were very few shops specializing in women's cultural works. No others provided an accessible, multimodal medium dedicated to increasing feminist connection.

Pleased with their new location, Vicki and Jocelyn scavenged appropriate display furniture for their wares, finding spinning racks and larger wall racks to hold cards. Bringing shelves from the garage in the country to fill with postcards, they created a mail order department in the middle room, adding a desk, plus large tables for fulfillment. Another smaller office space in the back had enough room for a couch, and there was an airy back porch where staff and volunteers could eat lunch, weather permitting. There was even space for parking in the back. As for in-store real estate, Helaine Victoria products occupied the walls and racks, while Vicki's cultural items were displayed on the counters and in a beautiful glass and wooden jewelry case they had found. Some items Vicki purchased wholesale and then resold; others she sold on consignment.

In 1983, Chicago Women's Graphics (CWG) had dissolved. Now that Helaine Victoria Press had a retail shop, Jocelyn and Julie Zolot, the CWG member who was tasked with the final dissolution of the silk screen shop, agreed on a purchase price, and the press added the remaining CWG feminist posters to the store's unique inventory. If Helaine Victoria Press was Queen of the Cards, Chicago Women's Graphics, at one time, held equal nobility in the realm of posters. Their colorful political and cultural silkscreen posters adorned the walls of feminist homes, offices, and women's centers, and now the Helaine Victoria Press Women's History Shop, as well.

While Jocelyn and Vicki worked to establish Helaine Victoria Press's presence in Bloomington, Jocelyn also reached out to IU Women's Studies faculty, informing them of the press's publishing plans and inviting them to consider how they might help guide the press's work. When Jocelyn and Nancy had started out in Los Angeles, they—and their customers—felt that every unsung or forgotten woman they located was a treasure, and each one was significant in her own right. Now, as they and others were searching the archives, writing articles and books, and constructing syllabi for courses on women's history, networks of women were discovered, movements were revealed, and patterns emerged. It was clear to Jocelyn that the young field was maturing quickly. It was time to involve more women who had developed deep knowledge of specific areas. Besides seeking additional scholarly expertise, Jocelyn was looking for more ways to share the load of the publishing work and to find new ways to collaborate. After an initial meeting with interested faculty, she conceived the idea of a publishing advisory board, which she would establish the next year.

Even with their concerted efforts and renewed vigor, not surprisingly, income continued to be an issue for the press. Although many customers were including donations with their orders, for which Jocelyn and the board of directors were very grateful, Lawrie informed the board that, in order to remain solvent and continue to grow, Helaine Victoria needed an infusion of grants totaling about $70,000.[6] So far, grants of that magnitude seemed about as likely as a visit to the Big Rock Candy Mountain.[7] A yard sale to benefit the press that fall did not do the job. Nonetheless, one very welcome grant came in. Anne Wilson, a longtime fan of the press, designated $3,000 via a donor-advised fund to support the printing of the Latina series.

The long-planned series of seven cards provided captions in both Spanish and English, another first for Helaine Victoria Press. Vicki coordinated production while Norma Alarcón served as advisor. While working on her doctoral thesis at IU, Norma had founded Third Woman Press to make available the work of women of color, and she was keen to see more attention given to the field. Chicano studies, in particular, was a fledging discipline, especially in the Midwest. The widely hailed anthology *This Bridge Called My Back: Writings by Radical Women of Color*, edited by Gloria Anzaldua and Cherrie Moraga, had appeared in 1981, with a second edition published in 1983. But, apart from this seminal text, there was little published at the time about Latinas. What's more, at the Women in Print conferences, the dearth of materials on Latinas—and especially the absence of published books on the subject—was well-noted, and Jocelyn returned from the conferences determined to use the resources of Helaine Victoria Press to address these gaps. It was not simply a matter of disseminating images, though that was an important aspect. Helaine Victoria Press aimed to create a communication medium for feminists of all ethnic backgrounds; the movement needed links that extended across cultures, and feminist memory needed to include all women's accomplishments.

When Jocelyn and Vicki approached Norma Alarcón, asking her to advise and participate in the series, she was most eager. Even though she had joined the Purdue foreign languages faculty in 1983, she continued to visit Bloomington regularly. As advisor for the series, Norma guided the selection of images in order to create a reasonable breadth of representation, given the many subcultures falling under the rubric of Latin America, although locations of the subjects of the cards were limited to the continental US, Puerto Rico, Mexico, and Central America. She also endeavored to ensure that a wide range of women's achievements were represented, covering medicine, journalism, electoral politics, and struggles for national sovereignty and labor rights. Because she was familiar with women working in related fields, she was able to assist in obtaining photographs and caption writers. This ability to draw on such connections proved to be a key asset academic advisors could bring to a series. Not only were they aware of those working in their area of expertise, but often they were personally acquainted with the individuals. Their academic positions carried clout, as well, when making a request on behalf of a nonprofit organization. The press, and Jocelyn in particular, hoped more people in the academic and feminist communities would begin to feel honored to submit a caption and be part of the publishing circle at Helaine Victoria Press.

The cards in the Latina series included one that had been previously published by Helaine Victoria Press and re-printed with the same design as the rest of the series: labor leader and educator Emma Tenayuca. Cards published for the first time in this series included: Soldaderas in the Mexican Revolution, with caption by Jocelyn H. Cohen; Dora María Téllez: Sandinista military officer, poet, feminist, and stateswoman, with caption by poet, photographer, and activist Margaret Randall; Jovita Idar: journalist, educator, and feminist, with caption by Vicki Leighty, composed after an interview with Jovita Lopez, Idar's niece; Lolita Lebrón, Puerto Rican independence activist incarcerated for twenty-five years for leading an armed attack on the US Congress in 1954, with caption by Linda Greene and Josefina Rodriguez; poet, novelist, essayist, journalist, and diplomat Rosario Castellanos, with caption by Norma Alarcón; and J. V. de Martinez-Alvarez: Puerto Rican physician, suffragist, and feminist, with caption by Susan Krieg.

## 78. Jovita Idar postcard

Jovita Idar (1885–1946), journalist, educator, feminist, humanitarian. Born in Laredo, TX, Idar wrote for the Spanish-language newspaper *La Crónica*, which was owned by her father, and which addressed the problems of Mexican Americans—discrimination, divestment of landholdings by Anglos, labor issues, lynchings and the Mexican Revolution. The Idars organized el Primer Congreso Mexicanista (First Mexican Congress) in Laredo in 1911. The first of its kind for Texas Mexicans, the meeting offered performances and workshops on Mexican history, culture, language, discrimination, criminal justice and women's issues. Idar and several other women formed la Liga Femenil Mexicanista (League of Mexican Women), an independent women's organization focusing mainly on education. When Mexican revolutionary troops attacked Nuevo Laredo, Mexico, in 1913, Idar joined Leonor Villegas de Magnon in providing medical aid to injured soldiers and civilians. She later became a war nurse for La Cruz Blanca (the White Cross), a medical relief organization founded by Villegas de Magnon. To the end of her life Idar stayed active in the cause of Mexican Americans as an educator, interpreter and journalist.

Locating subjects, images, and researchers was difficult, even with Norma Alarcón's expert assistance. In Chicago, Julie Zolot was ultimately able to connect the press with Josefina Rodriguez of Westtown Community Law Office, who, in turn, worked with Linda Greene to compose the caption for the card honoring Lolita Lebrón. All cards were translated into Spanish by Elena Tapia, an IU PhD student in linguistics. Each set also had a full page 8.5" x 14" bibliography inserted, offering pathways to more information and encouraging customers to continue building out feminist awareness.

The seven jumbo cards in the Latina set were designed to be printed offset. Press workers had made the difficult decision to shift to offset printing for many original cards as well as reprints, a decision driven by several factors: the volume of cards Helaine Victoria was attempting to keep in print; the increasing numbers of cards in each series; and the sense of urgency press workers felt as they attempted to keep up with the new findings on women who had been lost to history. This significant shift in operational conditions at Helaine Victoria Press did not impact the quality of the cards. If anything, some of the photographs were reproduced at a higher quality on a modern offset press than could have been done on what was by then a nearly 100-year-old platen press. Nonetheless, when it became clear that a division of labor would be necessary, the move to greater reliance on an outside printer meant another cultural change for the press. Although they continued to use the letterpress shop to produce both postcards and broadsides, the bulk of the cards printed henceforth, and especially the large multi-card series, were sent to an offset printer. Because Helaine Victoria's unique postcard logo was reserved solely for letterpress-printed cards, the offset-printed cards would not announce on the reverse side: "STILL PRINTING TODAY THE HISTORIC WAY."

Although Jocelyn was responsible for the majority of the design work after Nancy's departure, Laura Sparks, an IU art student volunteering at the press, was instrumental in creating some of the postcard designs, including the Latina series. Drawing from previous design elements, such as borders and tints to enhance the photos, she chose to have the cards printed in three colors: a rich sepia, chocolate brown, and a light peachy orange used both as a solid and a tint. When designing the card for Jovita Idar, Laura wrestled with the fact that the most evocative photograph they had did not accentuate Idar, showing her in her newspaper office with two male colleagues flanking her, one on each side. To deliver what is now a striking image of Idar, Sparks used a light tint of the orange for the background and Idar's colleagues. Idar herself, along with her worktable and proof press in the foreground, are in solid chocolate brown, linking her alone with the tools of the press and making her stand out prominently, her male colleagues receding into the background. The captions, too, brought new challenges. Translating the captions accurately proved complicated and time-consuming, given the nuanced differences in Spanish from diverse geographic areas.

Nonetheless, the breadth of activism and both historical and social significance represented in the series was outstanding, and Helaine Victoria Press workers had high expectations for this set. Jocelyn designed one of the signature public relations packets for a large promotional mailing, this one printed on crisp white bags with orange and green type announcing the series in both English and Spanish. Recipients found a descriptive flyer inside the bag along with several examples of the cards. The mailing went to over 200 English and Spanish language newspapers, magazines, and associated organizations.[8] Surely, this series would be joyfully embraced, even more so because it was available in both Spanish and English. But that was not to be the case. For reasons that are still unclear, the sets did not sell well. Even the promotional mailing failed to gain traction for the series.

While Helaine Victoria Press workers were designing and producing the Latin American Women and US Latinas series, they continued to solicit and print single jumbo cards. The press published several new cards in 1986, one featuring the girls' basketball team at the National Training School for Women and Girls in approximately 1915. The basketball team card offered another example of one of the press's methodologies: locate a gripping image, then research the story behind that image. In this case, Edith Mayo at the Smithsonian Institution had directed them to the photo. Then, seeking someone with expertise in African American women's history, Jocelyn had asked Erlene Stetson, associate professor of English at IU, if she would be interested in researching the National Training School for Women and Girls; she enthusiastically agreed. Photographer Marcelina Martin offered an image for a card celebrating Yoshiko Hayakawa, practitioner of *yumi*, the Japanese art of archery; Martin then collaborated with Edith Millikan, a Helaine Victoria Press volunteer with a graduate education in art history, to write the caption. These two new cards were printed in the same run as the seven Latina cards since the press sheet was large enough to print all nine cards, plus a bookmark, in the margin.

From the beginning, Helaine Victoria had made a practice of printing bookmarks in what was an extra inch or two on the large offset sheets. They always featured a woman or women who was already well-known—or who they hoped would be well-known. The bookmarks, given away to generate free publicity, served to link the press's postcard communication medium with the more widespread feminist book publishing movement in the hands of women across the country. With the Latina set, they included a bookmark titled "Latina History & Culture" with pictures of five of the seven women featured in the series, plus short notations about each.

Other revised and new cards appeared this year. In another press run, the press produced a card with three photos of Elsa Gidlow, including one by Marcelina Martin, and a new printing of Dian Fossey with Digit, the mountain gorilla. The press's original card about Dian Fossey had been negotiated with both Fossey and

### 79. Yoshiko Hayakawa postcard.

Yoshiko Hayakawa, born in Tokyo in 1944, has practiced yumi, the Japanese art of archery, for eight years. Yumi requires self-discipline, unwavering concentration, and inspired grace. The practice of yumi entails eight steps, each of which evolves from the one before. Hitting the target begins with picking up one's equipment and is one continuous rhythm until the arrow has hit its mark. As important as hitting the target are the movements and thoughts that carry the arrow to its destination. "I practice without a target," Hayakawa says, "for the goal is perfection of the individual. What you create inside is the target, but more than the target."

80. Helaine Victoria Press women's history bookmarks over the years, a sampling.

the National Geographic Society. This time, the new printing had to be captioned to tell readers that Dian Fossey had been killed, most likely by poachers exacting revenge for her vigilant protection of the small remaining gorilla population.

Despite the disappointing sales numbers for the Latina series, Helaine Victoria Press's efforts to recenter women in the historical record and generate an active feminist memory were showing more results by now, as the breadth of publicity for the press expanded and grew more inclusive. While acknowledgments of Helaine Victoria Press in local and regional publications increased, established national periodicals also began to recognize the press's work. In one instance, Jocelyn was asked to provide the postcards that were used to illustrate the Organization of American Historians' special issue of *Magazine of History* on the Progressive Era.[9] In March of 1986, Roy Rosenzweig devoted part of his column "Newsnotes" in the Spring issue of *Labor History* to a description

### 81. Latina History & Culture bookmark

Front: Latina History & Culture: Rosario Castellanos (1925-1974) Mexican writer and feminist; Josefina Villafañe de Martinez-Alvarez, M.D. (b. 1890), Puerto Rican physician; Emma Tenayuca (b. 1916) Chicana labor leader; Dora María Téllez (b. 1956) Nicaraguan minister of health; Jovita Idar (1885-1946) Texas-Mexican journalist and feminist. The back provides information on how to receive a Helaine Victoria Press catalog.

You say I am mysterious.
Let me explain myself:
In a land of oranges
I am faithful to apples.   *Elsa Gidlow*

### 82. Elsa Gidlow postcard

Elsa Gidlow (1898–1986), "The Poet Warrior," was a poet-philosopher and lesbian-feminist pioneer known through her love poetry, essays and autobiography, the film "Word is Out" and Druid Heights, her Zen-inspired retreat among the California redwoods. Elsa's writings challenge class privilege, religious and political dogmas, and sexism while celebrating all varieties of love and beauty as diverse flowers in a garden of unity. She insisted that daily life was the canvas of true art: "We consider the artist a special sort of person. It is more likely that each of us is a special sort of artist." Elsa led the precarious life of a freelance journalist, often supporting relatives and friends. Born in Yorkshire, England, Elsa emigrated with her family to French Canada. Raised in privation, she was mainly self-educated. She published *On a Grey Thread*, the first North American book to celebrate lesbian love (1923), and later expanded it into the poetry classic *Sapphic Songs* (1982). Elsa became a leading figure in San Francisco's bohemian, then psychedelic, New Age and feminist circles. The '50s saw her unsuccessful prosecution by McCarthyites. *ELSA: I Come with My Songs* is the first full-life, explicitly lesbian autobiography yet published, "the chronicle of an irrepressible free thinker."

of Helaine Victoria's Women in the American Labor Movement series.[10] Likewise, the Southeast Women's Employment Coalition, operating out of Lexington, Kentucky, publicized the Women in the American Labor Movement set in a long article in *Generations*, illustrated with three of the cards. Drawing from the captions on the cards and explaining their meaning in the history of the labor movement, the article's author quoted Jocelyn, saying, "According to Cohen, the set 'demonstrates that organized labor struggles definitely improve the workplace and workers' opportunities—

including job equity for women—and that women have made vital contributions to that change.'" The writer grasped the significance of the multimodal postcard medium, as well: "Thousands of people across the country see and use the cards for correspondence and library displays and as educational aids and inspirational icons for their home and workplace walls."[11] Similarly, when N. J. Stanley of regional publication *Arts Insight* asked "Why postcards?", Jocelyn explained again, as she and Nancy had many times before: "Women's history has always been hidden [ . . . ]. Like with a notecard, you stick it in an envelope, and that's where it stays. Postcards offer more exposure: to the giver, to the receiver, and who knows how many others in between."[12]

On November 8, 1986, the press's efforts to reveal women's history were enhanced by the grand opening of the Helaine Victoria Press Women's History Shop at 411 E. 4th Street in Bloomington. The celebration, from 4:00 to 9:00 p.m., featured a new exhibit of images of women on postcards entitled "Spinsters, Suffragettes, and Secretaries: The Stereotypical Image of Women on Early Postcards, 1890–1940." Jocelyn suggested the historical exhibit in order to visually frame where women's place in the postcard world had been versus where women were now. Edith Millikan wrote a curator's exhibit-style commentary that accompanied the display of the cards.

The grand opening was followed the next month by a holiday shopping open house, announced in another of the press's charming flyers. The exhibit was still on display, and someone at the press had thoughtfully anticipated all the gift shopping problems that could be solved at the Helaine Victoria Press Women's History Shop:

> The winter holidays are fast approaching—Chanukah, Christmas, Kwanzaa, New Year's, Solstice—and Helaine Victoria Press can help you do your holiday shopping. Wondering what to give your feminist friends? What would please your non-feminist friends

83. Donna Fay Reeves with photographer Lori Sudderth at the Helaine Victoria Press Women's History Shop opening, November 8, 1986

Opening celebration of Helaine Victoria Press Women's History Shop in Bloomington, IN.

84. Herschel and Toba Cohen at the Helaine Victoria Press Women's History Shop opening, November 8, 1986

Toba and Herschel Cohen gave priceless support to the press throughout its nearly two decades, and they always enjoyed sharing in the event's activities.

and give them a little feminist boost, too? What to give kids that's educational, enjoyable, and nonsexist? Perhaps you need to express a warm thank you to someone who helped you this year? We think we can help![13]

The store was not unlike a compact version of the crafts tent at the Michigan Women's Music Festival (minus the heat, humidity, dust, insects, and other wildlife), with many artistic offerings: the beautiful silkscreen posters from Chicago Women's Graphic Collective; pottery and glass from a variety of women, usually traded or purchased at festivals; jewelry from Lizzie Brown, Miriam Danu, and others; notecards, including Christine Eber's black-and-white illustrations of famous women and Sudie Rakusin's full-color goddess paintings; cassette tapes of women musicians distributed by Ladyslipper, the largest women's music distribution company; and T-shirts, not only those produced by Helaine Victoria Press, but hand-painted ones by Clsuf. The store also stocked buttons with progressive messages produced by Donnely/Colt, and hundreds of feminist and lesbian buttons from Ferne, a one-woman operation out of New Jersey. The inventory varied. Vicki's selections not only helped support colleagues all over the country creating material culture within the women's movement, but they also linked Vicki and Helaine Victoria Press with other women artists and craftswomen.

Even with this wealth of women's craft and artistry, the highlight of the shop was still the exceptionally large display of women's history postcards. Offerings included special gift packets, such as a collection of cards on working women, plus a Rosie the Riveter T-shirt and a 9 to 5 button. Store staff would even make up special gift packets according to a customer's interests and financial capabilities. Possible themes included literary women, women artists, or women athletes, and packets could include postcards, notecards, buttons, and first day covers. And, for only $2.00, the store would ship your order anywhere in the United States.

With Helaine Victoria Press's new presence close to the university, Jocelyn revisited her plan to involve IU faculty in the process of producing cards. At the meeting held the previous year, many women had indicated ongoing interest in the press and a desire to participate in postcard production. Writing now in the spring of 1987 to those who had attended the earlier meeting, Jocelyn described the rationale for moving the press's headquarters to Bloomington and discreetly reminded them of the resulting increased expenses. After describing the new Latina series and the exhibit that had been mounted at the new store, as well as plans for other exhibits, Jocelyn explained her plan for the Helaine Victoria Press Publishing Advisory Board. It would only meet once a year, she promised, though board members would be expected, "through classroom and community work[,] to support the press's work and keep the name alive." In return, board members would receive, by way of compensation, "a listing of their names in our catalogs, acknowledgment on grant applications, complimentary copies of all new and revised HV postcards—and the satisfaction of helping to further HV's overall purpose of educating the public about women's vital contributions to society and culture."[14] Almost two dozen women responded, joining the 1987 Helaine Victoria Press Publishing Advisory Board.[15] Most were IU faculty members, representing a wide variety of disciplines, with commitments to feminist scholarship and social change. The advisory board joined the working committee and the board of directors as an integral part of the Helaine Victoria Press structure. It continued its work over the next two years, several members offering considerable scholarly assistance as well as participating in fundraising efforts for the perennially cash-strapped press.

Although Helaine Victoria Press had always marketed cards in series as well as singly—the Bread & Roses series, the Women & Ecology series, the Jewish Women series—now the series concept had developed in such a way that greater expertise would help create sets of cards that cohered more closely, each card commenting on, in a sense, or enhancing the others in the set. At this time, Helaine Victoria Press was planning, or in the process of producing, series including Women and Social Protest, and Sisters of the Harlem Renaissance. Beyond these, the press still hoped to issue sets on Women's Presses, Women's Brigades and Auxiliaries, Women in Sports, and Women's Personal Narratives. Several members of the publishing advisory board stepped up to work in more depth on the various series the press was intent on publishing.

While attempting to streamline the work of the press with organizational reforms, primary staff and volunteers continued to keep the press running. "This spring and summer we attended more women's conferences and festivals than ever before in order to make our work known to new audiences," they told customers in "Viewy News." Meanwhile, back in Bloomington, the shop was promoting other work by women. "We feel it is essential to network with other 'like minds' and hope to do our part in keeping feminism alive on many fronts," they contended.[16] To advertise its bimonthly open houses, Donna Fay Reeves made several eye-catching, witty flyers using images from press postcards to entice local women into the store. And, to top it off, the press sponsored a girls' softball team coached by Ed Gubar, Susan Gubar's husband, sending the nine-year-olds out onto the field dressed in the best feminist fashion: T-shirts emblazoned with "Helaine Victoria Press, Inc." and the press's trademark image of Columbia, above the logo for the Girls Club of Monroe County—all elegantly printed in black on a white background, set off by a maroon neckband.

Although the shop on 4th Street needed to sell enough postcards, buttons, bumper stickers, jewelry, and T-shirts to pay the rent—and preferably support all the press's activities—it was also a key part of Helaine Victoria Press's feminist memory generating project. Thus, as they had planned, staff and volunteers mounted another exhibit in the shop in February. Replacing the images of women on historic postcards, the new show was titled "Black Women: History—Empowerment, Struggle, & Achievements." To

85. Professor Audrey McCluskey reading at Black Women: History opening, 1987

Women's History Month celebration at the Helaine Victoria Press Women's History Shop. Professor Audrey McCluskey read works by Black women writers and Professor Erlene Stetson appeared as Sojourner Truth. This event kicked off the opening of "Black Women: History—Empowerment, Struggle, & Achievement" exhibit.

celebrate the opening of this new exhibit, Vicki held an open house and program on February 13, a Friday evening from 4–8:00 p.m., the first of several bimonthly open houses she arranged in order to attract and serve members of the local community. Audrey McCluskey, publishing advisory board member and IU professor of African American and African Diaspora Studies, read work by Black writers; then Erlene Stetson, IU professor of English, appeared, performing as Sojourner Truth.

Despite the ongoing requirements and challenges of the shop and office in Bloomington, Helaine Victoria's primary mission continued to be designing and printing postcards and broadsides. In addition to her contribution to the exhibit, Prof. Audrey McCluskey also worked with the press on an individual card this year. Although several series of cards were underway, it was critical that the press offer at least a few new single accessible, modifiable cards each year in order to continue enabling feminist communication. Audrey McCluskey suggested a card for Mary Fields, also known as "Stagecoach Mary," for her intrepid work delivering mail near Cascade, Montana in the late nineteenth and early twentieth centuries. Largely forgotten except perhaps in Montana local history, Fields reappeared first in a 1959 issue of *Ebony* magazine. Jocelyn located an image of Stagecoach Mary at the Wedsworth Memorial Library in Cascade, and Audrey wrote the caption honoring Mary Fields, documenting her extraordinary life.

When Jocelyn designed the back of the 1987–88 catalog, she placed the image of Mary Fields next to a copy of the back of the card, writing in the message space:

Dear Friends—
 One of our new women from history jumbo postcards—Stagecoach Mary. Imagine how wonderful it would be to have her deliver all your mail, but here she is. Bringing you our 1987-88 catalog![17]

Who could resist that?

### 86. Mary Fields postcard

Mary Fields (1832?–1914), known also as "Stagecoach Mary," was a Montana pioneer and the second woman stagecoach driver on a U.S. mail route. Proud, independent, over 6′ tall and handy with a shotgun, Fields was born a slave in Tennessee but escaped to Toledo, OH, where she became a general handywoman at an Ursuline convent. After her close friend Mother Amadeus and other nuns left to start a mission school for Native American girls near Cascade, MT, Fields soon followed, resuming her old job and becoming the nuns' protector. When one of the mission's hired hands crossed her, she fired bullets past his ears and sent him hightailing it across the plains. This and other colorful tales surrounded the legendary Fields. She also worked as a servant, nurse, restaurateur, and freight hauler. Fields held her postal job for eight years, becoming a fixture along the trail, driving two teams of horses, and smoking big cigars. She is remembered not only for her zestful life but also for her kindness and eagerness to help others.

Combining two of Helaine Victoria's aims—focusing attention on women's words and celebrating the unnamed women who work to make the material necessities of our lives—the other card published this year offered part of a narrative transcribed from Corine Lytle Cannon, one of the first African American women to be hired to do production work in the Cannon Mills in Kannapolis, North Carolina.[18] Jocelyn was struck by the quote, and found it inspiring. Indeed, it seemed to describe the progress of the press quite well. She designed a continental-size card, hand-set with the quote on the front using Munder Venezian and italic typefaces and a silvery purple ink color. Part of the quotation reads:

My mother was a brilliant person. She came second to nobody. She was the rock of the family . . . She would never, never give up.
   She would always say:
   *Well, it could be worse. Let's get over this hurdle because there's another one coming. With this next one let's jump a little bit higher.*

Jocelyn also composed the caption for the back of the card. The caption begins with words that could have been written about any number of the women who appeared on Helaine Victoria postcards: "Always outspoken and assertive, Cannon is a political leader in her community." The caption continues to paint concisely the essence of Cannon's life, a clear message to anyone who might have thought feminist change was going to be easy.

At the same time, aware of Helaine Victoria's upcoming fifteenth anniversary, Jocelyn began working on new publications to celebrate the occasion: a collection of handmade broadsides reflecting Helaine Victoria's ideals and letterpress craft. Although Nancy and Jocelyn had been producing a large body of artistic works printed on their letterpress including the postcards, many in their customer base seemed not to appreciate fully the extraordinary amount of art and craft that went into the designs. As Jocelyn began incorporating handmade paper into some of her work, she hoped this would help distinguish Helaine Victoria Press as both a feminist press and a fine letterpress shop—which was, after all, one of the goals she and Nancy had listed in their 501(c)3 incorporation papers. The broadsides represented a range of women's voices, from an unknown folk figure to a Jewish immigrant writer to a political rebel. For each print, Jocelyn made sixty sheets of paper, 9 x 12 inches. In a continuing effort to provide a less expensive edition available to a larger audience, she used machine-made cover stock paper for another 200 copies, adjusting the design as necessary. Integrating the typographical design into the handmade sheets of paper meant an edition on machine-made paper required some design changes. For instance, the initial cap on one broadside was embedded in the paper itself; thus, it would not appear on the machine-made paper edition, and a different initial cap would have to be substituted. Using the press's Munder typeface, Jocelyn printed the broadsides on the Chandler & Price press.

The first print, "If I Had My Life to Live Over," was attributed to one "Nadine Stair." Jocelyn wanted the paper to be frolicsome, for several reasons. First, "Nadine Stair," allegedly an eighty-five-year-old woman from Louisville, Kentucky, had become something of a folk legend after one version of the poem was attributed to her. Earlier and later versions exist in both English and Spanish and also appear as the lyrics to a song. As in much folklore, we don't really know the source of the poem. In fact, the poem may not even have been written by a woman.[19] Well, never mind; we like the sentiment. The poem reminds us to have some fun in this life, not to worry about so many little details, and to be a bit crazy.

For this print, Jocelyn made a very clean sheet of white paper made from abaca and burlap. The burlap gave a soft look to the paper but by itself would not have made a sufficiently durable sheet, so Jocelyn added abaca, which makes a very strong sheet of paper. Using another vat of pulp and mould, she dipped a large pink initial capital "I" instead of printing it, and another pink oval for the headline. She squeezed on thin layers of pulp for a border, both a purple one and a yellow one. Then, she pressed and dried the sheets. The title and attributed author were printed in green Munder caps within the pink oval, and the body of the poem in dark blue using both Munder Venezian and italic. Registering handmade sheets made in this manner on a press is rather tricky. In the papermaking process, the positioning of the wet paper initial cap had to be measured on each sheet of paper from the top edge down and the left edge in, as there are slight variations on the edges of handmade paper with a deckle. The type for the poem locked up in the chase did not shift with each impression, but the edge of the paper coming in contact with the registration pins could have been off by a fraction of an inch, which would have made it appear out of register and thus not properly aligned. Despite these difficulties, Jocelyn created the requisite number of copies. Of the three broadsides, "If I Had My Life to Live Over" was by far the most popular, especially the handmade version.

The second print was drawn from Anzia Yezierska's 1925 novel, *Bread Givers:* "For the first time in my life I saw what a luxury it was for a poor girl to want to be alone in a room[.]" Although a better-known author has written about the necessity of having a room of one's own, Jocelyn liked the heart that Yezierska brought to her words about finding a "private room, a bargain cheap." She thought about the words, "I must have this room with the shut door. I must make this woman rent it to me," wondering how to translate them to paper.

Knowing she wanted the elegance of the words to contrast with a dingy environment, Jocelyn made a smaller white sheet couched on top of a larger gray one, leaving a one-inch gray border around the white deckle sheet. The little white squares in the four corners were the openings of light. She wanted to emphasize the words "private room, a bargain cheap," both because she enjoyed the syntax and because these words offered such hope to the novel's main character. She set the body of the text in Munder Venezian with three large initial caps for each paragraph, then used an old,

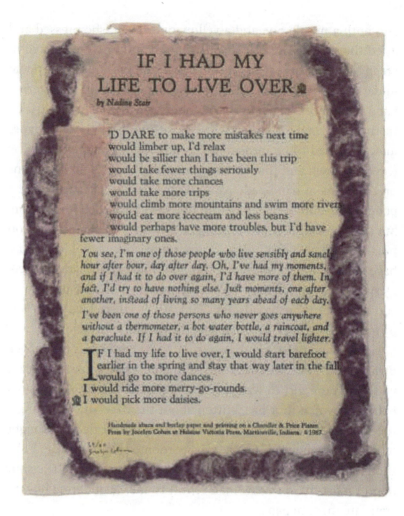

87. Nadine Stair, "If I Had My Life to Live Over" broadside
A lighthearted sentiment on equally frolicsome handmade paper. The reputed author reminds the reader of all the things worth doing in life ... climb more mountains, take more chances, relax, perhaps have more troubles but less imaginary ones ... a simple, wise and lively list of what she would do "If I Had My Life to Live Over."

nineteenth-century ornamental curlicue-type font for "private room, a bargain cheap." Jocelyn made the paper using two vats of pulp made from cotton rag, string, and jute, one for the white and the other for the gray. One mould was used to couche the gray sheet onto a felt, and another was used for the white sheet, which was registered and couched atop the gray. The four white squares in the corner were cut from a white sheet of wet paper and hand-placed in each corner; then, the entire sheet was pressed and dried.

The third print featured a quotation excoriating the practice of capital punishment taken from writing by Virginia Snow Stephen, a lapsed Mormon and University of Utah art faculty member during the early part of the twentieth century. She was also a Socialist Party activist who worked, unsuccessfully, to save the life of IWW organizer and songwriter, Joe Hill: "If it is evil to kill in the heat of passion, is it not a double evil to kill by a supine community consent called law?" Given the nature of Stephen's words, Jocelyn wanted a dramatic sheet. She chose to make black paper with a large red blotch. Because making a black sheet of paper without using pigments or dyes is quite difficult, she gathered as much cotton rag black clothing from friends as she could. She couched the black sheet onto the felt, then dipped the red abaca pulp from another vat on a mould that was masked off so only the pulp would stick to the one circular section. After registering and couching the red onto the black, she pressed and dried the sheet. The body of the text and the colophon were, as on the other broadsides, printed using the press's Munder type. She then tackled the process of letterpress printing white onto a black sheet. In order for the white to be opaque enough, she pulled two impressions of each sheet. A number of sheets were lost during this process because, if the second impression was off as much as a hair, the type looked slurred. She then changed to black ink and ran the sheets through again for the engraving of Justice, blindfolded with her scales, printed in black in the middle of the red blotch. Justice was one of many wonderful engravings Nancy and Jocelyn had collected from the Indianapolis printshops abandoning letterpress in favor of offset presses. With this print, Jocelyn had finally found the perfect place to use her.

After making the paper and printing the broadsides, Jocelyn was left with the task of making thirty folio covers to enclose the triplets—with every hope that a segment of the customer base would want to have all three of the beautiful handmade prints celebrating the fifteenth anniversary of the press. The folio was a large, 12" x 18" handmade sheet of mauve paper with a wraparound, two-inch wide strip for the spine. The cover read: "Helaine Victoria Press" above Columbia, enclosed by an ornamental leaf border. Below, "1973–1988" was followed by "In Celebration of 15 Years As a Feminist & Publisher." The colophon at the bottom gave "Special thanks to Joan Sterrenburg from Indiana University for opening up the world of papermaking to me, and to my friends and family who parted with clothing and snippets so I could make much of this paper. © 1987 Helaine Victoria Press, Martinsville, Indiana."

Helaine Victoria Press offered these three prints, in the folio, in the 1987-88 catalog with Mary Fields on the cover, pricing all three prints on handmade paper in the folio at $40. For those who did not want all three prints, each individual print on handmade paper was available for $15. Each print on machine-made paper sold for $5. "Because Helaine Victoria is one of the country's oldest feminist publishers and printers," Jocelyn announced in the catalog, "I decided to offer these three prints to begin our 15$^{th}$ year (three more prints to follow in spring '88). I felt it was a good time to draw attention to the fact that HV is not only a publisher but a small press as well. Since 1976, we've printed a large body of work we're very proud of on our 80-year-old Chandler & Price platen press."[20]

All involved with Helaine Victoria Press had every right to be proud. Against significant odds, they continued to upend conventional notions of art and place women at the center of history. Other fifteen-year offerings included a special Folio Collection with fifteen cards, one for each year, as well as bookplates, bookmarks, a first day cover, a print, and maybe a surprise or two. Collections varied and sold for $15. The press also offered Fifteenth Anniversary women's history celebration packs for $15. Customers could choose from four themes: Musicians who Stir the Soul & Calm the Heart, Issues of the 70s & 80s, An Explosion of Women's Power, and Women Writers & Their Visions. These packs contained an assortment of ephemera ranging from cards, prints, and posters to buttons and bumper stickers.

The cumulative effects of the 1980s' economic and political reversals, however, were becoming more and more apparent. Several women's presses—and there weren't that many to begin with—closed this year, including Iowa City Women's Press and San Francisco Women's Press. Book publishers, too, were struggling. Commercial publishers had determined that feminist and Lesbian topics offered possibilities for profit; however, the material they chose to publish was often moderated in various ways. Julie Enszer has pointed out that

> The first commercial publication of a lesbian poetry anthology is an anthology that deploys the identity of gay and lesbian, but not lesbian-feminist. *Gay & Lesbian Poetry in Our Time*, edited by Joan Larkin and Carl Morse and published by St. Martin's Press in 1987, crystallizes a new identity formation, gay and lesbian. *Gay & Lesbian Poetry in Our Time* expresses a co-gender identity formation and a denouement to the work and activities of lesbian-feminist publishing.[21]

Helaine Victoria Press, however, continued its ambitious publishing schedule, recruiting more women to research and write captions. The prints would be highlighted again in the 1988 Sale Catalog Supplement, printed on a 17" x 23" sheet and trifolded to 11.5" x 6", which would become a regular spring edition—or, tradition—along with a larger tabloid catalog produced the same year. Work had begun on the Women and Social Protest series even before the Latina series was completed. While she made paper and printed the broadsides for the fifteen-year folio, Jocelyn also collaborated with longtime press supporters and members of the publishing advisory board, Jean Robinson and Ellen Dwyer, both IU faculty with affiliations in Women's Studies, to produce the Social Protest cards, which would appear in September of 1989.

When she established the publishing advisory board in the spring of 1987, Jocelyn was envisioning just this sort of collaboration. Collaboration, after all, had been a core value of Helaine Victoria Press from the beginning. Ivan Illich's book *Tools for Conviviality* was published in 1973, the same year Nancy and Jocelyn established Helaine Victoria Press. Illich insisted that taking control over the tools and processes of production that shaped their lives would enable people to live in more meaningful ways.[22] Although collaborative relationships were not always easy to maintain within a dominant culture that promoted competition, especially between women, Helaine Victoria Press made every effort to celebrate and build new forms of personal and working relationships. Working together, Jean, Ellen, and Jocelyn conversed in-depth about what types of images should make up the series, what concepts should drive the content, and how many cards could be published, given time and money constraints. As Jean said later in an interview with Jocelyn,

> [W]orking together with others I have found really to be a wonderful experience [ . . . ] Helaine Victoria was my first time to do that, actually. As an academic, when you write [ . . . ], then you send it off to some journal or some press, and people you don't know decide whether it's going to be published or not. And then they decide whether they're going to emphasize it on their front page or the cover of the journal. And they make the decision about what it's going to look like in the end. At that time, probably, I didn't know as much as I now know about the way they change what you write.
>
> At Helaine Victoria Press, what you could do, what I could do, is work with you, and we could agree on what something was going to look like and what exactly, what words were going to be included [ . . . ]. It was being part of a whole process and working with you and others to make it happen.[23]

Jean and Ellen knew who in the field of women's studies was engaged in research in a specific area and could be called upon to

88. WWI Rivet-gang Workers postcard
WWI Rivet-gang Workers, Navy Shipyards. Higher wages beckoned working women into war-related industries. Women who worked in WWI trades rarely found skilled positions open to them when they left traditionally female jobs for higher paying traditionally male occupations like shipbuilding. Pictured are laborers from 4 or 5 riveting gangs. The four women at the left were "heaters." They plucked hot rivets from a portable furnace with tongs and threw them to the "passers," who caught them in small buckets and then inserted them into holes to be driven. Because of segregation on the job, the two Black women probably worked with Black men. Black laborers were the mainstay of the shipyard, but their wages were less than those of whites. Their work was often more dangerous and strenuous. Although the sexes did work together, the women experienced harassment and discrimination. Women's work during WWI never received support from unions or the government. Once the war ended most women returned to traditional female jobs.

write a particular caption, perhaps even contribute or locate a photograph. Altogether, nineteen different authors wrote captions for the twenty-two-card series. Some of the researchers were able to assist with photos; other images were provided by photographers working within the women's movement; still others were photographs Jocelyn and Nancy had collected on their archive trips. For Jocelyn, working with Jean and Ellen rekindled the kind of excitement about publishing and all the associated aspects involved in decision-making she had shared with Nancy.

While working on long-term projects, the press also brought

out two new individual cards in 1988, the WWI Rivet-gang Workers and Rosa Parks. Deborah Hoskins, an IU PhD student in history, wrote the caption for the rivet-gang workers card. Erlene Stetson, IU English faculty, wrote the caption for Rosa Parks. Both cards articulated the particular strengths displayed by Black women in the conditions they were required to negotiate.

Deborah Hoskins' caption for the rivet-gang workers card provides a clear example of this effort. To begin with, the photograph shows a group of unnamed young women, clearly dressed for work in the shipyard. After describing the work these women did, Hoskins pointed out the two African American women in the photo, explaining that because the workplace was segregated, they would not have been working with the white women in the picture but rather with African American men, and their jobs would have been more dangerous and more difficult. In contrast to this narrative of discrimination, the press published a card depicting Rosa Parks with Erlene Stetson's description of Parks's noncompliance with segregation on the buses in Montgomery, Alabama, a refusal, occurring some thirty-seven years after the photo of the rivet-gang workers was taken, that led to the 381-day Montgomery bus boycott and, ultimately, to a Supreme Court decision striking down segregation in public transportation.

Helaine Victoria Press had long ago mastered the arts of creating engaging press releases, anticipating some would lead to articles in newspapers—a.k.a. free publicity. Sometimes, publicity came about because publications used images from the cards as illustrations and provided the press's contact information in the credits. Such was the case when *Liberal Education,* published by the Association of American Colleges, illustrated an article entitled "Women's Studies: The Idea and the Ideas" by well-known feminist scholar Catherine Stimpson with an image from a Helaine Victoria card. At least a third of a page of the article, appearing in the September/October 1987 issue, was given over to the Trackwomen on the Baltimore & Ohio Railroad card, a cause for celebration at Helaine Victoria headquarters.[24]

*Practicing Anti-Racism,* another periodical with perhaps not quite the circulation of *Liberal Education,* listed Helaine Victoria Press under a subheading of "More Resources." The press, the article announced, has "[h]istorical and present-day postcards of women. [ . . . ] A dearth of Asian and Middle Eastern women," the editors added, "but they're undoubtedly working on it."[25] That was an optimistic assessment, but it also illustrates another aspect of the women's movement in the 1980s: because feminist organizations were, by definition, committed to creating social change, expectations were often unrealistically high. As a result, sometimes it became easier for people to criticize feminist groups for what they were *not* doing rather than supporting them in what they *were* doing.

Refreshingly, Carol Anne Douglas's column "Chicken Lady" in *off our backs* focused on Helaine Victoria's achievements, publicizing the Latina series in the April 1987 issue and listing each card and identifying the women pictured.[26] Likewise, Terry McCormick, editor and publisher of the *Vintage Clothing Newsletter,* gave Helaine Victoria Press a friendly acknowledgement, providing the press's address and saying that she "first encountered them when Nicole Hollander [feminist cartoonist, author of the 'Sylvia' series and longtime fan of the press] sent me one of their post cards that featured women in 1940s garb. I liked it so much I wrote to them and have been receiving their catalog ever since. Free catalog."[27] Staff members knew, however, that free publicity would not be sufficient, and they realized the importance of supporting other feminist publications, so they purchased ads in a variety of publications, ranging from *Spokewoman* to *Ms.* to *Lesbian Connection.*

With the welcome expansion of Women's History Week to Women's History Month in 1987, Helaine Victoria Press joined with other Bloomington organizations to celebrate. The Bloomington Commission on the Status of Women issued a lengthy and detailed list of activities, using Helaine Victoria cards as illustrations.[28] In the Helaine Victoria Press Women's History Shop, staff and volunteers organized an open house featuring a masquerade party. Attendees were encouraged to dress as their favorite "heroine from herstory," and on the evening of Friday, March 13, the shop filled with creatively costumed, festive partygoers. The flyer for the event, another Donna Fay creation, however, spelled out the reality behind the revelry. Headlined "Support Your Local Women's Press," it was illustrated with five items of clothing pinned on a line, reading, one after another: "Lots of Debts," "Increased Rent," "Payroll," "Big Ideas," and "Printing Costs."[29]

As noted before, the fundamental organization of Helaine Victoria Press had shifted from two women, both of whom shared the vision of the press in its entirety, to a larger organization taking in volunteers and part-time workers, each occupying a specific niche in the organization and each bringing a unique set of expectations. Even so, a core of committed women always existed, even if that core shifted. There also were women who had more-or-less involvement with the press on a day-to-day level but who were crucial in terms of ongoing support. With the added stressors of financial insecurity, however, disagreements began to fester, ultimately resulting in several staff members and volunteers leaving the press in late 1987.

Nonetheless, because many in the Bloomington community understood the significance of Helaine Victoria Press's unique contributions to the process of developing a participatory feminist memory, more volunteers, interns, and work-study students stepped up to add their support. The small army of recruits managed to get things done, although the paths of volunteers and staff often didn't cross. Most people worked one or two days a week, or a month; many worked from home. Yet their efforts made possible the publishing of new cards and new series. Sandra Runzo, for example, who had joined the English department faculty at Denison University in Granville, Ohio, helped to edit the captions

89. Jocelyn Cohen at the National Women's Music Festival in Bloomington, Indiana, 1986

The Helaine Victoria Press booth at the National Women's Music Festival. Behind and to the right of Jocelyn Cohen is Julie Zolot from Chicago Women's Graphics. At this time, the press had purchased the balance of inventory of posters from Chicago Women's Graphics to sell in the Helaine Victoria Press Women's History Shop. Assisting with sales behind the table is Linda Greene, another dedicated Helaine Victoria volunteer.

for nine cards from her new home, updating the language for style and accuracy.[30] Sandra and Jocelyn were close friends, and Jocelyn often discussed the politics and ongoing challenges of running the press with Sandy over pizza and beer—meeting halfway between Bloomington and the country at Morgan Monroe State Forest for quiet friendship and business gatherings.

Summer festivals and conferences also offered workers and volunteers opportunities to spend time together, staffing the Helaine Victoria Press booths. The National Women's Music Festival was conveniently located in Bloomington at that time—and, like the academic conferences, it was held indoors, eliminating the complications from weather so often found at outdoor festivals.

The outdoor festivals, though, specifically the Michigan Women's Music Festival and the Southern Women's Music & Comedy Festival, provided the twin senses of joy and liberation found

STOREFRONT IN BLOOMINGTON

nowhere else. Women shed restrictive clothing, soaking up the sun's warmth and laughing at the occasional incursion from nature. That summer, in 1987, Vicki and Bernice attended the Southern Women's Music & Comedy Festival in Georgia while Donna Fay and Jocelyn went to Michigan, where, Donna Fay recalled,

> I was working the HVP booth at Michigan one year wearing nothing but an apron when suddenly a field mouse ran across the ground in our space. Much screaming and running broke out from the nearby women, but I kept my cool. I pronounced that since I was wearing no pants, I did not think a mouse would run up my leg because there was no place to hide. No sooner had I said it than a mouse ran up my bare leg! I out-screamed and out-jumped the whole bunch of women I was talking to who were howling with laughter by this point![31]

In addition to worlds filled with laughter, the festivals offered the press one of the best opportunities to refill its coffers, although even the festivals couldn't provide enough sales to keep the press going strong.

Aware of Helaine Victoria's financial pressures, Sona Chambers, an energetic and optimistic woman committed to the visionary work of Helaine Victoria Press, proposed a plan to give the press a significant capital infusion. Although Chambers had not read Jocelyn and Nancy's article in *Sister* which asked whether women's businesses could succeed, she nonetheless clearly believed they could, and, as Jocelyn and Nancy had argued, it would be through women supporting other women.

Acquiring the Bloomington Unitarian Universalist church as a site for a gala evening event, she arranged for framed art—most by women artists—to be auctioned by New York City's Marlin Art, Inc. The work included lithographs, watercolors, and oils.[32] The event, celebrating Helaine Victoria's fifteenth year, also featured Erlene Stetson performing her one-woman show as Sojourner Truth, as well as the film *One Fine Day*, a six-minute film by Kay Weaver and Martha Wheelock made for Geraldine Ferraro's campaign as the first woman to be nominated to run for vice president by a major American political party.

> Kay Weaver's classic celebration of the American Woman from the 1800's to the present. Set to a rousing anthem written and sung by Kay Weaver, this fast-paced music-film uses over 100 scenes, beginning with black-and-white stills of Sojourner Truth, Emily Dickinson, and Harriet Tubman, which dissolves into live action suffrage parades that march us into present-day footage of Gloria Steinem, Shirley Chisholm, and Geraldine Ferraro.

According to the distributor's website, the film is "[g]uaranteed to lift your heart and bring you to your feet."[33] And, Chambers and other organizers fervently hoped, guaranteed to bring generous bids for the art auction. Sona Chambers threw herself into organizing the event, which raised enough money that Jocelyn was able to report in the next catalog that "[t]he Press feels more secure than ever before."[34]

However, the extraordinary efforts required to produce Helaine Victoria's cards—and the constant pressure to accomplish more—were beginning to tell on Vicki. She was studying for her bachelor's degree in folklore, was on the steering committee of the Indiana University Women's Studies program, was serving on the board of directors of the National Women's Music Festival, was the assistant director of Helaine Victoria Press, and was running a small business—the part of the Helaine Victoria Press Women's History Shop that marketed "material culture that affirms many women's identity."[35] By 1988, though, as Julie Enszer has pointed out, "[i]dentity categories were changing." Although many feminist bookstores were still open, most small feminist publishers had since closed. Increasingly, these bookstores began offering materials not so much for women as a group, but for lesbians and gay men.[36] The solidarity that any movement requires was not just mutating, but dissolving. While scholarship on topics related to women continued to be produced and books continued to be written, the societal changes were unmistakable.

In time, the comfortable liaison between Jocelyn and Vicki began to disintegrate as well, as the differences in experience, time, and life stages developed into rifts. What's more, the high enthusiasm and revolutionary zeal of the 1970s had been blunted by numerous social and economic forces for several years now, and people were simply not walking through the doors of the Helaine Victoria Press Women's History Shop in the necessary numbers. By the middle of 1988, Vicki had liquidated her part of the Helaine Victoria Press Women's History Shop and had left her position with the press, moving on to jobs that were less all-consuming. With superb organization skills, a gregarious nature, and a trained sense for social movements, Vicki had done exceptional work for the press and had enabled it to change and develop along with the cultural shifts taking place at the time. Her departure created both personal and work hardships, but Jocelyn and the organization moved on, with the publication of the Women in Social Protest series nearing completion.

Despite the deepening changes, the press still had a significant base of loyal fans, extending beyond the borders of the United States to include Canada, England, France, Germany, Italy, Japan, Mexico, New Zealand, Sweden, and Switzerland.[37] M. J. C. van Ryn from Tepoztlan, Mexico included a letter to the press with her order, praising the most recent catalog: "Your '88 catalogue is impressive. Such wealth of education in the form of postcards. Thank you for the wonderful work you are doing, giving visibility to womyn and womyn's art in such accessible form as postcards."[38] An equally touching letter came from Quincy Blackburn of Celebration! in Austin, Texas, thanking the press for allowing her to take Helaine Victoria cards to the 1988 Women in the Law conference. Although attendance was down at the conference, she said, the cards still sold fairly well. Dolores Huerta, she explained, was the keynote speaker, and Emma Tenayuca was present as well; nonetheless, the labor movement cards didn't sell as well as Blackburn had expected. However, there was a moment at the conference that seemed to make up for all the disappointments:

> There was an older Latina woman who kept coming back to look at the cards. She had a cane and it was obviously difficult for her to stand long to look at the cards. I gave her a chair and told her that she was welcome to look as long as she liked.
>
> About an hour later I noticed that she had tears in her eyes and was counting out change. When I went over to her, she told me that these may be just cards to us, but to her they were real memories.
>
> She went through the cards telling me whom she had worked with in various labor organizations, who had married, what their children, etc., were doing now. She wanted the cards to show her nephews and other family members that these were real & important people—that they were remembered.
>
> Her Social Security check had not come in time. The $26.00 honorarium check from the conference hadn't reached her. She had only the 3 or 4 dollars in change with her. She could not afford all the cards she wanted.
>
> I told her to take what she could afford—pick out what she wanted & that I would mail her the rest when she wanted. [That I should complain about burn-out—when this woman had been organizing since the 1920s!]
>
> Later that evening I was telling a Black woman attorney from New York how touched I had been by that episode. She volunteered to pay for the balance of the cards.[39]

Of course, for all the occasions the press found the best image and created the best design with the most appropriate colors, drawing participants into the project of generating feminist memory, occasionally a card slipped through with an inadvertent error.

In late 1988, a fellow from Rhode Island who had ordered 1,000 of the Two Irish Women cards to send to Ireland wrote to the press to point out what a bad idea it had been to reprint the four-leaf clovers from the original green on that card in *orange*.[40] Apparently no one at the press had had sufficient historical awareness, in that case, to understand the significance of their unfortunate color choice. From the documentation available, it seems likely that, after some negotiating, Helaine Victoria reprinted the offending cards for the customer.[41]

Minor disturbances aside, the press published two new jumbo cards this year: Queen Lili'uokalani and the Women's Land Army. Using a photograph from the Hawai'i State Archives, Karen Marie Frane, a longtime admirer of the press and volunteer, researched and wrote the caption for a card celebrating Hawai'i's last reigning monarch, Queen Lili'uokalani, a card long-planned by the press. Karen had a personal interest in the queen, as she herself was of Hawaiian descent; she passionately wanted to increase the public awareness of the truth of the overthrow of the Hawaiian government and its queen by the United States. Deborah Hoskins again volunteered to write a caption, this time for a photograph of the Women's Land Army, also called the "farmerettes," women who moved into agricultural work to fill the gaps left by men drafted into the military during World War I.

These two stellar new cards notwithstanding, Helaine Victoria Press's major accomplishment during 1989 was the completion and release of the Women in Social Protest: The US Since 1915 series. Having been awarded an Honors Division Undergraduate Non-Teaching Internship Award to work with the press during the spring semester of 1989, Laura Sparks designed the series.[42] The twenty-two cards were enclosed in a folder with a spine and ISBN, to facilitate bookstore sales and library acquisitions.[43] The editors, Jocelyn, Jean Robinson, and Ellen Dwyer, had sought contributions of photos and captions from a wide range of archives, scholars, and activists. In the press's continuing effort to enable all women to

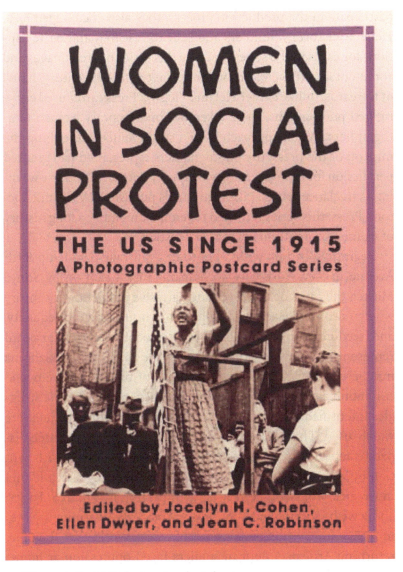

90. Women in Social Protest postcard set, front cover
Women in Social Protest Postcard: The US Since 1915, a Photographic Postcard Series.

participate in the production process, they also encouraged local Helaine Victoria volunteers and staff to research and write captions for cards in the series. Because this series offered images and commentary on events throughout the twentieth century, many of the cards, unlike earlier Helaine Victoria Press cards, used copyrighted photographs, some taken by contemporary women photographers. When approached by a staff member describing the mission of the press, the photographers represented had granted permission for reproduction, with appropriate fees for those working as freelance artists. Like many cards published by Helaine Victoria Press, this series returned to feminist memory a long history of women's commitments to social justice.

Beginning in 1915 with a photo of a suffrage parade up Fifth Avenue in New York City accompanied by a caption by Sonya Michel, the cards deliver a searing narrative of twentieth-century women's collective activism on behalf of human dignity, equality, and freedom from oppression. Jocelyn wrote the caption for a card representing the 1920s, documenting the 1921 Tulsa, Oklahoma massacre of African American residents of the Deep Greenwood community and destruction of their homes and businesses. Struggles intensified during the 1930s, and photography became more widely used. This meant the series was able to include three disparate actions: 1933 striking California cotton pickers, with caption by volunteer Jodi L. Hanna; women picketing a textile mill in Greensboro, Georgia in 1934, with caption by Philip S. Foner; and Jewish working women in New York City "learning to vote" in 1936, with caption by Jocelyn Cohen. As World War II ended, returning African American soldiers faced oppression at home, and the anti-lynching campaign intensified. The series included a card documenting a September 1946 anti-lynching protest held by African American women in front of the White House, captioned by Jocelyn Cohen and Ellen Dwyer. The next card, also captioned by Ellen Dwyer, recorded another response on the part of women to the ongoing oppression, showing an African American woman speaking in 1950 to a street crowd after the unprovoked police killing of a man in Harlem.

As resistance to legalized inequality as well as worries over increased militarism grew during the civil rights movement of the 1960s, women were major participants in protests. Five cards recorded some of the actions:

1. Adele Morrison, an English, film, and women's studies major at Indiana University, wrote the caption for a card showing women from the Jamaica, Queens chapter of the NAACP picketing Woolworth's in 1960 in support of the sit-in movement in the South.
2. Amy Swerdlow, scholar and peace activist, provided the caption for a card recording Women Strike for Peace members in 1962 trying to enter the Camp Mercury, Nevada nuclear test site.
3. Julia Kirk Blackwelder, history scholar, wrote the caption for a card of women sit-in demonstrators imprisoned in Greensboro, North Carolina in 1964.
4. Jenny Robertson, Helaine Victoria work-study student majoring in education, wrote the caption for "Jim Crow Can't Teach," a card detailing a 1964 New York City school boycott against separate and unequal education, photographed by Builder Levy.
5. Linking the civil rights and anti-war movements, Barbara Eisinger captioned a card documenting women participating in an anti-war demonstration, also photographed by Builder Levy, in the late 1960s.

The women's movement of the late 1960s and 1970s drew more women out of their homes and workplaces and into action for change. Additional captions included:

**91. Chinese American Garment Workers Strike**

The garment industry in the United States has long exploited women workers, including Chinese immigrant women who entered the trade in the 1920s. Their lack of English and other marketable job skills, combined with the pressures of low family income and the lack of childcare services, left many Chinese women no choice but to work long hours for piece-rate wages in Chinatown sweatshops, taking their children to work with them. A number of times they have organized to protest intolerable working conditions. In 1974, 128 Chinese garment workers at the Great Chinese American (Jung Sai) Company went on strike against Esprit de Corp to protest unsanitary working conditions and interference with unionization activities. Esprit responded by closing the plant. The workers, with the help of the International Ladies Garment Workers Union, persisted in fighting Esprit in the courts until they finally won a favorable settlement almost 10 years later in 1983.

1. Judy Yung, scholar specializing in Asian American and women's history, wrote two captions, one for a card with a photograph by Cathy Cade illustrating the 1974 strike of Chinese garment workers in San Francisco, and one for a card showing a photograph by Connie Hwang of a 1973 demonstration of Chinese-American women in support of maintaining childcare funding.
2. Brad Howard, IU doctoral student in anthropology and law, explained "The Longest Walk" in a caption for a card showing two women participants, photographed by JEB (Joan E. Biren), in the 1978 Native American walk

92. Disability Rights, Sharon Kowalski, Lesbian and Gay March postcard

In 1983 Sharon Kowalski suffered severe brain damage from a car accident. Karen Thompson, Sharon's lover for four years before the accident, was denied visitation rights by Kowalski's father when he was awarded legal guardianship in July 1985. Claiming that Sharon was incapable of making decisions, he placed her in a nursing home, where her condition deteriorated. Sharon's plight has been the catalyst for court action and demonstrations seeking to strengthen the rights of Lesbian, gay and disabled persons in relationships; to protect them from guardianship abuse; and to ensure that disabled people are allowed to speak for themselves. In February 1989 Sharon and Karen started visiting again; Sharon's father asked to resign as guardian; and in June 1989, Sharon moved to a rehabilitation center where she is now allowed to participate in making decisions about her life.

across the country, a demonstration for unity, peace, and liberation.

3. Doris-Jean Burton, political science scholar, tackled the difficult task of explaining the anti-pornography movement of the late 1970s in a caption for a card illustrating an anti-pornography demonstration, photographed by Bettye Lane.

4. Sandra Runzo, Denison University faculty member and Helaine Victoria Press volunteer, provided the caption for a card illustrating the Amazons Against Nukes activists also photographed by Bettye Lane, who joined others to create

a human chain around the New York Stock Exchange in 1979 to protest investments in the nuclear industry.

Conditions in the 1980s spurred more women to challenge social inequities.

1. Donna Fay Reeves, Helaine Victoria staff member, wrote the caption for a photo taken by JEB (Joan E. Biren) of women demonstrating for lesbian rights in 1987, long before marriage or domestic partnerships were available; in this instance, the issue was the right of a woman, Karen Thompson, to care for her injured partner, Sharon Kowalski.
2. Novelist and nonfiction writer Barbara Kingsolver, author of *Holding the Line,* contributed the caption and assisted with the photograph for a card featuring women picketing during the 1983 Phelps Dodge Copper strike in Arizona, photographed by Ron Chaff.
3. Karlyn Crowley, Women's Studies intern with Helaine Victoria Press, wrote the caption for the 1987 Lesbian and Gay March on Washington, photographed by JEB (Joan E. Biren).
4. Folklorist Jan Laude provided the caption for a card with a photograph by Patsy Lynch showing women students at Gallaudet University demonstrating in favor of hiring a deaf president. This last card drew a correction from a customer who pointed out to the press that rather than chanting "2-4-6-8, we want a deaf president now!" as the caption claimed, the students were actually signing the number four, which enumerated their demands, an unfortunate error.

With an eye to the future, Helaine Victoria Press included another card on the Social Protest press run, this one intended to

93. Dine (Navajo) Women, The Longest Walk postcard

These Dine (Navajo) women resting in Malcolm X Park at the end of The Longest Walk of 1978 are two of the hundreds of American Indian people who walked across Turtle Island (North America) from California's Alcatraz Island, symbol of the current American Indian spirit of liberation and site of its emergence, to Washington, D.C. They marched together to symbolize the unity of American Indian peoples in the fifth generation, when the Sacred Hoop comes together again as prophesied by Black Elk. Indian representatives met with government officials to demand the protection of human rights and the preservation of existing treaty relations between the United States and the Indian Nations. The Longest Walk had spiritual as well as political goals. At its end, the Dine, Lakota, and Haudenosaunee (Iroquois) nations called upon "all the peoples of the world to join us in seeking peace, and in seeking to ensure survival and justice for all indigenous peoples, for all the Earth's creatures and for all nations of the Earth."

draw attention to the plan to publish an International Social Protest series. Jean Robinson, series editor and professor of political science, contributed the caption for a card with a photograph by Catherine Allport of women pallbearers carrying the coffin of Victoria Mxenge, a South African anti-apartheid activist and lawyer who was murdered in 1985. Although the image was emotionally arresting and intensely thought-provoking, Helaine Victoria Press workers failed to consider the viability of this image as a postcard, a medium of communication; it did not sell well. That said, the image choice had nothing to do with the reasons the International Social Protest series was never completed. Larger forces were at work.

Pushing back against these forces, Helaine Victoria Press published the 17" x 22" folding Spring 1989 Sale Catalog, a truly collective affair produced by Jocelyn, Sandra Runzo, and Laura Sparks, with copywriting by Georg'ann Cattelona, Jocelyn Cohen, Donna Fay Reeves, Sandra Runzo, and Bernice Schipp and design by Laura Sparks. They ran a "Sneak Preview" on the back cover, picturing five postcards for customers to look forward to in the summer, including A'Lelia Walker (who would later be part of the Harlem Renaissance series), three cards that would be in the Social Protest Series, and a photo for a card of Bessie Coleman, the first African American woman aviator.[44]

Three editorials on the order form page reiterated the themes common to many Helaine Victoria Press catalogs: "Viewy News" by Jocelyn offered readers a close-up view of the people and current projects at the press; Georg'ann reminded those readers of the press's continuing financial struggles in a "$20,000 Goal for Publishing Costs" fundraiser request; and the "Sneak Preview Opportunity" announced an ambitious publishing schedule with several new series of postcards promised, including those also previewed on the catalog's back cover. Beyond "Women in Social Protest," the list drew readers' attention to more future sets: "Sisters of the Harlem Renaissance," "Sports and Adventure," "Personal Narratives and Oral Histories," and, depending upon the receipt of a pending grant, "In Our Own Way: A Celebration of Lesbian History and Culture."

In "Viewy News," Jocelyn wrote about the centrality of women's history to our emotional and intellectual lives, and, with more prescience than she realized at the time, about the fragility of life and the evanescence of women's accomplishments, noting that four of the women that Helaine Victoria Press had honored on postcards had died since their publication. She concluded, saying: "Combining our written and oral histories—of both 'exceptional' and 'ordinary' woman—weaves a story that not only deserves recognition, but also can be the key to our future, an opening to our dreams, an affirmation of our own experience, and a context in which we can view the reality of women's lives."[45]

Before the Social Protest set was released, the press had already begun working on the next series, Sisters of the Harlem Renaissance, which Sona Chambers had volunteered to coordinate. Jocelyn, meanwhile, was contemplating the needs of the press and her part therein. Bloomington's art and culture magazine, *The Ryder*, celebrated the press's work with an article pointing not only to the press's accomplishments, but also to the continuing need for the press's interventions in social consciousness:

> The Women in Social Protest series covers, among other things, women in the Black civil rights movement. Pictures include women picketing Woolworth's in the 1950s carrying signs that read "Apartheid exists in America, too." "It is startling how recent these events were," says Ms. Cohen. "To see women picketing the White House against lynching in the 1940s really makes you reflect and think about where we are today [ . . . ]."
>
> "I'm struck by how much mainstream history dictates what we know about someone, what's appropriate to know and what's hidden," she says. "The most hidden thing about women is Lesbianism. If all the wonderful, famous Lesbians were out, it could really make a difference. You can't even bring it up because people want to deny it." She cited the controversy that arose over Eleanor Roosevelt's relationships with women[.]
>
> "We've been at this sixteen years now, making an effort to uncover kinds of women's history that will get lost. I keep hoping that someone is going to jump on this and realize how essential it is. I still feel women's history isn't being valued, even by those of us who have the consciousness to understand."[46]

A month later, during National Women's History Month, the Bloomington Commission on the Status of Women and the Network of Career Women did articulate the value of women's history, recognizing the contributions of the press and of Jocelyn, in particular, to women's empowerment both locally and nationally.

In a letter of nomination, Helaine Victoria Press volunteer Karen Marie Frane wrote that "Helaine Victoria Press serves as an educational introduction of women's history to many young girls. It provides a vehicle to uncover and reclaim the contributions made by women."[47] Speaking in response to the recognition, Jocelyn emphasized two key elements that had driven the press's work over the years: the significance of recentering women in the historical record and the importance of challenging the cultural limits on women's relationships with each other.

> I see aspects [of women's lives] that are often central to our identity, values, politics, and motivation, minimized, obscured, and even denied because history and society do not at the moment feel comfortable with our being women. Couple that with being differently abled, poor, single mothers, Lesbians, incest survivors, Latinas, Jews, Asian or African American and our history is often retrievable only with persistence and tenacity.

Acknowledging and thanking all the women "who had helped fulfill the visions of the press in the past" and especially several of the press's workers and volunteers who were present at the March 7 event, she continued:

> All of us at the press work not only on our goal to research, publish, and distribute cards on women's history, but also I believe we recognize the importance we hold for each other in our working relationships [ . . . ]. The thrill of sharing skills and finding out about each other's abilities is never ending. The harmony of our working relationships is not taken for granted.[48]

At some point, after she finished working on the Spring folding 17" x 22" 1989 Sale Catalog, Bernice Schipp, loyal volunteer for more than seven years, decided she had done all she could for the press. In a heartfelt letter, Jocelyn thanked her "both personally and on behalf of the whole press for all the work, ideas, energy, and creativity you have given to the press over the years. You instigated programs which have become crucial to our operating and have helped make HV the success that it is." She went on, saying, "It's really difficult to put into words how much you have shared with the Press, the number of times you bailed me out and were there with emotional and financial support. Thank you for everything, Bernice."[49]

By the time the Social Protest series was released in September of 1989, Jocelyn was no longer in Bloomington to enjoy the celebration. She had informed the board of directors, staff, and volunteers earlier that year that she would be taking a five-month leave of absence in the fall to pursue graduate study in graphic design. With more advanced skills, she envisioned, she could create even more engaging cards, broadsides, and posters, energizing the press's work and increasing sales. Asked to assume the role of interim director, Donna Fay Reeves, perhaps sensing the enormity of the task, declined. Recent Indiana University graduate Lydia Bagwell then took on the role.

Jocelyn moved to San Francisco, where she enrolled in the graduate graphic design program at the Academy of Art College[50] and where longtime Helaine Victoria Press volunteer Anne Wilson offered to let her move in to her spare bedroom for the five-month period. Shortly after Jocelyn left, the landlord for the 4th Street space raised the rent, a bill that was already consuming too much of the press's budget. Donna, working with Toba Cohen, located a smaller space for the press's office in Bloomington, reducing the monthly rent from over $600 to $260.

When Jocelyn left for a semester at the Academy of Art College, the notion of closing the press was not part of her plan. Indeed, with a formal graphic arts education, she thought, she could enhance Helaine Victoria Press's offerings to compete with the commercial presses. Within a few weeks of her arrival in San Francisco, however, as the weight of the press's obligations lifted from her shoulders and the exciting new directions in graphic design became clear, Jocelyn began to question whether she could return to Indiana to continue directing Helaine Victoria Press.[51]

Despite great enthusiasm, visionary projects, the specialized expertise of many women who gave their time, contributions from outside consultants, and, not the least, the efforts of Jocelyn's family, larger forces were proving insurmountable. The press's financial condition aside, communication itself was undergoing a fundamental change as the internet shortened times of message transmission to fractions of a second and promised a future of unlimited images as well.

Helaine Victoria Press would continue operating in a limited fashion for another year and a half, sending out catalogs, filling orders, and working toward the publication of the Sisters of the Harlem Renaissance series, before ceasing operations in January, 1991.

# EPILOGUE

> [T]he post card format is a powerful mode of communication: both personal and public, verbal and visual, brief in length of message, but long lasting in its potential to endure.
> —Professor Beverly Stoeltje to Jocelyn Cohen, 4 March 1988

Over the next year and a half, Sona Chambers shepherded into print the twenty-six-card series Sisters of the Harlem Renaissance: The Found Generation, Helaine Victoria Press's last major publication. This project, another highly collaborative effort, as evidenced by the long list of women Chambers acknowledged in her introduction to the set, reaffirmed Helaine Victoria Press's longtime commitment to generating feminist memory and challenging cultural limits on women's relationships with one another. Chambers had embraced the project, not only coordinating all the people who contributed their expertise, but raising the funds, as well.

Jocelyn Cohen, Indiana University graduate student Jeanne Laurel, and English Department professor Erlene Stetson had initiated the project three years before, and had served as consultants during the ensuing years. With their assistance, Chambers said in her introduction to the set, she had organized a team of eighteen researchers and writers to locate the images and compose the captions for the series of cards.[1]

Chambers emphasized the significance of the series, saying,

94. Sisters of the Harlem Renaissance postcard set, front cover
Sisters of the Harlem Renaissance, the Found Generation 1920–1932, a Photographic Postcard Series.

"Sisters of the Harlem Renaissance: The Found Generation" uncovers the personal and political conflicts of our sisters, mothers, and grandmothers. They remind us of triumphs as well as ongoing struggles of African American women during 1920–1932, a time during which Harlem was the focus of a new spirit of race consciousness and pride, embodied in a veritable explosion of artistic, literary, political, and intellectual activity. Much of the mainstream work on this exhilarating period in African American history focuses on the accomplishments of men. This series uncovers the myriad contributions by women.[2]

The cards in the series illustrated the many forms that explosion of activity took and demonstrated, as well, the determination with which current scholars were seeking to discover and celebrate women from the past and to recenter women in the historical record. The list of those who researched and wrote the captions indicates the depth and breadth of knowledge that was invoked to create the series, with several scholars supplying more than one. Indiana University professor Erlene Stetson worked on three captions: pantomimist and comedian Florence Mills; singer, band leader, and trumpeter Valaida Snow; and, with Jeanne Phoenix Laurel, novelist and librarian Nella Larsen. University of Cincinnati professor Sharon G. Dean also provided three captions: writer and activist Alice Ruth Moore Dunbar-Nelson; poet Anne Spencer; and writer, dancer, and actor Josephine Baker. Historian and gay rights activist Eric Garber wrote captions for cards depicting poet Angelina Weld Grimke and pianist and blues singer Gladys Bentley. Artist, curator, and art historian Deirdre L. Bibby furnished captions for cards depicting the Harlem Community Art Center and sculptor Augusta Savage. Indiana University professor Winona L. Fletcher wrote captions for actor and theater organizer Rose McClendon and poet Georgia Douglas Johnson. Indiana University professor Phyllis Rauch Klotman provided captions for the cards depicting journalist Fay M. Jackson and writer Dorothy West.

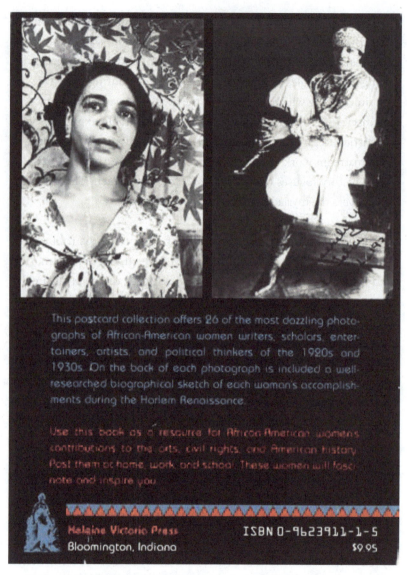

95. Sisters of the Harlem Renaissance postcard set, back cover
Sisters of the Harlem Renaissance, the Found Generation 1920–1932, a Photographic Postcard Series.

Both the image and the caption for the card illustrating actor Evelyn Preer were provided by her daughter, Sr. Francesca Thompson, O.S.F. Likewise, A'Lelia P. Bundles wrote the caption and supplied the photograph for her great-grandmother, Harlem salon hostess A'Lelia Walker.

Other contributors included feminist writer and jazz historian Rosetta Reitz, who wrote the caption for comedian Moms Mabley; University of North Carolina professor Kathy Perkins, who captioned the card for sculptor and theater designer Meta Vaux Warrick Fuller; and University of California, San Diego professor, novelist, and poet Sherley Anne Williams, who constructed the caption for a new Helaine Victoria Press card of Zora Neale Hurston. Joan Nestle, founder of the Lesbian Herstory Archives, wrote about her friend, Lesbian activist and dancer Mabel Hampton; University of North Carolina at Charlotte professor Sandra Y. Govan contributed the caption for poet Gwendolyn Bennett; and Harvard University research associate Joyce Flynn wrote the caption for author Marita Bonner. University of Wisconsin-Whitewater professor Carolyn Wedin supplied the caption for author and publisher Jessie Redmon Fauset; Professor T.J. Bryan, then-faculty at Coppin State College, wrote the caption for poet Helene Johnson (Hubbell); Indiana University professor Gloria J. Gibson-Hudson authored the caption for actress and film pioneer Anita Bush; and for singer and actress Ethel Waters, the series editors constructed a caption from the liner notes of one of her albums.

With the Sisters of the Harlem Renaissance: The Found Generation series, Helaine Victoria Press returned to its roots in art history, revealing more overlooked and erased women artists. Although many of the women represented in the set worked within traditional art forms, some pioneered new methods or new materials. To a one, however, they deployed these forms in ways certain to upend conventional notions of art.

Each card was framed in a turquoise and black African-influenced art deco border, in keeping with the artistic sensibili-

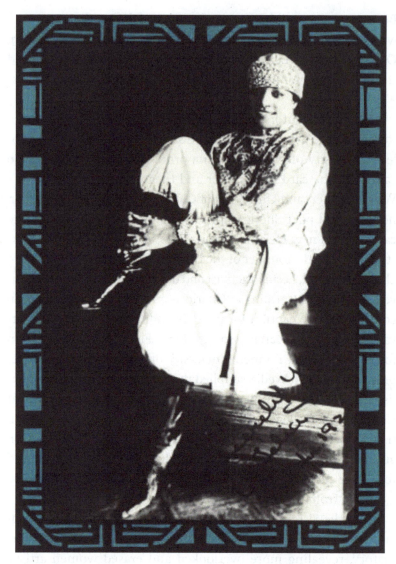

### 96. A'Lelia Walker postcard

A'Lelia Walker (1885–1931), the only child of Madam C. J. Walker, hosted one of the most memorable salons of the Harlem Renaissance. In "The Dark Tower," a converted floor of her New York townhouse, she entertained Harlem and Greenwich Village writers, artists, and musicians, as well as visiting African and European royalty. Her parties, along with her regal African beauty, lavish clothing, and glamorous lifestyle, inspired singers, poets, and sculptors. Langston Hughes called her the "joy goddess of Harlem's 1920's;" Zora Neale Hurston outlined a play about her and her mother; and Carl Van Vechten based his *Nigger Heaven* character, Adora Boniface, on her. She helped her mother found The Mme. C. J. Walker Mfg. Co. in 1905, then opened its New York office and beauty salon in 1913. Upon Madam Walker's death in 1919, A'Lelia Walker became president of the company. Her interest in Africa led her in 1922 to become one of the only westerners to visit Ethiopian Empress Waizeru Zauditu.

ties of the 1920s era. The folio folder format was modeled on the same design as that used for the Social Protest series, with a front and back cover and a spine so that it could be shelved alongside books with similar themes in bookstores or libraries. Columbia appeared on the spine and on the back cover, credits were listed on the inside cover, and the ISBN number was placed on the back, as is the practice for books. Sharon L. Sklar's design was dazzling, and, like the designs on all Helaine Victoria cards, it reflected the love and care that went into every aspect of developing the series.

Although it may have appeared as though more women than ever were involved in running Helaine Victoria Press, each had specific, delineated tasks, so much of the ongoing work central to the press languished. The accurate and precise system for monitoring and recording card sales that Bernice Schipp had constructed was not followed: no one was filing the documents produced and received by the press, nor was anyone maintaining and acquiring new cards for the postcard archive. Even the documents from the Harlem Renaissance series were never filed in the archive cabinets.

As the release date for the series neared, it became clear that this would be Helaine Victoria Press's last publication. In the final catalog, "Viewy News" contained two announcements: one, that Jocelyn would not be returning to Helaine Victoria Press, and two, the board's decision, made on July 14, 1990: "Our Spring sale catalog proudly proclaimed that we could do it, that we could march into the nineties and take the world by storm. In the intervening months, we at the Press have seriously evaluated our needs, resources, and wants. At a joint meeting of staff and the Board of Directors [ . . . ] we unanimously decided that the Press should close at the end of 1990."[3]

Nancy and Jocelyn's original vision continued to inform Helaine Victoria Press until it closed. They had envisioned creating a means of communication that was multimodal, participatory, and informative, one that not only illuminated a collective feminist ancestry, but that also drew back into the light the achievements of living women who had faded into obscurity. Speaking to the information the cards provided, Prof. Susan Gubar explained the ways in which the press was integral to the reshaping of knowledge, especially within educational institutions. Helaine Victoria Press, she said, "uncover[ed] women in politics, women and animals, women and nature, at a time when these areas were hardly subjects yet. So, in a sense, it was like [the press] was carving out certain territories [ . . . ]. And, with a modest form—a postcard. But the scope was really kind of promethean, very ambitious."[4] And while the press's influence on educational institutions of all levels was deeply significant, beyond that influence, the press was able to create linkages among women of all ages, classes, and backgrounds, as the cards were accessible and multidirectional, carrying messages inscribed by senders and traveling across the country, building feminist memory and fueling lines of possibility.

Throughout the lifespan of the press, those involved had struggled to answer the question that Jocelyn and Nancy had posed to readers of *Sister* in 1975: "Can Women's Businesses Succeed?" The answer to that question became more complicated than the two cofounders originally envisioned. Nancy and Jocelyn's plan for the press had always included a rural location with low overhead and a productive vegetable garden. However, they did not anticipate the ongoing need for considerable sacrifice on everyone's part. Nor did they anticipate the ability to shift to non-profit status and then recruit volunteers, interns, and work-study students, as well as accept grant funding and donations.

Nonetheless, the press had had a gloriously successful seventeen-year run. Writing in the final catalog, Donna Fay Reeves conceded that "[p]arts of my job have been very hard. Struggling to keep an organization alive with what seems like never enough help or money can feel very heavy, and the rewards were other than monetary." But, she continued, "I love what we do here, playing an active part in changing reality for women and working directly with women who feel the same as I do."[5]

Jocelyn, too, acknowledged the fundamental significance of the feminist ideology driving the press: "In our product, as well as our organization and functioning, HV has been a haven from the patriarchal mainstream, a place carefully crafted. It has allowed each of us to work in a unique women's atmosphere, sometimes alone and often in collaboration."[6] The effect of the press didn't end at the doors of the shop or the edges of the booths at festivals and conferences, however. The cards, as designed, had traveled widely, carrying in both images and captions, messages of solidarity. Jocelyn recalled:

> I'll always remember the letter from the trackwoman in the Midwest, expressing gratefulness for our postcard that showed five Black women working on the B&O railroad during [World War II]: when the winter wind blew cold during her solitary workdays, she could take joy from our cards, which strengthened her sense of identity and community and made life a little easier for her. At times when keeping the Press going seemed like a never-ending uphill struggle, words like those renewed our own sense of purpose and meaning.[7]

When the catalog had reached its recipients in the fall of 1990, letters poured in from across the country, sharing dismay at the closure as well as gratitude for the spirit and significance of the 200-some cards the press had produced over the years. Betty Gardner, manager of the Michigan Women's Historical Center gift shop, wrote to express her disappointment and gratitude, saying "Thank God there are people like you who are preserving the history of women down through the years."[8] June Swanston-Valdes, of Salt of the Earth, Inc., likewise said, "I am indeed in mourning and deeply sorry to hear you are closing. A distinct cultural void is being created with the demise of Helaine Victoria Press. Our children and grandchildren will have quite a time attempting to duplicate the fine quality and force which has kept you going over the past years."[9] Melody Ivins wrote from

Southern Sisters, Inc. in Durham, North Carolina, telling the staff and volunteers at the press that,

> Helaine Victoria was one of my first 'finds' as a budding feminist activist, a decade ago [ ... ]. You've continued to be a favorite resource, and I've recommended you to school teachers, other activists, and the grumpy delivery man who's recently decided that we're okay after all because we display your beautiful images of African American women [ ... ]. Thank you for all your hard work and your abundant and inclusive love for all kinds of women.[10]

During the years following the closing of the press, Jocelyn was determined to find the most appropriate place for the treasured Chandler & Price press and all the type and furniture that went with it. The press signified Jocelyn and Nancy's commitment to increasing women's access to technology; it could not just be sold to whomever might want to use it for hobby printing. Rather, it should go to a place where girls and women would have access to it, and where its historical significance would be acknowledged. With this in mind, Jocelyn sent out several query letters, and in late 1994, after some negotiations between her and Laura Rotegard, Assistant Park Superintendent from the Women's Rights National Historical Park in Seneca Falls, the National Park Service agreed to buy the press and printshop for a nominal amount and to set up The Suffrage Press, designed to introduce visitors—many of them schoolchildren—to the centrality of print communication and publishing in the struggle for voting rights for women.

Almost twenty years after Nancy and Jocelyn had bought the press, Paul Egenolf returned to the land in Martinsville and loaded it and all its accessories onto his truck for transport back to his shop in Indianapolis.

Jocelyn, Donna Fay Reeves, and former Helaine Victoria Press volunteer and intern Laura Sparks also returned to Martinsville to help pack the accessories for the move. From the Egenolf

**97. Chandler & Price press headed for Seneca Falls, NY**
Jocelyn Cohen sitting on the back of the flatbed truck for a final goodbye to the printshop in 1995, before it made its way to the Women's Rights National Historical Park in Seneca Falls, NY. Donna Fay Reeves and Laura Sparks came out to the Martinsville printshop for two days to help Jocelyn with the final packing and organizing for the next leg of the printshop's journey.

warehouse, a large van that the National Park Service had hired shipped all the equipment from Indianapolis to Seneca Falls, NY. The National Park staff, at Jocelyn's suggestion, had hired Laura Sparks to direct and re-create the shop in the new space, once the press had arrived.

The Rochester, NY *Democrat and Chronicle* anticipated the opening of the printshop with a front-page story announcing the new Suffrage Press located in the Women's Educational and Cultural Center headquarters of the Women's Rights National Historical Park. The article emphasized the importance of the park's new acquisition, quoting Assistant Park Superintendent Laura Rotegard: "We hope to help people understand the power of the press in effecting social change."[11] The press, she said, is similar to the one used by Amelia Bloomer in Seneca Falls in 1850 to print *The Lily*, the first suffrage newspaper.

98. Laura Sparks at the Women's Rights National Historical Park, The Suffrage Press printshop, 1995.

After the contents of the Helaine Victoria Press printshop were shipped off to Seneca Falls, Jocelyn Cohen had arranged with the Park Service for long-time volunteer, Laura Sparks, to go to Seneca Falls for two weeks and direct and assist in setting up the new Suffrage Press printshop.

With a grant from the National Park Foundation's Parks as Classrooms program, young students were already registered to come learn why and how women published their arguments in favor of suffrage. Becky Bly of WomanMade Products, who was familiar with Helaine Victoria Press from the festival circuit, was hired to assist in the educational program. Specifically, the fourth-graders

> will participate in the Social Advance Game, exploring how social change is advanced. Through a scripted program, they will re-enact the steps followed by organizers of the women's rights convention [ . . . ]. Pupils also will assemble lines of metal type from the bank-oak cases filled with drawers of nearly 60 fonts of type. They'll learn to fill the chase, or type frame, on the stone, a steel-top cabinet, and will select graphics and decorative bits to enhance their design.[12]

On April 29, 1995, the Women's Rights National Historical Park held a grand opening of the Suffrage Printshop. Jocelyn and her partner at the time, Patricia Antelles, flew out from San Francisco for the event. Toba Cohen flew in from Indianapolis. Lizzie Brown, a jeweler who Jocelyn also knew from the festival circuit, and her partner, Lydia Waltz, came from their home in Boston, as did Becky Bly and her partner at the time, Maureen Owens. Laura Sparks, of course, was already there, having arrived earlier to set up the shop. At least 120 people attended the opening ceremony, which included a ribbon-cutting with the mayor of Seneca Falls, speeches by local dignitaries, live music, dancing, and a table of elegant refreshments.

Later that night, Helaine Victoria Press surreptitiously printed a final broadside. Because Laura had a key to the printshop, the group of eight women went back to the shop after the festivities were over and ran the press one last time. They all huddled around and came up with the commemorative broadside text.[13]

From the *Lily Press*
In Seneca Falls, 1849

To

*Helaine Victoria Press*
In Indiana, 1973

Radical Dyke Printers
Passing it on
In Seneca Falls, 1995

Girls at Night

99. Lily Press to Helaine Victoria Press broadside
From the Lily Press in Seneca Falls, 1849 To Helaine Victoria Press In Indiana, 1973 • Radical Dyke Printers Passing it on In Seneca Falls 1995. Commemorative broadside made during a late-night printing in the new home for the Helaine Victoria Press printshop.

100. Jocelyn Cohen in front of the Women's Rights National Historical Park, The Suffrage Press printshop, 1995.

Of the group, only Jocelyn and Laura knew how to operate the press, so the event became a teaching and learning occasion for all of them. They chose the design, type, and ornament, and then gleefully set the type, each one with a composing stick setting a line. They locked it up, inked up the press, and took turns printing 100 copies or so.

And with that, Helaine Victoria Press ended its long run: recentering women in the historical record, upending conventional notions of art, insisting upon women's access to technology, and challenging cultural limits on women's relationships with one another.

Helaine Victoria Press products—cards, broadsides, posters, T-shirts—have, indeed, been "long-lasting in [their] potential to endure." As Ellen Dwyer commented recently, "Just a year ago, I sent the Women and Social Protest series to a niece after she was accepted to Boalt Hall Law School, where she is especially interested in their women and reproductive health track."[14] Cards still travel through the mail and adorn refrigerators and bulletin boards. Framed broadsides and posters still hang on walls. Libraries across the country hold cards and broadsides in special collections, sometimes included in the papers of individuals or organizations and sometimes as materials collected on their own. The over 5,000-item Postcard Archive of contemporary 1970–1990 postcards by and about women is held at the The Arthur and Elizabeth Schlesinger Library on the History of Women in America at the Radcliffe Institute for Advanced Study, Harvard University, as is the 500-card collection of early postcards spanning the late 1800s through the 1950s. The twenty-three-box archive of the press itself is held in the Special Collections at Smith College. Most significantly, Helaine Victoria Press cleared space for artists, writers, filmmakers, and others to generate a more complex and evocative feminist memory.

Helaine Victoria Press has begun to appear in books, articles, dissertations, and conference papers as enthusiastic scholars uncover the rich sources of multimodal print activism, as if they are peeling back the leaves of a Savoy cabbage. Much remains to be explored about those exuberant days of feminist activism that recovered the subjugated histories of the women's rights movements of the nineteenth and early twentieth centuries, as well as both earlier and later feminist challenges to traditional power arrangements. Such explorations will serve to illuminate and clarify the deep sources of feminist energy that fuel today's grassroots #MeToo, Payback, and Pink Wave movements, as they continue the efforts to remake the social norms and institutions of America.

*Glossary*

*Printing and Papermaking Terms Used in the Book*

**Abaca**: A high-cellulose plant in the banana family. High cellulose level in a plant provides a stronger paper strength. More commonly known for its use in making rope, twine, and hammocks. In Southeast Asia, banana leaves are being used as an eco-friendly substitute for plastic when wrapping fresh produce and then tied with abaca twine.[1,2]

**Broadside**: Historically used for political announcements, upcoming events, or news. Rather than in current forms such as a tweet, Evite, or email blast, broadsides were originally posted on walls in town squares or handed out on the street. They often voiced a strong opinion or belief. Always printed on one side and as a single sheet only, and often accompanied with a graphic such as a woodcut or, later, an engraving. In the fine press world today, the broadside may be lavishly produced to enhance poems and excerpts from literature or express political perspectives and social commentary, as well as show off the craft and design capability of the printer.[3]

**Case, job case, California job case, type case**: A compartmentalized wooden drawer used for storing foundry type or movable type for letterpress printing. The cases in the Helaine Victoria printshop were a style of case that evolved over time and coined as "California job cases" sometime in the 1800s. A case consists of eighty-nine compartments, each one assigned to specific letters, spacers, ligatures, and quads. The arrangement of the different kinds of cases was based on the idea of placing the letters most commonly used in the easiest positions for the typesetter to reach. The compartments were largest for letters most commonly used and smallest for those used least often.[4]

**Chase**: A metal frame made of cast iron or steel, used to hold type in place while printing, usually on a platen press but could be used on a flatbed press or a proof press. The size of a chase matches the specific press so, as the Chandler & Price press Helaine Victoria had was 10" x 15," the inside of the chase matched accordingly. The type, ornaments, engravings, and such are locked up in the chase using furniture to position them and quoins to apply pressure against all four sides of the chase. The forme is locked up on a composing stone to assure the type is level. Before quoins are tightened, a wooden plane is tapped gently on the surface of the type, ornaments, dingbats, etc., to make sure all the elements are flush against the stone, completely level. Helaine Victoria had several chases including one with handles at the top which made transporting the chase from the stone to the press easier. The more type in the chase, the heaver it was.

**Colophon**: An inscription at the bottom of a print or broadside or at the end of a book often including details about the production of the printed piece. It could include the printer's name, the name of the press, the typeface, the kind of paper—all kinds of information that otherwise would be lost forever.

**Composing stick**: A hand-sized, adjustable, tray-like tool used to set words and lines of foundry type or monotype. The typesetter can adjust the length of the lines. After a line is set, a lead or slug is dropped in to separate the lines. The stick is held in one hand,

and the other hand is used to select the letters out of the type case. The type is then transferred to the stone for lock up or to a galley for later use.[5]

**Couche, couch**: The term papermakers use to describe transferring a newly formed sheet of paper from the mould to the felts. "*Couch* comes from the French verb *se coucher*, to put to bed."[6] In Western papermaking, the sheets would be alternated with a felt, usually a small wool blanket much like one would put on a horse before the saddle or even like a thick wool blanket one might use in a yoga class. The felts separate the newly couched sheets from each other; otherwise, if they were just stacked on top of each other, the sheets would all bond together. They then are pressed to squeeze out the water before the sheets are laid out on drying racks.

**Deckle edge**: An uneven rough edge on handmade paper.

**Diatype**: In the early 1970s, the Diatype was a state-of-the-art typesetting machine that replaced foundry type. It was not used for newspapers or books, but more often for small sections of type, headlines, and similar. It was a cumbersome piece of equipment with individual fonts on an expensive glass disc. The user moved the machine bar to the desired character, one at a time. Inside the Diatype drum, a piece of light-sensitive film was exposed by means of a lamp.[7] After the letters were set, the film would be removed and taken to the darkroom to be processed.

**Die cut, die-cutting**: Die refers to a thin, sharp steel or brass blade that has been formed into a shape or pattern or even a simple line. Die-cutting for printing refers to using this die to cut paper into various shapes.[8] It is very much like a heavy-duty cookie cutter. Most printshops would have a case which would hold a selection of steel lengths that could be used for cutting a line. Dies can be made in any shape and generally would be jobbed out to a special shop.

In the Helaine Victoria shop, there was a case of steel dies from about six picas long to thirty-six picas long and also pieces that would perforate as well. In addition to cutting all the way through a printed piece, a die can be designed so that it cuts a perforated line. Known as perforated die-cutting, this allows the perforated shape—such as an ID card or coupon—to be easily removed by the consumer for use. Helaine Victoria used a perforated line for the accordion pages in the Women's History Album so that the cards could be separated.

**Dingbat**: A printer's ornament or character cast in lead or sometimes a small engraving. Current definitions consider what those of us at Helaine Victoria called typographical ornaments or piece borders to be dingbats, but we considered all the odd little treasures we found on galleys in old letterpress shops to be dingbats, everything from a cat to a bike to a fly.

**Distribute (type)**: Putting the type back in the case after use. Distributing type is like putting the dishes away after they are used and washed. Like dishes, type is reusable. Distributing type is often left undone if time and/or labor is short. If a shop had apprentices or a printer's devil, the task went to them. Because compositions often contained an assortment of fonts and sizes, and sometimes flowers, it was important to make sure the type went back in its proper location. Learning to hold five or six lines of type in one hand and distribute it with the other hand took a lot of practice. It was not unusual for shops to have galleys and galleys of undistributed type.[9] When Helaine Victoria acquired Munder, some of the type was still tied up on the galleys and had to be distributed back into the proper case.

**Embossing**: Embossing alters the surface of paper by providing a raised effect on selected areas, or a recessed effect called "debossing." A true emboss uses two dies: one that is raised, and one that is recessed. The dies fit together so that when the paper is pressed between them, the raised die forces the paper into the recessed die and creates the embossed impression.[10] It requires a very heavy duty press to emboss because of how much pressure it takes to make this impression. The embossing Helaine Victoria did was more of a debossing, and they used type and ornaments from their collection. Fine printing is reflected not just in the typography but also in how even the impression is. A perfect impression is referred to as a kiss impression. For the kind of embossing Helaine Victoria did, they built up the packing under the tympan paper, so the type pressed deeply into the sheet giving it an embossed effect, more of a smack than a kiss. Doing this was very hard on the type and made the nice sharp edges of the foundry type wear down, but it certainly had a beautiful effect.

**Engraving/photoengraving**: The process of taking a photograph and reproducing it into a form that can be printed on a letterpress. The tones of the photo are broken up into a pattern of dots called a halftone which corresponds to the light and shadow of the copy. The halftone is etched on a sensitized plate so the dots are raised enough for printing. These dots stand out in relief on the engraved plate which becomes the printing surface. The plates, originally copper and later made of zinc or magnesium, are mounted on wood so they are type-high—that is, the same height as foundry type. There are many processes involved in making a high-quality halftone engraving. A line engraving is similar except it is not broken down into halftone dots. A line engraving is a black and white sharp contrast drawing without shades of gray. The engraving is an exact reproduction of the lines or masses as they appear in the original.[11]

**Flourishes, fleurons, flowers**: Also called a printer's flower. In the Helaine Victoria shop, a flourish was more of an accent ornament rather than a flower. Flourishes, fleurons, or flowers were cast in the same way as other typographic elements: as individual metal sorts that could be fitted into the compositions with letters and numbers.[12] The Helaine Victoria shop had five or six type cases or drawers filled with all manner of these ornamental objects.

**Folio**: A packet, folder, or wrapping. Helaine Victoria designed many different types of folios: some more like an accordion album; others, a simple large sheet of cover stock with a folded edge at the bottom so items could be inserted inside; others still that folded in such a way so a large series of postcards could be inserted. This kind of folio would even have a spine on which the title could be printed, so it could then be placed on a bookshelf spine-out. Another folio Helaine Victoria created was the T-shaped sheet of paper, such as the one used for the Women and Papermaking set.

**Forme, form**: The loose components of a page that are composed inside the frame-like metal chase on top of the stone. The desired arrangement would be locked inside the chase, ready for printing.

**Foundry type, printers' type**: Letters of type cast in reverse so the printing surface of the letters, also known as the face of the type, stand out in relief above the type body, also called the shoulder. Foundry type is cast in individual letters or characters. The metal is an alloy of lead, antimony, and tin. All type is uniformly .918" high.[13]

**Furniture**: The wooden blocks that surround the forme inside the chase and hold it in place. They come in standard lengths and widths and are made to be shorter in height than type-high so they do not print along with the type or engraving. Furniture, like all the elements in a letterpress shop, is stored in a specific kind of cabinet, this one being wedge-shaped: wider at the bottom and narrower at top, housing all the different size pieces, five or so of each both in length and width. The shorter pieces would be at the top where it narrows and longer ones at the bottom.

**Galley:** A tray, usually brass or steel, for holding composed pages or in Helaine Victoria's case, often a caption, engraving, or type for the composition for a broadside. Often, galleys may be in a cabinet of their own, perhaps holding twenty or thirty trays. At the Helaine Victoria printshop, there was a small galley case like this and then the stone was designed to rest on top of four rows of galleys each holding about a dozen trays.[14]

**Gripper, gripper bars:** Metal bars that close down automatically against the platen when the press closes for an impression; they hold the paper flat against the tympan and platen. They are adjustable and must be moved outside the margins of the area being printed—that is, the forme—and also cannot come in contact with the paper guides or gauge pins so neither gets smashed.

**Guillotine-style paper cutter, manual lever paper cutter:** Paper cutter operated by putting a stack of paper in the bed of the cutter. On top of the cutter is a wheel you turn to bring a weight down on top of the stack of paper, holding it in place. Then pulling the lever down, the blade cuts through the stack of paper.

**Halftone:** The halftone process for printing, either the metal plates for offset or the photoengraving for letterpress, is a technique that breaks an image into a series of dots which give a continuous tone photograph a full range of tones that the printing press can read. The halftone screen converts the photograph first onto the film which is then transferred to either a metal plate for offset or an engraving for letterpress. The screens are made with a varying number of lines per inch, depending on the application; for newspapers, the range is usually sixty-five to eighty-five lines per inch because the paper is newsprint and cannot hold a fine set of dots. The halftone dots are small, so the human eye interprets the patterned areas as if they were smooth tones. The more lines per inch, the higher the quality of the reproduction. This is determined by both the paper and the printing press.[15, 16]

**Header**: A printed piece which contains information about what is inside a package or set. Typically, a set or series of cards would be packaged in a plastic bag and a header printed and stapled onto the top, the front side showing the name like Women's History Series 1, 12 cards, and the back listing the contents. Sets of cards needed to be packaged, and Helaine Victoria used both this method as well as folios.

**Job out**: Lingo for sending a job out to another printer.

**Lead snipper**: A lovely little printer's tool used only for cutting one- through four-point leads. Any thicker and you must use a trim saw. The gauge can be set for any length up to about a foot.

**Leads**: Strips of lead less than type-high used in composition as spacing material between lines of type or ornaments. They are made in given point thicknesses, from one to four points. When a lead is six points or more, it is called a slug. Leads are sold in long lengths that can be easily cut with a lead snipper.

**Letterpress**: Any one of several kinds of presses that all work on the concept in which impressions are made from raised surfaces such as type, or relief printing plates like line or photo engravings.[17]

**Ligature**: Many old-style Roman typefaces, like Munder in the Helaine Victoria Press printshop, included ligatures as part of the font. A ligature is two, or sometimes three, letters cast as a single letter. Ligatures were created for elegance and more graceful letter spacing. Munder included ct, st, fi and ffi ligatures.

**Line shot**: To copy or reproduce on film any kind of image that does not require a halftone screen. This includes type, a line drawing, any kind of image that is only solids with no gray scale. A line shot for printing is used in both offset and letterpress pre-press production.

**Linotype**: A keyboard-based machine for composing and casting type. It was a hot metal typesetting system that cast lines of metal type, thus replacing much of the hand typesetting.

Linotype is based on matrices for each letter, number, punctuation, and spacers that drop into a thirty-six-pica line, about five inches long, and are then cast. The linotype machine was invented by Ottmar Mergenthaler around 1880, revolutionizing typesetting. It is one of the most incredible machines ever made, and story has it that Mergenthaler went mad afterwards. The manual approaches the size of the *Encyclopedia Britannica*.[18]

**Lock up**: To assemble all the items to be printed in a forme. The extra space is filled with furniture, and two quoins, one for the vertical and one for horizontal direction, are inserted and turned to tighten, thus locking up the forme so that the composition does not fall out of the chase.

**Make-ready**: A detailed preparation before printing the forme in which layers of paper are added or subtracted so the final image has an even impression.[19] The platen of the press has two clamps in the front and back that the tympan sheet is attached to. The tympan consists of the waxed top manila sheet called the tympan sheet, and layers of packing, usually one or two sheets of very hard pressboard, and a few sheets of book paper. In the Helaine Victoria shop, there was a lot of coated enamel paper rescued from other shops, perfect for packing. The forme is put in the press, printed on the tympan sheet, then wiped off with paint thinner so only a light reproduction shows. A black and white proof is then made of the image to be printed. This proof is registered under the tympan paper, which will be used to balance the amount of pressure so the impression is even over all. When there are various typefaces, engravings, dingbats, or flowers, each element may not come up evenly, which would create an uneven impression. These discrepancies are addressed in the make-ready. The craft of fine letterpress printing requires a great deal of time adding underlays and overlays to ensure that the impression is even throughout the page when printed. Creating this perfectly even impression separates out the mediocre printers from fine printers.

**Mask off, mask out, knock out**: Using an opaque material, like an orange masking sheet or, often, film, in paste-up to outline photographs or in platemaking to withhold light from non-image areas. Intended to cover selected copy or art so it will not appear on the negative film or plate. Masking off is used to prevent light from reaching part of an image, therefore isolating the remaining part.[20]

**Mechanicals**: Generally, a paste-up of all the components of the job to be printed; often referred to as "camera-ready." Most often used for offset printing, a mechanical could be prepared for an engraving as well.[21]

**Monotype**: A composing machine that casts single letters, usually used for book work. Many foundries cast their ornamental piece borders out of monotype. The metal is softer and less expensive than foundry type. Often, fine book printers would have the copy set monotype so they could adjust letter spacing to perfection yet save time not setting foundry type. The type would then usually be sold as metal scrap after the press run was complete.

**Offset press**: Offset printing, or offset lithography, is a widely-used printing process where the inked image is transferred from a printing plate to a rubber blanket wrapped around a rubber cylinder, then finally transferred to the paper printing surface.[22]

**Ornaments**: Flourishes, dingbats, flowers or fleurons, and other typographic ornamentation. They are decorative motifs used to fill in page space in lieu of a long dash, or to signify the end of a chapter, book, or broadside. Ornaments add an aesthetic quality to the printed page. They have been around since moveable type printing in the fifteenth century, and, before that, monks drew them when illuminating manuscripts.[23]

**Paste-up**: Camera-ready copy with all the elements pasted into position for a job to be printed on an offset press. A dummy made for the printer's guidance, or in the case of the tabloid catalogs Helaine Victoria had printed, it could be the final layout from which the printer would shoot negatives and print. Paste-ups also could be made from a proof of a letterpress flower border that the printer wanted made into a line engraving.

**Pica and Points**: The two typographical units of measurement most commonly used for typesetting and design. Type is measured in points (pts). The family of type Helaine Victoria had, Munder, was cast in six- through seventy-two-point size in four styles, which constitutes a family of type. The leads and slugs for spacing are also measured in points, one through four for leads, and six through twelve for slugs. Furniture is measured in picas. Picas (pcs) are usually used to represent fixed horizontal measurements. A pica ruler typically shows points and picas on one side and inches on the other. One pica equals twelve points, six picas equal one inch, and seventy-two points equals one inch.

**Platen**: The smooth, metal surface that comes into contact with the flat bed part of the platen press. On a Chandler & Price press, the bed and the platen both move toward each other and smack together head on making a nice clean impression on the paper. On other presses, such as a clamshell press, the bed and the platen move forward like a clamshell opening and closing, sort of hinged at the bottom, which can cause slurring of the type.

**Point (type size)**: The basic typographical unit (a twelfth of a pica), about 1/72$^{nd}$ of an inch.

**Print broker**: Someone who works as a liaison between printshops and the public. This person would be familiar with all the local printers and associated trades and the services they provide. An individual, a business, or someone in the trades may call a print broker looking for a particular service such as offset printing, die-cutting, gold stamping, binding, and so on.

**Printer's devil**: A term applied to a junior apprentice in the printshop. Historically, often a young person, usually male, who did all kinds of clean up, redistributed type, and generally did lots of not-so-fun tasks. Like fence white-washing in *Tom Sawyer*, printer's devil work included the kinds of jobs Helaine Victoria could trick academics into thinking were really neat.

**Proof press**: Proof presses come in a wide range of different sizes, manual and automatic. The one in the Helaine Victoria shop was a large, flat bed with a hand-operated cylinder. The cylinder/drum was wrapped with a thin blanket and then tympan paper. There was a shelf for an ink palette for hand-inking using an ink roller called a "brayer." The bed could accommodate a large sheet of paper about 12" x 18". That meant that, besides making a proof, the proof press could print large signs for posters and information like price sheets hung at conferences. The type was placed on the bed and locked up, so it did not move. Then, using the brayer, ink was rolled over the type, a sheet of paper was laid atop the type and then, using the cylinder handle, the drum was rolled over the ink. A proof press is indispensable, as you always need to check the typesetting before putting it on the press. The proof would be read for mistakes and examined for design.

**Quoin**: Quoins are used to lock up all the elements in the chase. They originated as wooden wedges and evolved over the time into what became known as "high-speed quoins," which can be mechanically expanded or reduced to fit the space. Although the Helaine Victoria shop had some of the older metal wedge-type quoins, they had plenty of the high-speed ones in different lengths. In order to lock up the forme, the printer requires at least two quoins: one for pressure vertically, and another horizontally. A special key is required, which fits into the quoin and tightens or loosens it. The quoin then exerts pressure to hold all the elements inside the chase tightly.[24] The last thing you want is for the type to come loose in the chase either while moving it to the press or while printing.

**Register**: In printing, registration is the alignment of all the various inks in different press passes you are using. If you are printing something with more than one color, each color will be printed separately on the printing press, and they must overlap the others precisely. If not, the finished image will look fuzzy, blurred, or "out of register." When printing on handmade paper where an initial cap has been pressed into the paper, during printing the type must align correctly with the initial letter on the paper. Different systems of registration are necessary to assure the colors line up correctly.[25]

**Registration or gauge pins**: Little metal guides used to determine where the paper sits on the platen when printing. They lock into your tympan paper in a way that makes it virtually impossible to slip out of register during a letterpress printing run. These guides are positioned two on the bottom and one on the left-hand side of your tympan paper, setting the location to hold the paper. They fit in a space outside the forme so as to not interfere with the closing of the platen during letterpress printing, and do not come in contact with the type or engravings locked up in the chase or the gripper bars. Once the pins are in place exactly in register, they are waxed down with printer's sealing wax, which is the same or similar to the kind of wax used for wax seals, to fix the pins in place.[26]

**Reglets**: A form of spacing material made of wood and the same height as other spacing material like leads, slugs and furniture. Reglets are either six or twelve picas thick, of varying lengths, and are used for smaller spacing inside the chase and also on either side of the quoins in order to prevent injuring the furniture from the pressure.

**Rollers**: The rollers for a letterpress are precious and require care and attention. When the press is turned on, they move up and down over the bed of the press and up onto the ink disk. They also roll over the chase when it is in place with the forme, adding ink to the image. Some rollers are made of rubber, and if they get too hot, they will melt.

**Slugs**: Six- or twelve-point-wide pieces of lead used for spacing between lines of type.

**Stat camera, graphics process camera**: Used for shooting halftones and line shots. An indispensable piece of expensive equipment at the time of Helaine Victoria Press's operation. It consisted of the camera portion, which is inside the darkroom, and a long-extended platform where the camera person mounts the image to be shot/copied. That person would set the scale, focus, and mount the light-sensitive film from inside the darkroom. As they set the size and focus, the platform would move closer or farther away. After shooting the image, they took the negative and processed it in the photo chemicals.[27]

**Stone**: Originally, the stone was a large slab of just that: granite stone often set in a wood frame. More modern stones are made of smooth cast iron or steel with cabinets of some sort underneath. The Helaine Victoria shop cabinet held galleys, but others may hold furniture. The stone is where the printer assembles the forme in the chase, and it is paramount that the stone be perfectly flat and clean. Even a little bit of grit under a letter can make the type uneven in the forme and cause an uneven impression on the paper.

**Trim saw, type saw**: Very much like a small version of a woodworker's table saw. They are measured in picas instead of inches and are capable of very fine adjustments. They are used to cut both lead rule and wood, and they can quickly trim stacks of leading all to the same size.

**Tympan, drawsheet**: The tympan is a heavy oiled manila paper that comes in large rolls. It is used on top of the platen, a fresh sheet for each new printing job. It is held in place with the two clamps on the front and back of the platen that open and close to grip the paper snugly. Under this is a hanger sheet or "spot up sheet" that is also clamped, but only with the back. This way, it can be lifted up to put on or take off the make-ready sheet.

**Typeface**: A typeface includes all the fonts in the same style. Helaine Victoria's family of type was Munder. It contained four typefaces: Munder Venezian, Munder Venezian Italic, Munder Bold, and Munder Bold Italic. Each font was further described as Munder Venezian 12pt (twelve-point, etc.), 14pt, 36pt, or 72pt. Those are four different fonts all in the same typeface and part of the Munder type family.

**Waxed paper stencil or plate (Gestetner)**: A thin sheet of paper coated with wax that can be written upon with a special stylus, or typed on with a typewriter. Pressure from this writing cuts through the stencil by removing the wax coating. When the waxed plate was put on the drum of the Gestetner and the machine was turned on, ink was forced through the stencil where the wax was removed. This left the image on the sheet of paper.[28]

**Wood type**: Large letters for printing broadsides were in high demand with the expansion of the commercial printing industry in the first years of the nineteenth century. The process for mass producing wood type was invented in 1827. Metal type was too expensive to produce in larger than 72pt; also, because of the way the metal cooled, the lead type could become distorted. Wood cost half the price of metal, had a smooth even surface, and was much lighter, especially in large sizes. The letters were made from hard end-grain wood specially treated to prevent cracking and warping.[29]

*Helaine Victoria Press Chronological Publication Catalog: 1973–1994*

The Helaine Victoria Press Chronological Publication Catalog, organized by date, documents the editions of almost all postcards, prints, bookplates, notecards, and broadsides published by the press, plus a sampling of various special occasion items. Jocelyn reconstructed this list from handwritten pages she had saved. Each entry includes the year plus the edition, size, series, color, and manner of printing; the colors may include additional information, such as whether the edition was printed on handmade paper.

To view full-size images of Helaine Victoria Press cards, bookmarks, bookplates, photos, and other ephemera, see the Resources tab in the online open access edition of this book at www.leverpress.org. The open access edition also contains audio and video clips of commentary about the history and workings of the press. The last category in this catalog indicates whether the card is available for viewing in the open access EPUB edition under the "Resources" tab.

Although the authors digitized most of the Helaine Victoria Press publications, not every edition is included in either the print or the open access edition. For instance, the card memorializing Sojourner Truth may be listed multiple times in this appendix, yet only one edition may appear in the Resources section. Readers should also know that when Helaine Victoria Press reprinted a card, they did not necessarily note the new edition or reprint date on that card. A publication originally printed in 1974 and then reprinted in '75, '78, '82, and so on, may still say 1974. Moreover, when a card was reprinted, the title did not change, meaning multiple editions of a card all carry the same title, a fact readers should keep in mind when searching for a specific edition.

By examining this appendix, scholars can assess the frequency of interest in a publication, and if a collector or archivist finds that they have a different edition than one pictured in this volume's formats, this catalog will enable them to find the printing date of almost any given publication. Many of the original publications are held in the Special Collections at Smith College; the Schlesinger Library at Harvard University's Radcliffe Institute for Advanced Study; David M. Rubenstein Rare Book and Manuscript Library at Duke University; and other public collections.

Note: Most of the postcards were printed on 10–12pt. coated card stock; most broadsides and prints were published on assorted cover stock. From 1973–76, postcard press runs averaged 500 copies. Later press runs were larger.

## 1973

- "American Amazons" woodcut postcard. First edition. 4.25" x 6". Kitchen Table series. Black on rust. Offset printing. Available on Fulcrum: Yes
- "American Amazons" woodcut postcard. First edition. 4.25" x 6". Kitchen Table series. Black on white. Offset printing. Available on Fulcrum: No
- Rosa Bonheur postcard. First edition. 4.25" x 6". Kitchen Table series. Black on white, etching. Offset printing. Available on Fulcrum: Yes
- Rosa Bonheur postcard. First edition. 4.25" x 6". Kitchen Table series. Black on rust, etching. Offset printing. Available on Fulcrum: Yes

- Rosa Luxemburg postcard. First edition. 4.25" x 6". Kitchen Table series. Black on rust. Offset printing. Available on Fulcrum: Yes
- Rosa Luxemburg postcard. First edition. 4.25" x 6". Kitchen Table series. Black on white. Offset printing. Available on Fulcrum: Yes
- Sisterhood is Warm, Bobsledding postcard. First edition. 4.25" x 6". Kitchen Table series. Black on rust. Offset printing. Available on Fulcrum: Yes
- Sisterhood is Warm, Bobsledding postcard. First edition. 4.25" x 6". Kitchen Table series. Black on white. Offset printing. Available on Fulcrum: No
- Aimee Semple McPherson postcard. First edition. 4.25" x 6". Kitchen Table series. Black on tweedy fiber cardstock. Offset printing. Available on Fulcrum: Yes
- Emily Carr postcard. First edition. 4.25" x 6". Kitchen Table series. Black on tweedy fiber cardstock. Offset printing. Available on Fulcrum: Yes
- Mary Cassatt postcard. First edition. 4.25" x 6". Kitchen Table series. Black on tweedy fiber cardstock. Offset printing. Available on Fulcrum: Yes
- Radclyffe Hall and Una Troubridge postcard. First edition. 4.25" x 6". Kitchen Table series. Black on tweedy fiber cardstock. Offset printing. Available on Fulcrum: Yes
- Helaine Victoria mailer. 8.5" x 11". Black on bankers green or gold paper. Photocopy printing. Available on Fulcrum: No

## 1974

- "American Amazons" woodcut postcard. Second edition. 4.25" x 6". No series. Sepia. Offset printing. Available on Fulcrum: Yes
- Carrie Chapman Catt postcard. First edition. 4.25" x 6". No series. Sepia. Offset printing. Available on Fulcrum: Yes
- Carry Nation postcard. First edition. 4.25" x 6". No series. Sepia and blue-gray. Offset printing. Available on Fulcrum: Yes

- Belle Starr postcard. First edition. 4.25" x 6". No series. Sepia and blue-gray. Offset printing. Available on Fulcrum: No
- Helaine Victoria Enterprises postcard. First edition. 4.25" x 6". No series. Sepia and blue-gray. Offset printing. Available on Fulcrum: No
- Rosa Bonheur postcard. Second edition. 4.25" x 6". No series. Sepia, etching. Offset printing. Available on Fulcrum: Yes
- Rosa Luxemburg postcard. Second edition. 4.25" x 6". No series. Sepia and blue-gray. Offset printing. Available on Fulcrum: Yes
- Sisterhood is Warm, Bobsledding postcard. Second edition. 4.25" x 6". No series. Sepia. Offset printing. Available on Fulcrum: Yes
- Radclyffe Hall and Una Troubridge postcard. Second edition. 4.25" x 6". No series. Sepia. Offset printing. Available on Fulcrum: Yes
- Louise Sykes postcard. First edition. 4.25" x 6". No series. Sepia and blue-gray. Offset printing. Available on Fulcrum: No
- "American Amazons" woodcut postcard. Third edition. 4.25" x 6". No series. Sepia. Offset printing. Available on Fulcrum: No
- Carrie Chapman Catt postcard. Second edition. 4.25" x 6". No series. Sepia. Offset printing. Available on Fulcrum: No
- Carry Nation postcard. Second edition. 4.25" x 6". No series. Sepia. Offset printing. Available on Fulcrum: No
- Belle Starr postcard. Second edition. 4.25" x 6". No series. Sepia. Offset printing. Available on Fulcrum: Yes
- Helaine Victoria Enterprises postcard. First edition. 4.25" x 6". No series. Sepia. Offset printing. Available on Fulcrum: Yes
- Rosa Bonheur postcard. Third edition. 4.25" x 6". No series. Sepia, etching. Offset printing. Available on Fulcrum: No
- Rosa Luxemburg postcard. Third edition. 4.25" x 6". No series. Sepia. Offset printing. Available on Fulcrum: No
- Sisterhood is Warm, Bobsledding postcard. Third edition. 4.25" x 6". No series. Sepia. Offset printing. Available on Fulcrum: No
- Radclyffe Hall and Una Troubridge postcard. Third

edition. 4.25" x 6". No series. Sepia. Offset printing. Available on Fulcrum: No
- Louise Sykes postcard. First edition. 4.25" x 6". No series. Sepia. Offset printing. Available on Fulcrum: No
- 1893 Woman's Building & Sophia Hayden postcard. First edition. 5.5" x 7.25". No series. Dark green and golden. Offset printing. Available on Fulcrum: Yes
- Two Women in the Klondike, 1898 postcard. First edition. 5.5" x 7.25". No series. Dark green and golden. Offset printing. Available on Fulcrum: Yes
- Mary Walker with Rev. Susanna Harris & Belva Lockwood postcard. First edition. 5.5" x 7.25". No series. Dark green and golden. Offset printing. Available on Fulcrum: Yes
- Gertrude Stein & Alice B. Toklas postcard. First edition. 5.5" x 7.25". No series. Dark green. Offset printing. Available on Fulcrum: No
- Two Irish Women, Constance Markievicz and Maud Gonne postcard. First edition. 5.5" x 7.25". No series. Dark green. Offset printing. No
- Suffragettes and the Pankhursts postcard. First edition. 5.5" x 7.25". No series. Dark green. Offset printing. Available on Fulcrum: No
- Emily Carr postcard. First edition. 5.5" x 7.25". No series. Dark blue and golden. Offset printing. Available on Fulcrum: Yes
- Sojourner Truth postcard. First edition. 5.5" x 7.25". No series. Dark blue. Offset printing. Available on Fulcrum: Yes
- Amelia Earhart aviation class postcard. First edition. 5.5" x 7.25". No series. Dark blue and golden. Offset printing. Available on Fulcrum: Yes
- Susan B. Anthony & Elizabeth Cady Stanton postcard. First edition. 5.5" x 7.25". No series. Dark blue. Offset printing. Available on Fulcrum: Yes
- Women's Christian Temperance Union Officers postcard. First edition. 5.5" x 7.25". No series. Dark blue and golden. Offset printing. Available on Fulcrum: Yes

- Frances Willard in her study postcard. First edition. 5.5" x 7.25". No series. Dark blue. Offset printing. Available on Fulcrum: No
- Belle Starr postcard. First edition. 5.5" x 7.25". No series. Purple. Offset printing. Available on Fulcrum: Yes
- Carry Nation postcard. First edition. 5.5" x 7.25". No series. Purple, two photos. Offset printing. Available on Fulcrum: Yes
- Frances Willard in her study postcard. First edition. 5.5" x 7.25". No series. Purple. Offset printing. Available on Fulcrum: Yes
- Gertrude Stein & Alice B. Toklas postcard. Second edition. 5.5" x 7.25". No series. Purple. Offset printing. Available on Fulcrum: Yes
- Rosa Bonheur postcard. First edition. 5.5" x 7.25". No series. Purple, photo. Offset printing. Available on Fulcrum: Yes
- Two Irish Women, Constance Markievicz and Maud Gonne postcard. Second edition. 5.5" x 7.25". No series. Purple. Offset printing. Available on Fulcrum: Yes
- Mary Astell, title page to her 1694 treatise notecard. First edition. 5.5" x 4.25". Note-Ables series. Black on ivory ripple. Offset printing. Available on Fulcrum: Yes
- Fanny Bullock Workman notecard. First edition. 5.5" x 4.25". Note-Ables series. Black on ivory ripple. Offset printing. Available on Fulcrum: Yes
- Anti-Fur notecard. First edition. 5.5" x 4.25". Note-Ables series. Black on ivory ripple. Offset printing. Available on Fulcrum: Yes
- Birthday party at Vassar, 1903 notecard. First edition. 5.5" x 4.25". Note-Ables series. Black on ivory ripple. Offset printing. Available on Fulcrum: No
- British suffrage campaign wagon notecard. First edition. 5.5" x 4.25". Note-Ables series. Black on ivory ripple. Offset printing. Available on Fulcrum: No
- Bloomer costume cartoon Radcliffe College play, 1851 notecard. First edition. 5.5" x 4.25". Note-Ables series. Black on ivory ripple. Offset printing. Available on Fulcrum: No

- New woman gamblers, 1895 notecard. First edition. 5.5" x 4.25". Note-Ables series. Black on ivory ripple. Offset printing. Available on Fulcrum: No
- Radcliffe College play, 1900 notecard. First edition. 5.5" x 4.25". Note-Ables series. Black on ivory ripple. Offset printing. Available on Fulcrum: No
- Frances Willard bookmark. First edition. 8.5" x 1.5". No series. Dark green. Offset printing. Available on Fulcrum: Yes
- Helaine Victoria Press women's history bookmarks over the years, a sampling. 1974–1989. 7.5" x 1.5" appx. No series. Assorted colors. Offset and letterpress printing. Available on Fulcrum: Yes
- Three Singular Women in Concert, Margie Adam, Susan Gluck, and Judy Grahn flyer. First edition. 8.5" x 11". No series. Blue, red, and gray. Gestetner printing. Available on Fulcrum: Yes
- Helaine Victoria Enterprises catalog. 11.25" x 4.5", opens to 11.25" x 17.25". Black on ivory or golden. Offset printing. Available on Fulcrum: No

## 1975

- Elizabeth Gurley Flynn postcard. First edition. 5.5" x 7.25". No series. Dark green. Offset printing. Available on Fulcrum: Yes
- 1893 Woman's Building & Sophia Hayden postcard. Second edition. 5.5" x 7.25". No series. Dark green and pink. Offset printing. Available on Fulcrum: No
- Olive Schreiner postcard. First edition. 5.5" x 7.25". No series. Dark green and pink. Offset printing. Available on Fulcrum: Yes
- Pioneers in Education, Bethune, Willard, and Crandall postcard. First edition. 5.5" x 7.25". No series. Dark green and pink. Offset printing. Available on Fulcrum: Yes
- Suffragettes and the Pankhursts postcard. Second edition. 5.5" x 7.25". No series. Dark green. Offset printing. Available on Fulcrum: No

- Emily Carr postcard. Second edition. 5.5" x 7.25". No series. Dark green and pink. Offset printing. Available on Fulcrum: No
- Radclyffe Hall and Una Troubridge postcard. First edition. 5.5" x 7.25". No series. Charcoal and khaki. Offset printing. Available on Fulcrum: Yes
- Rosa Luxemburg and Clara Zetkin postcard. First edition. 5.5" x 7.25". No series. Charcoal and khaki. Offset printing. Available on Fulcrum: Yes
- Sojourner Truth postcard. Second edition. 5.5" x 7.25". No series. Charcoal. Offset printing. Available on Fulcrum: Yes
- Susan B. Anthony & Elizabeth Cady Stanton postcard. Second edition. 5.5" x 7.25". No series. Charcoal. Offset printing. Available on Fulcrum: Yes
- Amelia Earhart aviation class postcard. Second edition. 5.5" x 7.25". No series. Charcoal and khaki. Offset printing. Available on Fulcrum: No
- Women's Christian Temperance Union Officers postcard. Second edition. 5.5" x 7.25". No series. Charcoal and khaki. Offset printing. Available on Fulcrum: No
- Woman Voter bookplate. First edition. 3.5" x 4.25". Bookplate series. Black on ivory. Offset printing. Available on Fulcrum: Yes
- Folia bookplate. First edition. 3.5" x 4.25". Bookplate series. Black on ivory. Offset printing. Available on Fulcrum: No
- Lady's Library bookplate. First edition. 3.5" x 4.25". Bookplate series. Black on ivory. Offset printing. Available on Fulcrum: No
- Equal Rights Amendment poster. First edition. 17" x 22". No series. Black on ivory; over 20 editions on various color papers. Offset printing. Available on Fulcrum: Yes
- Lesbian History Exploration brochure cover. First edition. Folded 8.5" x 5.5". No series. Black. Offset printing. Available on Fulcrum: Yes
- NOW National Conference 1975 postcard set insert. First edition. 3.75" x 4.25". No series. Black with 2-3 stamps

celebrating women attached. Photocopy printing. Available on Fulcrum: Yes
- Helaine Victoria Enterprises catalog. 11.25" x 4.5", opens to 11.25" x 17.25". Black on pale pink. Offset printing. Available on Fulcrum: No

## 1976

- Radclyffe Hall and Una Troubridge postcard. Second edition. 5.5" x 7.25". No series. Maroon. Offset printing. Available on Fulcrum: Yes
- Carry Nation postcard. Second edition. 5.5" x 7.25". No series. Maroon, two photos. Offset printing. Available on Fulcrum: No
- Susan B. Anthony & Elizabeth Cady Stanton postcard. Third edition. 5.5" x 7.25". No series. Maroon. Offset printing. Available on Fulcrum: No
- Women's Christian Temperance Union Officers postcard. Third edition. 5.5" x 7.25". No series. Maroon. Offset printing. Available on Fulcrum: No
- Rosa Bonheur postcard. Second edition. 5.5" x 7.25". No series. Maroon. Offset printing. Available on Fulcrum: No
- Rosa Luxemburg and Clara Zetkin postcard. Second edition. 5.5" x 7.25". No series. Maroon. Offset printing. Available on Fulcrum: No
- Sojourner Truth postcard. Third edition. 5.5" x 7.25". No series. Maroon. Offset printing. Available on Fulcrum: No
- Amelia Earhart aviation class postcard. First edition. 5.5" x 7.25". No series. Maroon. Offset printing. Available on Fulcrum: No
- Madame Blanchard postcard. First edition. 4.25" x 6". Blue. Letterpress printing. Available on Fulcrum: Yes
- Madame Blanchard, First Day Cover. First edition. 3.5" x 6.5". Black with blue. Letterpress printing. Available on Fulcrum: Yes
- Book Sale Invitation notecard. First edition. 4" x 6". No series. Black. Letterpress printing. Available on Fulcrum: Yes

- Thanksgiving broadside. First edition. 9.5" x 8". No series. Black. Letterpress printing. Available on Fulcrum: Yes
- Helaine Victoria Guide & Price List to Books, summer catalog, no. 2. 8.5"x 5.5". Forty pages. No series. Black. Photocopy printing. Available on Fulcrum: Yes

## 1977

- Olive Schreiner postcard. Second edition. 5.5" x 7.25". No series. Dark green. Offset printing. Available on Fulcrum: No
- Elizabeth Gurley Flynn postcard. Second edition. 5.5" x 7.25". No series. Dark green. Offset printing. Available on Fulcrum: Yes
- Suffragettes and the Pankhursts postcard. Third edition. 5.5" x 7.25". No series. Dark green. Offset printing. Available on Fulcrum: No
- Frances Willard on her bicycle. First edition. 5.5" x 7.25". No series. Dark green. Offset printing. Available on Fulcrum: Yes
- Belle Starr postcard. Second edition. 5.5" x 7.25". No series. Dark green. Offset printing. Available on Fulcrum: No
- Susan B. Anthony & Elizabeth Cady Stanton postcard. Fourth edition. 5.5" x 7.25". No series. Dark green. Offset printing. Available on Fulcrum: No
- Rosa Luxemburg and Clara Zetkin postcard. Third edition. 5.5" x 7.25". No series. Dark green. Offset printing. Available on Fulcrum: No
- 1893 Woman's Building & Sophia Hayden postcard. Third edition. 5.5" x 7.25". No series. Dark green. Offset printing. Available on Fulcrum: No
- Radclyffe Hall and Una Troubridge postcard. Third edition. 5.5" x 7.25". No series. Dark green. Offset printing. Available on Fulcrum: No
- Ernestine Rose postcard. First edition. 5.5" x 7.25". No series. Blue with red rose. Offset and letterpress printing. Available on Fulcrum: Yes

- Amelia Earhart by propeller. Second edition. 5.5" x 7.25". No series. Blue. Offset and printing. Available on Fulcrum: No
- Suffragettes and the Pankhursts postcard. Third edition. 5.5" x 7.25". No series. Blue. Offset printing. Available on Fulcrum: No
- Frances Willard on her bicycle. Second edition. 5.5" x 7.25". No series. Blue. Offset printing. Available on Fulcrum: No
- Radclyffe Hall and Una Troubridge postcard. Fourth edition. 5.5" x 7.25". No series. Blue. Offset printing. Available on Fulcrum: No
- Pioneers in Education, Bethune, Willard, and Crandall postcard. Second edition. 5.5" x 7.25". No series. Blue. Offset printing. Available on Fulcrum: No
- Two Irish Women, Constance Markievicz and Maud Gonne postcard. Third edition. 5.5" x 7.25". No series. Blue. Offset printing. Available on Fulcrum: No
- Susan B. Anthony & Elizabeth Cady Stanton postcard. Fifth edition. 5.5" x 7.25". No series. Blue. Offset printing. Available on Fulcrum: No
- Sojourner Truth postcard. Fourth edition. 5.5" x 7.25". No series. Sepia. Offset printing. Available on Fulcrum: No
- 1893 Woman's Building & Sophia Hayden postcard. Fourth edition. 5.5" x 7.25". No series. Sepia. Offset printing. Available on Fulcrum: No
- Rosa Luxemburg and Clara Zetkin postcard. Fourth edition. 5.5" x 7.25". No series. Sepia. Offset printing. Available on Fulcrum: No
- Belle Starr postcard. Third edition. 5.5" x 7.25". No series. Sepia. Offset printing. Available on Fulcrum: No
- Amelia Earhart by propeller. Third edition. 5.5" x 7.25". No series. Sepia. Offset printing. Available on Fulcrum: No
- Gertrude Stein & Alice B. Toklas postcard. Fourth edition. 5.5" x 7.25". No series. Sepia. Offset printing. Available on Fulcrum: No
- Women of History postcard accordion album set. First edition.

4.5" x 6.5". Women of History. Red, blue, and silver detail. Letterpress printing. Available on Fulcrum: Yes
- Amelia Earhart & the 99's postcard. First edition. 4.25" x 6". Women of History. Black with silver. Letterpress printing. Available on Fulcrum: Yes
- Aphra Behn postcard. First edition. 4.25" x 6". Women of History. Black with silver. Letterpress printing. Available on Fulcrum: Yes
- George Sand postcard. First edition. 4.25" x 6". Women of History. Black. Letterpress printing. Available on Fulcrum: Yes
- Ida B. Wells-Barnett postcard. First edition. 4.25" x 6". Women of History. Black. Letterpress printing. Available on Fulcrum: Yes
- Isadora Duncan postcard. First edition. 4.25" x 6". Women of History. Black. Letterpress printing. Available on Fulcrum: Yes
- Margaret Fuller postcard. First edition. 4.25" x 6". Women of History. Black with silver. Letterpress printing. Available on Fulcrum: Yes
- Mother Jones postcard. First edition. 4.25" x 6". Women of History. Black. Letterpress printing. Available on Fulcrum: Yes
- Victoria Woodhull postcard. First edition. 4.25" x 6". Women of History. Black with silver. Letterpress printing. Available on Fulcrum: Yes
- Etta Macy broadside. First edition. 6.5" x 10.5". Sepia, cinnamon and, blue. Letterpress printing. Available on Fulcrum: Yes
- Mother Jones bookmark for 1977 NOW conference. First edition. 6.5" x 2.5". Brown. Letterpress printing. Available on Fulcrum: Yes
- Rosa Bonheur bookmark. First edition. 6.5" x 2.5". Brown. Letterpress printing. Available on Fulcrum: Yes
- All the Best of the Season postcard. First edition. 4.25" x 6". No series. Green and red. Letterpress printing. Available on Fulcrum: Yes
- Emily Carr postcard. Third edition. 5.5" x 7.25". No series.

Midnight blue and deep orange. Letterpress printing. Available on Fulcrum: Yes
- Amelia Earhart by propeller postcard. First edition. 5.5" x 7.25". No series. Sepia with silver. Letterpress printing. Available on Fulcrum: Yes
- Gertrude Stein & Alice B. Toklas postcard. Third edition. 5.5" x 7.25". No series. Mauve with silver. Letterpress printing. Available on Fulcrum: No
- Equal Rights Amendment postcard. First edition, multiple editions. 4.25" x 6". No series. Black. Letterpress printing. Available on Fulcrum: Yes
- Shalom notecard. First edition. 4.75" x 4". No series. Black with red on ivory. Letterpress printing. Available on Fulcrum: No
- Helaine Victoria catalog, with booklist #3 inserted. 8.5" x 11". 8 pages. Black. Letterpress printing with offset insert. Available on Fulcrum: No

## 1978

- Alice Paul postcard. First edition. 5.5" x 7.25". No series. Purple and green. Letterpress printing. Available on Fulcrum: Yes
- Alice Paul postcard. Second edition. 5.5" x 7.25". No series. Purple and caramel. Letterpress printing. Available on Fulcrum: Yes
- Elizabeth Gurley Flynn speaking postcard. First edition. 5.5" x 7.25". No series. Black with rust. Letterpress printing. Available on Fulcrum: Yes
- Elizabeth Gurley Flynn older postcard. First edition. 5.5" x 7.25". No series. Dark green with rust. Letterpress printing. Available on Fulcrum: Yes
- Emily Carr postcard. Fourth edition. 5.5" x 7.25". No series. Sepia with orange. Letterpress printing. Available on Fulcrum: No
- Winter Greeting postcard. First edition. 5" x 7". No series.

Red, green, silver, brown. Letterpress printing. Available on Fulcrum: Yes
- Alice Paul postcard. Third edition. 5.5" x 7.25". No series. Purple with poppy. Offset printing. Available on Fulcrum: No
- Amelia Earhart and Eleanor Roosevelt postcard. First edition. 5.5" x 7.25". No series. Purple with poppy. Offset printing. Available on Fulcrum: Yes
- Sojourner Truth postcard. Fifth edition. 5.5" x 7.25". No series. Purple and poppy. Offset printing. Available on Fulcrum: No
- Women's Christian Temperance Union Officers postcard. Fourth edition. 5.5" x 7.25". No series. Purple with poppy. Offset printing. Available on Fulcrum: No
- Carry Nation postcard. Third edition. 5.5" x 7.25". No series. Purple with poppy, two photos. Offset printing. Available on Fulcrum: No
- Olive Schreiner postcard. First edition. 5.5" x 7.25". No series. Purple with poppy, younger, new photo. Offset printing. Available on Fulcrum: No
- Amelia Earhart by propeller. Fourth edition. 5.5" x 7.25". No series. Purple with poppy. Offset printing. Available on Fulcrum: No
- Rosa Bonheur postcard. Second edition. 5.5" x 7.25". No series. Purple. Offset printing. Available on Fulcrum: No
- The Fairy Melusine broadside. First edition. 9" x 12". Black on firethorn orange cover stock. Letterpress printing. Available on Fulcrum: Yes
- Violet Trefusis to Vita Sackville-West broadside. First edition 11" x 14". Black and burnt orange and peach on green tweedy cover stock. Letterpress printing. Available on Fulcrum: No
- Violet Trefusis to Vita Sackville-West broadside. Second edition. 11" x 14". Black and burnt orange and blue on golden cover. Letterpress printing. Available on Fulcrum: Yes
- Mary Astell, title page to her 1694 treatise notecard. Second edition. 5.5" x 4.25". Note-Ables series. Black on ivory laid. Offset printing. Available on Fulcrum: No

- Fanny Bullock Workman notecard. Second edition. 5.5" x 4.25". Note-Ables series. Black on ivory laid. Offset printing. Available on Fulcrum: No
- Anti-Fur notecard. Second edition. 5.5" x 4.25". Note-Ables series. Black on ivory laid. Offset printing. Available on Fulcrum: No
- Birthday party at Vassar, 1903 notecard. Second edition. 5.5" x 4.25". Note-Ables series. Black on ivory laid. Offset printing. Available on Fulcrum: No
- British suffrage campaign wagon notecard. Second edition. 5.5" x 4.25". Note-Ables series. Black on ivory laid. Offset printing. Available on Fulcrum: No
- Bloomer costume cartoon Radcliffe College play, 1851 notecard. Second edition. 5.5" x 4.25". Note-Ables series. Black on ivory laid. Offset printing. Available on Fulcrum: No
- New woman gamblers, 1895 notecard. Second edition. 5.5" x 4.25". Note-Ables series. Black on ivory laid. Offset printing. Available on Fulcrum: No
- Radcliffe College play, 1900 notecard. Second edition. 5.5" x 4.25". Note-Ables series. Black on ivory laid. Offset printing. Available on Fulcrum: No
- ERA Cheer postcard. First edition. 3.5" x 5.5". Liberty Series. Blue and red. Letterpress printing. Available on Fulcrum: Yes
- Amelia Earhart & the 99s postcard. Second edition. 4.25" x 6". Women of History series. Black with red. Letterpress printing. Available on Fulcrum: No
- Berkshire Conference on the History of Women bookmark. First edition. 9" x 1". No series. Deep blue. Offset printing. Available on Fulcrum: Yes
- Helaine Victoria Press catalog. 8.75" x 6.25". 20 pages with booklist #4 insert. Black with red. Letterpress and offset printing. Available on Fulcrum: Yes

## 1979

- Elizabeth Gurley Flynn speaking postcard. Second edition. 5.5" x 7.25". No series. Charcoal. Offset printing. Available on Fulcrum: No
- Olive Schreiner postcard. Second edition. 5.5" x 7.25". No series. Charcoal, younger photo. Offset printing. Available on Fulcrum: No
- Ernestine Rose postcard. Second edition. 5.5" x 7.25". No series. Charcoal. Offset printing. Available on Fulcrum: No
- Gertrude Stein & Alice B. Toklas postcard. Fifth edition. 5.5" x 7.25". No series. Charcoal. Offset printing. Available on Fulcrum: No
- Sojourner Truth postcard. Sixth edition. 5.5" x 7.25". No series. Charcoal. Offset printing. Available on Fulcrum: No
- Rosa Bonheur postcard. Third edition. 5.5" x 7.25". No series. Charcoal. Offset printing. Available on Fulcrum: No
- Pioneers in Education, Bethune, Willard, and Crandall postcard. Third edition. 5.5" x 7.25". No series. Charcoal with red. Offset printing. Available on Fulcrum: No
- 1893 Woman's Building & Sophia Hayden postcard. Fifth edition. 5.5" x 7.25". No series. Charcoal. Offset printing. Available on Fulcrum: No
- Velma B. Johnston postcard. First edition. 3.5" x 5.5". Women & Ecology series. Black with yellow and orange. Letterpress printing. Available on Fulcrum: Yes
- Irene Herlocker postcard. First edition. 3.5" x 5.5". Women & Ecology series. Black with yellow and orange. Letterpress printing. Available on Fulcrum: Yes
- Ellen Swallow Richards postcard. First edition. 3.5" x 5.5". Women & Ecology series. Black with yellow and orange. Letterpress printing. Available on Fulcrum: Yes
- Hope Sawyer Buyukmihci postcard. First edition. 3.5" x 5.5". Women & Ecology series. Black with yellow and orange. Letterpress printing. Available on Fulcrum: Yes

- Women & Ecology postcard set. First edition. 3.5" x 5.5". Women & Ecology series. Brown with caramel and green. Letterpress printing. Available on Fulcrum: Yes
- Women & Ecology composite postcard. First edition. 3.5" x 5.5". Women & Ecology series. Brown with caramel and green. Letterpress printing. Available on Fulcrum: Yes
- Velma Johnston postcard. Second edition. 3.5" x 5.5". Women & Ecology series. Brown with caramel and green. Letterpress printing. Available on Fulcrum: Yes
- Irene Herlocker postcard. Second edition. 3.5" x 5.5". Women & Ecology series. Brown with caramel and green. Letterpress printing. Available on Fulcrum: Yes
- Ellen Swallow Richards postcard. Second edition. 3.5" x 5.5". Women & Ecology series. Brown with caramel and green. Letterpress printing. Available on Fulcrum: Yes
- Hope Sawyer Buyukmihci postcard. Second edition. 3.5" x 5.5". Women & Ecology series. Brown with caramel and green. Letterpress printing. Available on Fulcrum: Yes
- Bread & Roses Women in the American Labor Movement postcard set with cover. First edition. 4" x 8.25". Bread & Roses series. Red. Letterpress printing. Available on Fulcrum: Yes
- Bread & Roses composite postcard. First edition. 3.5" x 5.5". Bread & Roses series. Sepia. Letterpress printing. Available on Fulcrum: Yes
- Women's Trade Union League postcard. First edition. 3.5" x 5.5". Bread & Roses series. Sepia with blue and copper. Letterpress printing. Available on Fulcrum: Yes
- Women's Emergency Brigade postcard. First edition. 3.5" x 5.5". Bread & Roses series. Sepia with blue and copper. Letterpress printing. Available on Fulcrum: Yes
- Workers in an "Ideal" Factory postcard. First edition. 3.5" x 5.5". Bread & Roses series. Sepia with blue and copper. Letterpress printing. Available on Fulcrum: Yes
- Trackwomen on the Baltimore & Ohio Railroad postcard. First

edition. 3.5" x 5.5". Bread & Roses series. Sepia with blue and copper. Letterpress printing. Available on Fulcrum: Yes
- Lucy Parsons postcard. First edition. 3.5" x 5.5". Bread & Roses series. Sepia with blue and copper. Letterpress printing. Available on Fulcrum: Yes
- Crystal Lee Jordan Sutton postcard. First edition. 3.5" x 5.5". Bread & Roses series. Sepia with blue and copper. Letterpress printing. Available on Fulcrum: Yes
- Frances Perkins postcard. First edition. 3.5" x 5.5". Bread & Roses series. Sepia with blue and copper. Letterpress printing. Available on Fulcrum: Yes
- Rose Schneiderman and Dorothy Jacobs Bellanca postcard. First edition. 3.5" x 5.5". Bread & Roses series. Sepia with blue and copper. Letterpress printing. Available on Fulcrum: Yes
- Brookside bookplate. First edition. 3.5" x 4.25". Bookplate series. Black. Offset printing. Available on Fulcrum: Yes
- Circling Branch bookplate. First edition. 3.5" x 4.25". Bookplate series. Black. Offset printing. Available on Fulcrum: Yes
- Drinking Fawn bookplate. First edition. 3.5" x 4.25". Bookplate series. Black. Offset printing. Available on Fulcrum: Yes
- Phyllis Wheatley bookplate. First edition. 3.5" x 4.25". Bookplate series. Black. Offset printing. Available on Fulcrum: Yes
- Armchair Readers bookplate. First edition. 3.5" x 4.25". Bookplate series. Black. Offset printing. Available on Fulcrum: Yes
- Woman Voter bookplate. Second edition. 3.5" x 4.25". Bookplate series. Black. Offset printing. Available on Fulcrum: No
- Lady's Library bookplate. Second edition. 3.5" x 4.25". Bookplate series. Black. Offset printing. Available on Fulcrum: Yes
- Break-Time at the Defense Plant postcard. First edition. 5.5" x 7.25". No series. Sepia and silver-green. Letterpress printing. Available on Fulcrum: Yes

- Dian Fossey with Digit postcard. First edition. 5.5" x 7.25". No series. Sepia and green. Letterpress printing. Available on Fulcrum: Yes
- Margaret Sanger postcard. First edition. 5.5" x 7.25". No series. Dark blue and silver. Letterpress printing. Available on Fulcrum: Yes
- Jane Addams Hull House postcard. First edition. 5.5" x 7.25". No series. Dark blue and red. Letterpress printing. Available on Fulcrum: Yes
- "Do Something Rad-ish!" postcard. First edition. 3.5" x 5.5". No series. Red and green. Letterpress printing. Available on Fulcrum: Yes
- "Bidding You the Joys of Friendship & Love & All Life's Favors" postcard. First edition. 4.25" x 6". No series. Red with silver. Letterpress printing. Available on Fulcrum: Yes
- Susan B Anthony bookmark. First edition. 8.5" x 1.5". No series. Copper and blue. Offset printing. Available on Fulcrum: Yes
- Queen of the Cards bookmark. First edition. 8.5" x 1.5". No series. Brown and blue. Offset printing. Available on Fulcrum: Yes
- Ida B. Wells-Barnett postcard. Second edition. 4.25" x 6". Women of History. Black. Letterpress printing. Available on Fulcrum: No
- "Winter Greetings to You" postcard. Second edition. 5" x 7". No series. Blue, green, silver, brown. Letterpress printing. Available on Fulcrum: Yes
- "Do Something Rad-ish!" bumper sticker. First edition. 4" x 19". No series. Red and green. Letterpress printing. Available on Fulcrum: No
- "Come to a Country Celherbration for the Solstice" invitation notecard. First edition. 4.25" x 5.5". No series. Midnight blue on mustard. Letterpress printing. Available on Fulcrum: Yes
- Helaine Victoria Press Catalog, 1979-80. 6.25" x 9". 16 pages. Black with maroon. Offset printing. Available on Fulcrum: No

## 1980

- Helen May Butler & Her Ladies Brass Band postcard. First edition. 5.5" x 7.25". No series. Navy with sepia. Offset printing. Available on Fulcrum: Yes
- Break-Time at the Defense Plant postcard. Second edition. 5.5" x 7.25". No series. Sepia with blue. Offset printing. Available on Fulcrum: No
- Women of Colorado You Have the Vote postcard. First edition. 5.5" x 7.25". No series. Sepia and navy. Offset printing. Available on Fulcrum: Yes
- Amelia Earhart with Autogiro postcard. First edition. 5.5" x 7.25". No series. Blue and Sepia. Offset printing. Available on Fulcrum: Yes
- Trackwomen on the Baltimore & Ohio Railroad postcard. First edition. 5.5" x 7.25". No series. Sepia. Offset printing. Available on Fulcrum: Yes
- Students Making Barrel Furniture postcard. First edition. 5.5" x 7.25". No series. Sepia with navy. Offset printing. Available on Fulcrum: Yes
- Kimura Komako postcard. First edition. 3.5" x 5.5". No series. Sepia with navy. Offset printing. Available on Fulcrum: Yes
- Kimura Komako postcard. First edition. 3.5" x 5.5". No series. Navy with sepia. Offset printing. Available on Fulcrum: Yes
- Lucretia Mott postcard. First edition. 4.25" x 6". No series. Sepia with blue. Offset printing. Available on Fulcrum: Yes
- Suffragettes and the Pankhursts postcard. Fourth edition. 5.5" x 7.25". No series. Sepia with blue. Offset printing. Available on Fulcrum: Yes
- Susan B. Anthony in her study postcard. First edition. 4.25" x 6". No series. Black with gold. Letterpress printing. Available on Fulcrum: No
- "Bidding You the Joys of Friendship & Love & All Life's Favors" postcard. Second edition. 4.25" x 6". No series. Silver with red. Letterpress printing. Available on Fulcum: Yes

- The Woman Citizen postcard. First edition. 3.5" x 5.5". Liberty Series. Blue with red. Offset printing. Available on Fulcrum: Yes
- Ida B. Wells-Barnett postcard. Third edition. 4.25" x 6". Women of History. Black. Letterpress printing. Available on Fulcrum: No
- Bread & Roses composite postcard. Second edition. 3.5" x 5.5". Bread & Roses series. Sepia. Letterpress printing. Available on Fulcrum: Yes
- Women's Trade Union League postcard. Second edition. 3.5" x 5.5". Bread & Roses series. Sepia with blue and copper. Offset printing. Available on Fulcrum: Yes
- Women's Emergency Brigade postcard. Second edition. 3.5" x 5.5". Bread & Roses series. Sepia with blue and copper. Offset printing. Available on Fulcrum: Yes
- Workers in an "Ideal" Factory postcard. Second edition. 3.5" x 5.5". Bread & Roses series. Sepia with blue and copper. Offset printing. Available on Fulcrum: Yes
- Trackwomen on the Baltimore & Ohio Railroad postcard. Second edition. 3.5" x 5.5". Bread & Roses series. Sepia with blue and copper. Offset printing. Available on Fulcrum: Yes
- Lucy Parsons postcard. Second edition. 3.5" x 5.5". Bread & Roses series. Sepia with blue and copper. Offset printing. Available on Fulcrum: Yes
- Crystal Lee Jordan Sutton postcard. Second edition. 3.5" x 5.5". Bread & Roses series. Sepia with blue and copper. Offset printing. Available on Fulcrum: Yes
- Frances Perkins postcard. Second edition. 3.5" x 5.5". Bread & Roses series. Sepia with blue and copper. Offset printing. Available on Fulcrum: Yes
- Rose Schneiderman and Dorothy Jacobs Bellanca postcard. Second edition. 3.5" x 5.5". Bread & Roses series. Sepia with blue and copper. Offset printing. Available on Fulcrum: Yes
- Frances Perkins 1880–1965, First Day Cover postcard. First edition. 3.5" x 5.5". No series. Sepia with turquoise. Letterpress printing. Available on Fulcrum: Yes

- Frances Perkins 1880–1965, First Day Cover envelope. First edition. 3.5" x 6.5". No series. Sepia with turquoise. Letterpress printing. Available on Fulcrum: Yes
- Woman Citizen broadside. First edition. 9" x 12". No series. Dark blue and black with copper on Speckletone. Letterpress printing. Available on Fulcrum: Yes
- Cabbage print. First edition. 10" x 11.5". No series. Deep blue, yellow, brown, green, black. Letterpress printing. Available on Fulcrum: Yes
- Knock Knock, Jazz Age notecard. First edition. 4.25" x 5.5". Jazz Age series. Red, blue, and gray on ivory laid. Offset printing. Available on Fulcrum: Yes
- Bon voyage notecard. First edition. 4.25" x 5.5". Jazz Age series. Lime, blue, and black on ivory laid. Offset printing. Available on Fulcrum: No
- "I've been looking" notecard. First edition. 4.25" x 5.5". Jazz Age series. Black and red on ivory laid. Offset printing. Available on Fulcrum: No
- "Let's celebrate" notecard. First edition. 4.25" x 5.5". Jazz Age series. Black and pearl on ivory laid. Offset printing. Available on Fulcrum: No
- Mary Astell, title page to her treatise, 1694 notecard. Second edition. 4.25" x 5.5". Female Note-ables series. Black on ivory laid. Offset printing. Available on Fulcrum: No
- Birthday party at Vassar, 1903 notecard. Second edition. 4.25" x 5.5". Female Note-ables series. Black on ivory laid. Offset printing. Available on Fulcrum: No
- British suffrage campaign wagon notecard. Second edition. 4.25" x 5.5". Female Note-ables series. Black on ivory laid. Offset printing. Available on Fulcrum: No
- Radcliffe college play, 1900 notecard. Second edition. 4.25" x 5.5". Female Note-ables series. Black on ivory laid. Offset printing. Available on Fulcrum: No
- New woman gamblers on a train, 1895 notecard. Second

edition. 4.25" x 5.5". Female Note-ables series. Black on ivory laid. Offset printing. Available on Fulcrum: No
- Fanny Bullock Workman, "What can a woman do. . . ." notecard. Second edition. 4.25" x 5.5". Female Note-ables series. Black on ivory laid. Offset printing. Available on Fulcrum: No
- Anti-Fur notecard with the message notecard. Second edition. 4.25" x 5.5". Female Note-ables series. Black on ivory laid. Offset printing. Available on Fulcrum: No
- Bloomer costume cartoon notecard. Second edition. 4.25" x 5.5". Female Note-ables series. Black on ivory laid. Offset printing. Available on Fulcrum: No
- Folio, front. "Highlights from the History of Helaine Victoria Press." First edition. 10.5" x 6.5". No series. Black with maroon on ivory laid. Offset and letterpress printing. Available on Fulcrum: Yes
- Merchandise bag. Many editions (1980s). 7.5" x 11". No series. Black on brown bags. Letterpress printing. Available on Fulcrum: Yes
- "Winter Greetings to You" postcard. Second edition. 4.25" x 6". No series. Red, green, silver. Letterpress printing. Available on Fulcrum: No
- Helaine Victoria Press Catalog 1980–81. 6.25" x 9". Blue and black. Offset printing. Available on Fulcrum: Yes

## 1981

- May Massee postcard. First edition. 4.25" x 6". Muriel Fuller Memorial Series. Black with silver. Offset printing. Available on Fulcrum: Yes
- Minnie Earl Sears postcard. First edition. 4.25" x 6". Muriel Fuller Memorial Series. Black with silver. Offset printing. Available on Fulcrum: Yes
- Agnes Inglis postcard. First edition. 4.25" x 6". Muriel Fuller Memorial Series. Black with silver. Offset printing. Available on Fulcrum: Yes

- Eliza Atkins Gleason postcard. First edition. 4.25" x 6". Muriel Fuller Memorial Series. Black with silver. Offset printing. Available on Fulcrum: Yes
- Margaret E. Monroe postcard. First edition. 4.25" x 6". Muriel Fuller Memorial Series. Black with silver. Offset printing. Available on Fulcrum: Yes
- Amelia Earhart & the 99s postcard. Third edition. 4.25" x 6". Women of History series. Black with red. Offset and letterpress printing. Available on Fulcrum: Yes
- George Sand postcard. Second edition. 4.25" x 6". Women of History series. Black. Offset printing. Available on Fulcrum: No
- Aphra Behn postcard. Second edition. 4.25" x 6". Women of History series. Black with silver. Offset printing. Available on Fulcrum: No
- Isadora Duncan postcard. Second edition. 4.25" x 6". Women of History series. Black. Offset printing. Available on Fulcrum: No
- Mother Jones postcard. Second edition. 4.25" x 6". Women of History series. Black. Offset printing. Available on Fulcrum: No
- Margaret Fuller postcard. Second edition. 4.25" x 6". Women of History series. Black with silver. Offset printing. Available on Fulcrum: No
- Victoria Woodhull postcard. Second edition. 4.25" x 6". Women of History series. Black with silver. Offset printing. Available on Fulcrum: No
- Emily Carr postcard. Fifth edition. 5.5" x 7.25". No series. Sepia with copper. Offset printing. Available on Fulcrum: No
- Susan B. Anthony & Elizabeth Cady Stanton postcard. First edition, new photos. 5.5" x 7.25". No series. Sepia with copper. Offset printing. Available on Fulcrum: Yes
- Whiskey Crusade postcard. First edition. 5.5" x 7.25". No series. Sepia with blue. Offset printing. Available on Fulcrum: Yes
- Gertrude Stein & Alice B. Toklas postcard. Sixth edition. 5.5" x 7.25". No series. Sepia with blue. Offset printing. Available on Fulcrum: No

- 1893 Woman's Building & Sophia Hayden. Sixth edition. 5.5" x 7.25". No series. Sepia with blue. Offset printing. Available on Fulcrum: No
- Radclyffe Hall and Una Troubridge postcard. Fifth edition. 5.5" x 7.25". No series. Sepia with blue. Offset printing. Available on Fulcrum: No
- Rosa Bonheur postcard. Fourth edition. 5.5" x 7.25". No series. Sepia. Offset printing. Available on Fulcrum: No
- Trackwomen on the Baltimore & Ohio Railroad postcard. Second edition. 5.5" x 7.25". No series. Sepia. Offset printing. Available on Fulcrum: No
- Sojourner Truth postcard. Seventh edition. 5.5" x 7.25". No series. Sepia with blue. Offset printing. Available on Fulcrum: No
- Break-Time at the Defense Plant postcard. Third edition. 5.5" x 7.25". No series. Sepia with blue. Offset printing. Available on Fulcrum: No
- Susan B. Anthony in her study postcard. Second edition. 4.25" x 6". No series. Black with gold and red. Letterpress printing. Available on Fulcrum: Yes
- May Your Solstice Be Merry postcard. First edition. 4.25" x 6". No series. Purple with rose and silver. Letterpress printing. Available on Fulcrum: Yes
- "Women constitute half the world's population" postcard. First edition. 4.25" x 6". Women & Words. Burnt orange. Letterpress printing. Available on Fulcrum: Yes
- Too Much of a Good Thing postcard. First edition. 4.25" x 6". Women & Words. Magenta with deep blue. Letterpress printing. Available on Fulcrum: Yes
- "As a Woman," Virginia Woolf postcard. First edition. 4.25" x 6". Women & Words. Dark green. Letterpress printing. Available on Fulcrum: Yes
- Holiday Rebus broadside. First edition. 8.5" x 11". No series. Dark blue on assorted handmade papers. Letterpress printing. Available on Fulcrum: Yes

- Mary Astell, title page to her 1694 treatise notecard. Third edition. 5.5" x 4.25". Note-Ables series. Black on gold laid. Offset printing. Available on Fulcrum: No
- Fanny Bullock Workman notecard. Third edition. 5.5" x 4.25". Note-Ables series. Black on gold laid. Offset printing. Available on Fulcrum: No
- Anti-Fur notecard. Third edition. 5.5" x 4.25". Note-Ables series. Black on gold laid. Offset printing. Available on Fulcrum: No
- Birthday party at Vassar, 1903 notecard. Third edition. 5.5" x 4.25". Note-Ables series. Black on gold laid. Offset printing. Available on Fulcrum: No
- British suffrage campaign wagon notecard. Third edition. 5.5" x 4.25". Note-Ables series. Black on gold laid. Offset printing. Available on Fulcrum: No
- Bloomer costume cartoon Radcliffe College play, notecard. Third edition. 5.5" x 4.25". Note-Ables series. Black on gold laid. Offset printing. Available on Fulcrum: No
- New woman gamblers, 1895 notecard. Third edition. 5.5" x 4.25". Note-Ables series. Black on gold laid. Offset printing. Available on Fulcrum: No
- Radcliffe College play, 1900 notecard. Third edition. 5.5" x 4.25". Note-Ables series. Black on gold laid. Offset printing. Available on Fulcrum: No
- Helaine Victoria Press Picture Postcard Catalog Supplement. 5.5" x 7.5", opens to 15.75" x 15". Black. Offset printing. Available on Fulcrum: Yes

## 1982

- Elsa Gidlow postcard. First edition. 5.5" x 7.25". No series. Sepia with gold. Letterpress printing. Available on Fulcrum: Yes
- Harriet Tubman postcard. First edition. 4.25" x 6". No series. Sepia with blue. Letterpress printing. Available on Fulcrum: Yes
- Zora Neale Hurston postcard. First – Third edition. 5.5" x 7.25".

No series. Sepia with coral. Letterpress printing. Available on Fulcrum: Yes
- Susan B. Anthony in her study postcard. Third edition. 4.25" x 6". No series. Black with copper and red. Letterpress printing. Available on Fulcrum: Yes
- Agnes Vanderburg postcard. First edition. 5.5" x 7.25". No series. Sepia with green. Letterpress printing. Available on Fulcrum: No
- Phyllis Carter postcard. First edition. 5.5" x 7.25". No series. Deep blue with maroon. Letterpress printing. Available on Fulcrum: Yes
- Emma Goldman postcard. First edition. 5.5" x 7.25". No series. Dark blue with light blue. Letterpress printing. Available on Fulcrum: Yes
- Dian Fossey with Digit postcard. Second edition. 5.5" x 7.25". No series. Sepia and green. Letterpress printing. Available on Fulcrum: No
- Sojourner Truth postcard. First edition. 5.5" x 7.25". No series. Sepia with dark blue, new photo, sitting. Offset printing. Available on Fulcrum: No
- Kimura Komako postcard. First edition. 5.5" x 7.25". No series. Sepia with dark blue. Offset printing. Available on Fulcrum: No
- Break-Time at the Defense Plant postcard. Fourth edition. 5.5" x 7.25". No series. Sepia with dark blue. Offset printing. Available on Fulcrum: No
- Postcard Archives Project brochure. First edition. 7.5" x 9". No series. Black. Photocopy printing. Available on Fulcrum: Yes
- Postcard Archives Project certificate. First edition. 5.5" x 8". No series. Red and silver. Letterpress printing. Available on Fulcrum: Yes
- Postcard Archives Project envelope. First edition. 5.75" x 8.25". No series. Red. Letterpress printing. Available on Fulcrum: Yes
- Helaine Victoria Press Winter Supplement. 8.5" x 14". 4 pages. Black. Photocopy. Available on Fulcrum: No

- Helaine Victoria Press 1982-83 Postcard Catalog. 16" x 11.5". 20 pages. Black. Web press tabloid printing. Available on Fulcrum: No

1983

- Women and Papermaking folio. First edition. 5" x 6.5". Women and Papermaking series. Red, on tweedy gray handmade cotton rag paper. Letterpress printing. Available on Fulcrum: Yes
- Otomi Woman postcard. First edition. 4.25" x 6". Women and Papermaking series. Sepia, handmade burlap with cattail paper. Letterpress printing. Available on Fulcrum: Yes
- 18th Century Finishing Work postcard. First edition. 4.25" x 6". Women and Papermaking series. Sepia, on handmade white cotton rag with gray. Letterpress printing. Available on Fulcrum: Yes
- Rag Pickers postcard. First edition. 4.25" x 6". Women and Papermaking series. Sepia, on handmade white cotton rag with lavender. Letterpress printing. Available on Fulcrum: Yes
- Washi Papermaker postcard. First edition. 4.25" x 6". Women and Papermaking series. Sepia, on handmade burlap and white cotton paper with glitter. Letterpress printing. Available on Fulcrum: Yes
- Otomi Woman postcard. First edition. 4.25" x 6". Women and Papermaking series. Sepia. Letterpress printing. Available on Fulcrum: Yes
- 18th Century Finishing Work postcard. First edition. 4.25" x 6". Women and Papermaking series. Sepia. Letterpress printing. Available on Fulcrum: Yes
- Rag Pickers postcard. First edition. 4.25" x 6". Women and Papermaking series. Sepia. Letterpress printing. Available on Fulcrum: Yes

- Washi Papermaker postcard. First edition. 4.25" x 6". Women and Papermaking series. Sepia. Letterpress printing. Available on Fulcrum: Yes
- Zora Neale Hurston postcard. Fourth edition. 5.5" x 7.25". No series. Sepia with coral. Letterpress printing. Available on Fulcrum: No
- Celebrating Our 10th Year postcard. First edition. 4.25" x 6". No series. Blue with red. Letterpress printing. Available on Fulcrum: Yes
- Celebrating Our 10th Year postcard. First edition. 4.25" x 6". No series. Blue with red on handmade white cotton rag. Letterpress printing. Available on Fulcrum: Yes
- Celebrating Helaine Victoria Press's Tenth Year bookmark. First edition. 7.25" x 2". No series. Black on mixed color card stock. Letterpress printing. Available on Fulcrum: Yes
- Ten Year Retrospective Exhibit Opening Invitation postcard. First edition. 4.25" x 6". No series. Black. Letterpress printing. Available on Fulcrum: Yes
- Ten Year Retrospective Exhibit Opening poster. First edition. 10.5" x 16.25". No series. Black and red. Letterpress printing. Available on Fulcrum: Yes
- Equal Rights Amendment poster. First edition. 11" x 14". No series. Black on ivory, small. Offset printing. Available on Fulcrum: No
- 1983 Helaine Victoria Press Tenth Anniversary Resource Catalog. 16" x 11.5". 8 pages. Black with blue. Web press tabloid printing. Available on Fulcrum: No
- 1983 Helaine Victoria Press October mailer. 8.5" x 11". 4 pages. Black with orange. Photocopy and letterpress printing. Available on Fulcrum: No
- 1983–84 Helaine Victoria Press catalog. 16" x 11.5". 20 pages. Black with red. Web press tabloid printing. Available on Fulcrum: No

1984

- Mary Antin postcard. First edition. 5.5" x 7.25". Jewish series. Sepia with lavender. Offset printing. Available on Fulcrum: Yes
- Uprising of the 20,000 & Clara Lemlich postcard. First edition. 5.5" x 7.25". Jewish series. Sepia with lavender. Offset printing. Available on Fulcrum: Yes
- Rosa Sonneschein postcard. First edition. 5.5" x 7.25". Jewish series. Sepia with lavender. Offset printing. Available on Fulcrum: Yes
- The National Council of Jewish Women postcard. First edition. 5.5" x 7.25". Jewish series. Sepia with lavender. Offset printing. Available on Fulcrum: Yes
- Emma Tenayuca postcard. First edition. 5.5" x 7.25". No series. Sepia with lavender. Offset printing. Available on Fulcrum: Yes
- Mary McLeod Bethune postcard. First edition. 5.5" x 7.25". No series. Sepia with lavender. Offset printing. Available on Fulcrum: Yes
- Helen May Butler & Her Ladies Brass Band postcard. Second edition. 5.5" x 7.25". No series. Sepia with lavender. Offset printing. Available on Fulcrum: No
- Jane Addams & Mary McDowell postcard. First edition. 5.5" x 7.25". No series. Sepia with lavender. Offset printing. Available on Fulcrum: Yes
- Kimura Komako postcard. Second edition. 5.5" x 7.25". No series. Sepia with lavender. Offset printing. Available on Fulcrum: No
- Working for Women's Rights bookmark. Second edition. 7" x 2". No series. Sepia with lavender. Offset printing. Available on Fulcrum: Yes
- Latina History bookmark. First edition. 7" x 2". No series. Sepia with lavender. Offset printing. Available on Fulcrum: Yes
- Celebrating International Working Women's Day bookmark. First edition. 6" x 2". No series. Sepia with lavender. Offset printing. Available on Fulcrum: Yes

- Madam C. J. Walker postcard. First edition. 5.5" x 7.25". No series. Black with silvery lavender. Letterpress printing. Available on Fulcrum: Yes
- Madam C. J. Walker postcard. Second edition. 5.5" x 7.25". No series. Black with red. Letterpress printing. Available on Fulcrum: No
- Phyllis Carter postcard. Second edition. 5.5" x 7.25". No series. Deep blue with maroon. Letterpress printing. Available on Fulcrum: Yes
- The Woman Citizen postcard. Second edition. 3.5" x 5.5". Liberty Series. Purple with deep orange. Letterpress printing. Available on Fulcrum: No
- Adrienne Rich, "Split at the Root" broadside. First edition. 10.5" x 16". No series. Black with deep red on handmade white cotton rag paper with a hint of blush. Letterpress printing. Available on Fulcrum: Yes
- Michelle Cliff from Abeng broadside. First edition. 12.5" x 18". No series. Black with deep red on handmade off-white cotton rag paper with a blue burlap ribbon and beige manila hemp ribbon. Letterpress printing. Available on Fulcrum: Yes
- Adrienne Rich, "Split at the Root" broadside. First edition. 10.5" x 16". No series. Black with deep red on white. Letterpress printing. Available on Fulcrum: Yes
- Michelle Cliff from Abeng broadside. First edition. 12.5" x 18". No series. Black with deep red on white. Letterpress printing. Available on Fulcrum: Yes
- Labyris handmade paper art print. First edition. 8.5" x 11". No series. Lavender and white. Available on Fulcrum: Yes
- Peace Dove handmade paper art print. First edition. 8.5" x 11". No series. Gray and white. Available on Fulcrum: Yes
- Helaine Victoria Press 1984 Summer Supplement. 16" x 11.5". 8 pages. Black with green. Web press tabloid printing. Available on Fulcrum: No
- 1984–85 Helaine Victoria Press Catalog. 16" x 11.25". 20 pages.

Black with green. Web press tabloid printing. Available on Fulcrum: No

## 1985

- Women in the American Labor Movement folio. First edition. 4.5" x 6.25". Women in the American Labor Movement series. Black with blue, red, and rose. Offset printing. Available on Fulcrum: Yes
- Sit-down Strikes postcard. First edition. 4.25" x 6". Women in the American Labor Movement series. Black with blue and rose. Offset printing. Available on Fulcrum: Yes
- Voltairine de Cleyre postcard. First edition. 4.25" x 6". Women in the American Labor Movement series. Black with blue and rose. Offset printing. Yes
- Dolores Huerta postcard. First edition. 4.25" x 6". Women in the American Labor Movement series. Black with purple and red. Offset printing. Available on Fulcrum: Yes
- Blue Collar Asian Women (BCAW) postcard. First edition. 4.25" x 6". Women in the American Labor Movement series. Black with blue and rose. Offset printing. Available on Fulcrum: Yes
- Rose Pesotta postcard. First edition. 4.25" x 6". Women in the American Labor Movement series. Black with rose. Offset printing. Available on Fulcrum: Yes
- Maida Springer-Kemp postcard. First edition. 4.25" x 6". Women in the American Labor Movement series. Black with blue and rose. Offset printing. Available on Fulcrum: Yes
- Haymarket postcard. First edition. 4.25" x 6". Women in the American Labor Movement series. Black with red. Offset printing. Available on Fulcrum: Yes
- May Day Parade postcard. First edition. 4.25" x 6". Women in the American Labor Movement series. Black with blue and red. Offset printing. Available on Fulcrum: Yes
- Lucy Gonzales Parsons postcard. First edition. 4.25" x 6".

Women in the American Labor Movement series. Black with red. Offset printing. Available on Fulcrum: Yes
- Zora Neale Hurston postcard. Fifth edition. 5.5" x 7.25". No series. Sepia with blue. Offset printing. Available on Fulcrum: No
- Madam C. J. Walker postcard. Third edition. 5.5" x 7.25". No series. Sepia with blue. Offset printing. Available on Fulcrum: No
- Trackwomen on the Baltimore & Ohio Railroad postcard. Third edition. 5.5" x 7.25". No series. Sepia. Offset printing. Available on Fulcrum: No
- Sojourner Truth postcard. Second edition. 5.5" x 7.25". No series. Sepia with blue, photo sitting. Offset printing. Available on Fulcrum: No
- Break-Time at the Defense Plant postcard. Fifth edition. 5.5" x 7.25". No series. Sepia with blue. Offset printing. Available on Fulcrum: No
- Edmonia Lewis postcard. First edition. 4.25" x 6". No series. Black with blue and red. Offset printing. Available on Fulcrum: Yes
- Mother Jones postcard. Third edition. 4.25" x 6". Women of History Series. Black with blue. Offset printing. Available on Fulcrum: No
- Rosie the Riveter postcard. First edition (multiple editions). 4.25" x 6". No series. Full color. Offset printing. Available on Fulcrum: Yes
- Connie Marsh Memorial print. First edition. 12"x 18". No series. Deep green, sky blue, light green, black, yellow, tangerine, rose, purple, and brown. Letterpress printing. Available on Fulcrum: Yes
- Zora Neale Hurston T-shirt. First edition. No series. Sepia and black with red on white. Silkscreen printing. Available on Fulcrum: No
- Rosie the Riveter T-shirt. First edition. No series. Blue, red,

beige, and brown on gold. Silkscreen printing. Available on Fulcrum: No
- 1985 Helaine Victoria Press Catalog. 15.5" x 11". 20 pages. Black with lavender. Web press tabloid printing. Available on Fulcrum: No

## 1986

- Emma Lazarus and the New Colossus postcard. First edition. 4.25" x 6". No series. Black with rose and turquoise. Letterpress printing. Available on Fulcrum: Yes
- Sum•Her Soul•Stice Wishes postcard. First edition. 4.25" x 6". No series. Black with pink and blue. Letterpress printing. Available on Fulcrum: Yes
- Zora Neale Hurston postcard. Sixth edition. 5.5" x 7.25". No series. Sepia with coral red. Offset printing. Available on Fulcrum: Yes
- Amelia Earhart and Eleanor Roosevelt postcard. Second edition. 5.5" x 7.25". No series. Sepia with coral red. Offset printing. Available on Fulcrum: Yes
- Harriet Tubman postcard. First edition. 5.5" x 7.25". No series. Sepia with coral red. Offset printing. Available on Fulcrum: Yes
- Madam C. J. Walker postcard. Fourth edition. 5.5" x 7.25". No series. Sepia with coral red. Offset printing. Available on Fulcrum: Yes
- Trackwomen on the Baltimore & Ohio Railroad postcard. Fourth edition. 5.5" x 7.25". No series. Sepia. Offset printing. Available on Fulcrum: No
- Sojourner Truth postcard. Eighth edition. 5.5" x 7.25". No series. Sepia with coral red, quote. Offset printing. Available on Fulcrum: No
- Susan B. Anthony in her study. Fourth edition. 4.25" x 6". No series. Sepia with coral red. Offset printing. Available on Fulcrum: No

- Frances Willard on her bicycle. Third edition. 5.5" x 7.25". No series. Sepia. Offset printing. Available on Fulcrum: No
- Soldaderas postcard. First edition. 5.5" x 7.25". The History and Culture of US Latinas and Latin American Women series. Sepia duotone with peach. English version. Offset printing. Available on Fulcrum: Yes
- Emma Tenayuca postcard. First edition. 5.5" x 7.25". The History and Culture of US Latinas and Latin American Women series. Sepia duotone with peach. English version. Offset printing. Available on Fulcrum: Yes
- Dora María Téllez postcard. First edition. 5.5" x 7.25". The History and Culture of US Latinas and Latin American Women series. Sepia duotone with peach. English version. Offset printing. Available on Fulcrum: Yes
- Rosario Castellanos postcard. First edition. 5.5" x 7.25". The History and Culture of US Latinas and Latin American Women series. Sepia duotone with peach. English version. Offset printing. Available on Fulcrum: Yes
- Jovita Idar postcard. First edition. 5.5" x 7.25". The History and Culture of US Latinas and Latin American Women series. Sepia duotone with peach. English version. Offset printing. Available on Fulcrum: Yes
- Lolita Lebrón postcard. First edition. 5.5" x 7.25". The History and Culture of US Latinas and Latin American Women series. Sepia duotone with peach. English version. Offset printing. Available on Fulcrum: Yes
- Josefina Villafañe de Martínez-Alvarez postcard. First edition. 5.5" x 7.25". The History and Culture of US Latinas and Latin American Women series. Sepia duotone with peach. English version. Offset printing. Available on Fulcrum: Yes
- Soldaderas postcard. First edition. 5.5" x 7.25". The History and Culture of US Latinas and Latin American Women series. Sepia duotone with peach. Spanish version. Offset printing. Available on Fulcrum: Yes

- Emma Tenayuca postcard. First edition. 5.5" x 7.25". The History and Culture of US Latinas and Latin American Women series. Sepia duotone with peach. Spanish version. Offset printing. Yes
- Dora María Téllez postcard. First edition. 5.5" x 7.25". The History and Culture of US Latinas and Latin American Women series. Sepia duotone with peach. Spanish version. Offset printing. Available on Fulcrum: Yes
- Rosario Castellanos postcard. First edition. 5.5" x 7.25". The History and Culture of US Latinas and Latin American Women series. Sepia duotone with peach. Spanish version. Offset printing. Available on Fulcrum: Yes
- Jovita Idar postcard. First edition. 5.5" x 7.25". The History and Culture of US Latinas and Latin American Women series. Sepia duotone with peach. Spanish version. Offset printing. Available on Fulcrum: Yes
- Lolita Lebrón postcard. First edition. 5.5" x 7.25". The History and Culture of US Latinas and Latin American Women series. Sepia duotone with peach. Spanish version. Offset printing. Available on Fulcrum: Yes
- Josefina Villafañe de Martínez-Alvarez postcard. First edition. 5.5" x 7.25". The History and Culture of US Latinas and Latin American Women series. Sepia duotone with peach. Spanish version. Offset printing. Available on Fulcrum: Yes
- Yoshiko Hayakawa postcard. First edition. 5.5" x 7.25". No series. Sepia duotone with peach. Offset printing. Available on Fulcrum: Yes
- Girls' Basketball Team postcard. First edition. 5.5" x 7.25". No series. Sepia duotone with peach. Offset printing. Available on Fulcrum: Yes
- Latina History and Culture bookmark. Second edition. 7.5" x 2". No series. Sepia duotone with peach. Offset printing. Available on Fulcrum: Yes

- Elsa Gidlow bookmark. Second edition. 7" x 2". No series. Sepia duotone with peach. Offset printing. Available on Fulcrum: Yes
- Helaine Victoria Press Women's History Shop bookmark. First edition. 7" x 2". No series. Sepia duotone with peach. Offset printing. Available on Fulcrum: No
- History & Culture of US Latinas and Latin American Women mailing bag. First edition. 6.5" x 9.5". No series. Green and orange. Letterpress printing. Available on Fulcrum: Yes
- Store Opening Invitation postcard. First edition. 4.25" x 6". No series. Black with red. Letterpress printing. Available on Fulcrum: Yes
- Helaine Victoria Press Spring Supplement. 15.5" x 11". 4 pages. Black with yellow. Web press tabloid printing. Available on Fulcrum: No
- 1986–87 Helaine Victoria Press Catalog. 15.5" x 11". 16 pages. Black with blue. Web press tabloid printing. Available on Fulcrum: No

## 1987

- Mary Fields postcard. First edition. 5.5" x 7.25". No series. Sepia with turquoise. Offset printing. Available on Fulcrum: Yes
- Ernestine Rose (new) postcard. First edition. 5.5" x 7.25". No series. Sepia with turquoise. Offset printing. Available on Fulcrum: Yes
- Emma Goldman postcard. Second edition. 5.5" x 7.25". No series. Sepia with turquoise. Offset printing. Available on Fulcrum: No
- Susan B. Anthony & Elizabeth Cady Stanton postcard. Second edition. 5.5" x 7.25". No series. Sepia with turquoise. Offset printing, new photo. Available on Fulcrum: Yes
- Mary McLeod Bethune postcard. Second edition. 5.5" x 7.25". No series. Sepia with turquoise. Offset printing. Available on Fulcrum: No

- Elizabeth Gurley Flynn speaking postcard. Third edition. 5.5" x 7.25". No series. Sepia with turquoise. Offset printing. Available on Fulcrum: Yes
- Rosa Luxemburg and Clara Zetkin postcard. Fifth edition. 5.5" x 7.25". No series. Sepia with turquoise. Offset printing. Available on Fulcrum: No
- Amelia Earhart with Autogiro postcard. Second edition. 5.5" x 7.25". No series. Sepia with turquoise. Offset printing. Available on Fulcrum: Yes
- Agnes Vanderburg postcard. Second edition. 5.5" x 7.25". No series. Sepia with turquoise. Offset printing. Available on Fulcrum: Yes
- Blue Collar Asian Women (BCAW) postcard. Second edition. 4.25" x 6". Women in the American Labor Movement series. Sepia with turquoise. Offset printing. Available on Fulcrum: Yes
- Hard Times Cotton Mill Girls, Corine Lytle Cannon postcard. First edition. 4.25" x 6". No series. Silvery lavender. Letterpress printing. Available on Fulcrum: Yes
- Rosie the Riveter postcard. Second - Fourth editions. 4.25" x 6". No series. Full color. Offset printing. Available on Fulcrum: No
- Winter Greeting postcard. First edition. 5" x 7". No series. Green, silver, and red. Letterpress printing. Available on Fulcrum: Yes
- 15 Year Anniversary Handmade Folio Cover. First edition. 9" x 12". 15 year series. Black with silvery lavender on handmade mauve paper. Letterpress printing. Available on Fulcrum: Yes
- Virginia Snow Stephen, Anti-Capital Punishment broadside. First edition. 8.5" x 11". 15 year series. White with black and red on handmade dark gray cotton rag paper with red abaca blotch. Letterpress printing. Available on Fulcrum: Yes
- Nadine Stair, "If I Had My Life to Live Over" broadside. First edition. 8.5" x 11". 15 year series. Blue with green on handmade white abaca and burlap paper with purple, yellow, and pink squeegee layers. Letterpress printing. Available on Fulcrum: Yes

- Anzia Yezierska, "First Time in My Life" broadside. First edition. 8.5" x 11". 15 year series. Dark blue with maroon on handmade white cotton rag, string, and jute paper with gray cotton rag border. Letterpress printing. Available on Fulcrum: Yes
- Virginia Snow Stephen, Anti-Capital Punishment broadside. First edition. 8.5" x 11". 15 year series. Black with red on white. Letterpress printing. Available on Fulcrum: No
- Nadine Stair, "If I Had My Life to Live Over" broadside. First edition. 8.5" x 11". 15 year series. Blue with green and pink on white. Letterpress printing. Available on Fulcrum: No
- Anzia Yezierska, "First Time in My Life" broadside. First edition. 8.5" x 11". 15 year series. Dark blue with maroon on white. Letterpress printing. Available on Fulcrum: No
- Latina History and Culture bookmark. Second edition. 7.5" x 2". No series. Sepia with turquoise. Offset printing. Available on Fulcrum: No
- Rosie the Riveter bookmark. Second edition. 6" x 2". No series. Sepia with turquoise. Offset printing. Available on Fulcrum: No
- 1987–88 Helaine Victoria Press Catalog. 15.5" x 11". 16 pages. Black with red. Web press tabloid printing. Available on Fulcrum: Yes

## 1988

- Rosa Parks. First edition. 5.5" x 7.25". No series. Sepia with light orange. Offset printing. Available on Fulcrum: Yes
- Zora Neale Hurston postcard. Seventh edition. 5.5" x 7.25". No series. Sepia with light orange. Offset printing. Available on Fulcrum: No
- WWI Rivet-gang Workers postcard. First edition. 5.5" x 7.25". No series. Sepia with light orange. Offset printing. Available on Fulcrum: Yes
- Phyllis Carter postcard. Third edition. 5.5" x 7.25". No series. Sepia with light orange. Offset printing. Available on Fulcrum: No

- Elsa Gidlow postcard. First edition. 5.5" x 7.25". No series. Sepia with light orange, three photos. Offset printing. Available on Fulcrum: Yes
- Dian Fossey (posthumous) with Digit postcard. Third edition. 5.5" x 7.25". No series. Sepia and light orange. Offset printing. Available on Fulcrum: No
- Two Irish Women, Constance Markievicz and Maud Gonne postcard. Fourth edition. 5.5" x 7.25". No series. Sepia with light orange. Offset printing. Available on Fulcrum: No
- Sojourner Truth postcard. Ninth edition. 5.5" x 7.25". No series. Sepia with light orange. Offset printing. Available on Fulcrum: No
- Rosa Bonheur postcard. Fourth edition. 5.5" x 7.25". No series. Sepia. Offset printing. Available on Fulcrum: No
- Amelia Earhart T-shirt. First edition. No series. White on black. Silkscreen printing. Available on Fulcrum: No
- Sojourner Truth T-shirt. First edition. No series. Sepia, black, and red on white. Silkscreen printing. Available on Fulcrum: No
- Art Auction Featuring International Contemporary Art by Women poster. First edition. 10.5" x 16.25". No series. Black and deep red. Letterpress printing. Available on Fulcrum: Yes
- Helaine Victoria 1988-89 Catalog. 11.25" x 16". 16 pages. Black with green. Web press tabloid printing. Available on Fulcrum: No

## 1989

- Queen Liliuokalani postcard. First edition. 5.5" x 7.25". No series. Sepia with light rose. Offset printing. Available on Fulcrum: Yes
- Women's Land Army postcard. First edition. 5.5" x 7.25". No series. Sepia with rose and deep rose. Offset printing. Available on Fulcrum: Yes
- Jane Addams & Mary McDowell postcard. Second edition. 5.5" x

7.25". No series. Sepia with deep rose. Offset printing. Available on Fulcrum: No
- Uprising of the 20,000 & Clara Lemlich postcard. Second edition. 5.5" x 7.25". Jewish series. Sepia with deep rose. Offset printing. Available on Fulcrum: No
- Alice Paul postcard. Fourth edition. 5.5" x 7.25". No series. Sepia with deep rose. Offset printing. Available on Fulcrum: No
- Break-Time at the Defense Plant postcard. Sixth edition. 5.5" x 7.25". No series. Sepia with deep rose. Offset printing. Available on Fulcrum: No
- Students Making Barrel Furniture postcard. Second edition. 5.5" x 7.25". No series. Sepia with deep rose. Offset printing. Available on Fulcrum: No
- Harriet Tubman postcard. Second edition. 5.5" x 7.25". No series. Sepia with deep rose. Offset printing. Available on Fulcrum: No
- Trackwomen on the Baltimore & Ohio Railroad postcard. Fifth edition. 5.5" x 7.25". No series. Sepia. Offset printing. Available on Fulcrum: No
- Women in Social Protest postcard set, front cover. First edition. 4.5" x 6.25". Women in Social Protest: The US Since 1915 series. Sepia with deep rose and black. Offset printing. Available on Fulcrum: Yes
- Gallaudet University Women Students Protest postcard. First edition. 4.25" x 6". Women in Social Protest: The US Since 1915 series. Sepia with black. Offset printing. Available on Fulcrum: Yes
- Disability Rights, Sharon Kowalski, Lesbian and Gay March postcard. First edition. 4.25" x 6". Women in Social Protest: The US Since 1915 series. Sepia with black. Offset printing. Available on Fulcrum: Yes
- Lesbian & Gay March on Washington postcard. First edition. 4.25" x 6". Women in Social Protest: The US Since 1915 series. Sepia with black. Offset printing. Available on Fulcrum: Yes

- Anti-Pornography March postcard. First edition. 4.25" x 6". Women in Social Protest: The US Since 1915 series. Sepia with black. Offset printing. Available on Fulcrum: Yes
- Chinese American Women Demonstrate Against Childcare Cutbacks postcard. First edition. 4.25" x 6". Women in Social Protest: The US Since 1915 series. Sepia with black. Offset printing. Available on Fulcrum: Yes
- Dine (Navajo) The Longest Walk postcard. First edition. 4.25" x 6". Women in Social Protest: The US Since 1915 series. Sepia with black. Offset printing. Available on Fulcrum: Yes
- Chinese American Garment Workers Strike postcard. First edition. 4.25" x 6". Women in Social Protest: The US Since 1915 series. Sepia with black. Offset printing. Available on Fulcrum: Yes
- African American Women Anti-War postcard. First edition. 4.25" x 6". Women in Social Protest: The US Since 1915 series. Sepia with black. Offset printing. Available on Fulcrum: Yes
- "Jim Crow Can't Teach," School Boycott postcard. First edition. 4.25" x 6". Women in Social Protest: The US Since 1915 series. Sepia with black. Offset printing. Available on Fulcrum: Yes
- Makeshift Jail, Greensboro, NC postcard. First edition. 4.25" x 6". Women in Social Protest: The US Since 1915 series. Sepia with black. Offset printing. Available on Fulcrum: Yes
- Women Strike for Peace postcard. First edition. 4.25" x 6". Women in Social Protest: The US Since 1915 series. Sepia with black. Offset printing. Available on Fulcrum: Yes
- NAACP Woolworth's Picket postcard. First edition. 4.25" x 6". Women in Social Protest: The US Since 1915 series. Sepia with black. Offset printing. Available on Fulcrum: Yes
- Anti-Lynching Demonstration postcard. First edition. 4.25" x 6". Women in Social Protest: The US Since 1915 series. Sepia with black. Offset printing. Available on Fulcrum: Yes
- Jewish Women Voter Registration postcard. First edition. 4.25" x 6". Women in Social Protest: The US Since 1915 series. Sepia with black. Offset printing. Available on Fulcrum: Yes

- Mill Workers Strike, Greensboro, GA postcard. First edition. 4.25" x 6". Women in Social Protest: The US Since 1915 series. Sepia with black. Offset printing. Available on Fulcrum: Yes
- California Cotton Pickers postcard. First edition. 4.25" x 6". Women in Social Protest: The US Since 1915 series. Sepia with black. Offset printing. Available on Fulcrum: Yes
- Tulsa Massacre 1921 postcard. First edition. 4.25" x 6". Women in Social Protest: The US Since 1915 series. Sepia with black. Offset printing. Available on Fulcrum: Yes
- Suffrage Parade 1915, NYC postcard. First edition. 4.25" x 6". Women in Social Protest: The US Since 1915 series. Sepia with black. Offset printing. Available on Fulcrum: Yes
- Phelps Dodge Copper Strike postcard. First edition. 4.25" x 6". Women in Social Protest: The US Since 1915 series. Sepia with black. Offset printing. Available on Fulcrum: Yes
- Amazons Against Nukes postcard. First edition. 4.25" x 6". Women in Social Protest: The US Since 1915 series. Sepia with black. Offset printing. Available on Fulcrum: Yes
- End Police Murders Demonstration postcard. First edition. 4.25" x 6". Women in Social Protest: The US Since 1915 series. Sepia with black. Offset printing. Available on Fulcrum: Yes
- Women's Equality & Women's Lives March postcard. First edition. 4.25" x 6". Women in Social Protest: The US Since 1915 series. Sepia with black. Offset printing. Available on Fulcrum: Yes
- Victoria N. Mxenge postcard. First edition. 4.25" x 6". No series. Sepia with black. Offset printing. Available on Fulcrum: Yes
- Ida B. Wells-Barnett postcard. Fourth edition. 4.25" x 6". Women of History. Sepia with black. Offset printing. Available on Fulcrum: No
- Dolores Huerta postcard. Second edition. 4.25" x 6". Women in the American Labor Movement series. Sepia with black. Offset printing. Available on Fulcrum: Yes
- Segregation Protest bookmark. First edition. 7" x 2". No series. Black and deep rose. Offset printing. Available on Fulcrum: Yes

- Women in Social Protest bookmark. First edition. 7" x 2". No series. Black and deep rose. Offset printing. Available on Fulcrum: Yes
- Zora Neale Hurston bookmark. First edition. 7" x 2". No series. Sepia orange and peach. Offset printing. Available on Fulcrum: Yes
- Helaine Victoria Press 1989 Spring Sale Catalog. 6" x 11.5", opens to 17.5" x 23". Black with orange. Offset printing. Available on Fulcrum: No
- Helaine Victoria Press 1989-90 Catalog. 11.25" x 16". 16 pages. Black with turquoise. Web press tabloid printing. Available on Fulcrum: No

1990

- Helaine Victoria Press Fall 1990 Catalog. 7" x 9". Black with turquoise. 20 pages. Offset printing. Available on Fulcrum: No
- Helaine Victoria Press 1990 Spring Sale Catalog. 6" x 11.5". Opens to 17.5" x 23". Black with Magenta. Offset printing. Available on Fulcrum: No

1991

- Sisters of the Harlem Renaissance postcard set, front cover. First edition. 4.5" x 6.25". Sisters of the Harlem Renaissance series. Black with silvery blue and red. Offset printing. Available on Fulcrum: Yes
- Alice Ruth Moore Dunbar-Nelson postcard. First edition. 4.25" x 6". Sisters of the Harlem Renaissance series. Black with turquoise. Offset printing. Available on Fulcrum: Yes
- Anne Spencer postcard. First edition. 4.25" x 6". Sisters of the Harlem Renaissance series. Black with turquoise. Offset printing. Available on Fulcrum: Yes
- Rose McClendon postcard. First edition. 4.25" x 6". Sisters of

the Harlem Renaissance series. Black with turquoise. Offset printing. Available on Fulcrum: Yes
- Anita Bush postcard. First edition. 4.25" x 6". Sisters of the Harlem Renaissance series. Black with turquoise. Offset printing. Available on Fulcrum: Yes
- Helene Johnson Hubbell postcard. First edition. 4.25" x 6". Sisters of the Harlem Renaissance series. Black with turquoise. Offset printing. Available on Fulcrum: Yes
- Ethel Waters postcard. First edition. 4.25" x 6". Sisters of the Harlem Renaissance series. Black with turquoise. Offset printing. Available on Fulcrum: Yes
- Evelyn Preer postcard. First edition. 4.25" x 6". Sisters of the Harlem Renaissance series. Black with turquoise. Offset printing. Available on Fulcrum: Yes
- Meta Vaux Warrick Fuller postcard. First edition. 4.25" x 6". Sisters of the Harlem Renaissance series. Black with turquoise. Offset printing. Available on Fulcrum: Yes
- Fay M. Jackson postcard. First edition. 4.25" x 6". Sisters of the Harlem Renaissance series. Black with turquoise. Offset printing. Available on Fulcrum: Yes
- Georgia Douglas Johnson postcard. First edition. 4.25" x 6". Sisters of the Harlem Renaissance series. Black with turquoise. Offset printing. Available on Fulcrum: Yes
- Gwendolyn Bennett postcard. First edition. 4.25" x 6". Sisters of the Harlem Renaissance series. Black with turquoise. Offset printing. Available on Fulcrum: Yes
- Josephine Baker postcard. First edition. 4.25" x 6". Sisters of the Harlem Renaissance series. Black with turquoise. Offset printing. Available on Fulcrum: Yes
- Moms Mabley postcard. First edition. 4.25" x 6". Sisters of the Harlem Renaissance series. Black with turquoise. Offset printing. Available on Fulcrum: Yes
- The Harlem Community Art Center postcard. First edition. 4.25" x 6". Sisters of the Harlem Renaissance series. Black with turquoise. Offset printing. Available on Fulcrum: Yes

- Augusta Savage postcard. First edition. 4.25" x 6". Sisters of the Harlem Renaissance series. Black with turquoise. Offset printing. Available on Fulcrum: Yes
- Florence Mills postcard. First edition. 4.25" x 6". Sisters of the Harlem Renaissance series. Black with turquoise. Offset printing. Available on Fulcrum: Yes
- Jessie Redmon Fauset postcard. First edition. 4.25" x 6". Sisters of the Harlem Renaissance series. Black with turquoise. Offset printing. Available on Fulcrum: Yes
- Marita Bonner postcard. First edition. 4.25" x 6". Sisters of the Harlem Renaissance series. Black with turquoise. Offset printing. Available on Fulcrum: Yes
- Valaida Snow postcard. First edition. 4.25" x 6". Sisters of the Harlem Renaissance series. Black with turquoise. Offset printing. Available on Fulcrum: Yes
- Nella Larsen postcard. First edition. 4.25" x 6". Sisters of the Harlem Renaissance series. Black with turquoise. Offset printing. Available on Fulcrum: Yes
- A'Lelia Walker postcard. First edition. 4.25" x 6". Sisters of the Harlem Renaissance series. Black with turquoise. Offset printing. Available on Fulcrum: Yes
- Dorothy West postcard. First edition. 4.25" x 6". Sisters of the Harlem Renaissance series. Black with turquoise. Offset printing. Available on Fulcrum: Yes
- Mabel Hampton postcard. First edition. 4.25" x 6". Sisters of the Harlem Renaissance series. Black with turquoise. Offset printing. Available on Fulcrum: Yes
- Angelina Weld Grimke postcard. First edition. 4.25" x 6". Sisters of the Harlem Renaissance series. Black with turquoise. Offset printing. Available on Fulcrum: Yes
- Gladys Bentley postcard. First edition. 4.25" x 6". Sisters of the Harlem Renaissance series. Black with turquoise. Offset printing. Available on Fulcrum: Yes

- Zora Neale Hurston postcard. First edition. 4.25" x 6". Sisters of the Harlem Renaissance series. Black with turquoise. Offset printing. Available on Fulcrum: Yes
- Helaine Victoria Press Harlem Renaissance mailer. 8.5" x 11". Black. 2 pages, announcing Harlem Renaissance series and Press closing. Offset printing. Available on Fulcrum: No

## 1993

- Helaine Victoria Press Inventory Close-out catalog. 5.5" x 8.5". Black. 10 pages. Photocopy printing. Available on Fulcrum: No

## 1994

- Helaine Victoria Press Inventory Close-out catalog. Second edition. 5.5" x 8.5". Black. 10 pages. Photocopy printing. Available on Fulcrum: No

# Notes

## INTRODUCTION

1. Nancy Poore, telephone interview with Julia Allen, 21 August 2018.
2. For a brief narrative of the events leading to the establishment of Womanspace, see Judy Chicago, *Through the Flower* (New York: Penguin, 1975), 102–3. See also Faith Wilding, *By Our Own Hands* (Double X: Santa Monica, CA, 1977), 47–57.
3. Prior to moving to Los Angeles, Nancy worked for the *Chicago Tribune* and for the British Consulate in San Francisco. Shortly after the art gallery opened, participants started publishing *Womanspace*, a journal devoted to women's art; Nancy volunteered to do paste-up for that journal, too.
4. Miriam Schapiro was a painter, sculptor, and printmaker who dissolved boundaries between art and craft as part of her feminist celebration of women's art-making. Judy Chicago is known for her large art installations exploring women's history and culture. Chicago founded the original Feminist Art Program at Fresno State College in 1970; the following year, 1971, she and Shapiro collaborated and cofounded a similar FAP at California Institute for the Arts. Arlene Raven was an art historian who pioneered the recuperation of women artists throughout history.
5. For a brief, cogent explanation of public memory, see Roger C. Aden, "Public Memory," in *The SAGE Encyclopedia of Communication Research Methods*, edited by Mike Allen (Sage Publications online ed., 2020). http://dx.doi.org.sonoma.idm.ock.org/10.4135/9781483381411.n467.
6. Lara Kelland acknowledged briefly the work of Helaine Victoria Press in *Clio's Foot Soldiers* (Amherst and Boston: University of Massachusetts Press, 2015), 86–91.
7. Jocelyn Cohen and Nancy Poore, "Can Women's Businesses Succeed?" *Sister* (April 1975): 1.

8. The name is a combination of Jocelyn Cohen's middle name, Helaine, and Nancy Poore's pen name, Victoria.
9. See Eleanor Flexner, *Century of Struggle: The Woman's Rights Movement in the United States* (Cambridge, MA: Belknap Press of Harvard University, 1959); Sheila Rowbotham, *Hidden from History: 300 Years of Women's Oppression and the Fight Against It* (London: Pluto Press, 1973).
10. Michel Foucault, *"Society Must Be Defended"* (New York: Picador, 2003), 7.
11. Foucault, *"Society,"* 8.
12. Greg Dickinson, Carole Blair, and Brian Ott, Introduction, *Places of Public Memory: The Rhetoric of Museums and Memorials,* edited by Greg Dickinson, Carole Blair, and Brian Ott (Tuscaloosa: University of Alabama Press, 2010), 8.
13. Marita Sturken, *Tangled Memories: The Vietnam War, the AIDS Epidemic, and the Politics of Remembering* (Berkeley: University of California Press, 1997), 3. Quoted in Dickinson, et al., Introduction, 9.
14. Dickinson, et al., Introduction, 6.
15. Interview in the film *Radical Harmonies,* dir. Dee Mosbacher. Quoted in Bonnie J. Morris, *The Disappearing L: Erasure of Lesbian Spaces and Culture* (Albany, NY: State University of New York Press, 2016), 30.
16. Mary Mackey, "Models," from an unpublished essay, used by permission of the author.
17. Jacques Le Goff explains that "[t]o make themselves the master of memory and forgetfulness is the great preoccupation of the classes, groups, and individuals who have dominated and who continue to dominate historical societies." *History and Memory*, trans. Steven Rendall and Elizabeth Claman (New York: Columbia University Press, 1992), 54.
18. John E. Bodnar, *Remaking America: Public Memory, Commemoration, and Patriotism in the Twentieth Century* (Princeton, NJ: Princeton University Press, 1997), 15. Quoted in Dickinson, et al., Introduction, 10.
19. Mary Powers, "Postcards give mini-lessons on women throughout history," *Louisville Courier-Journal,* April 4, 1977, in Box 5, Publicity 1977 folder, Helaine Victoria Press Records, Sophia Smith Collection, SSC-MS-00209, Smith College Special Collections, Northampton, MA.
20. Now California State University, Fresno.
21. One of the largest feminist public art installations was Womanhouse, an entire house "redecorated" by Feminist Art Program students and faculty to articulate the realities of women's lives. Although only available for six weeks, Womanhouse was documented in several films, most notably by Johanna Demetrakas in *Womanhouse.*

22. Arlene Raven, *Crossing Over: Feminism and Art of Social Concern* (Ann Arbor, MI: University of Michigan Press, 1988), 129.
23. Marguerite Elliot and Maria Karras, eds., *The Woman's Building & Feminist Art Education, 1973–1991: A Pictorial History* (Los Angeles: Ben Maltz Gallery, Otis College of Art and Design, 2011), 40.
24. Norma Broude and Mary D. Garrard, "Introduction: Feminism and Art in the Twentieth Century," in *The Power of Feminist Art*, ed. Norma Broude and Mary D. Garrard (New York: Harry N. Abrams, Inc., 1994), 22.
25. For an argument supporting the value and importance of reproducibility in art, see Walter Benjamin, "The World of Art in the Age of Reproducibility," in *Walter Benjamin: Selected Writings, Volume 4, 1938–1940*, trans. Edmund Jephcott and others, ed. Howard Eiland and Michael W. Jennings (Cambridge, MA: The Belknap Press of Harvard University Press, 2003), 251–283.
26. Dickinson, et al., Introduction, 22ff.
27. Roland Barthes, "The Rhetoric of the Image," in *Image, Music, Text*, trans. Stephen Heath. (New York: Hill and Wang, 1967), 36.
28. Barthes, "Rhetoric of the Image," 39.
29. Barbie Zelizer, "The Voice of the Visual in Memory," in *Framing Public Memory*, ed. Kendall R. Phillips (Tuscaloosa: University of Alabama Press, 2004), 163–64.
30. It is this very dispersal of art to those with no other means of access that Walter Benjamin applauds in "The Reproducibility of Art."
31. Donna Fay Reeves, personal interview with Jocelyn Cohen, Bloomington, IN, 8 August 2016.
32. Alexa Freeman and Jackie MacMillan, "Prime Time: Art and Politics," *Quest: A Feminist Quarterly* 2, no. 1 (Summer 1975): 29.
33. Freeman and Macmillan, "Prime Time," 30.
34. Freeman and Macmillan, "Prime Time," 33.
35. Gunther Kress, *Multimodality: A Social Semiotic Approach to Contemporary Communication* (New York: Routledge, 2010), 6.
36. Sheila de Bretteville, quoted in Ellen Lupton, "Reputations: Sheila Levrant de Bretteville," *Eye* (Autumn 1993), http://www.eyemagazine.com/feature/article/reputations-sheila-levrant-de-bretteville.
37. Kress, *Multimodality*, 79.
38. Printing ornaments are any of the design features not part of the typefaces. Also called dingbats. For more on printing ornaments or dingbats, see the Glossary.
39. See Kress, 88, for a discussion of the question of whether font and color can be considered modes. Answer: it depends. In the case of Helaine Victoria Press, the answer would be yes, because both were used to create meaning.

40. Bernhard Siegert, *Relays* (Stanford, CA: Stanford UP, 1999), 148.
41. Kress, *Multimodality*, 119.
42. Kress, *Multimodality*, 49.
43. Kress, *Multimodality*, 43.
44. *Womanspace* (Summer 1973): 3.
45. Sheila de Bretteville, "A reexamination of some aspects of the design arts from the perspective of a woman designer." From notes for a lecture given at Hunter College in November 1972. Typescript in possession of Jocelyn Cohen.
46. To compensate for the spine problem, Helaine Victoria Press began packaging some of the series of cards in book-like folios which could be displayed more successfully in bookstores. These series extended the linkages to longer, more detailed explorations of related subjects.
47. Donna Fay Reeves, personal interview with Jocelyn Cohen, Bloomington, IN, 8 August 2017.
48. Judy Chicago, qtd. in Norma Broude and Mary D. Garrard, "Conversations with Judy Chicago and Miriam Schapiro," in *The Power of Feminist Art*, ed. Norma Broude and Mary D. Garrard (New York: Harry N. Abrams, 1994), 72.
49. For a discussion linking the early feminist understanding of the importance of craft with current discussions of the relationship between maker and material, see Melissa Potter, "Material Engagements: Craft and Feminist Futures," *BOMB*, (June 28, 2019), https://bombmagazine.org/articles/material-engagements-craft-and-feminist-futures/.
50. Miriam Schapiro, qtd. in Broude and Garrard, "Conversations with Judy Chicago and Miriam Schapiro," 83.
51. Women in other fields, particularly the trades, formed similar alliances, blending politics and skill-sharing and learning ways to navigate and transform male dominated venues. Tradeswomen, Inc. was "founded in 1979 as a grassroots recruitment, retention and leadership & development for women in blue-collar skilled craft." https://tradeswomen.org/.
52. For a photo of Alm and several students using the press, see Faith Wilding, *By Our Own Hands*, 91.
53. Gunseli Berik and Cihan Bilginsoy, "Unions and Women's Training for the Skilled Trades in the U.S." *The Review of Black Political Economy* (Spring 2002): 100–1.
54. Dickinson, et al., Introduction, 10. Le Goff, attributing the creation of family albums to women, asks, "Should we see in this a relic of the feminine function of the conservation of remembrance or, on the contrary, a conquest of the group memory by feminism?" He also suggests that "[i]n addition to the

photos people take, we should also consider postcards they buy." *History and Memory*, 90.

55. For a brief narrative of four feminist publishing houses, see Julie R. Enszer, "Feverishly Lesbian-Feminist: Archival Objects and Queer Desires, in *Out of the Closet, Into the Archives: Researching Sexual Histories*, ed. Amy L. Stone and Jaime Cantrell (Albany, NY: SUNY Press, 2015), 157–164. Junko R. Onosaka has explored the flourishing of feminist bookstores in *Feminist Revolution in Literacy: Women's Bookstores in the United States* (New York: Routledge, 2006). Although Onosaka limits her discussion to the United States, it should be noted that during the 1970s–90s, women's bookstores could be found in many major cities around the world. See also Kristen Hogan, *The Feminist Bookstore Movement: Lesbian Antiracism and Feminist Accountability* (Durham, NC: Duke University Press, 2016).

56. Dickinson, et al., Introduction, 15. For a clear description and analysis of the women's print movement, see Carol Seajay, "Our Words in Our Hands: A Brief History of Women's Presses and Bookstores," in *The Woman-Centered Economy: Ideals, Reality, and the Space In Between*, ed. Loraine Edwalds and Midge Stocker (Chicago: Third Side Press, 1995), 77–86.

57. June Arnold, "Feminist Presses and Feminist Politics," *Quest: A Feminist Quarterly* III, no. 1 (Summer 1976): 18.

58. Fran Moira, "Women in Print," *off our backs* 11, no. 11 (December 1981): 2.

59. Moira, 2.

60. See Dickinson, et al., Introduction, 23 for a discussion of the metonymic function of places and objects in public memory.

61. Several commentators from the Women in Print movement attribute the saying about the "power of the press" to KNOW, Inc., a feminist publisher located in Pittsburgh. The phrase undoubtedly predates KNOW, however.

62. Radicalesbians, "The Woman Identified Woman," (Pittsburgh, PA: KNOW, INC., 1970), 4. Although Radicalesbians did not continue to exist as a group for long, the ideas they articulated had considerable influence and longevity.

63. Helen and Scott Nearing, *Living the Good Life: How to Live Sanely and Simply in a Troubled World* (New York: Schocken Books, 1970).

64. Mary Astell, *A Serious Proposal to the Ladies*, ed. Sharon L. Jansen, (Steilacoom, WA: Saltar's Point Press, 2014), 65.

65. Astell, "Serious Proposal," 52–53.

66. Astell, "Serious Proposal," 66.

67. Astell, "Serious Proposal," 89–90.

68. Sarah Scott, *Millennium Hall*, ed. Gary Kelly (Peterborough, Ontario, Canada: Broadview Literary Texts, 1995).

69. For several analyses of the constraints affecting women-run businesses, see *The Woman-Centered Economy: Ideals, Reality, and the Space In Between*, ed. Loraine Edwalds and Midge Stocker (Chicago: Third Side Press, 1995). Mary Byrne's article, "Business Within Women's Culture," 133–158, offers the most specific explanation of the issues confronted by women attempting to provide goods and services within the women's movement.

## CHAPTER 1

1. Susan Gubar, personal interview with Jocelyn Cohen, Bloomington, IN, 15 August 2015.
2. Smithsonian National Postal Museum, https://postalmuseum.si.edu/about/frequently-asked-questions/us-domestic-postcard-rates.html.
3. So-called funny themes included a fat woman overbearing a tiny husband, often looking scary with a household weapon like a rolling pin; a secretary smiling on the boss's lap at work; the disappointed and ugly spinster or "old maid"; or the angry wife catching the husband flirting with the "help" all abounded. Domestic violence was never portrayed as it was in the real world, but rather, the postcards turned the table, making the poor husband the brunt of the violence. Racial and ethnic bigotry portrayed immigrants as stupid. And the card displays were filled with objectifying images of women's bodies as "bathing beauties."
4. Annette Polan, "Reflecting on women in the visual arts in 1972 vs. today," *Forest Hills Connection* (October 27, 2014), https://www.foresthillsconnection.com/news/reflecting-on-women-in-the-visual-arts-in-1972-vs-today/.
5. *Sister* was a feminist tabloid newspaper published by the Los Angeles Women's Center.
6. Nancy Poore, "An Alphabet Soup of Heroes," *Sister*, special supplement: women in art, (August 1973): 5.
7. Poore, "Alphabet Soup," 5.
8. Jocelyn Cohen, "Opening: A Personal Gallery," *Sister*, special supplement: Women in Art, (August 1973): 6.
9. Cohen, "Opening," 6.
10. Approximately $350/month in 2018 dollars.
11. "Few women have lived more multiple lives than I have: as editor; as that anomaly, an American president's personal representative, decorated by six governments; as a writer of thirteen books and contributor to six others; as a painter, with fifty-one one-man exhibitions throughout the world; patron of the arts and sciences, irrepressible traveller and, more importantly, friend-gatherer . . . ." Quoted in Dan Piepenbring, "Fleurs *Flair*," *The Paris Review*

(January 20, 2015), https://www.theparisreview.org/blog/2015/01/20/fleurs-fl air/.

12. Nancy Poore, telephone interview with Julia Allen, 22 August 2018.
13. Charles Morris has coined the term *mnemonicide* to describe this systematic, power-driven erasure. See Charles E. Morris III, "My Old Kentucky Homo: Abraham Lincoln, Larry Kramer, and the Politics of Queer Memory," in *Queering Public Address*, edited by Charles E. Morris III (Columbia, SC: University of South Carolina Press, 2007), 103–4.
14. They also designed the cards, using antique and vintage border and ornamental motifs. Sometimes they found interesting border motifs among the old books or magazines they were using during research. Important sources were the Dover publications, especially the two-volume set, Clarence P. Hornung's *Handbook of Early Advertising Art*, Vol 1, Pictorial and Vol 2, Typographical (NY: Dover Publications, 1956). They wanted the images to be enhanced with a designed border, not just be a photo on a piece of card stock.
15. Jocelyn Cohen, "Art in L.A.: Current Shows and Current Criticism," *Sister* (August 1973): 6.
16. *Art: Anonymous Was A Woman: A Documentation of the Women's Art Festival – A Collection of Letter to Young Women Artists*, ed. Miriam Schapiro (Los Angeles: Feminist Art Program, California Institute of the Arts, 1974). "A member of our program, Connie Marsh, mysteriously disappeared last March while out painting near Cal Arts. It is with great sadness that we dedicate this book to her."
17. No one was ever apprehended for the murder. See "Search for Missing Coed Will Expand," *Los Angeles Times* (April 13, 1974): 15; "Cal Arts Family Won't Give Up Hope for Missing Coed," *Los Angeles Times* (April 25, 1974): 215, 227; "Skull Identified as Missing Student," *The Signal* (December 18, 1974): 1, 8; "Head Blow Killed Student," *The Signal* (December 20, 1974): 1, 6; Sherry Wheeler, "A Case of Rape," Letter to the Editor, *The Signal* (August 19, 1977): 10; "5 Years After: No Clue," *The Signal* (April 1, 1979): 1, 9.
18. Jocelyn sent a print to Miriam Schapiro, who responded, saying, "I can't tell you what seeing the print for Connie Marsh did for me. I shall treasure it." Mimi to Jocey, 12 October 1985, Box 2, Miriam Schapiro Folder, Helaine Victoria Press Records. Although the prints, with the accompanying inscription, should be part of feminist awareness and memory, most remain—160 of them—in a box in Jocelyn's studio.
19. Judy Chicago, *Beyond the Flower* (New York: Penguin, 1996), 35.
20. Terry Wolverton, *Insurgent Muse: Life and Art in at the Woman's Building* (San Francisco: City Lights Books, 2002), xvi.
21. When an image that has more than one color is printed, each color is printed

separately, but each must overlap the others precisely where the designer specifies. If this is not done, the finished image will look fuzzy, blurred, or "out of register." Every system of printing has a methodology for registering colors. On the Gestetner, each waxed paper stencil had one color on it, and all three waxed paper stencils, when printed, aligned. Each sheet of paper went through the Gestetner three times to produce the final flyer.

22. Terry Wolverton narrates a similar story regarding the Woman's Building: "Like many of my sisters in the women's movement, I was ill-prepared for the social convulsion that split the seventies from the eighties, as if the ever-expanding universe had, in a sudden spasm, contracted. That countercultural lifestyle I'd been so smug about living—easy bohemianism laced with anti-Establishment politics—was revealed to be largely dependent on a climate of economic prosperity and political largesse.... The funding sources on which the Woman's Building had relied dried up as well.... The policies of Reaganism cut a wide swath in the social fabric of Los Angeles." Wolverton, *Insurgent Muse*, 170.

23. Partnership Agreement between Nancy Taylor Poore and Jocelyn Helaine Cohen dated September 17, 1974, Box 13, Structure of HV folder, Helaine Victoria Press Records.

24. "Focus on Freedom: Heroes for Women," *California News-Banner* 1, no. 7, (May 11, 1975): 10, Box 5, Publicity 1974 Folder, Helaine Victoria Press Records.

25. Editorial, *Greetings* (July 1974): 1, Box 5, Publicity 1974 Folder, Helaine Victoria Press Records.

26. Nancy Poore and Jocelyn Cohen, letter to the editor, *Greetings* (October 1974): 30, Box 5, Publicity 1974 Folder, Helaine Victoria Press Records.

27. Jocelyn H. Cohen, letter to the editor, *Feminist Art Journal* 4, no. 1 (Fall 1974): 46–7.

28. The quote is commonly attributed to A. J. Liebling, columnist for the *New Yorker*, in "The Wayward Press: Do You Belong in Journalism?" *New Yorker* (May 14, 1960): 109.

29. Lesbian History Exploration, Invitational Packet, November 1, 1974, Box 5, Outgoing Corr./Special Events/Projects/1970s–1980s Folder, Helaine Victoria Press Records. The reference to suicide would become especially poignant for Jocelyn when she learned that her close friend from the Feminist Art Program, Barbara England, had taken her own life in November 1979. Miriam Schapiro wrote to Jocelyn years later, memorializing Barbara, saying, "I particularly remember the tender relationship between you and Barbara. I am sure none of us will ever get over Barbara's suicide." Mimi to Jocey, 11 January 1985, Box 2, Miriam Schapiro Folder, Helaine Victoria Press Records.

30. Norna Labouchere, *Ladies' Book-plates: An Illustrated Handbook for Collectors and Book-lovers* (London: George Bell & Sons, 1895).
31. Helaine Victoria Enterprises Catalog, n.d. [1974], in possession of Jocelyn Cohen.
32. Kathleen Walkup, "Books in a New Language," *From Site to Vision: The Woman's Building in Contemporary Culture*, ed. Sondra Hale and Terry Wolverton (Los Angeles: Otis College of Art and Design, 2011), 280.
33. Qtd. in Wolverton, *Insurgent Muse*, 124.
34. Walkup refers to Helaine Victoria Enterprises as "the Helaine Victoria Collective," an example of the way in which Helaine Victoria continues to elude traditional categories.
35. First day covers are envelopes with a picture, called a cachet, that provides more information about the stamp. The envelope(s) is sent to the particular post office prior to the specific day the stamp is made available, and the post office adds the stamp and postmarks it from that location. The post office cancels the stamp on the envelope and either returns the first day cover to the sender or sends it to the addressee.
36. A cachet is the illustration or design printed on the envelope of a first day cover.
37. Jocelyn Cohen and Nancy Poore, "Can Women's Businesses Succeed?" *Sister* (April 1975): 1.
38. Elsa Gidlow, *ELSA I Come With My Songs: The Autobiography of Elsa Gidlow*. A Druid Heights Book. (San Francisco: Booklegger Press, 1986), 384.
39. "Lesbian History Exploration, 1975, part 2." *Dyke: A Quarterly* (April 3, 2015), https://www.dykeaquarterly.com/2015/04/.
40. "Historical Post Cards," *College Store Executive*, January 1975, Box 5, Publicity 1975 folder, Helaine Victoria Press Records.
41. *The New Women's Survival Sourcebook*, ed. Kirsten Grimstad and Susan Rennie (New York: Knopf, 1975), 146–7.
42. [Carol Anne Douglas], "Chicken Lady," *off our backs*, November 1975, http://www.jstor.org/stable/25784119.
43. Ellen Dwyer to Jocelyn, 1 December 1975, Box 1, Colleges and Universities Folder, Helaine Victoria Press Records.
44. Ellen Dwyer, personal communication to Julia Allen and Jocelyn Cohen, 16 March 2017.
45. The Arts and Crafts movement sprang from anti-industrial sentiments in mid-nineteenth-century England. Some key tenets of the movement include a high value placed on working and being in touch with the land; being thoroughly familiar with the materials and methods being used; the freedom of

all people to be creative; and a blurring of the lines between art and craft. Many movement adherents were active in the Socialist Party. The center of Arts and Crafts movement thinking in the United States was Chicago at the turn of the twentieth century. For a good introduction to the movement, see Gillian Naylor, *The Arts and Crafts Movement* (Cambridge, MA: The MIT Press, 1971).

46. "Helaine Victoria Press," an interview by Maida Tilchen, *Sinister Wisdom* 13 (Spring 1980): 89.

## CHAPTER 2

1. Later they would learn about Bessie Coleman, the first African American and Native American woman to hold an international aviator license. Thanks to the efforts of women such as Judy Kaplan, the USPS issued a stamp honoring Coleman in 1995.
2. Nancy Poore, telephone interview with Julia Allen, 22 August 2018.
3. Should you ever happen upon a used book with some combination of these letters on the first page, you will know that it probably at some time was owned and sold by Helaine Victoria Press.
4. The two earlier catalogs were printed on single sheets of paper, front and back, and then folded for mailing, more like a flyer. Later catalogs were far more substantial.
5. Over the next few years, they printed seven different Educated Female bookplate designs.
6. Christine Eber to Nancy and Jocelyn, 29 March n.y. [1976], Box 1, D-F Correspondence, Helaine Victoria Press Records.
7. Helaine Victoria Enterprises Catalog [wholesale], n.d. [1975], one page, center column, in possession of Jocelyn Cohen.
8. They planted 100 white pine, 100 red pine, and 100 autumn olive. The autumn olive trees were at that time considered a good backup food source for birds in the winter. Unfortunately, time has shown that this tree has crowded out native plantings; it is now considered an invasive species.
9. $2,230.38 in 2018 dollars.
10. See Glossary for definitions of these printing terms. The only differentiating factor between a New Series and an Old Series Chandler & Price press was the rotating direction of the fly wheel.
11. The platen on Nancy and Jocelyn's press had been used so much that it was no longer even. The press exerted about 250 pounds of pressure per square inch to make an impression, which led to uneven wear in the areas where there

was most often a form or image or body of type, usually in the middle of the platen.

12. *Helaine Victoria Guide & Price List to Books By and About Women*, Summer Catalog no. 2 (Summer 1976): 3, in possession of Jocelyn Cohen.
13. *Helaine Victoria Guide*, 25.
14. Helaine Victoria Enterprises Catalog [wholesale], n.d., [1976], back page, in possession of Jocelyn Cohen.
15. Helaine Victoria Enterprises Autumn Brochure [retail], n.d., [1976], back page, in possession of Jocelyn Cohen.
16. Tax returns, 1975 & 1976, Box 7, Helaine Victoria Enterprises folder, Helaine Victoria Press Records.
17. Although the theoretical framework of the Feminist Art Program clearly transcended the biological, too frequently it has been labeled "essentialist," (which is to say, rooted in physiology).
18. Arlene Raven and Ruth Iskin. "Through the Peephole: Toward a Lesbian Sensibility in Art," *Chrysalis* 4 (1977): 21
19. Raven and Iskin, "Peephole," 21.
20. Raven and Iskin, "Peephole," 21.
21. 99percentinvisible. Episode 244. The Revolutionary Post. Jan 24, 2017. Writing more recently, Winifred Gallagher, author of *How the Post Office Created America: A History*, has argued that the post office is not simply a method of transporting a letter. Beginning with its founding, the post office was the primary way people got information. The service was designed to connect otherwise separate towns and people, and, in doing so, Gallagher posits, the post office created the United States of America. From their rural outpost, Nancy and Jocelyn developed a profound understanding of the functions of the US Postal Service. https://99percentinvisible.org/episode/the-revolutionary-post/.
22. 99percentinvisible. Episode 244.
23. Donna Fay Reeves, personal interview with Jocelyn Cohen, Bloomington, IN, 8 August 2016. Technically, Dynasty Lane was Rural Route 1 in 1976; it did not become Dynasty Lane until a few years later.
24. Helaine Victoria Enterprises Winter 1976–77 Catalog, 2 in possession of Jocelyn Cohen.
25. A die cut is often done on a specialized press that is more heavy duty and used for embossing and die cutting. This is because of the enormous pressure needed for either. But small die cuts are quite easy to do on any platen press; elaborate die cuts would be sent out to a specialized craftsperson to form, but simple ones can be assembled in any shop. There are special pieces of brass

that are higher than type high. For a simple slit for a flap, one chooses a piece of brass the length needed and locks it up in the chase just as one does for printing type. So, they selected a brass about three inches long that had a very sharp top edge for cutting, and locked it up in the chase. After the folio cover was printed in three colors so that it looked embossed, they took the postcard folio cover and, rather than printing, they ran the press without ink, and as they dipped each printed sheet into the press, the cut was made from the die or die cut. They made the V-shaped cut flap itself with their paper cutter, a small guillotine paper cutter they had acquired.

26. Apart from the obvious fact that their professional responsibilities mean providing access to materials, librarians usually need to justify their budget requests by tallying the numbers of requests they receive and the publications supported by their collections.

27. Betty H. Gillies to Ms. Cohen, 30 March 1977, Box 1, Complaints folder, Helaine Victoria Press records.

28. Alfreda Duster to Jocelyn Cohen and Nancy Poore, 14 March 1977, Box 1, Folder D-F Correspondence, Helaine Victoria Press Records.

29. Helaine Victoria Enterprises 1976-1977 Catalog, unpaginated [p. 7], in possession of Jocelyn Cohen.

30. Mary Powers, "Postcards give mini-lessons on women throughout history," *Louisville Courier-Journal* (April 4, 1977), Box 5, Publicity 1977 folder, Helaine Victoria Press Records.

31. It may be difficult for those who were not part of this revolution to grasp its significance, yet many benefit today from the trailblazing efforts cultivated for a few decades by hundreds of thousands of Lesbians.

32. Notecards, Helaine Victoria Enterprises, in possession of Jocelyn Cohen.

33. Helaine Victoria Press 1978 Catalog, 2, in possession of Jocelyn Cohen. $6.50 is approximately $26 in 2018 dollars.

34. Helaine Victoria Press 1978 Catalog, 2.

35. The following summer they made one last attempt and created the Phyllis Wheatley bookplate, before giving up the bookplate endeavor entirely.

36. Sheila (de Bretteville) to Helaine Victoria Press, 28 November 1978, Box 2, W Correspondence, Helaine Victoria Press Records.

37. Nancy Poore, email communication to Julia M. Allen, 27 February 2019.

38. Deed of Gift to the National Museum of History and Technology of the Smithsonian Institution, 15 June 1980, Washington, DC, Box 11, Smithsonian folder, Helaine Victoria Press Records.

39. Emma Goldman, early twentieth century American anarchist and feminist, deported to the Russian Soviet Republic in December of 1919 for her anti-war activities.

40. "Helaine Victoria Press," an interview with Maida Tilchen, *Sinister Wisdom* 13 (Spring 1980): 90.
41. Although considerable material was collected, this series was never published. A folder in the Helaine Victoria Press Records contains over a dozen photos (some photocopies) and potential research material for the planned Women's Auxiliaries & Brigades series. Items in this folder document the critical role women played in supporting various causes through these brigades and auxiliaries. See Box 20, Women's Brigades and Auxiliaries folder, Helaine Victoria Press Records.
42. Lucy Parsons was an American free speech and labor organizer. After her husband, Albert, was hanged following the infamous Chicago Haymarket "riot" in 1886, she devoted herself to labor organizing, becoming one of the cofounders of the Industrial Workers of the World and later active in Communist Party efforts.
43. Their experience trying to keep the cards in print illustrates some of their difficulties with the vagaries of the printing trade at that time. Not having the equipment, time, or expertise to make their own engravings, Helaine Victoria Press outsourced the making of engravings from the photographic images. In this case, the engraver had changed over from zinc to magnesium plates without informing Nancy and Jocelyn. A few years later, when they wanted to reprint the cards, they found that the magnesium plates had corroded. They decided to job out the series to an offset shop, but were unhappy with the results. Finally, for other cards, they were able to find an engraver who used zinc. In the past, all engravings had been copper, but copper had become obsolete due to the cost.
44. Nancy (Poore) to Elsa (Gidlow), 22 February 1978, Box 2, Elsa Gidlow folder, Helaine Victoria Press Records.
45. Gloria (Kaufman) to Nancy (Poore) and Jocey (Cohen), 4 January 1979, Box 4, Susan B. Anthony Celebration South Bend folder, Helaine Victoria Press Records.
46. Helaine Victoria Press: Postcards that Mirror Women's Progress Through History," typescript, Box 5, Publicity 1979 folder, Helaine Victoria Press Records,
47. Helaine Victoria Press 1979–80 Catalog, 3, in the possession of Jocelyn Cohen.
48. Helaine Victoria Press 1979–80 Catalog, 2.
49. As they were researching the life of journalist and anti-lynching activist Ida B. Wells-Barnett, Jocelyn and Nancy learned that Francis Willard had not only accepted the racist turn of the suffrage movement in the late nineteenth century, a move that was designed to attract the support of southern white women, she had made offensive statements herself, singling out Black men as

abusers of alcohol. Publicly challenged by anti-lynching activist Ida B. Wells-Barnett, Willard did not back down.
50. Nancy Poore, telephone conversation with Julia Allen, 10 February 2019.
51. Nancy Poore, telephone interview with Julia Allen, 17 November 2018.
52. Poore, Interview, 17 November 2018.
53. In the "It's always something" department, the mailing service that the press had begun to use in Indiana to respond to requests for catalogs lost all the requests that came in from the *Publishers Weekly* notice—and didn't tell Nancy and Jocelyn until months later. See Nancy Poore to Ms. Daisy Maryles, 25 January 1980, Box 5, Publicity 1980 folder, Helaine Victoria Press Records.
54. Julie R. Enszer, "'What Made Us Think They'd Pay Us for Making a Revolution?': Women in Distribution (WinD), 1974–1979," *This Book is an Action: Feminist Print Culture and Activist Aesthetic*, ed. Jaime Harker and Cecelia Konchar Farr (U of Illinois P, 2015). ProQuest Ebook Central.

## CHAPTER 3

1. Fred Whitehead, "U.S. women and labor," *Daily World* (April 18, 1980): 3.
2. Lucretia Coffin Mott was a Quaker abolitionist and feminist who, with Elizabeth Cady Stanton, organized the 1848 Seneca Falls convention where they read the "Declaration of Sentiments," demanding a series of rights for women, including the right to vote. This event is generally taken to be the inception of the first wave of feminism.
3. This collection is now housed at The Arthur and Elizabeth Schlesinger Library on the History of Women in America at Harvard University. Helaine Victoria Press letter to Anne Engelhart from Jocelyn Cohen, February 3, 2008, and response from Kathryn Allamong Jacob and Johanna-Maria Fraenkel, Curator of Manuscripts March 18, 2009, in the possession of Jocelyn Cohen.
4. Early second-wave feminism often focused on the negative representations of women in fiction, film, and advertising, alerting women to the ways in which their lives were circumscribed by these widely held expectations. See, for example, Kate Millett's 1968 ground-breaking book, *Sexual Politics*, developed from her Columbia University dissertation. Another key text was Susan Koppelman Cornillon's *Images of Women in Fiction*, published in 1972. Susan Koppelman was an enthusiastic customer of Helaine Victoria Press. Jean Kilbourne is credited with providing the first detailed analysis of images of women in advertising and related media through her lectures, which were developed into the documentary film *Killing Us Softly* in 1979.
5. The record of Nancy's presentation at the NWSA meetings has been lost.

6. Barbara Ann [Caruso] to J. & N., 12 May 1980, Box 3, Earlham College folder, Helaine Victoria Press Records.
7. Barbara Ann Caruso, telephone interview with Jocelyn Cohen and Julia Allen, 7 January 2019.
8. Jean Robinson, personal interview with Jocelyn Cohen, Bloomington, IN, 28 August 2016. The existence of women's and gender studies programs and feminist scholarship in general is the result of much hard work, struggle, and sacrifice on the part of women faculty and students during the 1970s and 1980s.
9. Caruso, telephone interview, 7 January 2019.
10. Caruso, telephone interview, 7 January 2019.
11. Helaine Victoria Press 1980–81 Catalog, 8, in possession of Jocelyn Cohen.
12. See Lauren Berlant, "Cruel Optimism: On Marx, Loss, and the Senses," *New Formations* 63 (Winter 2007/2008): 33. Proquest.
13. Teresa D. Bergen to Sisters, 5 May 1980, Box 1, Correspondence A-C, Helaine Victoria Press Records.
14. However, owning their press enabled them to set up a re-print quickly when inventory ran low on a single card.
15. For more on headwraps, see https://www.naturallycurly.com/curlreading/hairstyles/the-history-of-headwraps-then-there-and-now.
16. Merry Bateman, written response to mailed questionnaire, envelope dated 21 February 2017, in possession of Julia M. Allen.
17. Helaine Victoria Press 1980–81 Catalog, 8, in the possession of Jocelyn Cohen. The cost of gasoline had skyrocketed in 1979 due to cutbacks during the Iranian Revolution. The following year, during the Iran-Iraq War, oil production fell again, causing shortages in the United States.
18. Goldenrod insert, Helaine Victoria Press 1980–81 Catalog, in possession of Jocelyn Cohen.
19. Folio, Highlights from the History of Helaine Victoria Press, Box 5, 10-year folio folder [label missing], Helaine Victoria Press Records.
20. Helaine Victoria Press 1980–81 Catalog, 9. At the time, Martha Vicinus was on the faculty of the English Department at Indiana University.
21. This account of Helaine Victoria Press owes much to Vicki Leighty's filing system, which is now part of the Helaine Victoria Press Records.
22. Adrienne [Rich] to Jocelyn, 18 August 1980, Box 2, Adrienne Rich folder, Helaine Victoria Press records.
23. Tricia Vita to Nancy and Jocelyn, 4 November 1980, Box 5, Publicity 1980 folder, Helaine Victoria Press Records.

24. Nancy Poore to Judy Harvey Sahak, Librarian, The Ella Strong Denison Library, Scripps College, 6 August, 1980, Box 4, Scripps College Exhibit 1980 folder, Helaine Victoria Press Records.
25. Jo Feldman to Helaine Victoria Press, quoted in Views from our Friends & Customers, Helaine Victoria Press 1980–81 Catalog, 9, in possession of Jocelyn Cohen.
26. "Views," Helaine Victoria Press 1980–81 Catalog, 9. Professor Ruth Perry founded Women's and Gender Studies at MIT; she has written extensively on eighteenth-century women writers. See https://chawtonhouse.org/2015/06/chawton-house-library-conversations-junes-podcast/ for a brief discussion of Mary Astell by Professor Perry.
27. "Helaine Victoria Press," an interview with Maida Tilchen, *Sinister Wisdom* 13 (Spring 1980): 90.
28. Helaine Victoria Press Spring 1981 Catalog, [single sheet, folded], in possession of Jocelyn Cohen.
29. Diane Sands to H.V.P/Nancy, February 18, 1981, Box 4, Susan B. Anthony Celebration '81 folder, Helaine Victoria Press Records.
30. Chicago Women's Graphics was the only other major producer of accessible print art documenting or reflecting feminist memory at the time. They, too, were printers of a different sort, producing silkscreened posters brazenly striking in both content and colors. They did not have the same educational goal as did Helaine Victoria Press, but Jocelyn, in particular, found a special camaraderie with members of the Collective, because they were printers who were not producing books but rather working in a popular art form.
31. Susan Gubar, personal interview with Jocelyn Cohen, Bloomington, IN, 15 August, 2015.
32. For a discussion of the role of bookstores, see Kristen Hogan, *The Feminist Bookstore Movement: Lesbian Antiracism and Feminist Accountability* (Durham, NC: Duke University Press, 2016).
33. For a detailed account of the efforts of Howard University librarian Dorothy Porter to design a cataloging system that functioned for African Americans as agents, not just as subtopics (if at all) of the activities of others, see Laura E. Helton, "On Decimals, Catalogs, and Racial Imaginaries of Reading," *PMLA* 134, no. 1 (2019): 99–120.
34. Ms. B. Sykes to The Secretary, Helaine Victoria Press, Inc., 30 November 1981, Cambridge, MA, Box 1, Catalog Correspondence, Helaine Victoria Press Records.
35. Toni Cade Bambara to Somebody, n.d., Box 1, Catalog Correspondence, Helaine Victoria Press Records.

36. Sheila de Bretteville, quoted in Ellen Lupton, "Reputations: Sheila Levrant de Bretteville," *Eye* (Autumn 1993), http://www.eyemagazine.com/feature/article/reputations-sheila-levrant-de-bretteville.
37. Randy Harelson, *SWAK: The Complete Book of Mail Fun for Kids* (New York: Workman Publishing Co., 1981), 118.
38. Elizabeth Isadora Gold to Helaine Victoria Press, 14 December 1983. Box 1, Catalog Correspondence folder, Helaine Victoria Press Records.
39. Mary [Ruthsdottir] to Nancy and Jocelyn, 5 November 1981, Box 4, NWHP NWHW 1981–1987 folder, Helaine Victoria Press Records. Rep. Barbara Mikulski served as Democratic Representative from Maryland in the US House of Representatives from 1977–87. She then served in the Senate from 1987–2017. She was known for, among other things, her support for women's issues. Senator Orrin Hatch served as US Senator from Utah for forty-two years, from 1976 to 2019. He was known especially for drawing conservative Christians and Mormons into political work through the Republican party. He was an outspoken opponent of the Equal Rights Amendment.
40. Mary [Ruthsdottir] to Jocelyn, 15 December, 1981, Box 4, NWHP NWHW 1981–1987 folder, Helaine Victoria Press Records.
41. When they arrived, Jocelyn and Nancy had been advised by their friendly neighbors, the Amys, that they should arm themselves for protection. They acquired a shotgun for the purpose. When the teenage harassers showed up one time too many, Jocelyn took out the shotgun, opened the front door, and blasted a shot into the air. That was the last visit from the young louts.
42. Patty Parchem, "Helaine Victoria Press," *Womensource* 5, no. 4 (April 22, 1981): 4–5, Box 5, Publicity 1981 folder, Helaine Victoria Press Records.
43. Helaine Victoria Press Winter 1982 Picture Postcard Supplement, Box 12, Catalogs 1982–1984 folder, Helaine Victoria Press Records. The NWML project was instrumental in helping Helaine Victoria build their mailing list as well. Deborah Brecher and Jill Lippitt, founders of the National Women's Mailing List, The Women's Information Exchange (WIE): A National Feminist Communication Network, and The Women's Computer Literacy Project, were both friends of the press and business associates. The WIE was founded in 1980 both to make computer literacy accessible to women in the early days of information technology and to also create a database of individuals and organizations, including some 2,500 services, organizations, institutions, and programs for women. The aim was to present a broad representation of the available women's resources, and the founders envisioned it becoming an international network. See multiple sources in Box 13, National Women's Mailing List folder, Helaine Victoria Press Records. See also "The Women's Information Exchange," Electra Pages, http://www.electrapages.com/.

44. Throughout the 1970s and into the 1980s, white women who worked full-time, year-round made fifty-nine cents on average for every dollar earned by men; women of color made much less.
45. *Missouri Valley Socialist* 2, no. 1 (Winter 1981–2): back cover, Box 5, Publicity 1981 folder, Helaine Victoria Press Records.
46. A box at the foot of the page informed readers that Sara N. Cleghorn, a Vermont feminist and writer from the early twentieth century was responsible for coining the word "viewy": "The protagonist of her autobiographical novel, *The Spinster*, is often called 'viewy' or 'too viewy' by other characters. That is, she has too many decided opinions and points of view for a proper young lady. Good for her. We hope you will enjoy this catalog of our viewy postcards." Helaine Victoria Press 1982–83 Catalog, 1, in possession of Jocelyn Cohen.
47. "Viewy News," Helaine Victoria Press 1982–83 Catalog, 1, in possession of Jocelyn Cohen.
48. Helaine Victoria Press 1982–83 Catalog, back cover.
49. A rebus, the concept for which originated in the 1500s, is a message, puzzle, or story that uses pictures in lieu of words to convey the message. For words with no visual possibilities, a letter and an image may be used to make up a word. For instance, a "T" and a hat might combine to become *that*.
50. Jocey [Cohen] to Michelle [Cliff] & Adrienne [Rich], 17 January 1982, Box 2, Rich, Adrienne folder, Helaine Victoria Press Records. "The Life and Times of Rosie the Riveter," released in 1980, was directed by Connie Field. "Four Women Artists," released in 1977, was directed by William Ferris.
51. Helaine Victoria Press, Request for Outreach Program Support, Indiana Committee for the Humanities, Box 3, ICH Project 1982 folder, Helaine Victoria Press Records.
52. Jean Jenson, "Rosie the Riveter Was On The Job," *Indianapolis News*, June 11, 1982, 12, http://www.newspapers.com/.
53. Ellen [Dwyer] to Josie [Cohen] and Nancy [Poore], 24 May 1982, Box 3, ICH Project 1982 folder, Helaine Victoria Press Records.
54. Susan [Gubar] to Nancy [Poore] and Jocey [Cohen], 19 May 1982, Box 3, ICH Project 1982 folder, Helaine Victoria Press Records.
55. After the card was published, Beverly Robinson contacted the press again with concerns about one line in the caption, specifically questioning a line about an ex-slave cook serving a family a meal in which a poisonous snake had been cooked. Jocelyn was quite sure she had quoted correctly from the biographical sketch in the Library of Congress Robinson had written; a librarian also confirmed the accuracy of Helaine Victoria's caption. Robinson then

wrote a congenial letter to the press, commenting that the issue was one of "who planted the harm." She apologized for a lack of clarity in her biographical sketch and praised the card as "such a symbol of pride." In her reply, Jocelyn offered a caption rewritten to reflect the exact circumstances as Robinson had explained them; the card would be reprinted soon. See correspondence between Beverly Robinson, Brett Topping (writer/editor, Library of Congress), and Jocelyn Cohen, Box 2, Beverly Robinson folder, Helaine Victoria Press Records.

56. Colleen Whalen to Helaine Victoria Press, Inc., n.d., Box 1, Catalog Correspondence folder, Helaine Victoria Press Records.
57. Maureen Goggin to Helaine Victoria Press, Inc., 18 January 1982, Washington, DC, Box 1, Catalog Correspondence folder, Helaine Victoria Press Records.

## CHAPTER 4

1. The nineteenth-century set included: Sojourner Truth, Pioneers in Education (Emma Willard, Prudence Crandall and Mary McLeod Bethune), Ernestine Rose, Susan B. Anthony and Elizabeth Cady Stanton, Temperance 1873 and Forward, Emma Goldman, Harriet Tubman, Lucy Parsons, and "Old Washee," a Native American Indian-Navajo Medicine Woman. This last card was published by Kustom Quality, a company that specialized in early images of the western United States. The card had a short descriptive caption to accompany the striking image: "Old Washee, Medicine Woman, Toqui-Naachai or Old Washee, was a Navajo 'medicine woman.' She was believed to be more than 103 years old when this photo was taken in the 1880s. Her silver beads and crescent shaped naja reveal the Spanish colonial influence. More traditional are the strings of turquoise nuggets and hishi beads. Acoma pottery was widely used by Navajos. (Wittick photo: Ft. Wingate, N. Mex. Terr.)" The twentieth-century set contained cards featuring Jane Addams, Alice Paul, Amelia Earhart, Frances Perkins, Eleanor Roosevelt and Amelia Earhart, Ida B. Wells, Zora Neale Hurston, Phyllis Carter, Agnes Vanderburg, and Kimura Komako.
2. Nancy Poore to Claire Moses, 21 February 1982, Box 5, Feminist Studies folder, Helaine Victoria Press Records.
3. Cathy Loeb & Linda Shult, "First Midwest Regional Women in Print Conference, Woodstock, Illinois, September 10–12, 1982," *Feminist Collections* 4, no. 1 (Fall 1982): 6–7. FC_4.1_Fall1982.pdf (1.122Mb).
4. Nancy [Poore] to Adrienne [Rich], 9 September 1982, Box 2, Rich, Adrienne folder, Helaine Victoria Press Records.

5. Joan Sterrenburg, email communication to Jocelyn Cohen, 20 February 2017.
6. Adrienne [Rich] to Jocey [Cohen], 23 December 1982, Box 2, Rich, Adrienne folder, Helaine Victoria Press Records.
7. Readers should bear in mind that all record keeping had to be done by hand, as Helaine Victoria Press predated computer availability and software systems for small businesses.
8. Toba Cohen had been keeping the press's books, but she also worked at the family's shoe store, and as the press's orders grew, her volunteer time could not increase accordingly.
9. Lawrie [Hamilton], in "Viewy News," Helaine Victoria Press 1983–84 Catalog, 18, in the possession of Jocelyn Cohen.
10. Cheryl Scutt, "Postcards tell history of women," *Sunday Herald-Times*, January 9, 1983, Section E: n.p., Box 5, Publicity 1983 folder, Helaine Victoria Press Records.
11. Paula [Worley], in "Viewy News," Helaine Victoria Press 1983–84 Catalog, 18, in the possession of Jocelyn Cohen.
12. Typescript, brief description of the press's activities, sent to Susan Blosser of the Indiana University Women's Studies Department, for inclusion in the department's newsletter, 8 August 1983, Box 3, Short overview of the PC archives folder, Helaine Victoria Press Records. When the press stopped accepting cards in 1990, the collection numbered over 5,000.
13. Seeking to take advantage of the new computer-based archiving possibilities, Helaine Victoria Press applied for a grant from Apple; however, the project was not funded. Researchers should be aware that, unfortunately, as of 2019, the index cards and numerical log of the 5,000 or so cards have been misplaced at the Schlesinger Library, the repository of the collection.
14. Karen [Schollenberger], in "Viewy News," Helaine Victoria Press 1983–84 Catalog, 18, in the possession of Jocelyn Cohen.
15. Kirsten [Johnson], in "Viewy News," Helaine Victoria Press 1983–84 Catalog, 18, in the possession of Jocelyn Cohen.
16. Attention Feature Editor, "Join the National's Celebration of National Women's History Week—March 6–12, 1983," February 25, 1983, Box 12, Press Releases 1974–1987 folder, Helaine Victoria Press Records.
17. *Women and Language News* 6, no. 2/3 (1982): 9, Box 5, Publicity 1982 folder, Helaine Victoria Press Records.
18. Helaine Victoria Press Announces Call for Research, August 1983, Box 3, 10 Year Retrospective Exhibit folder, Helaine Victoria Press Records.
19. *Abeng* was published by The Crossing Press in 1984, then reissued by Penguin the following year.

20. Michelle [Cliff] to Jocey [Jocelyn Cohen], March 15, n.y. [1984], Box 1, Cliff, Michelle folder, Helaine Victoria Press Records.
21. Michelle [Cliff] to Vicki [Leighty] n.d., ca. 1986, Box 1, Cliff, Michelle folder, Helaine Victoria Press Records. Rich and Cliff had moved to Santa Cruz, CA in 1984.
22. The School of Fine Arts Gallery is now the Grunwald Gallery.
23. Helaine Victoria Press 1973–1983 Catalog, unpaginated [back page], in possession of Jocelyn Cohen.
24. Ten-Year Text, in the possession of Jocelyn Cohen.
25. [Jocelyn Cohen] to Susan Stamberg, 11 August 1983, Box 12, Press Releases 1974–1987 folder, Helaine Victoria Press Records.
26. Telegram from Anne Wilson to Jocey Cohen and Nancy Poore, care Helaine Victoria Show, DLR, The Fine Arts Gallery, Indiana University, Bloomington, IN, September 29, Box 3, Tenth Year Anniversary folder, Helaine Victoria Press Records.
27. Helaine Victoria Press 1983 Holiday Catalog, single page, Box 12, Catalogs 1982–84 folder, Helaine Victoria Press Records.
28. A strong drink that Jocelyn and Nancy concocted for just such occasions.
29. Helaine Victoria Press, 1984 Directory Summer Supplement of Women's Postcards: Women's History and Culture in Print, unpaginated [back page], in possession of Jocelyn Cohen.
30. Helaine Victoria Press, "For Immediate Release: Madam C.J. Walker – Proud, Determined & Independent—HV's Newest Publication," March 12, 1984, Box 5, Publicity 1986 folder, Helaine Victoria Press Records.
31. Every researcher received 100 copies of the card for which they provided the caption, plus a $5 honorarium.
32. LeLe [A'Lelia Bundles] to Jocelyn Cohen, 25 January 1985, Box 6, Bundles, A'Lelia folder, Helaine Victoria Press Records.
33. Marcia McNair, "Where to Find," *Essence* (September 1983): 40, Box 5, Publicity 1983 folder, Helaine Victoria Press Records.
34. Mrs. A Gaskins to Wonderful People, Pittsburgh, PA, n.d., Box 1, Catalog Correspondence folder, Helaine Victoria Press Records.
35. Donna B. Powe to To Whom It May Concern, 23 January 1985, Box 1, Catalog Correspondence folder, Helaine Victoria Press Records.
36. Nancy [Poore], in "Viewy News," Helaine Victoria Press, 1983–84 Catalog, 18, in the possession of Jocelyn Cohen.
37. Vicki Leighty, "Structure and Ideology: The Workings and the Changings of a Feminist Press," paper written for W480, Practicum in Women's Studies, undated, Box 6, Historical Papers on HVP folder, Helaine Victoria Press Records.

38. Bernice to Vicki, Jocey, Lawrie, 28 March 1984, Box 13, Source Code Summaries folder, or possibly in an adjoining folder that lost its label, Helaine Victoria Press Records.
39. Dave Long, "Chrome Collecting: Small Talk," *The Postcard Collector* (May 1984): 11, Box 5, Publicity 1984 folder, Helaine Victoria Press Records.
40. Interview with Jocelyn Cohen, *Feminist Teacher* 1, no. 1 (Fall 1984): 12.
41. Unfortunately, Helaine Victoria Press's enthusiasm for re-use means that these audio cassettes are no longer available.
42. The October 28, 1983 issue of *The Texas Observer,* included a long article on Tenayuca and the pecan shellers that served as a good foundation for Vicki's interviews. *The Texas Observer* (28 October 1983): cover, 7–15, copy in possession of Vicki Leighty.
43. Emma [Tenayuca] to Vicki [Leighty], 17 December 1984, Box 2, Tenayuca, Emma folder, Helaine Victoria Press Records.
44. Emma to Vicki, 17 December 1984.
45. Sandra Cisneros, "Cactus Flowers: Women's Books and Periodicals and Where to Find Them," *San Antonio Woman's Magazine*, n.d.: 22, Box 5, Publicity 1985 Tearsheets folder, Helaine Victoria Press Records.
46. In her book, *They Who Knock at Our Gates: A Complete Gospel of Immigration* (Boston: Houghton Mifflin, 1914), Antin argues "that open immigration is integral to the ideal of American democracy." Quotation taken from caption on Helaine Victoria Press card honoring Mary Antin.
47. During the late 1980s, Bonnie Denny and Jenny Robertson worked for the press as work-study students. Like the other students who had worked for the press, they put their hearts into their work, helping wherever they were needed—answering the telephone, filling orders, staffing the shop, and packaging cards. Jules Unsel served as assistant office manager, bookkeeper, grant writer, and promotions coordinator in the last two years of the press's existence.
48. By the summer of 1985, Nancy Poore and Chris Johnson had acquired a century-old Pearl letterpress for Metis Press in Chicago. With the acquisition of this press, Nancy was able to continue her fine letterpress printing. "Metis Press: Starting Our Second Decade," *Women Printers Newsletter* (Summer 1985): 5, Box 11, Print Hers News folder, Helaine Victoria Press Records.
49. Jocey [Jocelyn Cohen] to Linda [Preuss], 22 October 1985, Box 2, P Correspondence folder, Helaine Victoria Press Records.
50. Jean Robinson, interview with Jocelyn Cohen, Bloomington, IN, 28 August 2016.

51. Joan Corbett to Helaine Victoria Press, printed in Helaine Victoria Press 1984–85 Catalog, 18, in possession of Jocelyn Cohen.
52. Yvonne Forrest to Helaine Victoria Press, printed in Helaine Victoria Press 1984–85 Catalog, 18, in possession of Jocelyn Cohen.
53. Joanne Forman to Helaine Victoria Press, 22 February 1985, Box 1, Catalog Correspondence folder, Helaine Victoria Press records.
54. Jocelyn Cohen, "Viewy News," Helaine Victoria Press 1984–85 Catalog, 18, in possession of Jocelyn Cohen.
55. Third National Women in Print Conference Program, Box 4, Women in Print 1981 folder, Helaine Victoria Press Records.
56. Tricia Lootens, "Third National Women in Print Conference," *off our backs* (August–September 1985): 23. http://www.jstor.org/stable/25775543.
57. Jocelyn H. Cohen, "Women, History, and Postcards," *Belles Lettres* 1, no. 2 (November–December 1985): 11, Box 5, Publicity 1985 folder, Helaine Victoria Press Records.
58. Bernice Schipp, Caption, Edmonia Lewis card, Helaine Victoria Press, 1985.
59. Later research has uncovered the original source of the poster. That research, however, has not stopped the continuing widespread use of the image as Helaine Victoria Press defined it: as a recognition of women's strength and contributions to the fight against fascism. See Gwen Sharp and Lisa Wade, "secrets of a feminist icon," *Contexts* 10, no. 2 (Spring 2011): 82–83, https://doi.org/10.1177/1536504211408972.

## CHAPTER 5

1. Although the amendment passed in the House in 1971 and in Senate in 1972, it failed to be ratified by enough states by the deadline in 1982.
2. See Suzanne Staggenborg, "Beyond Culture versus Politics: A Case Study of a Local Women's Movement," *Gender and Society* 15, no. 4, (August 2001): 507–530 for a more detailed discussion of the changes that took place in the feminist movement in Bloomington, IN.
3. G. Sue Sullivan Bales, *The Dirty Dozen, Plus Three* (Bloomington, IN: Author-House, 2008), 43. This was the first year the award was presented. Jeanine Rae was a prominent figure for her support of the arts and contributions to the women's community, especially in Indianapolis where she was a co-owner with her partner, Joyce Borne, of The Woman's Touch, a bookstore and community hub. Jeanine was a minister and therapist and Joyce a nurse, both dividing time between their new establishment and previous professional work. When Nancy and Jocelyn first arrived in Indiana, Jeanine and Joyce

were two of the first to welcome them, and they continued to be supportive. Jeanine became ill and died in 1984, which led to the eventual closing of The Woman's Touch. The award was established in Jeanine Rae's memory.

4. Marlene Mannella, interview with Vicki Leighty, Columbia, MO, 15 May 2019.
5. The sign is now stored in San Francisco, awaiting the right museum or collection to acquire it.
6. Jocelyn H. Cohen, "Viewy News," Helaine Victoria Press 1984 Summer Supplement Catalog, 1, in possession of Jocelyn Cohen.
7. Those unfamiliar with the folk song can find a rendition here: https://www.youtube.com/watch?v=JqowmHgxVJQ
8. List for Latina PR Mailing, Box 17, Latina Press Release folder, Helaine Victoria Press Records.
9. *OAH Magazine of History* 1, no. 3/4, The Progressive Era (Winter–Spring, 1986).
10. Roy Rosenzweig, "Newsnotes," *Labor History* 27, no. 2 (Spring 1986): 313–315.
11. "Women in the American Labor Movement, 1886–1986," *Generations* (Winter 1986): 10, Box 5, Publicity 1986 folder, Helaine Victoria Press Records.
12. N. J. Stanley, "Backwoods HV Press Tackles Foreign Postcard Markets," *Arts Insight* (October 1986): 23, Box 5, Publicity 1986 folder, Helaine Victoria Press Records.
13. Letter to Bloomington-area friends from Your Sisters at Helaine Victoria Press, 1 December 1986, Box 3, Open House Flyers folder, Helaine Victoria Press Records.
14. Letter to prospective Publishing Advisory Board members from Jocelyn H. Cohen, 22 March 1987, Box 13, Board of Directors folder, Helaine Victoria Press Records.
15. Final List for 3/87 Meeting, Advisory Board. Box 13, Board of Directors folder, Helaine Victoria Press Records.
16. "Viewy News," Helaine Victoria Press 1987–88 Catalog, 14, in possession of Jocelyn Cohen.
17. Helaine Victoria Press 1987–88 Catalog, back cover, in possession of Jocelyn Cohen.
18. The selection for the card by and about Corine Lytle Cannon was transcribed by Victoria Byerly for her book *Hard Times Cotton Mill Girls: Personal Histories of Womanhood and Poverty in the South*, published by I.LR. Press at Cornell University in 1986.
19. For a discussion of the source of the poem, see "Moments (poem)," https://en.m.wikipedia.org/wiki/Moments_(poem).
20. Jocelyn Cohen, "A Keepsake in Celebration of Our 15th Year," Helaine Victoria Press 1987–88 Catalog, 14, in possession of Jocelyn Cohen.

21. Julie R. Enszer, "The Whole Naked Truth" (dissertation, University of Maryland, College Park, 2013), 297. ProQuest.
22. Ivan Illich. *Tools for Conviviality* (New York: Harper & Row, 1973).
23. Jean Robinson, personal interview with Jocelyn Cohen, Bloomington, IN, 28 August 2016.
24. Catherine Stimpson, "Women's Studies: The Idea and the Ideas," *Liberal Education* 71, no. 4 (September–October 1987): 34–38, Box 5, Publicity 1987 folder, Helaine Victoria Press Records.
25. "More Resources," *Practicing Anti-Racism* (Fall 1987): 18, Box 5, Publicity 1987 folder, Helaine Victoria Press Records.
26. [Carol Ann Douglas], "Chicken Lady," *off our backs* (April 1987): 23. http://www.jstor.org/stable/25795664.
27. Terry McCormick, editor, *Vintage Clothing Newsletter* (March–April, 1987): 7, Box 5, Publicity 1987-2 folder, Helaine Victoria Press Records.
28. Bloomington Commission on the Status of Women, National Women's History Month Calendar, March 1987, Box 4, National Women's History Month folder, Helaine Victoria Press Records.
29. "Support Your Local Women's Press," Box 13, Board of Directors folder, Helaine Victoria Press Records.
30. Jocelyn Cohen to Sandy [Runzo], 27 November 1987, Box 2, P-R Correspondence folder, Helaine Victoria Press Records.
31. Donna Fay Reeves, email communication to Julia Allen, 19 July 2019.
32. "Women's art in auction," *Indianapolis News* (April 15, 1988): 16. www.newspapers.com.
33. "One Fine Day," www.wildwestwomen.org.
34. "Viewy News," Helaine Victoria Press 1988–1989 Catalog, 1, in possession of Jocelyn Cohen.
35. "Viewy News," 1988–89 Catalog, 1.
36. Enszer, "Whole Naked Truth," 36.
37. Organizational Information, Box 13, Structure of HV folder, Helaine Victoria Press Records.
38. M. J. C. van Ryn to Dear Womyn, Tepoztlan, Mexico, 15 March 1988, Box 1, Catalog Correspondence folder, Helaine Victoria Press Records.
39. Quincy Blackburn to Dear Women, Austin, TX, 18 March 1988, Box 1, Correspondence A-C folder, Helaine Victoria Press Records.
40. Orange is the sash color worn by the Orangemen, members of a Protestant political organization in Northern Ireland; the color comes from the name of William of Orange, a seventeenth-century Dutch Protestant prince who deposed James II, a Catholic, to become king of England.

41. Albert J. McAloon to Jocelyn [Cohen], Middletown, R.I., 27 July 1988; Sandra Runzo to Albert [McAloon], 2 August 1988, Box 2, M Correspondence folder, Helaine Victoria Press Records.
42. James S. Ackerman, Director, University Honors Division, to Laura L. Sparks, 15 November 1988, Box 10, Laura Sparks folder, Helaine Victoria Press Records.
43. The addition of a spine and an ISBN overcame what had long prevented Helaine Victoria Press from selling postcards through bookstores. Many bookstores were reluctant to engage in the card business. However, the ISBN, along with a folder large enough for the title to go on the spine, meant a packaged card series could be displayed on a bookshelf. This satisfied some of the bookstores' key requirements.
44. Bessie Coleman also held the distinction of being the first aviator with Native American ancestry and first person of African American descent to receive an international pilot's license.
45. "Viewy News," Helaine Victoria Press Spring 1989 Sale Catalog, n.p. in possession of Jocelyn Cohen.
46. Jana McGee and D. Self, "Women's History, Women's Spaces," in *The Ryder Magazine* (February 1989): 28–29, Box 5, 1985–1990 Publicity folder, Helaine Victoria Press Records.
47. Dana Denny, "Work of five women to be recognized at Women's History Month luncheon." *Herald-Telephone* (March 2, 1989), Section D: n.p., copy in possession of Jocelyn Cohen.
48. Jocelyn Cohen, text of brief speech given upon being recognized by the Bloomington Commission on the Status of Women and the Bloomington Network of Career Women, 7 March 1989, in possession of Jocelyn Cohen.
49. Jocey [Cohen] to Bernice [Schipp], n.d., ca. 1989, Box 10, Bernice Schipp folder, Helaine Victoria Press Records.
50. Now called the Academy of Art University.
51. Although she was beginning to doubt the likelihood that she could return to Indiana and to Helaine Victoria Press, Jocelyn had brought with her a determination to continue honoring women otherwise lost to history. As a student in the MFA program at the Academy of Art College, in one of her courses utilizing computer-aided design, she produced five small booklets honoring women in history: "Sylvia Pankhurst: Artist, Suffragette and Political Activist"; "Elaine Gray, a Pioneer and an Original, Designer and Architect"; "Jane Grabhorn: Fine Letterpress Printer, Designer, Bookbinder and Publisher"; "Anna Simmons: Type Designer and Calligrapher"; and "Clearing the View: Black Women Photographers in the Early 1900s." These booklets appeared in Helaine Victoria Press's Fall 1990 Catalog under the headline: "Limited

Editions of HV Director's newest work!" In a class on early photographic techniques, she created a large story quilt of favorite Helaine Victoria postcard images, experimenting with different processes to reproduce the images.

## EPILOGUE

1. Gail Cohee and Leslie Lewis edited the captions. Susan Gubar, Gloria Gibson-Hudson, and Phyllis Klotman reviewed images for selection. Student intern Wendy Fishman carried out key tasks for the project. Bernadette Beekman not only combed through photographs, looking for the best images, but, along with Vicky Young, helped to raise funds for the endeavor. Shirley Chisholm participated in the fundraising effort, as well. The Network of Career Women, especially Charlotte Zietlow and Jane Jenkins, helped to come up with funds, and Anne Wilson also contributed. Another devoted fan of the press from Boston sent a check for $2,500.
2. Sona Chambers, Project Coordinator, Introductory card, Sisters of the Harlem Renaissance: The Found Generation, in possession of Jocelyn Cohen.
3. "Viewy News," Helaine Victoria Press Fall 1990 Catalog, 1, in possession of Jocelyn Cohen.
4. Susan Gubar, personal interview with Jocelyn Cohen, Bloomington, IN, 15 August 2015.
5. Donna Fay Reeves, "Personal Statement," Helaine Victoria Press Fall 1990 Catalog, 15, in possession of Jocelyn Cohen.
6. Jocelyn H. Cohen, "Personal Statement," Helaine Victoria Press Fall 1990 Catalog, 15, in possession of Jocelyn Cohen.
7. Cohen, "Personal Statement," 1990 Catalog, 15.
8. Betty Gardner to Dear Mesdames, Lansing, MI, 9 November 1990, Box 6, Letters from people about closing folder, Helaine Victoria Press Records.
9. June Swanston-Valdes to Dear Sisters, Greensboro, NC, 29 November 1990, Box 6, Letters from people about closing folder, Helaine Victoria Press Records.
10. Melody Ivins to Dear Sisters, Durham, NC, 7 November 1990, Box 6, Letters from people about closing folder, Helaine Victoria Press Records.
11. Doris Wolf, "Fourth-graders to study power of 1890s press," *Democrat and Chronicle* (April 11, 1995): 1. http://www.newspapers.com/.
12. Wolf, "Fourth-graders," 1.
13. The 5.5" x 8.5" broadside was printed on reclaimed cover stock.
14. Ellen Dwyer, personal communication to Jocelyn Cohen and Julia Allen, 16 March 2017.

## GLOSSARY

1. "Philippine Markets Ditch Plastic for Leaves Following Thailand & Vietnam With Organic Wrapping," BrightVibes.com, https://brightvibes.com/1256/en/philippine-supermarkets-ditch-plastic-for-leaves-following-thailand-vietnam-with-organic-wrapping. Accessed August 31, 2021.
2. "LOOK: Albay supermarket uses banana leaves, abaca instead of plastic," Rappler.com, https://www.rappler.com/science-nature/environment/229215-albay-supermarket-uses-banana-leaves-abaca-instead-of-plastic. Accessed August 31, 2021.
3. "Broadside (printing)," Wikipedia, https://en.wikipedia.org/wiki/Broadside_(printing). Updated 25 July 2021. See also "The Popularity of Broadsides," Printed Ephemera: Three Centuries of Broadsides and Other Printed Ephemera, Library of Congress, https://www.loc.gov/collections/broadsides-and-other-printed-ephemera/articles-and-essays/introduction-to-printed-ephemera-collection/the-popularity-of-broadsides/. Accessed September 1, 2021.
4. Ralph W. Polk and Edwin Polk, *The Practice of Printing Letterpress and Offset*, rev. ed. (Peoria, IL: Chas. A. Bennett Co., 1926), 26–30.
5. "Composing stick," Wikipedia, https://en.wikipedia.org/wiki/Composing_stick. Last modified 5 June 2019.
6. "Couch It! Papermaking Tutorial for Embedding Materials," Paperslurry, https://www.paperslurry.com/2016/02/24/couch-it-papermaking-tutorial-for-embedding-materials/. Accessed September 1, 2021.
7. "Diatype (machine)," Wikipedia, https://en.wikipedia.org/wiki/Diatype_(machine). Last modified 29 May 2021.
8. "Printing Lingo: What is Die-Cutting?" Formax Printing Solutions, https://www.formaxprinting.com/blog/2014/04/printing-lingo-what-is-die-cutting/.
9. Polk and Polk, 64–66.
10. "Paper Embossing," Wikipedia, https://en.wikipedia.org/wiki/Paper_embossing. Last modified 12 May 2021.
11. Polk and Polk, 273–4.
12. "Fleuron (typography)," Wikipedia, https://en.wikipedia.org/wiki/Fleuron_(typography). Last modified 19 December 2020.
13. Polk and Polk, 18–25.
14. Oliver Simon, *Introduction to Typography* (London: Faber & Faber, 1963), 149.
15. Polk and Polk, 273–5. See also John F. J. Cabibi, *Copy Preparation for Printing* (New York: McGraw-Hill, 1973), 143.
16. "Halftone Process Printing," *Encyclopedia Britannica Online*. https://www.br

itannica.com/technology/halftone-process. Last modified 20 July 1998.
17. Cabibi, 144.
18. "Linotype Machine," Wikipedia, https://en.wikipedia.org/wiki/Linotype_machine. Last modified 6 August 2021.
19. Polk and Polk, 123–4.
20. "Glossary of Printing Terms," Trumbull Printing, https://www.trumbullprinting.com/printterms.
21. *Pocket Pal: A Graphic Arts Digest for Printers and Advertising Production Managers* (New York: International Paper Company, 1973), 165.
22. "Offset Printing, Offset Lithography," Whatis.com, https://whatis.techtarget.com/definition/offset-printing-offset-lithography. Last updated January 2019.
23. "Printer's Ornaments," Cultures of the Book, http://digitalbookhistory.com/culturesofthebook/Printer%27s_Ornaments. Last modified 18 December 2018.
24. Polk and Polk, 98–9.
25. "Registration, what is that?" CutPasteandPrint, https://www.cutpasteandprint.com/registration. Accessed August 31, 2021.
26. Polk and Polk, 125.
27. "Process camera," Wikipedia, https://en.wikipedia.org/wiki/Process_camera. Last modified 9 October 2020.
28. "Gestetner," Wikipedia, https://en.wikipedia.org/wiki/Gestetner. Last modified 3 June 2021.
29. Polk and Polk, 19.

# Bibliography

99percentinvisible. Episode 244. The Revolutionary Post. Jan 24, 2017. https://99percentinvisible.org/episode/the-revolutionary-post/.

Aden, Roger C. "Public Memory." In *The SAGE Encyclopedia of Communication Research Methods*, edited by Mike Allen. Sage Publications, 2020; online ed. http://dx.doi.org.sonoma.idm.ock.org/10.4135/9781483381411.n467.

Antin, Mary. *They Who Knock at Our Gates: A Complete Gospel of Immigration*. Boston, MA: Houghton Mifflin, 1914.

Arnold, June. "Feminist Presses and Feminist Politics." *Quest: A Feminist Quarterly*, III, no. 1 (Summer 1976): 18–26.

Astell, Mary. *A Serious Proposal to the Ladies*. Edited by Sharon L. Jansen. Steilacoom, WA: Saltar's Point Press, 2014.

Bales, G. Sue Sullivan. *The Dirty Dozen, Plus Three*. Bloomington, IN: AuthorHouse, 2008.

Barthes, Roland. "The Rhetoric of the Image." In *Image, Music, Text*, translated by Stephen Heath. New York, NY: Hill and Wang, 1977.

Benjamin, Walter. "The World of Art in the Age of Reproducibility." In *Walter Benjamin: Selected Writings, Volume 4, 1938–1940*, translated by Edmund Jephcott and others; edited by Howard Eiland and Michael W. Jennings. Cambridge, MA: The Belknap Press of Harvard University Press, 2003.

Berik, Gunseli and Cihan Bilginsoy, "Unions and Women's Training for the Skilled Trades in the U.S." *The Review of Black Political Economy* (Spring 2002): 100-1. DOI:10.1007/BF02717299

Berlant, Lauren. "Cruel Optimism: On Marx, Loss, and the Senses." *New Formations* 63 (Winter 2007/2008): 33–51.

Broude, Norma and Mary D. Garrard. "Conversations with Judy Chicago and Miriam Schapiro." In *The Power of Feminist Art*, edited by Norma Broude and Mary D. Garrard, 66–85. New York, NY: Harry N. Abrams, Inc., 1994.

———. "Introduction: Feminism and Art in the Twentieth Century." In *The Power of Feminist Art*, edited by Norma Broude and Mary D. Garrard, 10–29. New York, NY: Harry N. Abrams, Inc., 1994.

Byerly, Victoria. *Hard Times Cotton Mill Girls: Personal Histories of Womanhood and Poverty in the South*. Ithaca, NY: ILR Press, 1986.

Byrne, Mary. "Business Within Women's Culture." In *The Woman-Centered Economy: Ideals, Reality, and the Space In Between*, edited by Loraine Edwalds and Midge Stocker, 133–158. Chicago, IL: Third Side Press, 1995.

Cabibi, John F. J. *Copy Preparation for Printing*. New York: McGraw-Hill, 1973.

Chicago, Judy. *Beyond the Flower*. New York, NY: Penguin, 1996.

———. *Through the Flower*. New York, NY: Penguin, 1975.

Cohen, Jocelyn. "Art in L.A.: Current Shows and Current Criticism." *Sister* (August 1973): 6.

———. Letter to the editor. *Feminist Art Journal* 4, no. 1 (Fall, 1974): 46–7.

———. "Opening: A Personal Gallery." *Sister*, special supplement: women in art. (August, 1973): 6–9.

Cohen, Jocelyn and Nancy Poore, "Can Women's Businesses Succeed?" *Sister* (April 1975): 1.

de Bretteville, Sheila. "A reexamination of some aspects of the design arts from the perspective of a woman designer." Notes for a lecture given at Hunter College in November 1972.

Dickinson, Greg, Carole Blair, and Brian Ott. Introduction to *Places of Public Memory: The Rhetoric of Museums and Memorials*, edited by Greg Dickinson, Carole Blair, and Brian Ott, 1–54. Tuscaloosa, AL: University of Alabama Press, 2010.

[Douglas, Carol Ann]. "Chicken Lady" *off our backs* (November 1975): 11. https://www.jstor.org/stable/community.28041825

———. "Chicken Lady" *off our backs* 17, no. 4 (April 1987): 22–23. http://www.jstor.org/stable/25795664

Edwalds, Loraine and Midge Stocker, eds. *The Woman-Centered Economy: Ideals, Reality, and the Space In Between*. Chicago, IL: Third Side Press, 1995.

Elliot, Marguerite and Maria Karras, eds. *The Woman's Building & Feminist Art Education, 1973-1991: A Pictorial History*. Los Angeles, CA: Ben Maltz Gallery, Otis College of Art and Design, 2011.

Enszer, Julie R. "Feverishly Lesbian-Feminist: Archival Objects and Queer Desires." In *Out of the Closet, into the Archives: Researching Sexual Histories*, edited by Amy L. Stone and Jaime Cantrell, 157–164. Albany, NY: State University of New York Press, 2015.

———. "'What Made Us Think They'd Pay Us for Making a Revolution?': Women in Distribution (WinD), 1974-1979." In *This Book is an Action: Feminist Print Culture and Activist Aesthetic*, edited by Jaime Harker and Cecelia Konchar Farr, 99-111. Champaign, IL: University of Illinois Press, 2015. ProQuest Ebook Central.

Enszer, Julie R. "The Whole Naked Truth." PhD diss., University of Maryland, College Park, 2013. ProQuest Dissertations & Theses Global: The Humanities and Social Sciences Collection. (1432764937).

Feminist Teacher and Jocelyn Cohen. "An Interview with Jocelyn Cohen." *Feminist Teacher* 1, no. 1 (Fall, 1984): 12. http://www.jstor.org/stable/25684349

Flexner, Eleanor. *Century of Struggle: The Woman's Rights Movement in the United States*. Cambridge, MA: Belknap Press of Harvard University, 1959.

Foucault, Michel. *"Society Must Be Defended": Lectures at the Collège de France 1975-1976*. New York, NY: Picador, 2003.

Freeman, Alexa and Jackie MacMillan. "Prime Time: Art and Politics." *Quest: A Feminist Quarterly* 2, no. 1 (Summer 1975): 27-39.

Gallagher, Winifred. *How the Post Office Created America: A History*. New York, NY: Penguin Books, 2016.

Gidlow, Elsa. *ELSA I Come With My Songs: The Autobiography of Elsa Gidlow*. San Francisco, CA: Booklegger Press, 1986.

Grimstad, Kirsten and Susan Rennie, eds. *The New Women's Survival Sourcebook*. New York, NY: Knopf, 1975.

Harelson, Randy. *SWAK: The Complete Book of Mail Fun for Kids*. New York, NY: Workman Publishing Co., 1981.

"Helaine Victoria Press," an interview by Maida Tilchen. *Sinister Wisdom* 13 (Spring 1980): 87-90.

Helaine Victoria Press Records. Smith College Special Collections, Smith College, Northampton, MA.

Helton, Laura E. "On Decimals, Catalogs, and Racial Imaginaries of Reading." *PMLA* 134, no. 1 (2019): 99-120.

Hogan, Kristen. *The Feminist Bookstore Movement: Lesbian Antiracism and Feminist Accountability*. Durham, NC: Duke University Press, 2016.

Hornung, Clarence P. *Handbook of Early Advertising Art*. Vol. 1 Pictorial and Vol. 2 Ornamental and Typographical. New York, NY: Dover Publications, 1956.

Illich, Ivan. *Tools for Conviviality*. New York, NY: Harper & Row, 1973.

Kelland, Lara. *Clio's Foot Soldiers*. Amherst, MA: University of Massachusetts Press, 2015.

Kress, Gunther. *Multimodality: A Social Semiotic Approach to Contemporary Communication*. New York, NY: Routledge, 2010.

Labouchere, Norna. *Ladies' Book-plates: An Illustrated Handbook for Collectors and Book-Lovers.* London, UK: George Bell & Sons, 1895.

Le Goff, Jacques. *History and Memory,* translated by Steven Rendall and Elizabeth Claman. New York, NY: Columbia University Press, 1992.

"Lesbian History Exploration, 1975, part 2." *Dyke: A Quarterly* (April 3, 2015). https://www.dykeaquarterly.com/2015/04/.

Loeb, Cathy and Linda Shult. "First Midwest Regional Women in Print Conference, Woodstock, Illinois, September 10–12, 1982." *Feminist Collections* 4, no. 1 (Fall 1982): 6–7, FC_4.1_Fall1982.pdf.

Lootens, Tricia. "Third National Women in Print Conference." *off our backs* (August–September 1985): 23. http://www.jstor.org/stable/25775543.

Lupton, Ellen. "Reputations: Sheila Levrant de Bretteville," *Eye* (Autumn 1993). http://www.eyemagazine.com/feature/article/reputations-sheila-levrant-de-bretteville.

Mackey, Mary, "Models," from an unpublished essay, used by permission of the author.

Moira, Fran. "Women in Print." *off our backs* 11, No. 11 (December 1981): 2.

Morris, Bonnie. *The Disappearing L: Erasure of Lesbian Spaces and Culture.* Albany, NY: State University of New York Press, 2016.

Morris, Charles E., III. "My Old Kentucky Homo: Abraham Lincoln, Larry Kramer, and the Politics of Queer Memory." In *Queering Public Address,* edited by Charles E. Morris III, 93–120. Columbia, SC: University of South Carolina Press, 2007.

Naylor, Gillian. *The Arts and Crafts Movement.* Cambridge, MA: The MIT Press, 1971.

Nearing, Helen and Scott. *Living the Good Life: How to Live Sanely and Simply in a Troubled World.* New York, NY: Schocken Books, 1970.

*OAH Magazine of History* 1, no. 3/4, The Progressive Era (Winter–Spring, 1986).

Onosaka, Junko. *Feminist Revolution in Literacy: Women's Bookstores in the United States.* New York, NY: Routledge, 2006.

Perry, Ruth. Interviewed in "June's Podcast." *Chawton House Library Conversations.* https://chawtonhouse.org/2015/06/chawton-house-library-conversations-junes-podcast/.

Piepenbring, Dan. "Fleurs *Flair.*" *The Paris Review* (January 20, 2015). https://www.theparisreview.org/blog/2015/01/20/fleurs-flair/.

*Pocket Pal: A Graphic Arts Digest for Printers and Advertising Production Managers.* 10th ed. New York, NY: International Paper Company, 1973.

Polan, Annette. "Reflecting on women in the visual arts in 1972 vs. today." *Forest Hills Connection* (October 27, 2014). https://www.foresthillsconnection.com/news/reflecting-on-women-in-the-visual-arts-in-1972-vs-today/.

Polk, Ralph W. and Edwin Polk. *The Practice of Printing Letterpress and Offset*, revised ed. Peoria, IL: Chas. A. Bennett Co., 1926.

Poore, Nancy. "An Alphabet Soup of Heroes." *Sister*, special supplement: women in art. (August, 1973): 5, 11.

Potter, Melissa. "Material Engagements: Craft and Feminist Futures." *BOMB* (June 28, 2019). https://bombmagazine.org/articles/material-engagements-craft-and-feminist-futures/

Radicalesbians, "The Woman Identified Woman." Pittsburgh, PA: KNOW, INC., 1970.

Raven, Arlene. *Crossing Over: Feminism and Art of Social Concern*. Ann Arbor, MI: University of Michigan Press, 1988.

Raven, Arlene and Ruth Iskin. "Through the Peephole: Toward a Lesbian Sensibility in Art." *Chrysalis* 4 (1977): 19–28.

Rosenzweig, Roy. "Newsnotes." *Labor History* 27, no. 2 (Spring 1986): 313–315.

Rowbotham, Sheila. *Hidden from History: 300 Years of Women's Oppression and the Fight Against It*. London, UK: Pluto Press, 1973.

Schapiro, Miriam, ed. *Art: Anonymous Was A Woman: A Documentation of the Women's Art Festival – A Collection of Letter to Young Women Artists*. Los Angeles, CA: Feminist Art Program, California Institute of the Arts, 1974.

Scott, Sarah. *Millennium Hall*. Edited by Gary Kelly. Peterborough, Ontario, Canada: Broadview Literary Texts, 1995.

Seajay, Carol. "Our Words in Our Hands: A Brief History of Women's Presses and Bookstores." In *The Woman-Centered Economy: Ideals, Reality, and the Space In Between*, edited by Lorraine Edwalds and Midge Stocker, 77–93. Chicago: Third Side Press, 1995.

Sharp, Gwen and Lisa Wade. "secrets of a feminist icon." *Contexts* 10, no. 2 (Spring 2011): 82–83.

Siegert, Bernhard. *Relays*. Stanford, CA: Stanford UP, 1999.

Simon, Oliver. *Introduction to Typography*. London: Faber & Faber, 1963.

Staggenborg, Suzanne. "Beyond Culture versus Politics: A Case Study of a Local Women's Movement." *Gender and Society* 15, no. 4, (August 2001): 507–530. http://www.jstor.org/stable/3081920

Travis, Trysh. "The Women in Print Movement: History and Implications." *Book History* 2 (2008): 275–300. http://www.jstor.org/stable/30227421.

Walkup, Kathleen. "Books in a New Language." In *From Site to Vision: The Woman's Building in Contemporary Culture*, edited by Sondra Hale and Terry Wolverton. Los Angeles, CA: Otis College of Art and Design, 2011.

Whitehead, Fred. "U.S. women and labor." *Daily World* (April 18, 1980): 3.

Wilding, Faith. *By Our Own Hands*. Santa Monica, CA: Double X, 1977.

Wolf, Doris. "Fourth-graders to study power of 1890s press," *Democrat and Chronicle* (April 11, 1995): 1. http://www.newspapers.com/.

Wolverton, Terry. *Insurgent Muse: Life and Art in at the Woman's Building.* San Francisco, CA: City Lights Books, 2002.

*Womanspace.* Summer 1973.

"The Women's Information Exchange." Electra Pages. http://www.electrapages.com/.

Zelizer, Barbie. "The Voice of the Visual in Memory." In *Framing Public Memory*, edited by Kendall R. Phillips, 157–186. Tuscaloosa, AL: University of Alabama Press, 2004.

# Index

Acres of Books bookstore, 46, 64, 83, 118
Abbey Press, 166, 210
Abbott, Berenice, 213
abolition movement, 50, 177
Academy of Art College, 317
Adam, Margaret (Margie), viii, 57, 58
Addams, Jane, 146, 203, 236, 239, 419n1
aesthetics, xxix, 7–8, 52–53. *See also* feminist aesthetics
*Aframerican Woman's Journal,* 237
Aiken, Loretta Mary, 323
Alarcon, Norma, 239, 271–72, 274
Alexander, Becky, 168
Allen, Julia, xviii; *and* collaboration, xxviii
Allport, Catherine, 313
Alm, Helen, 18, 44, 46, 47, 57, 93
Alvarez, Sonya, 181
American Folklife Center, 198–200
*American Jewess, The,* 250
American, Sadie, 250
Amy, Chuck and Polly, xxii, xxiii, 91, 131, 417n41
Anguissola, Sofonisba, 34
Antelles, Patricia, xvi, xvii, 331
Anthony, Susan B., xii, 49, 49, 51, 61, 68, 85, 110, 144, 150, 176–77, 191, 413n45, 416n29, 419n1
Antin, Mary, 250, 422n46
antiracism, 180–182, 184–86, 196, 198, 245–46, 249–50
Anzaldua, Gloria, 271
Arnold, June, 19–20, 405n57
art establishment, 32, 37, 65–67
Arts and Crafts movement, 17, 78, 128, 140, 253, 409n45
*Arts Insight,* 281
Astell, Mary, 24–26, 76–78, 102, 127, 128, 172, 201, 253, 405n64–67, 416n26
Athena women's arts collective, 263, 268
Aura, Jan, 61–62
Avrich, Paul, 239, 253

back to the land movement, 24, 128, 130
Bagwell, Lydia, 317
Baker, Josephine, 321
Banks, Louis Albert, D.D.: *Hall of Fame,* 94
Barnard Center for Research on Women's 1982 Scholar and Feminist Conference, 264

Barnes, Djuna, 124–126
Barney, Natalie, 71
Barthes, Roland, 8, 403n27, 403n28
Bateman, Merry, xi, xviii, 163–66, 168, 209, 415n16
Behn, Aphra, 36, 106, 108
Bellanca, Dorothy, 138
*Belles Lettres*, 256–60
Bambara, Toni Cade, 185, 242
Beck, Evelyn Torton, 194
Beekman, Bernadette, 427n1
Bennett, Gwendolyn, 323
Bentley, Gladys, 321
Bergen, Teresa, 159
Berkshire Conference on the History of Women, xxviii, 115, 127, 243
Berlant, Lauren, 158
Bethune, Mary MacLeod, 71, 85, 182, 237–239, 242, 419n1
Bibby, Deirdre L., 321
bicentennial celebration, 67
Biddle, Mary, xviii
Bird, Betty, 181
Biren, Joan E., 5, 259, 310, 312
Blackwelder, Julia Kirk, 309
Black Elk, 313
Black Women in the Middle West Project at Purdue, 243
Blanchard, M., 82–83
Blair, Carole, 4
Bloch, Alice, 62, 63
Bloomer, Amelia, 329
Bloomington Commission on the Status of Women, 299–300, 315
Bloomington, Indiana, xviii, 90, 105–6, 156, 196, 228; *and* Helaine Victoria Press storefront, 28, 263–70, 281–82, 285
Bly, Becky, 331

Bonaparte, Napoleon, 82, 83
Bonheur, Rosa, 37, 41, 46, 48, 85
Bonner, Marita, 323
bookmarks, xvi, 3, 29, 65, 83, 103, 113, 211, 227–228, 276–279, 294,
bookplates, 3, 29, 64–66, 83, 86, 100, 112–114, 122, 233, 351, 362, 364, 294. *See also* Educated Female Bookplates
Bouloukos, Beth, xviii
Brady, Maureen, 181
de Bretteville, Sheila, 12, 15, 56, 126, 186
Brittain, Vera, 83
Brooks, Nancy (Nan), 229–31
Brooks, Romaine, 40
Brown, Lizzie, 283, 331
Brown, Rita Mae, 102
Bryan, T.J., 323
Bundles, A'Lelia P., 240, 242, 323
Burton, Doris-Jean, 311
Bush, Anita, 323
Butler, Helen May, 160–61
Buyukmihci, Hope Sawyer, 142
Byrd, Caroline, 70

Cade, Cathy, 310
Calder, Barbara, 60
California Institute of the Arts. *See* Feminist Art Programs
*California News-Banner*, 59–60
Cannon, Corine Lytle, 289, 424n18
Carr, Emily, 37, 41, 51, 71, 72, 213
Carriera, Rosalba, 37
Carter, Jimmy, 160
Carter, Phyllis, 183, 198–200, 371n1
Caruso, Barbara Ann, xviii, 156, 157–58, 179
Cassatt, Mary, 37, 41, 49

Castellanos, Rosario, 239, 245, 272, 279
Cattelona, Georg'Ann, 252, 314
Catt, Carrie Chapman, 47, 68
Chaff, Ron, 312
Chambers, Sona, 302–03, 319–21
Chandler & Price letterpress. *See* communication technologies
Chaney, William, xxiii
Chicago, Judy, xxi, xxii, xxvii, 1, 6–7, 16, 17, 32–33, 39, 53–54, 56, 57, 100; *and* collaboration with Miriam Schapiro, xxii, xxvii, 32–33, 53, 57, 88, 100, 401n4
*Chicago Tribune,* 18, 41, 354n3
Chicago Women's Graphic Collective, 204, 270, 283, 301, 416n30. *See also* Zolot, Julie.
Chisholm, Shirley, 200, 303, 427n1
Cisneros, Sandra, 249
de Cleyre, Voltairine, 239–40, 245, 253
Cliff, Michelle, 181, 194, 220–23
Clinton, Kate, 227
Clsuf, 283
Cohen, Herschel, 91, 92, 130, 164, 209, 282
Cohen, Jocelyn: *and* aesthetic, 52–53; *and* collaboration with Julia Allen, xxviii–ix; *and* collaboration with Nancy Poore, xxi–xxvii, 1–6, 59; *and* education, xxi, 6, 36, 46, 57, 317, 426n51; *and* family of origin, xxii, xxiii, 60, 83, 88, 90–92, 130, 282; *and* Jewish identity, xxiii–xxiv; *and* recognition, 264, 315–16; *and* relationship with Nancy Poore, 1, 23–27, 100, 104, 188–89, 202–03; *and* relationship with Vicki Leighty, 204, 304
Cohen, Marty, xxi, xxiii, 88, 91, 131
Cohen, Toba, 83, 84, 88, 90, 96, 130, 163, 168, 209, 219, 232, 234–35, 244, 282, 317, 331, 420n8
Cohee, Gail, 427n1
Coleman, Bessie, 314, 410n1, 426n44
Colette, 249
collaboration, xxvii–xxx, 7–8, 21–22, 32–35, 54, 67, 106, 216, 219–20, 244–45, 250, 327; *and* Judy Chicago and Miriam Schapiro, 54, 88, 406n4
collective memory. *See* generating feminist memory
*College Store Executive,* 72
communication technologies: 34, 36, 44–48, 51, 57, 78–9, 87, 98–100, 103, 116–17, 177–78, 274, 403n38, 411n25, 413n43; *and* biases 18–19, 22, 44, 63–64, 79, 90–91, 93, 207, 404n51; *and* Chandler and Price letterpress, 22, 23, 81, 92–94, 112, 125, 140, 147, 158, 160, 167, 192, 200, 294, 328, 410n11; *and* feminism, 17–20, 22–23, 191, 192, 207, 328–31; *and* letterpress, 145–146, 171–72, 174, 186, 216, 289–90, 290; *and* Munder, 93–94, 146–147, 148, 167, 186, 208, 221, 226, 289; *and* offset printing, 44, 78–79, 146, 160, 192; *and* Parsons, 148; *and* Pearl letterpress, 243; *and* postcards, 10–14, 38, 41, 47, 172, 186, 191, 192, 281, 319; *and* Rotaprint offset press, 17–18, 44, 46–47, 51; *and* T-shirts, 3, 264; *and* United States Post Office, 13, 411n21
Communist Party, 73, 155, 247, 249, 413n42
consciousness raising, 7. *See also* second wave feminism
Convivial Design, xvii

INDEX 439

Corcoran Conference on Women in the Visual Arts, 32–33
Corbett, Joan, 255
*Cosmopolitan,* Japanese edition, 171
Cowan, Liza, 70–71
Cowles, Fleur, 43
Crandall, Prudence, 71, 85, 419n1
Crowley, Karlyn, 312

Danu, Miriam, 283
Dare, Virginia, 67
Daughters, Inc, 20
Davis, Elizabeth Gould, 123–124
*Daily World,* 155
Dean, Sharon G., 321
Deviant Productions, 213
*Dial, The,* 108
Diana Press, 5, 151
Dickinson, Emily, 303
Dickinson, Greg, 4
disability issues, xviii, 311
Djuna Books, 171
Douglas, Carol Anne, 75, 299
Douglass, Frederick, 123
Dunbar-Nelson, Alice, 321
Duncan, Isadora, 36, 106, 107, 108, 187
Duster, Alfreda, 110–112, 113, 134, 148–50, 152
Dwyer, Ellen, xviii, 75–76, 153, 196–97, 295–97, 306–09, 333

Earlham College, 155, 179
Earhart, Amelia, 51, 82, 84, 106, 108, 109, 146, 218, 264, 419n1
Eber, Christine, 87, 113, 118–20, 283
*Ebony,* 287
economics, xxi, xxiv, xxvi, 38, 39, 43, 59, 63–64, 68–70, 84, 88, 91, 92, 100, 156–60, 179, 185–86, 190, 208, 218, 235, 266, 268, 271, 284, 295, 300–03, 314, 317, 326, 460n69, 408n22; *and* feminist publishing, 151–52, 205, 256, 295–96, 303–04; *and* nonprofit status, 152, 153–54, 158, 173–74, 179, 211, 218; *and* recycling, 86, 96, 172; *and* subsistence living, 23, 27–28, 91, 97, 128–31, 158, 188, 209, 410n8
Educated Female Bookplates, 64–66, 412n35
Egenolf, Paul, 92–94, 328, 329
Eliot, George, 36
Elwell, Sue Levi, 250
Enszer, Julie R., 152, 295, 303
environmental movement, 140–42
Eisinger, Barbara, 309
Esprit de Corp, 310
*Essence* magazine, 242
Equal Rights Amendment, 51–52, 69, 70, 86, 109, 263, 417n39, 423n1
*Equal Times,* 218

Fauset, Jessie Redmon, 323
Feldman, Jo, 172
feminist aesthetics, xxix, 6–11, 32–34, 37, 52–54, 100–02, 118, 186
*Feminist Art Journal,* 61
Feminist Art Movement, 2, 8, 15, 37, 54, 88, 126
Feminist Art Programs at Fresno State College and California Institute for the Arts, xiii–xiv, xxi, 1, 6–7, 12, 16, 17–18, 20, 33, 34, 36, 39, 44, 53, 54–56, 88, 100–101, 253, 254, 410n4, 402n21, 408n29, 411n17
*Feminist Bookstore News,* 151
*Feminist Collections,* 204
feminist memory. *See* generating feminist memory

440  INDEX

*Feminist Studies,* 203
*Feminist Teacher,* 245
Feminist Studio Workshop, 56, 57, 101
feminist print culture, 15, 19–20, 23, 180, 405n55, 405n56, 405n61
Ferne, 283
Ferraro, Geraldine, 200, 303
Fields, Mary, 287–88, 294
finances. *See* economics
First day covers, 67–68, 71, 82, 84, 87, 112, 114, 118, 409n32
Fishman, Wendy, 427n1
*Flair,* 41–43, 140, 194, 406n11
Fletcher, Winona L., 321
Flexner, Eleanor, 4
Flynn, Elizabeth Gurley, 71–74, 85, 133
Flynn, Joyce, 323
Foner, Philip S., 253, 308
Forman, Joanne, 255
Forrest, Yvonne, 255
Fossey, Dian, 146, 172, 276–7
Foucault, Michel, 4
Frane, Karen, 306, 316
Freeman, Alexa, 12
Freeman, Elizabeth, 122–123
Fresno State College. *See* Feminist Art Programs
Freidman, Florence. *See* Cowles, Fleur
*From Handicrafts to Factory Work,* 195–97, 201, 217, 232
Fuller, Margaret, 106, 108
Fuller, Meta Vaux Warrick, 323

Gair, Cynthia, 151, 158
Gallaudet University, 312
Garber, Eric, 321
Gardner, Betty, 327
gay liberation movement, 23
generating feminist memory, 3–8, 16, 19, 22–23, 29, 34, 37–38, 41, 46, 61, 65, 90, 132, 140, 154, 161, 163, 171, 178, 182–183, 186, 190, 195–97, 202–3, 213–14, 218, 220, 226, 241, 243, 249, 263, 269, 278, 285–86, 300, 305, 308, 319, 326, 334, 404n54, 407n13, 416n30
*Generations,* 280
Gibson-Hudson, Gloria J., 323, 427n1
Gidlow, Elsa, 70, 87, 144, 198, 276, 280
Gilman, Charlotte Perkins, 70
Gillies, Betty, 106, 109
Goggin, Maureen, 200
Gold, Elizabeth Isadora, 187
Goldman, Emma, 137, 198, 249, 412n39, 419n1
Gonne, Maud, 48–49, 59, 85
Good Taste Productions, 57–58, 61, 63
Gossett, Hattie, 181
Govan, Sandra Y., 323
Gluck, Susan, 57, 58
Grahn, Judy, 57, 58
Greene, Linda, 252, 272, 274, 301
*Greetings,* 60
Grier, Barbara, 181
Grimke, Angelina Weld, 321
Grimstad, Kirsten, 72
Gubar, Susan, xviii, 31, 180, 197, 285, 326, 427n1

Hale, Sarah, 104
Hall, Radclyffe, 40, 41, 48, 85
Hamilton, Lawrie, 211–12, 228, 230, 244, 266, 268, 271
Hampton, Mabel, 323
Hampton Normal and Agricultural Institute, 133
Hanna, Jodi L., 308
Harelson, Randy, 186–187

*Harper's Magazine*, 76
Harris, Helaine, 151, 158
Harris, Susanna, 49
Hayakawa, Yoshiko, 276, 277
Hayden, Sophia, 48, 49, 51, 61, 84
Helaine Victoria Enterprises, xxii, 4, 39, 43, 59, 65, 71, 75, 76, 87, 116; *and* Southern California, xxii, 32, 38, 45, 61, 69, 78, 79, 81, 88–90, 102
Helaine Victoria Press Board of Directors, 28, 154, 173–74, 179, 202, 211, 244, 271, 284, 317, 325
Helaine Victoria Press Catalogs, 23, 27, 65–66, 84, 85–86, 87, 99–100, 106, 112–13, 116–18, 121, 145–47, 158, 165–68, 173–74, 188, 189–92, 208, 211, 219, 233, 242, 244, 249, 252, 255, 261, 263, 279, 284, 287, 294–95, 299, 304, 314, 316, 325, 327, 347, 410n4, 414n53, 418n46
Helaine Victoria Press Columbia logo, xi, 94–95, 116, 147, 165, 167, 190, 264–65, 269, 285, 294, 325
Helaine Victoria Press in the media, 59–60, 61, 72, 75, 113, 144, 155, 168, 171, 187, 190, 211–12, 218–19, 231, 242, 245, 249, 278–81, 298–99, 315–16
Helaine Victoria Press Postcard Archive Project, 212–15, 332
Helaine Victoria Press postcard logo, 140, 147, 241, 274
Helaine Victoria Press Postcards. *See* Helaine Victoria Press Chronological Publication Catalog, 351ff.
Helaine Victoria Press Postcard Series: Bread and Roses, 134, 136–140, 142, 143, 146, 155, 160, 161, 163, 233, 254, 284; Jewish Women, 250, 284; Kitchen Table, 40–41, 112, 227; Latinas, xxvi, 219, 245, 271–76, 278, 295, 299; Sisters of the Harlem Renaissance, The Found Generation, xxvi, 285, 314, 315, 318, 319–25; Women and Papermaking, 223–26, 342; Women in Social Protest, xxvi, 285, 295, 304, 306–09, 312–13, 314, 315, 317, 325, 333; Women in Ecology, xxvii, 140–143, 146, 161, 284; Women in the American Labor Movement, 202, 219–20, 243, 251, 253–55, 259, 280; Women of History, 14, 106–08, 110, 112, 114
Helaine Victoria Press Publishing Advisory Board, 270, 285, 287, 295–96
Helaine Victoria Press T-shirts, 3, 264, 266, 283, 285, 333
Helaine Victoria Press Working Committee, 244, 245, 284
Helaine Victoria Press Women's History Shop, 28, 268–70, 281–82, 285–86, 300
Herlocker, Irene, 142
Hess, Melinda, xvii
Hill, Joe, 72, 293
Hine, Darlene Clark, 243
Hitchcock, Mary Evelyn, 49
Holiday, Billie, 136
Hollander, Nicole, 299
Horn, Rosa, 149
Hoskins, Deborah, 298, 306
Howard, Brad, 310
Hwang, Connie, 310
Huerta, Dolores, 254, 305
Hull House, 146, 236, 239
Hurston, Zora Neale, 122–123, 158, 183–86, 264, 323, 324, 419n1

Idar, Jovita, 272, 273, 275
Illich, Ivan, 296
inclusive politics, xxix
Indiana Committee for the Humanities, 195–97, 218, 238
Indiana Department of Agriculture, 131
Indiana Endowment for the Humanities, 217
Indiana University, 75, 209, 276, 284, 287; *and* Handmade Paper Facility, 192, 205–06, 207, 216, 224, 294; *and* School of Fine Arts, 226; *and* Women's Studies Program, 226–27, 254, 266, 295–96, 420n12
Industrial Workers of the World, 73, 139, 413n42
Internal Revenue Service, 152
International Ladies Garment Workers Union, 239
International Women's Year Conference, 114, 115
Institute of Texan Cultures at University of Texas at San Antonio, 246
Iowa City Women's Press, 295
Iskin, Ruth, 101, 118
Ivins, Melody, 327–28

Jackson, Fay M., 321
Jane Addams Bookstore, 5, 203
Jenkins, Carol, 148
Jenkins, Jane, 427n1
Jewish Women's Congress of the 1893 World's Columbian Exposition, 250
Johnson, Chris, 203, 422n48
Johnson, Georgia Douglas, 321
Johnson, Helene, 323

Johnson, Kirsten, 216
Johnson, Sonia, 213
Johnston, Frances Benjamin, 133
Johnston, Velma, 142

Kalep, Elvy, 106
Kaplan, Judy, 66–67, 82, 84, 87
Kaufman, Gloria, 144, 179
O'Keeffe, Georgia, 37, 71, 213, 249
Kelland, Lara, 2, 401n6
Kingsolver, Barbara, 312
Klotman, Phyllis Rauch, 321, 427n1
Kollwitz, Käthe, 37, 87
Komako, Kimura, 165–66, 169–71, 187, 419n1
Koppelman, Susan, 259
Korn, Susan, 153, 179
Kowalski, Sharon, 311–12
Kress, Gunther, 12, 14–16. *See also* rhetoric
Krieg, Susan, 272
Krolik, Jill, 181
Ku Klux Klan, xxiii–xxiv, 90, 148–149, 190. *See also* Chaney, William

Labor Movement, 73, 138
*La Crónica*, 273
*Ladies Book-plates*, 64
Ladyslipper Music, 283
Lane, Bettye, 311
Lange, Dorothea, 87, 133
Larsen, Nella, 321
Laude, Jan, 312
Laurel, Jeanne, 319
Lazarus, Emma, 178
Lebron, Lolita, 272, 274
Leeder, Elaine, 239, 253, 259
Le Goff, Jacques, 19, 402n17, 404n54

Leighty, Vicki, xviii, xxix, 28, 168, 194, 204, 209, 212–213, 217–19, 222, 232, 243, 244, 246, 249, 254, 259, 260, 263, 267–72, 283, 286, 302–04
Lemlich, Clara, 248, 250
Lesbian aesthetics. *See* feminist aesthetics
Lesbian Feminism, xxi, 5, 21, 23, 26–27, 33–34, 53, 57, 90, 118, 151, 156, 168, 180, 201, 253, 268–69, 280, 295
Lesbian Herstory Archives, 71
Lesbian History Collective, 61
Lesbian History Exploration, 61–64, 70–71, 126, 198
Lesbian sensibility. *See* feminist aesthetics
Letterpress. *See* communication technologies
Levitt, Perrie, xvii
Levy, Builder, 309
Lewis, Edmonia, 257, 260
Lewis, Leslie, 427n1
*Liberal Education,* 298, 299
Library of Congress, 132–133, 183, 198–200, 418n55
*Lily Press, The,* 329, 332
Lippard, Lucy, 7–8
Lockwood, Belva, 49
Lomax, Allen, 183
Long, Dave, 144, 245
Long, Marjorie, 136–37
Longest Walk, The, 310–11, 313
Lootens, Tricia, 256
Lopez, Jovita, 272
Los Angeles. *See* Helaine Victoria Enterprises
Los Angeles Technical College, 79
Louisville *Courier-Journal,* 113
Lovelace, Richard, 51
Luxemburg, Rosa, xxv 41, 48, 71, 85
Lynch, Patsy, 312

Mabley, Jackie "Moms." *See* Aiken, Loretta Mary
Mackey, Mary, 5
Macy, Etta, 103, 172
*Magazine of History,* 278
*Majority Report,* 67, 72
Mallory, Mary, 132, 137, 217, 244, 253
Markievicz, Constance, 48–49, 59, 85
Marsh, Connie, 54–56, 407n17, 407n18
Martin, Marcelina, 276
de Martinez-Alvarez, J.V., 272, 279
Martinsville, Indiana, xviii, xxiii–xxiv, 88, 90, 104–05, 148–149; *and* Lesbian feminist community 104–105
Marsalis, Frances, 106
Massachusetts Institute of Technology, 49,141, 172
Mayo, Edith, 134, 161, 276
Melusine, the Fairy, 123–124
Metis Press, 203, 204, 422n48
Mexican Revolution, 272, 273
Michel, Sonya, 308
Middleton, R. Hunter, 189
Mills, Florence, 321
Mikulski, Barbara Ann, 188, 200, 417n39
Miller, Alice Duer, 118–120, 144
Millikan, Edith, 252, 276, 281
Mitchell, Maria, 191
Modersohn-Becker, Paula, 259
Moira, Fran, 20, 21
Montagu, Lady Barbara, 26
Montgomery bus boycott, 298
Moraga, Cherrie, 181, 271

Morrison, Adele, 309
Moses, Claire, 203
Mother Jones, 106, 108, 109, 212
Mott, Lucretia, 68, 155–56, 414n2
*Ms.* Magazine, 72, 84, 299
Mullaney, Janet, 256
multimodality. *See* rhetoric
Munder typeface. *See* communication technologies
Mxenge, Victoria, 313
MacMillan, Jackie, 12, 403n32
Macpherson, Ida Rust, 46
McClendon, Rose, 321
McCluskey, Audrey, 286–87
McCormick, Terry, 299
McDowell, Mary, 236, 239
McPherson, Aimee Semple, 41

Naiad Press, 181
Nanny, 221–22
Nation, Carry, 48, 85, 156, 175
National Archives, 132–133, 260–61
National Association of Colored Women, 175
National Council of Jewish Women, 250
National Council of Negro Women, 237
National Negro Business League Convention, 240–41
National Organization for Women, 52, 66, 68, 109, 131–32, 159
National Training School for Women and Girls, 276
National Women's History Month, 286, 299, 315
National Women's History Project, 187–88, 202–03
National Women's History Week, 187–88, 195, 217–19, 231, 238, 299, 420n16
National Women's Mailing List, 190, 417n43
National Women's Studies Association, 115, 156, 219
Nearing, Helen and Scott, 128–131, 201; *and Living the Good Life,* 24, 128, 201. *See also* Back to the Land Movement
Nestle, Joan, 323
Network of Career Women, 315, 281n1
*New Directions for Women,* 150
*New Women's Survival Sourcebook, The,* 75
notecards, 3, 29, 47, 59, 72, 75, 76, 77, 83, 85, 87, 100, 116, 118, 168, 172, 233, 281, 283

*off our backs,* 20, 43, 72, 75, 180, 256, 299
offset printing. *See* communication technologies
Organization of American Historians, 278
Otomi woman, 223–24
Ott, Brian, 4
Oxenberg, Jan, 57, 61–62, 63

Pankhurst, Emmeline, 49, 84, 426n51
Pankhurst, Sylvia, 49
Palmer, Bertha Honore, 49, 61
papermaking, 192–194, 205–08, 216, 223–226, 232, 290–94
Parks, Rosa, 5, 298
Parsons, Lucy, 137, 138, 139, 253–54, 413n42, 419n1
Paul, Alice, 133, 146, 419n1
Paxton, Evan, 57–58, 61–62

Perkins, Frances, 135, 138, 163, 419n1
Perkins, Kathy, 323
Perry, Ruth, 127, 172, 416n26
Persephone Press, 5, 181, 194
Pesotta, Rose, 239, 245, 253, 259
Philipsborn, General Postal Director, 13
Planned Parenthood, 114, 150–151
Polan, Annette, 32
Poore, Nancy: *and* career history, 18, 41, 60, 88, 401n3; *and* Chris Johnson, 203, 422n48; *and* collaboration with Jocelyn Cohen, xxii–xxvii, 35, 59, 125; *and* departure from HVP, 28, 253; *and* education, 6, 45–46, 78; *and* family of origin, 18, 90; *and* Metis Press, 422n48; *and* relationship with Jocelyn Cohen, 1, 23–27, 100, 104, 188–89, 201–03
Posener, Jill, 213
postcard medium, 38, 41, 187; *and* history of, 13, 31–32, 47, 155–56, 191, 281, 406n3. *See also* communication technologies
*Postcard Collector,* 245
posters, 47, 51, 57, 63, 65, 69, 83, 86, 98, 100, 108, 112, 114, 126, 150, 154, 159, 165, 187, 200, 218, 228, 375, 260, 270, 283, 295, 301, 317, 334, 416n30, 423n59
Powers, Mary, 113
*Practicing Anti-Racism,* 299
Preer, Evelyn, 323
Preuss, Linda, 254
print trades. *See* communication technologies
Printer's Devil, 127, 235
public memory, 402n17, 405n60. *See also* generating feminist memory

*Publishers Weekly,* 150, 168, 171
Purdue University, 109, 239, 243, 272
Putnam, Emily, 70

Queen Liliʻuokalani, 306
*Quest: A Feminist Quarterly,* 12
Quintanales, Mirta, 181

Radicalesbians, 23
Rae, Jeanine, 264, 423n3
Rakusin, Sudie, 283
Ramos, Juanita, 181
Randall, Margaret, 272
Raven, Arlene, 1, 7, 36, 41, 56, 65, 81, 101, 115, 118, 233, 401n4
Reagan, Ronald, 160, 173, 249, 263, 408n22
recycling. *See* economics
Reeves, Donna Fay, xx, xxxi, 10, 16, 104–06, 234, 264, 267, 282, 285, 300, 302, 312, 314, 317, 326–27, 329
Reitz, Rosetta, 323
Rennie, Susan, 75, 233
rhetoric, 8–15; *and* multimodality, 12–15, 79, 163, 239, 241, 332, 403n39; *and* post cards, 10–16, 38, 105, 325–26; *and* T-shirts, 264; *and* United States Postal Service, 13
Rich, Adrienne, 127, 168–69, 194, 195, 202, 203–06, 208, 221
Richards, Ellen Swallow, 141, 142
Robertson, Jenny, 309, 422n47
Robinson, Beth, 219, 232, 233–35, 244
Robinson, Beverly, 200, 371n55
Robinson, Jean, xviii, 157, 253, 254, 295–97, 306–09, 313
Rodriguez, Josefina, 272
Roosevelt, Eleanor, 113, 146, 218, 315, 419n1

Roosevelt, Franklin D., 135
Rose, Ernestine, 118, 419n1
Rose, Margaret, 254
Rosenzweig, Roy, 280
Rosie the Riveter, 195–97, 258, 260–61, 264, 283
rotaprint offset press. *See* communication technologies
Rotegard, Laura, 328, 329
Rowbotham, Sheila, 4
Runzo, Sandra, 252, 300–01, 311, 314
Ruthsdottir, Mary, 187–88
*Ryder, The*, 315

Saad, Camille, xviii, 163–66, 168, 209
Saar, Betye, 213
Sackville-West, Vita, 124–26
Sahak, Judy Harvey, 171–72
*San Antonio Light*, 246
*San Antonio Woman*, 249
San Francisco Women's Press, 295
Sand, George, 106, 108
Sands, Diane, 176
Sanger, Margaret, 146
Sangster, Margaret E., 94
Santa Monica, 38, 57, 75, 89, 90, 268
Santa Monica City College, 79
Savage, Augusta, 321
Schapiro, Miriam, xxii, xiv, xxix, 1, 6–7, 16, 32–33, 53, 54, 100, 407n17, 408n29; *and* collaboration with Judy Chicago, xxvii54, 88, 401n4
Schlesinger Library at Harvard University, 215, 334, 414n3, 420n13
Schipp, Bernice, 166, 209–212, 219, 232, 235, 244, 260, 267, 302, 314, 316–17, 325
Schneiderman, Rose, 138
Schollenberger, Karen, 216

Schreiner, Olive, 71, 85, 129–30
Schroeder, Patricia, 200
Scott, Sarah, 26, 102, 128, 201, 253
Scripps College, 6, 24, 45, 46, 78, 171
Scutt, Cheryl, 211–12
second wave feminism, xxxi 1–2, 5, 7, 16, 17, 19, 20, 24, 81, 176, 202–03, 253, 414n4; *and* arts, 16–17, 263–64; *and* diversity and inclusion, xxviii–xxix, xxxii, 21–22; 23–24, 32, 33–34, 113–14, 181–82; *and* language, 102; *and* publishing, 151–52, 179–81, 181–82, 202–03; *and* colleges and universities, 20, 151, 156–58, 173, 415n8
Seneca Falls, 28, 191, 328–32, 368n2. *See also* Women's Rights National Historical Park
Silverwoman, Judith, 62, 63
*Sister*, 1, 3, 27, 34–36, 39, 43, 52, 68–69, 181, 302, 326, 360n5
Sklar, Sharon L., 325
Smith, Barbara, 181
Smith College, xviii, 334
Smithsonian Institution, 4, 132–34, 147, 276
Snow, Valaida, 321
Solomon, Hannah Greenbaume, 250
Somerset, Lady, 9
Sonneschein, Rosa, 250
Sparks, Laura, 252, 2754 306, 314, 328–30, 331, 333
Spencer, Anne, 321
*Spokeswoman*, 150
Springer-Kemp, Maida, 254, 259, 260
Stagecoach Mary. *See* Fields, Mary
Stair, Nadine, 290, 292
Stamberg, Susan, 228–231, 235
Stanley, N. J., 281

Stanton, Elizabeth Cady, 51, 68, 83, 85, 187, 414n2, 419n1
Starr, Belle, 47, 59, 85, 105
Starr, Ellen Gates, 236
Statue of Liberty, 118–120, 144
Stein, Gertrude, 49, 71, 84
Stephen, Virginia Snow, 293
Sterrenburg, Joan, xviii, 192, 205, 207, 226, 294
Stetson, Erlene, 276, 286–87, 298, 302, 319, 321
Stimpson, Catherine, 298
Stirrat, Betsy, 226
Stoeltje, Beverly, 319
Stonewall rebellion, 23
Sturken, Marita, 4
subsistence living, xxiv, 27, 78, 97, 128–31. *See also* economics
Sudderth, Lori, 282
Suffrage, 6, 9, 13, 28, 32, 69, 70, 118–19, 170, 174, 328-331, 413n49
Suffrage Press, The, 328–330, 329, 333
Sutton, Crystal Lee Jordan, 138
Swanston-Valdes, June, 327
Swerdlow, Amy, 309
Sykes, Louise, 47
Sykes, Ms. B., 185
St. Joan, Jackie, 181

T-shirts, 3, 264, 266, 283, 286
Tapia, Elena, 274
Tellez, Dora Maria, 272, 279
temperance movement, 8, 11, 46, 150, 174–76
Tenayuca, Emma, 213, 245–49, 260, 272, 305
Third Woman Press, 271
*This Bridge Called My Back: Writings by Radical Women of Color,* 271
Thompson, Sr. Francesca, 323

Thompson, Karen, 311–12
Thurman, Lucy, 175
Tilchen, Maida, 153
Title IX, 19, 79
Toder, Nancy, 61–62
Toklas, Alice B., 49, 71, 84
Trefusis, Violet, 124–126, 172
Triangle Shirtwaist Factory fire, 163
Troubridge, Una, 40, 41, 48, 85
Truth, Sojourner, 50, 51, 84, 182, 218, 242, 264, 286, 287, 302–03, 413n1
Tulsa, Oklahoma massacre, 1921, 308
Tubman, Harriet, 50, 122–23, 198, 303, 419n1
Tutu, Bishop Desmond, 149–50

United Methodist Church, 154–55
United States Alliance of Lesbian and Feminist Printers, 20, 204
United States Postal Service, 13, 31, 102–03, 122, 136, 187–88, 218, 230, 410n1, 411n21
University of California, Los Angeles, 34, 41, 45, 132
University of Michigan, Joseph A. Labadie Collection, 134, 137

Van Buren, Edith, 49
Van Ryn, M. J. C. 304
Van Vechten, Carl, 324
Vanderburg, Agnes, 198, 200, 419n1
Vassar College, 141
Vicinus, Martha, 156–57, 168, 179, 415n20
Villegas de Magnon, Leonor, 273
*Vintage Clothing Newsletter,* 299
Walker, A'Lelia, 240, 314, 323, 324
Walker, Madam C.J., 238–41, 324
Walker, Mary, 49
Waters, Ethel, 323

Wayne State University, Walter P. Reuther Library, Archives of Labor and Urban Affairs, 134, 135
Weaver, Kay, 303
Wedin, Carolyn, 323
Wells-Barnett, Ida B., 106, 108, 110–12, 113, 122–23, 134, 148, 149, 241, 413n49, 419n1
West, Dorothy, 321
Whalen, Colleen, 200
Wheelock, Martha, 303
Whitehead, Fred, 155
Wilding, Faith, 7
Wilkinson, Robert, 19, 79, 93, 207
Willard, Emma, 71, 85, 419n1
Willard, Frances, 9, 11, 46, 51, 65, 83, 84–85, 150, 155, 175, 413n49, 419n1
Williams, Sherley Anne, 323
Wilson, Anne, 217, 233, 244, 271, 317, 427n1
Wisconsin Women Library Workers, 178–79
Woman's Building of the 1893 World's Columbian Exposition, 48, 49, 51, 56, 61
Woman's Touch, The, 423n3
Womanspace Art Gallery, 1, 31, 56
*Womanspace* journal, 15, 401n2, 401n3
*Women and Language News,* 219
Women in Distribution (WinD), 151–52, 158–59, 266
Women in Law, 115, 304–05
Women in Print, xxv–xxvi, 2, 17, 20–22; *and* diversity and inclusion, 21–22, 179–182, 271; *and* conferences, 20–21, 179–80, 185, 204, 205, 211, 256–58
Women and the Printing Arts exhibit, 65
*Women Printers Newsletter,* 151
Woman's Building on Grandview Boulevard, 56–57, 65, 90, 126, 408n22
Women's Christian Temperance Union, 9, 11, 46, 51, 85, 150, 155, 175
Women's Educational Equity Act, 187
Women's Graphic Center at the Los Angeles Woman's Building, 76, 78, 90, 126
Women's International League for Peace and Freedom, 236
Women's Land Army, 306
Women's Liberation Movement. *See* second wave feminism
Women's Music Festivals, 16, 27, 103, 106, 114–16, 132, 148, 150–51, 154, 244, 254, 263, 264–65, 267, 283, 301–02
Women's Rights National Historical Park at Seneca Falls, 28, 328, 329–31, 333
Women's Trade Union League, 138, 248
Woodhull, Victoria, 106, 108
Workers Alliance, 247
World War II, 109, 135–36, 161–63, 194, 196, 258, 261, 308, 327
Workman, Fanny Bullock, 76–77
Works Progress Administration, 133, 161
Worley, Paula, 212, 213–16, 232, 244

Ylla, 213
Yezierska, Anzia, 291
Young, Vicky, 427n1
Yumi, 276, 277
Yung, Judy, 310

Zetkin, Clara, 71, 85
Zietlow, Charlotte, 427n1
Zolot, Julie, 270, 274, 301